User Experience
Re-Mastered

The Morgan Kaufmann Series in Interactive Technologies

Series Editors: Stuart Card, PARC; Jonathan Grudin, Microsoft; Jakob Nielsen, Nielsen Norman Group

User Experience Re-Mastered
Your Guide to Getting the Right Design

Edited by
Chauncey Wilson

AMSTERDAM • BOSTON • HEIDELBERG • LONDON
NEW YORK • OXFORD • PARIS • SAN DIEGO
SAN FRANCISCO • SINGAPORE • SYDNEY • TOKYO

Morgan Kaufmann Publishers is an imprint of Elsevier

MORGAN KAUFMANN PUBLISHERS

Morgan Kaufmann Publishers is an imprint of Elsevier.
30 Corporate Drive, Suite 400, Burlington, MA 01803, USA

This book is printed on acid-free paper. ⊗

Chapter 1 was originally published in *Usability Engineering*, by Jakob Nielsen (Elsevier Inc. 1993).

Chapter 2 was originally published in *Usability for the Web: Designing Web Sites that Work*, by Tom Brinck (Elsevier Inc. 2002).

Chapter 3 was originally published in *Understanding Your Users: A Practical Guide to User Requirements Methods, Tools, and Techniques*, by Catherine Courage and Kathy Baxter (Elsevier Inc. 2005).

Chapter 5 was originally published in *Sketching User Experience: Getting the Design Right and the Right Design*, by Bill Buxton (Elsevier Inc. 2007).

Chapter 6 was originally published in *The Persona Lifecycle: Keeping People in Mind Throughout Product Design*, by John Pruitt and Tamara Adlin (Elsevier Inc. 2006).

Chapter 7 was originally published in *Effective Prototyping for Software Makers*, by Jonathan Arnowitz, Michael Arent, and Nevin Berger (Elsevier Inc. 2006).

Chapters 8, 9, 11, 12 were originally published in *User Interface Design and Evaluation*, by Debbie Stone, Caroline Jarrett, Mark Woodroffe, and Shailey Minocha. Copyright © The Open University 2005.

Chapter 10 was originally published in *Observing the User Experience*, by Mike Kuniavsky (Elsevier Inc. 2003).

Notices
Knowledge and best practice in this field are constantly changing. As new research and experience broaden our understanding, changes in research methods, professional practices, or medical treatment may become necessary.

Practitioners and researchers must always rely on their own experience and knowledge in evaluating and using any information, methods, compounds, or experiments described herein. In using such information or methods they should be mindful of their own safety and the safety of others, including parties for whom they have a professional responsibility.

To the fullest extent of the law, neither the Publisher nor the authors, contributors, or editors, assume any liability for any injury and/or damage to persons or property as a matter of products liability, negligence or otherwise, or from any use or operation of any methods, products, instructions, or ideas contained in the material herein.

Library of Congress Cataloging-in-Publication Data
User experience re-mastered: your guide to getting the right design/edited by Chauncey Wilson.
    p. cm.
  ISBN 978-0-12-375114-0
  1. User interfaces (Computer systems)—Design. 2. Human-computer interaction. 3. Web sites—Design. I. Wilson, Chauncey.
  QA76.9.U83U833 2009
  006.7—dc22
                        2009028127

British Library Cataloguing-in-Publication Data
A catalogue record for this book is available from the British Library.

ISBN: 978-0-12-375114-0

> For information on all Morgan Kaufmann publications,
> visit our Web site at *www.mkp.com* or *www.elsevierdirect.com*

Printed in the United States of America
Transferred to Digital Printing, 2014

Typeset by diacriTech, Chennai, India

Contents

Contributors

Jakob Nielsen   User Advocate and Principal, Nielsen Norman Group.

Tom Brinck   Creative Director, A9.com.

Darren Gergle   Assistant Professor, Northwestern University.

Scott D. Wood   Soar Technology, Inc.

Kathy Baxter   Senior User Experience Researcher, Google.

Catherine Courage   Vice President of User Experience, Citrix Systems.

Chauncey Wilson   Senior User Researcher, Autodesk.

Bill Buxton   Principal Researcher, Microsoft.

John Pruitt   Senior Program Manager, Microsoft.

Tamara Adlin   Founding Partner, Fell Swoop.

Michael Arent   Vice President of User Interface Standards, SAP Labs.

Jonathan Arnowitz   User Experience Strategist, Stroomt Interactions.

Nevin Berger   Senior Director of User Experience, TechWeb of United Business Media.

Dr. Debbie Stone   Project Manager, Infinite Group, and former Lecturer, Open University.

Caroline Jarrett   Director, EffortMark.

Shailey Minocha   Senior Lecturer of Human–Computer Interaction, Open University.

Mark Woodroffe   Deputy Head of the Computing Department, Open University.

Michael Kuniavsky   Cofounder and Head of Design, ThingM Corp.

PART 1
Defining Usability

CHAPTER 1

What Is Usability?

3

Jakob Nielsen

EDITOR'S COMMENTS

Jakob Nielsen has been a leading figure in the usability field since the 1980s and this chapter from his classic book, *Usability Engineering* (Nielsen, 1993), highlights the multidimensional nature of usability. To be usable, a product or service must consider, at a minimum, these five basic dimensions:

- Learnability
- Efficiency
- Memorability
- Error tolerance and prevention
- Satisfaction

An important point made by Nielsen and other usability experts is that the importance of these dimensions will differ depending on the particular context and target users. For something like a bank automated teller machine (ATM) or information kiosk in a museum, learnability might be the major focus of usability practitioners. For complex systems such as jet planes, railway systems, and nuclear power plants, the critical dimensions might be error tolerance and error prevention, followed by memorability and efficiency. If you can't remember the proper code to use when an alarm goes off in a nuclear power plant, a catastrophic event affecting many people over several generations might occur.

In the years since this chapter was published, the phrase "user experience" has emerged as the successor to "usability." User experience practitioners consider additional dimensions such as aesthetics, pleasure, and consistency with moral values, as important for the success of many products and services. These user experience dimensions, while important, still depend on a solid usability foundation. You can design an attractive product that is consistent with your moral values, but sales of that attractive product may suffer if it is hard to learn, not very efficient, and error prone.

Jakob's chapter describes what is needed to establish a solid foundation for usability – a timeless topic. You can read essays by Jakob on topics related to many aspects of usability and user experience at http://www.useit.com.

Back when computer vendors first started viewing users as more than an inconvenience, the term of choice was "user friendly" systems. This term is not really appropriate, however, for several reasons. First, it is unnecessarily anthropomorphic – users don't need machines to be friendly to them, they just need machines that will not stand in their way when they try to get their work done. Second, it implies that users' needs can be described along a single dimension by systems that are more or less friendly. In reality, different users have different needs, and a system that is "friendly" to one may feel very tedious to another.

Because of these problems with the term *user friendly*, user interface professionals have tended to use other terms in recent years. The field itself is known under names like computer–human interaction (CHI), human–computer interaction (HCI), which is preferred by some who like "putting the human first" even if only done symbolically, user-centered design (UCD), man-machine interface (MMI), human-machine interface (HMI), operator-machine interface (OMI), user interface design (UID), human factors (HF), and ergonomics,[1] etc.

I tend to use the term *usability* to denote the considerations that can be addressed by the methods covered in this book. As shown in the following section, there are also broader issues to consider within the overall framework of traditional "user friendliness."

USABILITY AND OTHER CONSIDERATIONS

To some extent, usability is a narrow concern compared with the larger issue of system acceptability, which basically is the question of whether the system is good enough to satisfy all the needs and requirements of the users and other potential stakeholders, such as the users' clients and managers. The overall acceptability of a computer system is again a combination of its social acceptability and its practical acceptability. As an example of social acceptability, consider a system to investigate whether people applying for unemployment benefits are currently gainfully employed and thus have submitted fraudulent applications. The system might do this by asking applicants a number of questions and searching their answers for inconsistencies or profiles that are often indicative of cheaters. Some people may consider such a fraud-preventing system highly socially desirable, but others may find it offensive to subject applicants to this kind of quizzing and socially undesirable to delay benefits for people fitting certain profiles. Notice that people in the latter category may not find the system acceptable even if it got high scores on practical acceptability in terms of identifying many cheaters and were easy to use for the applicants.

EDITOR'S NOTE: SOCIAL NETWORKING AND SOCIAL RESPONSIBILITY

In the years since the publication of this chapter, social networking and other collaboration technologies, such as Facebook, Twitter, and blogs, have become popular with millions of users. These new technologies have great promise for bringing people together but also pose new issues around social acceptability. Take Twitter as an example. Messages about conditions at work or how bad one's managers are might be considered socially accept-able whining by the originator, but the person's managers might view the same whining on Twitter as detrimental to the company. Comments on social networking sites can persist for years and a single photo or comment could harm someone's chances for a new job or affect revenue for a company. Human resource personnel can Google much personal information when they screen candidates, but is that socially acceptable? Social network-ing can be a boon or a disaster for individuals and organizations.

Given that a system is socially acceptable, we can further analyze its practical acceptability within various categories, including traditional categories such as cost, support, reliability, compatibility with existing systems, as well as the cat-egory of usefulness. *Usefulness* is the issue of whether the system can be used to achieve some desired goal. It can again be broken down into the two categories, utility and usability (Grudin, 1992), where utility is the question of whether the functionality of the system in principle can do what is needed and usabil-ity is the question of how well users can use that functionality. Note that the concept of "utility" does not necessarily have to be restricted to the domain of hard work. Educational software (courseware) has high utility if students learn from using it, and an entertainment product has high utility if it is fun to use. Figure 1.1 shows the simple model of system acceptability outlined here. It is clear from the figure that system acceptability has many components and that usability must trade-off against many other considerations in a development project.

Usability applies to all aspects of a system with which a human might interact, including installation and maintenance procedures. It is very rare to find a computer feature that truly has no user interface components. Even a facility to transfer data between two computers will normally include an interface to trouble-shoot the link when something goes wrong (Mulligan, Altom, & Simkin, 1991). As another example, I recently established two electronic mail addresses for a committee I was managing. The two addresses were `ic93-papers-administrator` and `ic93-papers-committee` (for e-mail to

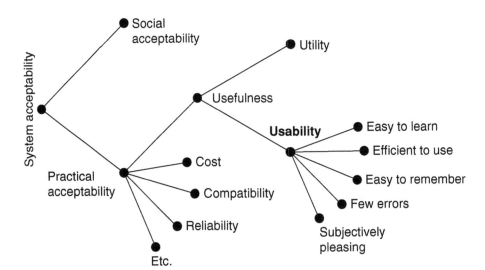

FIGURE 1.1
A model of the attributes of system acceptability.

my assistant and to the entire membership, respectively). It turned out that several people sent e-mail to the wrong address, not realizing where their mail would go. My mistake was twofold: first in not realizing that even a pair of e-mail addresses constituted a user interface of sorts and second in breaking the well-known usability principle of avoiding easily confused names. A user who was taking a quick look at the "To:" field of an e-mail message might be excused for thinking that the message was going to one address even though it was in fact going to the other.

DEFINITION OF USABILITY

It is important to realize that usability is not a single, one-dimensional property of a user interface. Usability has multiple components and is traditionally associated with these five usability attributes:

- Learnability: The system should be easy to learn so that the user can rapidly start getting some work done with the system.
- Efficiency: The system should be efficient to use so that once the user has learned the system, a high level of productivity is possible.
- Memorability: The system should be easy to remember so that the casual user is able to return to the system after some period of not having used it without having to learn everything all over again.
- Errors: The system should have a low error rate so that users make few errors during the use of the system, and so that if they do make errors they can easily recover from them. Further, catastrophic errors must not occur.
- Satisfaction: The system should be pleasant to use so that users are subjectively satisfied when using it; they like it.

Each of these usability attributes will be discussed further in the following sections. Only by defining the abstract concept of "usability" in terms of these more precise and measurable components can we arrive at an engineering discipline where usability is not just argued about but is systematically approached, improved, and evaluated (possibly measured). Even if you do not intend to run formal measurement studies of the usability attributes of your system, it is an illuminating exercise to consider how its usability could be made measurable. Clarifying the measurable aspects of usability is much better than aiming at a warm, fuzzy feeling of "user friendliness" (Shackel, 1991).

Usability is typically measured by having a number of test users (selected to be as representative as possible of the intended users) use the system to perform a prespecified set of tasks, though it can also be measured by having real users in the field perform whatever tasks they are doing anyway. In either case, an important point is that usability is measured relative to certain users and certain tasks. It could well be the case that the same system would be measured as having different usability characteristics if used by different users for different tasks. For example, a user wishing to write a letter may prefer a different word processor than a user wishing to maintain several hundred thousands of pages of technical documentation. Usability measurement, therefore, starts with the definition of a representative set of test tasks, relative to which the different usability attributes can be measured.

To determine a system's overall usability on the basis of a set of usability measures, one normally takes the mean value of each of the attributes that have been measured and checks whether these means are better than some previously specified minimum. Because users are known to be very different, it is probably better to consider the entire distribution of usability measures and not just the mean value. For example, a criterion for subjective satisfaction might be that the mean value should be at least 4 on a 1–5 scale; that at least 50 percent of the users should have given the system the top rating, 5; and that no more than five percent of the users gave the system the bottom rating, 1.

Learnability

Learnability is in some sense the most fundamental usability attribute, because most systems need to be easy to learn and because the first experience most people have with a new system is that of learning to use it. Certainly, there are some systems for which one can afford to train users extensively to overcome a hard-to-learn interface, but in most cases, systems need to be easy to learn.

Ease of learning refers to the novice user's experience on the initial part of the learning curve, as shown in Fig. 1.2. Highly learnable systems have a steep incline for the first part of the learning curve and allow users to reach a reasonable level of usage proficiency within a short time. Practically all user interfaces have learning curves that start out with the user being able to do nothing (have zero efficiency) at time zero (when they first start using it). Exceptions include the so-called walk-up-and-use systems, such as museum information systems,

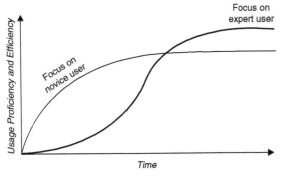

FIGURE 1.2
Learning curves for a hypothetical system that focuses on the novice user, being easy to learn but less efficient to use, as well as one that is hard to learn but highly efficient for expert users.

that are only intended to be used once and therefore need to have essentially zero learning time, allowing users to be successful from their very first attempt at using them.

The standard learning curve also does not apply to cases where the users are transferring skills from previous systems, such as when they upgrade from a previous release of a word processor to the new release (Telles, 1990). Assuming that the new system is reasonably consistent with the old, users should be able to start a fair bit up on the learning curve for the new system (Polson, Muncher, & Engelbeck, 1986).

Initial ease of learning is probably the easiest of the usability attributes to measure, with the possible exception of subjective satisfaction. One simply picks some users who have not used the system before and measures the time it takes them to reach a specified level of proficiency in using it. Of course, the test users should be representative of the intended users of the system, and there might be a need to collect separate measurements from complete novices without any prior computer experience and from users with some typical computer experience. In earlier years, learnability studies focused exclusively on users without any computer experience, but because many people now have used computers, it is becoming more important to include such users in studies of system learnability.

The most common way to express the specified level of proficiency is simply to state that the users have to be able to complete a certain task successfully. Alternatively, one can specify that users need to be able to complete a set of tasks in a certain, minimum time before one will consider them as having "learned" the system. Of course, as shown in Fig. 1.2, the learning curve actually represents a continuous series of improved user performance and not a dichotomous "learned"/"not learned" distinction. It is still common, however, to define a certain level of performance as indicating that the user has passed the learning stage and is able to use the system and to measure the time it takes the user to reach that stage.

When analyzing learnability, one should keep in mind that users normally do not take the time to learn a complete interface fully before starting to use it. On the contrary, users often start using a system as soon as they have learned a part of the interface. For example, a survey of business professionals who were experienced personal computer users (Nielsen, 1989a) found that four of the six highest-rated usability characteristics (out of 21 characteristics in the survey) related to exploratory learning: easy-to-understand error messages, possible to do useful work with program before having learned all of it, availability of undo, and confirming questions before execution of risky commands. Because of users' tendency to jump right in and start using a system, one should not just measure how long it takes users to achieve complete mastery of a system but also how long it takes to achieve a sufficient level of proficiency to do useful work.

Efficiency of Use

Efficiency refers to the expert user's steady-state level of performance at the time when the learning curve flattens out (Fig. 1.2). Of course, users may not necessarily reach that final level of performance any time soon. For example, some operating systems are so complex that it takes several years to reach expert-level performance and the ability to use certain composition operators to combine commands (Doane, McNamara, Kintsch, Polson, & Clawson, 1992; Doane, Pellegrino, & Klatzky, 1990). Also, some users will probably continue to learn indefinitely, though most users seem to plateau once they have learned "enough" (Carroll & Rosson, 1987; Rosson, 1984). Unfortunately, this steady-state level of performance may not be optimal for the users who, by learning a few additional advanced features, sometimes would save more time over the course of their use of the system than the time it took to learn them.

To measure efficiency of use for experienced users, one obviously needs access to experienced users. For systems that have been in use for some time, "experience" is often defined somewhat informally, and users are considered experienced either if they say so themselves or if they have been users for more than a certain amount of time, such as a year. Experience can also be defined more formally in terms of number of hours spent using the system, and that definition is often used in experiments with new systems without an established user base: test users are brought in and asked to use the system for a certain number of hours, after which their efficiency is measured. Finally, it is possible to define test users as experienced in terms of the learning curve itself: a user's performance is continuously measured (e.g., in terms of number of seconds to do a specific task), and when the performance has not increased for some time, the user is assumed to have reached the steady-state level of performance for that user (Nielsen & Phillips, 1993).

A typical way to measure efficiency of use is thus to decide on some definition of expertise, to get a representative sample of users with that expertise, and to measure the time it takes these users to perform some typical test tasks.

Memorability

Casual users are the third major category of users besides novice and expert users. Casual users are people who are using a system intermittently rather than having the fairly frequent use assumed for expert users. However, in contrast to novice users, casual users have used a system before, so they do not need to learn it from scratch, they just need to remember how to use it based on their previous learning. Casual use is typically seen for utility programs that are only used under exceptional circumstances, for supplementary applications that do not form part of a user's primary work but are useful every now and then, as well as for programs that are inherently only used at long intervals, such as a program for making a quarterly report.

Having an interface that is easy to remember is also important for users who return after having been on vacation or who for some other reason have temporarily stopped using a program. To a great extent, improvements in learnability often also make an interface easy to remember, but in principle, the usability of returning to a system is different from that of facing it for the first time. For example, consider the sign "Kiss and Ride" seen outside some, Washington, DC, Metro stations. Initially, the meaning of this sign may not be obvious (it has poor learnability without outside assistance), but once you realize that it indicates a drop-off zone for commuters arriving in a car driven by somebody else, the sign becomes sufficiently memorable to allow you to find such zones at other stations (it is easy to remember).[2]

Interface memorability is rarely tested as thoroughly as the other usability attributes, but there are in principle two main ways of measuring it. One is to perform a standard user test with casual users who have been away from the system for a specified amount of time and measure the time they need to perform some typical test tasks. Alternatively, it is possible to conduct a memory test with users after they finish a test session with the system and ask them to explain the effect of various commands or to name the command (or draw the icon) that does a certain thing. The interface's score for memorability is then the number of correct answers given by the users.

The performance test with casual users is most representative of the reason we want to measure memorability in the first way. The memory test may be easier to carry out but does have the problem that many modern user interfaces are built on the principle of making as much as possible visible to the users. Users of such systems do not need to be actively able to remember what is available, since the system will remind them when necessary. In fact, a study of one such graphical interface showed that users were unable to remember the contents of the menus when they were away from the system, even though they could use the same menus with no problems when they were sitting at the computer (Mayes, Draper, McGregor & Oatley, 1988).

Few and Noncatastrophic Errors

Users should make as few errors as possible when using a computer system. Typically, an error is defined as any action that does not accomplish the desired goal, and the system's error rate is measured by counting the number of such actions made by users while performing some specified task. Error rates can thus be measured as part of an experiment to measure other usability attributes.

Simply defining errors as being any incorrect user action does not take the highly varying impact of different errors into account. Some errors are corrected immediately by the user and have no other effect than to slow down the user's transaction rate somewhat. Such errors need not really be counted separately, as their effect is included in the efficiency of use if it is measured the normal way in terms of the user's transaction time.

Other errors are more catastrophic in nature, either because they are not discovered by the user, leading to a faulty work product, or because they destroy the user's work, making them difficult to recover from. Such catastrophic errors should be counted separately from minor errors, and special efforts should be made to minimize their frequency.

Subjective Satisfaction

The final usability attribute, subjective satisfaction, refers to how pleasant it is to use the system. Subjective satisfaction can be an especially important usability attribute for systems that are used on a discretionary basis in a nonwork environment, such as home computing, games, interactive fiction, or creative painting (Virzi, 1991). For some such systems, their entertainment value is more important than the speed with which things get done, because one might *want* to spend a long time having fun (Carroll & Thomas, 1988). Users should have an entertaining and/or moving and/or enriching experience when using such systems because they have no other goal.

Note that the notion of subjective satisfaction as an attribute of usability is different from the issue of the public's general attitudes toward computers. Even though it is likely that a person's feelings toward computers as a general phenomenon will impact the extent to which that person likes interacting with a particular system, peoples' attitudes toward computers in general should probably be seen as a component of the social acceptability of computers rather than their usability. See (LaLomia & Sidowski, 1991) for a survey of such computer attitude studies. Computer enthusiasts may hope that steady improvements in computer usability will result in more positive attitudes toward computers. Little is currently known about the relation between attributes of individual computer systems and users' general attitudes, though users who perceive that they have a high degree of control over the computer have been found also to have positive attitudes toward computers (Kay, 1989).

In principle, certain objective measures might be used instead of asking the users' subjective preference to assess the pleasing nature of an interface. In a few cases, psychophysiological measures such as electroencephalograms (EEGs), pupil dilation, heart rate, skin conductivity, blood pressure, and level of adrenaline in the blood have been used to estimate the users' stress and comfort levels (Mullins & Treu 1991; Schleifer, 1990; Wastell, 1990). Unfortunately, such measures require intimidating experimental conditions such as wiring the user to an EEG machine or taking blood samples. Because test users are normally nervous enough as it is and because a relaxed atmosphere is an important condition for much user testing, the psychophysiological approach will often be inappropriate for usability engineering studies.

Alternatively, subjective satisfaction may be measured by simply *asking* the users for their subjective opinion. From the perspective of any single user, the replies to such a question are subjective, but when replies from multiple users are averaged together, the result is an objective measure of the system's pleasantness. Because the entire purpose of having a subjective satisfaction usability attribute is to assess whether users like the system, it seems highly appropriate to measure it by asking the users, and this is indeed what is done in the overwhelming number of usability studies.

To ensure consistent measurements, subjective satisfaction is normally measured by a short questionnaire that is given to users as part of the debriefing session after a user test. Of course, questionnaires can also be given to users of installed systems in the field without the need to have them go through a special test procedure first. For new systems, however, it is important not to ask the users for their subjective opinions until after they have had a chance to try using the system for a real task. The answers users give to questions before and after having used a system are unfortunately not very highly correlated (Root & Draper, 1983).

Users have been known to refuse to use a program because the manual was too big (Nielsen, Mack, Bergendorff & Grischkowsky, 1986), without even trying to read it to see whether it was in fact as difficult as they thought. Therefore, it is certainly reasonable to study the approachability of a system (this is especially important from a marketing perspective) (Angiolillo & Roberts, 1991). To do so, one can show the system to users and ask them, "How difficult do you think it would be to learn to use this?" – just don't expect the answers to have much relation to the *actual* learnability of the system.

Even when users do have experience using a system, their subjective ratings of its difficulty are much more closely related to the peak difficulty they experienced than to mean difficulty; the most difficult episode a user experienced is the most memorable for that user. In one experiment, the peak experienced difficulty while performing a task accounted for 31 percent of the users' subjective rating of the system's difficulty, whereas the task time only accounted for 7 percent (Cordes, 1993). One conclusion is that one cannot rely solely on user ratings if the goal is to improve overall system performance. On the other hand, sales considerations imply a need to have users *believe* that the system is easy to generate positive word-of-mouth, and such impressions might be improved more by a bland interface with no extreme peak in difficulty than by a system that is mostly excellent but has one really hard part for users to overcome.

Subjective satisfaction questionnaires are typically very short, though some longer versions have been developed for more detailed studies (Chin, Diehl & Norman, 1988). Typically, users are asked to rate the system on 1–5 or 1–7 rating scales that are normally either Likert scales or semantic differential scales (LaLomia & Sidowski, 1990). For a *Likert scale*, the questionnaire postulates some statement (e.g., "I found this system very pleasant to use") and asks the users to rate their degree of agreement with the statement. When using a 1–5 rating scale, the reply options are typically 1 = strongly disagree, 2 = partly disagree, 3 = neither agree nor disagree, 4 = partly agree, and 5 = strongly agree.

A *semantic differential scale* lists two opposite terms along some dimension (e.g., very easy to learn vs. very hard to learn) and asks the user to place the system on the most appropriate rating along the dimension. Table 1.1 and Table 1.2 list some sample questions that are often asked to measure subjective satisfaction. One could add a few questions addressing issues of special interest, such as "the quick reference card was very helpful," but it is normally best

Table 1.1	Questions Users Might Be Asked to Measure Subjective Satisfaction Using a Likert Scale

Please Indicate the Degree to Which You Agree or Disagree with the Following Statements About the System:

"It was very easy to learn how to use this system."

"Using this system was a very frustrating experience."

"I feel that this system allows me to achieve very high productivity."

"I worry that many of the things I did with this system may have been wrong."

"This system can do all the things I think I would need."

"This system is very pleasant to work with."

Users would typically indicate their degree of agreement on a 1–5 scale for each statement. One would normally refer to the system by its name rather than as "this system."

Table 1.2	Some Semantic Differential Scales to Measure Subjective Satisfaction with Computers

Please Mark the Positions That Best Reflect Your Impressions of This System:

Pleasing	——————	Irritating
Complete	——————	Incomplete
Cooperative	——————	Uncooperative
Simple	——————	Complicated
Fast to use	——————	Slow to use
Safe	——————	Unsafe

See Coleman, Williges, and Wixon (1985) for a list of 17 such scales.

to keep the questionnaire short to maximize the response rate. A final rating for subjective satisfaction is often calculated simply as the mean of the ratings for the individual answers (after compensating for any use of reverse polarity), but it is also possible to use more sophisticated methods, drawing upon rating scale theory from sociology and psychometrics.

No matter what rating scales are used, they should be subjected to pilot testing to make sure that the questions are interpreted properly by the users. For example, a satisfaction questionnaire for a point-of-sales system used a dimension labeled "human contact versus cold technology" to assess whether users felt that it was impersonal to be served by a machine. However, because no humans were present besides the user, many users felt that it was logically impossible to talk about "human contact" and did not answer the question in the intended manner.

When rating scales are used, one needs an anchor or baseline to calibrate the scale before it is possible to assess the results. If subjective satisfaction ratings are available for several different systems or several different versions of the same system, it is possible to consider the ratings in relation to the others and thus to determine which system is the most pleasant to use. If only a single user interface has been measured, one should take care in interpreting the ratings, because people are often too polite in their replies. Users normally know that the people who are asking for the ratings have a vested interest in the system being measured, and they will tend to be positive unless they have had a really unpleasant experience. This phenomenon can be partly counteracted by using reverse polarity on some of the questions, that is, having some questions to which an agreement would be a negative rating of the system.

Nielsen and Levy (1994) found that the median rating of subjective satisfaction for 127 user interfaces for which such ratings had been published was 3.6 on a 1–5 scale with 1 being the worst rating and 5 the best. Ostensibly, the rating 3 is the "neutral" point on a 1–5 rating scale, but because the median is the value where half of the systems were better and half were poorer, the value 3.6 seems to be a better estimate of "neutral" or "average" subjective satisfaction.

If multiple systems are tested, subjective satisfaction can be measured by asking users which system they would prefer or how strongly they prefer various systems over others. Finally, for systems that are in use, one can measure the extent that users choose to use them over any available alternatives. Data showing voluntary usage is really the ultimate subjective satisfaction rating.

EXAMPLE: MEASURING THE USABILITY OF ICONS

To clarify the slightly abstract definition of usability in the previous section, this section gives several examples of how to measure the usability of a concrete user interface element: icons. Icons have become very popular elements in graphical user interfaces, but not all icons have equally good usability characteristics.

A systematic approach to icon usability would define measurable criteria for each of the usability attributes of interest to the system being developed. It is impossible to talk about the usability of an icon without knowing the context in which it will be shown and the circumstances under which it will be used. This section presents a few of the approaches to icon usability that have been published in the user interface literature. For some other examples, see (Green & Barnard, 1990; Hakiel & Easterby, 1987; Magyar, 1990; Nolan, 1989; Salasoo, 1990; Stammers & Hoffman, 1991; Zwaga, 1989).

A classic study of icon usability was described by Bewley, Roberts, Schroit, and Verplank (1983). Four different sets of icons were designed for a graphical user interface with 17 icons. All the icons were tested for ease of learning, efficiency of use, and subjective satisfaction. Ease of learning was assessed by several means: First, the intuitiveness[3] of the individual icons was tested by showing them to the users, one at a time, asking the user to describe "what you think it is." Second, because icons are normally not seen in isolation, the understand-ability of sets of icons was tested by showing the users entire sets of icons (one of the four sets that had been designed). Users were then given the name of an icon and a short description of what it was supposed to do and asked to point to the icon that best matched the description. Users were also given the complete set of names and asked to match up all the icons with their names. The score for all these learning tests was the proportion of the icons that were correctly described or named.

EDITOR'S NOTE: USING BRAINDRAWING TO GENERATE IDEAS FOR ICONS

Braindrawing is a method of visual brainstorming and problem-solving where participants create and modify rough sketches quickly to generate ideas or solve visual layout prob-lems. For example, braindrawing could be used to come up with ideas for icons that will represent abstract functions in toolbars, menus, or ribbons. You can also use braindrawing to explore layouts for dialogue boxes or Web pages.

The basic procedure for braindrawing involves the following steps:

1. Each member of a group is invited to explore solutions to a visual problem state-ment by sketching ideas for a designated period of time.
2. Each sketch is passed to another person who then enhances or adds something to the sketch or creates a new sketch. After a designated time, each person passes the sketches on to yet another person.
3. The sketch-then-pass process is repeated for three to six iterations.
4. At the end of a braindrawing session, all the sketches created by the group are posted in an "art gallery," where colleagues and participants can review the sketches and discuss which ideas should be considered further.
5. (Optional) The group votes on the best ideas and then prioritizes them further at the end of the session or at a separate session.

Two efficiency tests were conducted. In the first test, users who had already learned the meaning of the icons through participation in the learning tests were given the name of an icon and told that it might appear on the computer display. A random icon then appeared, and the users pressed a "yes" button if it was one they were looking for and a "no" button if it was some other icon. In the second test, users were shown a randomized display of icons and asked to click on a specific icon. Both these tests were timed, and the score for an icon was the users' reaction time in seconds.

Subjective satisfaction was measured in two ways. First, users were asked to rate each icon one at a time for how easy it was to pick out. Second, for each of the 17 concepts, the users were shown the four possible icons and asked to choose the one they preferred. The subjective score for an icon was the user rating for the first test and the proportion of users who preferred it for the second test.

Given the results from all these tests, it was possible to compare the four icon sets. One set that included the names of the commands as part of the icon got consistently high scores on the test where users had to describe what the icon represented. This result may not be all that surprising and has indeed been confirmed by later research on other interfaces (Egido & Patterson, 1988; Kacmar & Carey, 1991). Unfortunately, this set of icons was not very graphically distinct, and many of the icons were hard to find on a screen with many similar icons. For the final system, a fifth set of icons was designed, mostly being based on one of the four original sets, but with some variations based on lessons from the tests as well as the aesthetic sensibilities of the graphic designers.

Icons are probably easier to design for objects than for operations since many objects can be depicted representationally. Rogers (1986) studied the usability of icon sets for operations by testing gradually more complex icons with more and more elements. The only usability parameter measured was comprehensibility, which was assessed by a matching test. For each level of icon complexity (e.g., icons with few elements), an entire set of icons was designed to represent the commands in the system. For each such set, 10 users were shown all the icons as they went through a list of textual descriptions of the command functions.[4] For each textual description, the users picked the one icon they believed matched it best, and the total comprehension score for an icon set was then calculated as the number of correct matches.

The best icons showed both the concrete object being operated upon (e.g., a sheet of paper) and an abstract representation of the operation (e.g., an arrow). Icons with only one of these elements were harder to understand as were icons with even more information (such as replacing the arrow with a pointing finger with little cartoon-like lines denoting movement). So, a medium level of complexity was best for comprehension. Also, icons for commands with a visual outcome (such as the movement of text in a word processor) were much easier to comprehend than were icons for commands with a nonvisual outcome (such as "save a file").

Icons that are intended for critical or widely used applications may need to satisfy more stringent quality criteria than other icons. International standards is certainly one area where one would want a high level of usability. Lindgaard, Chessari, and Ihsen (1987) report on a case where the International Standards Organization (ISO) required that icons should be correctly interpreted by at least 66 percent of the subjects in a test for the icon to be considered for adoption as an international standard. Only half of the proposed icons actually passed this criterion when they were tested with technically knowledgeable users, and for naive subjects, only one of 12 icons was good enough. Iterative design resulted in improved icons, but the important lesson from this study is the benefit of deciding on a reasonable criterion for measurable usability and then testing to see whether the goal has been met before releasing a product.

The examples in this section have shown that icon usability can be defined and measured in many different ways. The main conclusion from the examples is the need to refine the basic usability criteria listed in Section 1.2 with respect to the circumstances of each concrete project. There are many different ways of measuring usability, and no single measure will be optimal for all projects.

> **EDITOR'S NOTE: ISO STANDARD FOR TESTING GRAPHIC SYMBOLS**
>
> ISO 9186-2:2008, Procedures for the Development and Testing of Public Information Symbols, defines testing methods and criteria for adopting symbols as an international standard. If you haven't done icon testing before, this standard is a good resource.

USABILITY TRADE-OFFS

The learning curves in Fig. 1.2 may give the impression that one can have *either* a system that is easy to learn *or* one that is eventually efficient, though initially hard to learn. In fact, often a system that will give good novice learning will also be good for the experts. Also, it is often possible to ride the best parts of both learning curves by providing a user interface with multiple interaction styles such that the user starts by learning one interaction style that is easy to learn and later changes to another that is more efficient for frequently used operations.

The typical way to achieve this "best-of-both-worlds" effect is to include *accelerators* in the user interface. Accelerators are user interface elements that allow the user to perform frequent tasks quickly, even though the same tasks can also be performed in a more general, and possibly slower, way. Typical examples of accelerators include function keys, pop-up menus in the work area, command name abbreviations, and the use of double-clicking to activate an object. Users of such a dual interface who are on the part of the learning curve where they are changing to expert mode may suffer a small dip in performance, so the learning curve will not necessarily be continuously increasing. Also, one should keep in mind that the increased interface complexity inherent in having both novice and expert modes can be a problem in itself. It is, therefore, important to design the interface in such a way that the novice users can use it without being confronted with the expert mode and the accelerators. For example, a command language system that allows abbreviations should always spell out the full name of the commands in any help and error messages. Also, any operation that is activated by double-clicking should also be made available as a menu choice or in some other visible fashion.

The trade-off between learnability for novice users and efficiency of use for expert users can sometimes be resolved to the benefit of both user groups without employing dual interaction styles. For example, unless the application involves a very large number of fields, one might as well use descriptive field labels in a dialogue box, even though they would make it a little larger than if cryptic abbreviations were used. The expert users would not be hurt by such a concession to the novices.[5] Similarly, both user groups would benefit from appropriate choice of default values – experts because they would need to change the value less often and novices because the system would conform to their typical needs without the need for them to learn about the nondefault options.

Even so, it is not always possible to achieve optimal scores for all usability attributes simultaneously. Trade-offs are inherent in any design process and apply no less to user interface design. For example, the desire to avoid catastrophic errors may lead to the decision to design a user interface that is less efficient to use than otherwise possible: typically because extra questions are asked to assure that the user is certain about wanting a particular action.

In cases where a usability trade-off seems necessary, attempts should first be made at finding a win-win solution that can satisfy both requirements. If that is not possible, the dilemma should be resolved under the directions set out by the project's usability goals, which should define which usability attributes are the most important given the specific circumstances of the project.

Furthermore, considerations other than usability may lead to designs violating some usability principles. For example, security considerations often require access controls that are decidedly nonuser friendly, such as not providing constructive error messages in case of an erroneously entered password. As another example, museum information systems and other publicly used systems may have hidden options, such as a command to reboot the system in case of trouble, in cases where the options are not intended to be used by the regular users.

CATEGORIES OF USERS AND INDIVIDUAL USER DIFFERENCES

The two most important issues for usability are the users' tasks and their individual characteristics and differences. An analysis of 92 published comparisons of usability of hypertext systems found that four of the 10 largest effects (including all the top three effects) in the studies were due to individual differences between users and that two were due to task differences (Nielsen, 1989b). It is therefore an important aspect of usability engineering to know the user. Understanding the major ways of classifying users may also help (Potosnak, Hayes, Rosson, Schneider & Whiteside, 1986), though often the same system design will be good for many categories of users.

Figure 1.3 shows the "user cube" of the three main dimensions[6] along which users' experience differs: experience with the system, with computers in general, and with the task domain.

The users' experience with the specific user interface under consideration is the dimension that is normally referred to when discussing user expertise, and users are normally considered to be either novices or experts or somewhere in between. The transition from novice to expert user of a system often follows a learning curve somewhat like those shown in Fig. 1.2.

Most of the usability principles discussed in this book will help make systems easier to learn, and thus allow users to reach expert status faster. In addition to general learnability, there are several user interface elements that can prod users to acquire expertise. A classic example is the way many menu systems list the appropriate shortcut for menu options as part of the menu itself. Such shortcuts are often function keys or command name abbreviations but, in any case, they can be mentioned in a way that does not hurt novice users while still encouraging them to try the alternative interaction technique. Online help systems may encourage users to broaden their understanding of a system by providing hypertext links to information that is related to their specific queries. It may even be possible for the system to analyze the user's actions and suggest alternative and better ways of achieving the same goal.

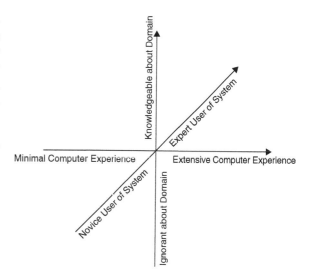

FIGURE 1.3
The three main dimensions on which users' experience differs: knowledge about computers in general, expertise in using the specific system, and understanding of the task domain.

Some user interfaces are only intended to be used by novices, in that almost nobody will use them more than a few times. This is true for most walk-up-and-use systems, like a kiosk for making dinner reservations in an amusement park, but also for interfaces that may require a little reading of the instructions, such as installation programs, disk formatting routines, and tax return programs that change every year. Most interfaces, however, are intended for both novice and expert users and thus need to accommodate both usage styles.

A common way to cater to both expert and novice users is to include accelerators in the interface to allow expert users to use faster, but less obvious, interaction techniques. Several widely used systems come with two sets of menus, one for novice users (often called "short menus" to avoid any stigma) and one for expert users "long menus." This allows the system to offer a wide range of features to the experts without confusing the novices. Online help can assist the novice users without getting in the way of the experts. Interfaces that are solely intended for novices may not need special help systems, as they should include all the necessary user assistance in the primary interface itself.

EDITOR'S NOTE: SHORT VERSUS LONG MENUS

The use of "short menus" and "long menus" for supporting both novice users and expert users requires detailed usage data about what novice and expert users require for their particular usage patterns. For some products like word processors, mail merge, a complex feature, may be perceived as an expert item by a design team, but the reality is that many novices might be required to do mail merge because they have a large volume of e-mail or paper mail to send. The use of explicit short and long menus has diminished in popularity since this chapter was published.

In spite of the common simplistic distinction between expert and novice users, the reality is that most people do not acquire comprehensive expertise in all parts of a system, no matter how much they use it. Almost all systems of some complexity have so many features and so many uses that any given user only makes extensive use of a small subset (Draper, 1984). Thus, even an "expert" user may be quite novice with respect to many parts of the system not normally used by that user. As a consequence, expert users still need access to help systems for those parts of the interface that they do not use as often, and they will benefit from increased learnability of these features.

The users' general experience with computers also has an impact on user interface design. As a simple example, consider a utility program distributed to systems administrators as compared with one that is to be used by home computer owners. Even though the two utilities may be intended for somewhat the same purpose, such as disk defragmentation, the interfaces should be very different. Even with more application-oriented interfaces, users with extensive experience from many other applications will normally be better off than users who have only used a single system, because experienced users will have some idea of what features to look for and how a computer normally deals with various situations. For example, a user with experience of a spreadsheet and a database program might try to look for a "sort" command in a new word processor. Furthermore, a user's programming experience will to a large degree determine the extent to which that user can use macro languages and other complex means of combining commands and whether the resulting structures will be easily maintainable and modifiable when the user's needs change at a later date.

The final important dimension is the user's knowledge of the task domain addressed by the system. Interfaces for users with extensive domain knowledge can use specialized terminology and a higher density of information in the screen designs. Users with little domain knowledge will need to have the system explain what it is doing and what the different options mean, and the terminology used should not be as abbreviated and dense as for domain specialists. Consider, for example, the design of a financial planning system. The interface obviously needs to be very different depending on whether the intended users are finance professionals or whether the system is intended to help professionals from other fields invest and keep track of their money.

Users also differ in other ways than experience. Some differentiating factors are easy to observe, such as age (Czaja, 1988) and gender (Fowler & Murray, 1987; Teasley, Leventhal, Blumenthal, Instone & Stone, 1994). Other factors are less immediately obvious, such as differences in spatial memory and reasoning abilities (Gomez, Egan & Bowers, 1986) and preferred learning style (Sein & Bostrom, 1989), where some people learn better from abstract descriptions and others learn better from concrete examples. The important lesson from studies of these and other differences is that one needs to consider the entire spectrum of intended users and make sure that the interface is usable for as many as possible and not just for those who happen to have the same characteristics as the developers themselves. For example, the developers may find it easy to remember where everything is located in a hierarchical file system, but users with lower spatial memory abilities may find the user interface significantly easier to use if it included an overview map (Vincente & Williges, 1988).

In addition to differences between groups of users, there are also important differences between individual users (Egan, 1988). The most extreme example may be in programming, where the difference in productivity between the best and the worst programmers typically is a factor of 20 (Curtis, 1981). That is, the program that one person can write in two weeks will take another person a year – and the two-week program will often be of better quality. A practical implication of this result that has been found in several studies is that the most important aspect of improving software projects is to employ fewer, but better programmers. Even for nonprogramming tasks, the ratio between the best and the worst users' performance is typically a factor of between four and 10.

Attitude differences can also impact how people use computers. For whatever reason, some people simply love using computers and will go to extreme efforts to learn all about their system. I once interviewed a business professional who said that she liked to learn a new software package every month just to stay in shape, and many other "super-users" spend as much time as many hackers learning about obscure details in their computers, even though they are business professionals and not programmers (Nielsen, et al., 1986). Such super-users (also known as "power users" or "gurus") often serve an important function as liaisons between the regular users and new computer developments as introduced by an information management department or outside software vendors. The super-users' role as technology champions not only helps introduce new systems but also provides the regular users with a local means of finding sympathetic and task-specific help (Gantt & Nardi, 1992; Nardi & Miller, 1991). Because they often like to talk, super-users can also serve as a way for software developers to get feedback about changing user needs before the majority of users have reached a stage where these new needs have become apparent. Just remember that most users will be different from the super-users, so do not design the user interface purely on the basis of their desires.

Given the many differences between groups of users and between individual users, it might be tempting to give up and just allow the users to customize their interfaces to suit their individual preferences. However, it is not a good idea to go too far in that direction either, since users are not designers. Most often, it is possible to design user interfaces to accommodate several kinds of users as long as attention is paid to all the relevant groups during the design process. It is rare that an interface change that is necessary to help one group will be a major problem for another or that it is at least not possible to work around the second group's difficulties.

END NOTES

1. Human factors (HF) and ergonomics have a broader scope than just HCI. In fact, many usability methods apply equally well to the design of other complex systems and even to simple ones that are not simple enough.
2. "Kiss and Ride" is an analogy with "Park and Ride" areas where people can leave their cars. The sign refers to commuters who are driven by their spouses and will kiss them before getting out of the car to take the train.
3. An early activity aimed at getting intuitive icons is to ask some users to draw icons they would like for each of the concepts that need to be depicted. The results will probably not look very good, but they can serve as a pool of ideas for the graphic designer.
4. Users were shown the command descriptions one at a time, thus preventing them from matching icons to descriptions by exclusion. If the users had been able to see all the command descriptions at the same time as they were seeing all the icons, they could have assigned the last (and probably most difficult) icon to the remaining, unmatched command description.
5. Actually, Fitts' Law implies that it would be a little slower to move the mouse between fields in the larger version of the dialogue box, because the time to point at an object is proportional to the logarithm of the distance to the object (Card, English, & Burr, 1978). However, expert users would be likely to move between the fields in the dialogue box with the Tab key (another accelerator) if speed was of the essence, and they would therefore not be subject to Fitts' Law.
6. Note that the classification dimensions used here are different from those used in the "user cube" of Cotterman and Kumar (1989). Their dimensions concerned the degree to which the user was the producer or consumer of information, whether the user had any part in developing the system, and the user's degree of decision-making authority over the system. These dimensions are certainly also of interest.

CHAPTER 2

User Needs Analysis

Tom Brinck, Darren Gergle, and Scott D. Wood

EDITOR'S COMMENTS

Many software and Web projects fail because of missing, wrong, or ambiguous requirements. Usability practitioners can play a major role in defining requirements for the users and other stakeholders that will improve the chances of product success. Usability practitioners can determine which usability dimensions (see Chapter 1 in this book) are most critical for the success of a product or service, and define the specific usability requirements for learnability, satisfaction, error rates, and overall task completion. Field visits, interviews, and other methods of determining the needs of users can also reveal functional, interoperability, and scalability requirements that can be used by product and development managers. For example, you might learn through a series of site visits that your primary users often deal with databases with millions of items. Knowing that it is millions, rather than tens of thousands, would be important for understanding the performance requirements and designing the specific user interface used to access those millions of items. Providing your colleagues on the project team with information that would improve the quality of requirements is a way to improve collaboration and your standing in the team.

The first part of this chapter provides a rich set of methods for understanding the user needs early in the product development cycle when you can have a significant impact on the product development. The second part of this chapter explains in clear terms how task analysis methods can help user experience practitioners understand workflow, improve efficiency, and eliminate pain points that cause frustration.

INTRODUCTION

User needs analysis sets the groundwork for the entire design process. The principal purpose of this stage of design is to define the design goals and constraints and develop an understanding of your audience and what they do. This chapter covers the basic process of setting the goals and objectives, and then it discusses the methods of background research necessary to elaborate and clarify these goals: surveys, competitive analysis, interviews, and focus groups.

Four primary activities are involved in user needs analysis:

1. Investigation: Do the background research to understand your audience and business needs.
2. Analysis: Analyze this information to understand the priorities.
3. Specification: Specify your objectives, assumptions, and design constraints.
4. Documentation: Document all your lessons learned, goals, and design decisions.

THE OBJECTIVES OF USER NEEDS ANALYSIS

At the end of the process, your goal is to emerge with clear statements about the following issues, informed as much as possible by the objective data from your target users:

1. Define your audience: Who are the users?
2. Identify user goals: What do your users want and need? How do they solve their problems now?
3. Define your business goals: What do the users need to do for this Web site or application to be a viable investment?
4. Set the usability objectives: To what extent does the site need to satisfy both the user and the business goals? How do we measure success?
5. Identify the design constraints: Define the budget, the timeline, and the project team. Investigate the target platforms and their technical limitations. Identify which platforms will not be targeted and the possible constraints that will not apply.
6. Define functional specifications: Based on all your goals and design constraints, specify the detailed functionality of the Web site.

Spelling out this information early in the design process avoids costly redesign and repair later in the process and focuses all future work toward these goals.

Many Web design firms use a form like the Form 2.1 to help identify the project goals during an initial client interview. (Download from http://www.mkp.com/uew/.) This worksheet can be a useful shortcut when in-depth user research is not possible.

SETTING YOUR OBJECTIVES

After defining your audience, you need to define the goals for the Web site. Why are you creating a Web site? Who is it for and what do they need to do on the site?

A form like the Form 2.2 can be used to help you clarify the stakeholders, business goals, user goals, and usability objectives for the site. (Download from http://www. mkp.com/uew/.) Feel free to expand on it if it isn't quite the right list for your site.

The Stakeholders

Who will be affected by the existence of your Web site, and why do they care? Your clients? Your design team? The end users? For an e-commerce site, the stakeholders include the vendors, the distributors, the shipping company, business partners, advertisers, investors, all the departments (marketing, purchasing, billing, shipping, customer support) within the e-commerce company, the customers, the person they're buying for, the customers' spouses who get ignored while the customers are using the computer, and their friends who are trying to call while they're monopolizing the phone line.

You've got to factor in the concerns of all these people in a complex set of design trade-offs. If you ignore some stakeholders, someday they're going to walk in and play their trump card, and an otherwise careful design will be shot full of holes. If you've never bothered to consider what information the shipping company wants, and you don't have what they want, then you may find yourself with hundreds of orders (or worse yet, millions) with no way to fill them. For instance, you may have assumed a flat shipping rate or a rate scaled to the purchase quantity, but your shipping department may surprise you with extra charges for fragile items, hazardous chemicals, or biological waste.

Stakeholders who are affected by your site design but don't actually use it themselves are sometimes called *indirect users.* Excellent usability means working for the indirect and the direct users.

Client Interview/Web Site Information Worksheet

Project Name _____ Date _____

Client Contacts

Name	Role	Phone	Fax	Email
	Principal Contact			

Project Team

Name	Role	Phone	Fax	Email
	Account Rep			
	Project Manager			
	Lead Designer			
	Lead Developer			

FORM 2.1.
*Client Interview/
Web Site Information
Worksheet.*

Project Schedule and Milestones

Date	Milestone
_____	Initial Meeting
_____	1st Mockups Delivered
_____	Feedback from Mockups
_____	2nd Mockups Delivered
_____	Focus Groups
_____	Final Mockup Approval
_____	User Testing
_____	Final QA
_____	Launch

Description of Business/Organization (Current Web site address, primary market, primary products/services, competitive advantages)

_____
_____
_____

Competitors (Web site addresses, why they're good or bad, differentiators)

_____
_____
_____

Other Web Sites You Like (Web site addresses, why you like them)

_____
_____
_____

Web Site Goals (Primary reasons for and goals of this project, and how you will measure success)

_____
_____

Target Audience (Business or consumer, narrow or mass audience, age range, computer skills, platform considerations, screen sizes, accessibility concerns)

_____

Development Considerations (Hosting platform and software, plans for maintenance)

_____

Design Considerations

What is your logo? _____

What fonts do you use? _____

What colors do you use? (Pantone, RGB, etc.) _____

What other elements constitute your design identity?

(Slogans, bylines, illustrations, etc.) _____

Sections of Your Site (e.g., Home, About, Products/Services, Contact, Privacy Policy, Help, Site Map)

Page   *Requirements*

_____   _____

_____   _____

_____   _____

_____   _____

_____   _____

Goals Checklist

Identify the Stakeholders

Stakeholder   *Needs*

_____

_____

_____

Business Goals of the Site

❑ Brand image marketing   ❑ Sales
❑ Customer support   ❑ Lead development
❑ Interactive service   ❑ Persuasion: alter ideas or behavior
❑ Provide a free community service: ❑ Sell advertising
   information, entertainment, etc.   ❑ Other_____

User Goals

❑ Have fun   ❑ Find information
❑ Purchase something   ❑ Ask a question
❑ Meet people   ❑ Get a job done
❑ Other_____

Usability Objectives

Primary task   *Time to do it*   *Number of mistakes users can make*

_____

_____

_____

How long it takes to learn the system _____

Subjective Impressions

How well should the average user rate the web site on each of these dimensions?

Easy to use	1 2 3 4 5 6 7	Hard to use
Attractive	1 2 3 4 5 6 7	Unattractive
Useful	1 2 3 4 5 6 7	Waste of time
Efficient	1 2 3 4 5 6 7	Tedious
Well organized	1 2 3 4 5 6 7	Haphazard
Entertaining	1 2 3 4 5 6 7	Boring
Valuable information	1 2 3 4 5 6 7	No information
Responsive	1 2 3 4 5 6 7	Slow

FORM 2.2.
Goals Checklist.

Business Goals

What are the business reasons for this Web site? What's the value proposition? How is the business going to determine whether the site was a success? For some sites, the evaluation is simply, "How much money did we make from customers of the Web site?" In the large number of marketing Web sites, the value is assessed based on the indirect effects on purchasing, lead generation, and company reputation and valuation.

For many first-time sites, the criterion for success is that the business gains a better understanding of the role the Internet can play in its business. In redesigning or expanding an existing Web site (or developing a large initial Web site), a cost justification is in order, without which the site is destined for failure. Business goals have to be factored into consideration with the user goals. For example, if the usability goals aren't tempered by the business goals, the most usable e-commerce site is one where users get everything for free (it's not only cheaper but also a lot simpler)!

User Goals

Why will users come to your site? To be entertained or to get work done? To learn something or to create something? To interact with other people or to avoid having to talk to one of your salespeople? Set up your initial expectations and refine them as you learn more about the users.

If you can't think of a reason for why users would come, then they probably won't. Some Web sites try to lure users by providing portals or news, but if you can't think of a reason for why users would *prefer* your portal or news service over another source, then they probably still won't come. So consider how your service can be more useful – for example, greater relevance (e.g., local news), more up-to-date information, or easier use. Try adding value to your core services rather than throwing in unrelated extras.

Define the Usability Objectives

Determine how well the site needs to work for the users. Consider how often they're likely to come to your site and how much time they can spend there. Based on that, how much time can they afford to spend learning how to use your system? How many times can they afford to make mistakes? If they get confused, will they simply leave your site and never return? How much do the users need to be impressed? What activities do they need to perform? How often do they need to come back? These questions will be elaborated as you learn more about your users. Table 2.1 shows some common types of usability objectives that may apply to your site. Chapter 1 in this book provides some additional details on defining usability objectives.

Don't be overly simplistic or unrealistic in setting these objectives. A three-click rule is a popular target (the user should be able to get to any page within three clicks), but it's not a realistic objective for large sites. It's good to minimize the number of clicks that users have to make to get something done, but it's more

Table 2.1	Examples of Usability Objectives
Category	**Examples of Specific Objectives**
Learning time/ task time	Users will be able to use this site the first time without any training
	First-time users will be able to find their topic of interest within two minutes of visiting the site; expert users (five or more visits) will be able to find a topic within 30 seconds
Number of errors	Users will not visit more than three incorrect pages (on average) in completing a task
	Users will make no fatal errors at least 99 percent of the time (such as entering an incorrect credit card or shipping address)
Subjective impressions	On a scale of 1 (really appealing) to 7 (really unappealing), users will rate the site at least a 2.5
Accomplished tasks	At least 75 percent of users who add an item to a shopping cart will complete a purchase
	At least 95 percent of users who complete their credit card information will complete a purchase
Revisits	At least 50 percent of registered users will return to the site at least once per month

important to consider how long it takes them and how many mistakes they may make than to worry about the specific number of clicks. Similarly, it's good to aim for fast downloading of pages, but you should be realistic about how fast they can possibly be.

EDITOR'S NOTE: TESTING THE THREE-CLICK RULE

Joshua Porter of User Interface Engineering (http://www.uie.com/articles/three_click_rule/) put the three-click rule to an empirical test with 44 users who tried to complete 620 tasks. The results showed that users often clicked well beyond three clicks to find the content they desired. Porter concluded that the number of clicks is not as important to users as finding what they wanted. The goal of minimizing clicks in a Web site is a reasonable goal, but trying too hard to enforce the three-click rule might create other problems.

EDITOR'S NOTE: ALIGNING BUSINESS, USABILITY (OR USER EXPERIENCE), AND FUNCTIONS

A technique for aligning business goals, usability goals, and functions that will help achieve those goals is a simple matrix (Donoghue, 2002) where you list each type of goal and the specific functions that support that goal. In the table below, an important goal is to "grow the business" by improving learnability. Functions that support both the business goal and the user experience goal include progressive tooltips and wizards for navigating the more complex features that are important for initial setup.

Business Goal	User Experience Goal	Functions to Support Goals
Grow the business by getting more new users to adopt our service	Improve the learnability	Progressive tooltips
		Wizards to get people started
Reduce support costs	Reduce/prevent errors	▪ Formatting information for text fields
		▪ Error message enhancements
		▪ Diagnostic features
Inspire loyalty among existing users	Reduce navigational requirements	▪ Shortcuts to frequently used content or features

Define the Functional Specifications

While functionality is sometimes considered outside the domain of the usability specialist, it's clear that if users simply *can't* do something they need to do, then the system isn't usable. As such, much of the work done in user studies during user needs analysis is focused on uncovering the capabilities and functionality that the users will need.

A traditional requirements' document in software engineering focuses on functional specifications, or specs. These list each subsystem of the software and all functional requirements within each subsystem. This document is revised throughout the requirements analysis phase, and additional functional requirements may be added during the development as the functionality is understood more intimately or as the usability studies show that a feature needs to be added, modified, or removed. Later changes are reviewed carefully to understand their impact on schedule and budget. Functional requirements are explicitly prioritized and the desired features are scheduled for later releases of the Web site.

The functional specs are referenced throughout the design and production of the site to verify that the system being produced corresponds to the necessary functionality. In addition, the quality assurance team uses the functional specs as the basis for the majority of its testing.

A large site will have hundreds, thousands, or even more functional requirements specified. Some examples of the functional requirements for the site visitor include the following:

- Site contains a help system that can be brought up from any screen.
- Site contains links to contact information on every screen.

- Error pages include a customer service phone number.
- Searches that return zero matches include suggested products to view.
- Product listings include product name, description, size, and weight.
- Site sends e-mail to buyers when orders are back-ordered, and when back-ordered products are received.
- Site e-mails a welcome message to users when they register.

Many sites need an administrative interface for those who must update the site content or process orders. Don't forget to plan the features for these users also. Some examples of the functional requirements for the administrative (or back-end) portion of the Web site include the following:

- Ability to add, modify, and delete the product listings on the site.
- Ability to add, modify, or delete the banner advertisements posted throughout the site.
- Notification system that e-mails copies of all orders to the shipping department and to the site administrator.
- Nightly transaction reports listing all orders through the site.
- Reports upon request for
  - the money made per period – by advertisements and by orders
  - the user demographics by the product category
  - the products sold by the user category
  - the banner advertisements hit counts by company purchasing the banner advertisements
- Ability to tell if the system is down and send an alert to the system administrator and to the manager responsible for the site.

BACKGROUND RESEARCH

Several forms of background research are used to uncover user needs including: surveys, scenarios, competitive analysis, interviews, and focus groups. These give us a better idea of our true user profile, user needs, and user preferences. Most of these methods are also good at generating conceptual design ideas. Designers don't have to rely on their own ingenuity to solve the design problems but can use background research to elicit the considerable knowledge and domain expertise of the target users.

With most of these methods, you'll want to work closely with the marketing department because of the large overlap of interests between the usability concerns and marketing. You'll also find that there are some distinct interests: although marketing is interested in how much people are willing to pay, what magazines they read, and how they make purchasing decisions, the usability specialist is more interested in their disabilities, computer skills, physical and social environments, and work practices. As a result, while many of these techniques are also part of traditional marketing practice, such as competitive analysis and focus groups, you'll see that the way we carry them out is somewhat different than the traditional methods, stressing the usability concerns.

SURVEYS

The first method of background research that we'll discuss is conducting a user survey. Because most people have answered a marketing survey at one time or another, this method is likely to be the most familiar.

What to Ask About

What kinds of information are surveys particularly good at collecting? Surveys work well for issues that are clear-cut and easy to categorize, such as basic demographics. They should also focus on questions that directly resolve design dilemmas, helping to guide your design decisions.

DEMOGRAPHICS

Surveys are a good way to collect the demographics of your users, especially to help uncover the breadth of diversity. A questionnaire can determine the general age, gender, profession, education, computer skill, type of computer, and nationality of the target population. The first use of demographics is to verify that you have properly sampled your target population. The second use is to find out the basic data about the skills, experience, and lifestyle of your audience. For instance, if you are building a gaming site for young men, you can first check to make sure that your responses are actually from young men, and then you want to find out what those young men are like: what computers do they use, what games do they play, what types of game controllers do they have, what is their reading (or education) level, and how much time do they spend on Internet gaming sites?

> ### EDITOR'S NOTE: DEMOGRAPHICS AT THE END, PLEASE!
>
> Demographics are important for user needs analysis, but don't make the mistake of placing a large block of standard demographic questions (e.g., age, job title, salary, gender, state, and country) at the beginning of your survey. These questions, while important to you, are not interesting to the respondent or connected to the main purpose of your survey. Place your standard demographic questions at the end of the survey (Dillman, 2007). Use your early questions (unless you need to do some screening) to capture the interest of the respondents – something that questions about age, gender, and job title are not likely to do.

NEEDS AND PREFERENCES

Surveys explore people's preferences with questions such as "What kinds of products would you like to buy online?" Surveys explore the problems people have with Web sites by asking questions such as "Which of these issues would you consider to be the *worst* aspect of browsing the Web: download speed, browser incompatibility, getting lost." And surveys also explore the problems that users have with the job task for which they are using the Web by asking questions such as "What are the most common problems you have with tracking inventory today?"

DESIGN IMPACT

In crafting your survey, choose questions that will have a direct impact on your design. If you can't decide how an answer would affect your design, then delete the question.

For instance, if your design wouldn't be affected by gender, don't bother asking users to specify their gender. And definitely do not depend on stereotypes of how gender should influence the design. Your stereotypes may be wrong, so rely on user data. If you think men prefer black backgrounds on their Web sites, you're much better off asking "What background color do you prefer on Web sites?" than asking their gender. Similarly, don't assume technical people want a design with elaborate technical wizardry or that children prefer talking animals before you've actually asked them.

While it may be interesting to ask about gender and find out how gender correlates with other responses, this is mostly useful if you're trying to do a long-term research rather than a practical design. For solving the design problem at hand, keep the survey short and precise, skipping questions you won't apply directly, and design your Web site to work across the spectrum of responses you get. Occasionally, it may be useful to ask general questions to look at how users' backgrounds may affect their responses. This may lead you to broaden your survey sample if the pattern of responses suggests that you had a biased sample. Form 2.3 is a sample survey template that can be modified according to the kind of information that is needed. (Download from http://www.mkp.com/uew/.)

How to Structure the Survey Responses?

The type of response you allow – checkbox, multiple choice, free response – is guided by several concerns: keeping the survey short and making the responses fast, enabling straightforward analysis with statistical tools, encouraging accurate and complete responses, and encouraging new information that you could not have anticipated.

FREE RESPONSE

A free response option asks an open question and lets respondents enter any response they like. Because this takes more effort than most types of questions, free response questions tend to get the fewest responses. In addition, because the responses can be in any form the respondent chooses, it can be difficult to tally up the answers and to compare them. You may be able to categorize typical responses, but it is quite likely that exceptional cases don't fit categories well.

EDITOR'S NOTE: TIPS FOR WHEN TO USE FREE RESPONSE (OPEN) QUESTIONS IN SURVEYS

Free response questions are useful when:

- You don't know much about a particular topic and thus can't generate credible response categories.
- The known list of responses is very long.
- You are doing exploratory studies at the beginning of a project.
- You want to follow up on a closed question response.
- You have questions that can be easily recalled without a list of responses.
- You have dedicated customers (e.g., a customer council) who really want to tell you why they rated something as good or bad. Dedicated groups of users are often very willing to provide details in the hope that you will fix the problems.

You generally want to avoid starting a survey with a tough open question that will give your respondents the feeling that the survey is taxing and time-consuming. Start with a closed question that is relevant, but not threatening. For example, you might ask the person to choose a job role, but you would not have the first question ask "How much money do you make?"

Free response questions can include those that encourage specific answers, such as asking for specific quantities. These are obviously easier to tally and compare.

Use free response questions at the end of your survey to see if the respondents have any other comments that go beyond what you were looking for. Make sure there is some place for respondents to write in concerns about your survey: how it will be used, ways in which they chose to interpret your questions, and the response options you may have left out.

Free response items can be a very useful way to get ideas from potential users at a very low cost. Use these responses as directions to explore as you investigate more deeply with other methods: interviews, focus groups, user testing, and so forth.

CHECKBOXES AND CHECKLISTS

Checkboxes and checklists allow the respondent to quickly answer a large number of questions (often called "closed" or "close-ended" questions), keeping writing to a minimum. A checklist might, for instance, list products that a respondent owns or would be interested in purchasing through your Web site. A checklist can list possible problems that people have in doing their jobs. A checklist could ask the users what features they'd like on your Web site.

While no other response is quite as fast, respondents often skip reading long checklists or overlook the checklist options. It's difficult to tell whether an unchecked box was explicitly left unchecked or was simply ignored. For this reason, in counting up the number of people who responded to a particular checklist item, you should view the total as a likely underestimate of what might have been the actual interest in that item. A checkbox can usually be replaced with a Yes/No response, which eliminates the problem of interpreting whether the item was skipped but may still have a relatively low-response rate.

MULTIPLE CHOICE

Multiple choice responses enable you to restrict the response set to easily understood categories, making analysis of responses more straightforward than with free response questions. Providing choices requires that you anticipate what responses are possible. When you believe you may be missing important alternatives, leave an option to choose "Other" and space to write in a response.

For online surveys, make sure that all the multiple choice items, typically displayed as radio buttons, default to a "No Response" option or have none of the radio buttons selected.

Likert scales are multiple choice responses like "strongly disagree 1 2 3 4 5 6 7 strongly agree," which have a numerical range of choices with typically five or seven options in a range. You can label each option, omitting the numbers (e.g., "strongly disagree disagree neutral agree strongly agree"). This is most useful when you have an uncommon response dimension (e.g., "cool" versus "uncool," which is not recommended) or where the intermediate levels could be interpreted differently by each respondent. It's most accurate to include a neutral or middle option, but in some types of surveys you may find respondents will tend to gravitate toward a "no opinion" stance (out of politeness, for instance). When you omit the middle option (leaving four or six options), you can draw out small preferences. Because of their numerical interpretation, Likert scales enable you to take an average of the responses.

FORM 2.3.
Sample Survey.

Web Site Survey

This survey is designed to gather information about the users and potential users of our web site in order to make sure we serve your needs as well as possible.

Please answer the questions as completely as you can. Do not include your name—your participation in this survey is anonymous.

Your Experience
How long have you used computers?
    under 1 year   1–3 years   more than 3 years

Which computer systems have you used regularly?
    DOS   Windows   Mac   Unix   Other _____

Which browsers have you used regularly?
    Internet Explorer   Netscape Navigator   Other _____

Our Web Site
The following questions are about your experiences of our Web site at
www.examplewebsite.com.

How many times have you visited our Web site? _____

List any other sites you have used that are similar

_____
_____
_____
_____
_____

Please rate our site on the following dimensions

Easy to use	1 2 3 4 5 6 7	Hard to use
Attractive	1 2 3 4 5 6 7	Unattractive
Useful	1 2 3 4 5 6 7	Waste of time
Efficient	1 2 3 4 5 6 7	Tedious
Well organized	1 2 3 4 5 6 7	Haphazard
Entertaining	1 2 3 4 5 6 7	Boring
Valuable information	1 2 3 4 5 6 7	No information
Responsive	1 2 3 4 5 6 7	Slow

What do you consider the most valuable aspect of the Web site?

_____
_____

What is the biggest problem with the site?

_____
_____

Which features would you like us to add to this site?
❏ Ability to purchase products online
❏ Online discussion boards
❏ An announcements mailing list
❏ Additional online help
❏ Ability to place classified ads on our site
❏ A jobs board

About You
Your job title _____

Your age   under 18   18–29   30–39   40–49   50 or over

Gender   female   male

Highest level of education
  high school   some college   bechelor's degree   graduate work

Do you have any other comments about our Web site you would like to offer?
_____
_____
_____

Thank you for participating in our survey.

INTERPRETING RESPONSES

When analyzing responses to your survey, you'll generally look for the average or most common response. You can count the total number of responses to a checked item. Low response to an individual question may indicate that the question is unclear and the responses should be interpreted cautiously. Surveys can provide extremely useful data, but remember to document the limitations to the data, such as a low-response rate, sampling problems, or biases, discussed later.

Exceptional responses should not be ignored. You're not simply looking for an average response. While it's useful to know how an "average" person responds, it's also very useful to understand the spectrum of responses. How much do people vary in their responses? You may want to create a design that serves two or more divergent audiences. Also, some outlier populations may be extremely important to your site design. For instance, two percent of your users may be millionaires, but they may buy your most expensive products and account for more than a two percent portion of your profits. And some small populations may require extra attention to serve more challenging needs, such as providing an accessible design for people with disabilities.

Sampling

How many survey responses do you need to collect? Even a small number of responses can be useful. Designing from *any* information is better than designing with *none*, so long as you're careful not to be overconfident in a limited sample. If you're trying to achieve statistical significance, the degree of significance will depend on both your sample size and the range of responses you get to each question. You'll need to consult with a statistician to work out a good number for your case. A helpful rule of thumb is that fewer than 10 returned surveys is not likely to be useful, and 50 returned surveys is a good target. Solid scientific research may, in some cases, require more surveys, but 50 should be more than adequate for most practical design situations.

RETURN RATE

To get 50 surveys back, you'll need to send out quite a few more than that. Online surveys can expect as few as one to two percent of site visitors actually to respond. E-mail and snail mail surveys typically are returned at a rate of five to 10 percent, meaning that you need to send out as many as 1,000 to get 50 returned. People who are highly motivated to be involved in the design will return the surveys at a much higher rate. It's not unusual to get 100 percent return rate when surveying within a small organization that will be using your Web site in its daily work.

You can improve the rate of return of mail surveys in several ways:

- Offer a small gift or prize drawing for those who return your survey.
- Include a small gift with the survey, whether or not they return it.
- Make sure that the survey does not look like junk mail: address envelopes by hand, lick stamps rather than using a machine, sign cover letters by hand (or even write the cover letters by hand), personally address the cover letter to the recipient. For e-mail surveys, make sure each e-mail is personally addressed rather than sent to a list.
- Use unusual paper and envelopes to make the survey stand out in the mail.
- Include a referral letter in cases where you are contacting members of a specific organization. For instance, surveys going out to employees of a company should include a letter from a relevant manager.
- Keep the survey short and say how long it is likely to take to fill out the questionnaire.
- Include a self-addressed stamped envelope.
- Emphasize that the responses will be kept confidential.
- Emphasize the benefits to users of having a Web site design reflecting their needs and interests.
- Specify a date by which you'd like the survey to be returned. Otherwise, respondents may procrastinate.
- Follow up the initial survey with a written or online query to those who haven't responded, encouraging them to participate.

EDITOR'S NOTE: OFFERING PRIZE DRAWINGS HAS LEGAL IMPLICATIONS

If you are considering a prize drawing ("fill out our survey for a chance at winning one of 50 iPods®"), consult your organization's attorney. In the United States, each state has different rules about how sweepstakes must be run. Even prize drawings within a single company with offices in different states might present legal problems. If you are offering something on the Internet, you have to consider international laws on prize drawings or restrict your drawing to specified countries. There are companies that specialize in running lotteries and sweepstakes. If you are planning a major survey with significant prizes or monetary awards, consult a reputable company that will help you avoid any legal problems.

EDITOR'S NOTE: INCREASING THE RATE OF RETURN OF E-MAIL AND ONLINE SURVEYS

If you want to increase the rate of return of e-mail and online surveys you should:

- Personalize e-mail and Internet requests so people don't think that they are part of a mass mailing. Include a real contact person's name, affiliation, and e-mail. Including this type of personal information will help respondents trust the survey.
- For Web surveys, create an introduction page that will motivate respondents to fill out the survey and assure them that it will be easy to answer. The introduction page should have a personal contact for any questions about the survey.
- Start with an easy first question.
- Provide specific instructions for each question.
- Test your survey on a range of browsers and resolutions. Design your questions so they will be readable on systems with different resolutions.
- Conduct a small pilot test of your online survey with actual respondents before you release it broadly. Verify that there are no technical or usability problems.
- Provide some form of progress on Web surveys so the respondents know where they are in the survey.

SELECTING SURVEY RECIPIENTS

When dealing with a small number of customers or a small number of users, as with an intranet, you can send the survey to everyone; your only limiting factor is the cost of distributing the survey and analyzing the responses. If the survey can be created online, the cost of distributing the survey and collecting the data is minimized, and development time is your only significant cost.

It is trickier when you're targeting a mass market, an ill-defined group, or prospective customers. You may not have an appropriate mailing list to start out with. Here are some ideas for getting started. Advertise the survey on your current site or on another Web site in the industry. If there are appropriate mailing lists or newsgroups, send your survey to them. Make sure this is within the usage policy of the list; identify yourself and your purposes clearly at the beginning of the message; keep the message short; and post only once. Go where your users congregate. If it's a local site, hand out surveys on a street corner. If it's an industry site, visit an industry convention. Use the *snowball sampling* technique: ask each respondent to suggest another appropriate recipient (gathering respondents like a snowball accumulates snow rolling down a hill).

For e-mail surveys, ask respondents to forward surveys to their friends and colleagues. In your e-mail, be sure to specify by what date the survey needs to be returned, or you may end up getting surveys coming to you for years as they circulate around the Internet. While you should avoid creating a survey that *looks like* junk mail, you also need to avoid the perception that your survey *is* junk mail. Be careful not to abuse mailing lists that were clearly not intended for the purpose of your survey. Ask permission of organization leaders before sending it to the members of their group. Make sure that your company has decided that it's okay to send surveys to customers before the surveys go out, and include appropriate cover letters from the account representatives.

EDITOR'S NOTE: EXAMPLES OF OTHER SAMPLING TECHNIQUES

In addition to snowball sampling, there are other approaches to sampling for surveys as well as other data collection methods. Here are some other sampling approaches:

- **Quota sampling** where you try to obtain respondents in relative proportion to their presence in the population.
- **Dimensional sampling** where you try to include respondents who fit the critical dimensions of your study (e.g., time spent on the Internet, age, shops online for gifts).
- **Convenience sampling** where you choose the easiest and most accessible people who meet the basic screening criteria.
- **Purposive sampling** where you choose respondents by interest or typicality. Samples that meet the specific goals of the study are sought out, for example, if you are trying to understand how experts in a particular field make decisions, you might seek out the "best of the best" and use them for your interviews.
- **Extreme samples** where you want people who have some exceptional knowledge, background, or experience that will provide a special perspective.
- **Heterogeneous samples** in which you choose the widest variety of people possible on the dimensions of greatest interest (e.g., you might choose people from many industries and experience ranges).

SELF SELECTION

You usually can't control who responds to your survey, so the people who take the time to fill out the questionnaire are the people who *choose* to do so. These motivated people may be exactly the people who are sufficiently interested in your Web site that they'll be your regular users, but there are many reasons for not returning a survey. For instance, people who have been dissatisfied with your Web site may not want to waste their time providing you with information, but you especially want to know what problems caused their dissatisfaction. People who are motivated to provide feedback may have significantly different usage behavior than other users.

Self selection should be a concern, and you want to minimize it, but don't view it as a reason not to conduct a survey. Any user study will have some limitations, and sampling problems are a common one. Carefully document which target groups did and did not receive the survey, and write down the reasons you think people may not have responded. Include this information in your survey results, and factor these limitations into your design recommendations based on the survey. You will often find that you can have fairly high confidence in your results despite self-selection problems.

Avoiding Bias

Survey questions need to be carefully worded to avoid biasing the responses. Respondents will actively try to understand and interpret the purpose of your questions and will often try to determine what answers you're expecting and how they think you'll use those answers. Often, the way they respond will not correspond to the question you were hoping to ask.

Pretest the survey to identify questions that are misleading, ambiguous, insulting, or just plain nonsense. The pretest will identify questions that are always skipped and answers that are always the same. The pretesters will often give you insights into how to fix the questions. Below are some tips for minimizing these biases.

QUESTION SKIPPING

People have a tendency to skip questions in surveys because they don't understand the questions, don't consider them relevant, can't figure out an appropriate answer, or are just bored with a long questionnaire. As a result, surveys need to be kept short and relevant to maximize the quality of responses. In addition, asking respondents to answer every question can increase the completeness of their responses.

RESPONSE ORDER

Put response options in their natural order, say from the lowest to highest value. Or, if there is no natural order, scramble them. You will have the tendency to place possible responses in the order that you think of them, and because of this, you'll want to rearrange the responses to avoid implying that some responses are "better" than the others. Respondents may also have a tendency to choose either the first or last item, so watch for this in pretesting or rearrange the order on different versions of the survey. Don't rearrange the order between questions if some of the questions involve negatives, or else the respondents will likely become very confused.

ROTE ANSWERS

One problem with arranging all the answers in a consistent order is that respondents may fall into a pattern of marking all low or high responses in a series, without thinking through each question. Without confusing the respondent, vary the responses. To keep people thinking, switch often between types of responses: multiple choice, free response, and checklist.

NEGATIVE QUESTIONS

Avoid all uses of negatives, such as "Which of the following is not a problem in using our Web site?" If you have to use a negative term, emphasize it as "NOT." Watch out for subtle implied negatives, such as "Which of the following are you least likely to consider as your most delightful fantasy: ice cream, world peace, or pots of gold?" Among such great alternatives, the word "least" can easily be missed.

LEADING QUESTIONS

Nobody loves a *terrorist*, but *freedom fighters* can be pretty popular. Your choice of words may imply a certain response that is the opposite you'd get by phrasing it differently.

AMBIGUITY

The same question or response may mean different things to different people. Make your responses as specific and concrete as possible. If you choose to imitate the phrasing of an older questionnaire (one you dug out of a book, for instance), make sure that the language is contemporary and that words haven't shifted meaning. A common example is the use of the word "fair" as a response option: some people feel that "fair" is a positive term and others feel that it's a negative term.

RANGE BIAS

If you ask, "How many times per week do you use the Internet?" you've already implied that the respondent uses the Internet at least once a week. Instead ask, "How often do you use the Internet?" If your response options are "15 hours/day or more; 10–15 hours/day; 5–10 hours/day; and less than 5 hours/day," you'll arrive at more frequent use than if your options are "at least once per day; 1–5 times per week; 1–5 times per month; and less than once per month." Requiring a write-in response may minimize the bias but will reduce the comparability of responses, frustrating your analysis. This bias can't be avoided entirely, but be sure to choose sensible ranges and pretest to make certain that you get an effective range of responses.

EDITOR'S NOTE: AVOID DOUBLE QUESTIONS – THEY MAKE DATA UNINTERPRETABLE

Design questions so that they address a single issue. "Double questions" – two questions posing as a single question – are difficult to answer and should be split into two separate questions with the appropriate response alternatives. Here are examples of double questions, which should be split into two questions.

- Rate the usability and reliability of the system.

This first example is a double question because it asks one question about usability and a second question about reliability. There is often a connection between reliability and usability, (if something crashes a lot, it might be viewed as unusable; however, it may be quite usable most of the time, but crashes once in awhile), but this double question would produce muddled results. You wouldn't quite know if you needed to work on the user interface or the underlying code for improved reliability or both. Here is another example of a double question:

■ How satisfied were you with the performance and usability of the BookBuyer.com Web site?

In this second example, the performance of the site could have been great, but the usability was poor or vice versa. This question could be split into one question about performance and another question about usability. This type of mistake renders the data uninterpretable because it is not clear which "question" (performance or usability) the participant is answering.

Fowler and Mangione (1990; 84) describes another category of double questions called "hidden questions" where an implied question is part of an explicit question. For example, the question "Who will you vote for in the next Usability Professionals' Association (UPA) election?" has an implied question, "Will you vote in the next UPA election?" and an explicit question "Who will you vote for in the UPA election?"

When to Use Surveys

Surveys can be an inexpensive way to gather large amounts of data from potential users. Because you can get a large sample size, a good survey can provide you with the most reliable demographics possible. Surveys are especially useful before a project starts, and once the Web site has gone live they can be used to inexpensively gather the feedback online. They are less successful when you have trouble identifying who the target users will be or when the target users have a very low motivation to return the survey. Surveys often come back with incomplete data. By contrast, direct user contact in interviews and focus groups can provide both more complete feedback and more in-depth, thoughtful responses. However, the complete anonymity of a survey can give you personal information that wouldn't come across in a face-to-face interview.

COMPETITIVE ANALYSIS

A competitive analysis can be one of the fastest ways to hone in on a workable design paradigm for your product. If you are designing a portal, take a look at Yahoo! If you're designing a shopping site, look at Amazon. If you're building an auction system, look at eBay. One caveat: Yahoo, Amazon, and eBay are all multimillion-dollar systems, so you may find some excellent features on their sites that are not possible within your budget.

The traditional competitive analysis will focus on the market niche being targeted, the price of the product, and the unique selling point being promoted. In analyzing for the usability, we're looking for the user interface ideas. What categories, labels, icons, processes, and features are they using? What audience are they targeting, and what user goals are they trying to serve? We want to examine their good ideas and apply them to our design. This can be as simple as visiting the competitors' sites and listing all the features they support as a first step to writing a functional specification for your site.

Examining ideas from your competitors is a time-honored technique for innovation, but it needs to be done with a serious respect for intellectual property. Copyright law protects the way Web sites express their look and feel – the creative aspects of their design, such as their exact words or images and the way they've chosen to combine them. Don't copy text or images directly, although it's usually safe to copy an individual label, and it's okay to show a dog if another site has shown a dog, even the very same dog. You just can't use the same picture of the dog. If it's the same dog (or a similar one), watch out for trademarks. Similarly, if you copy a label, make sure it's not a label that is trademarked, such as a brand name or service mark. Don't assume it's safe to copy just because there's no copyright notice. Copyright and trademarks don't have to be explicitly declared to be protected. If there's only one *optimal* way to do something, copyright law would not protect it because there's no creativity involved in choosing the *unique* optimal solution. However, in this case, the patent law may apply. Someone may have patented a specific process that enables users to perform a task or a specific way of computing results. If you have any doubts about which, if any, intellectual property laws apply, you'll need to consult with your lawyer.

EDITOR'S NOTE: COPYRIGHT AND US INTELLECTUAL PROPERTY

Copyright, patent, and trademark laws are complex and are often misunderstood. As noted in this chapter, copyright occurs when a work is created – you don't have to register your copyright. Copyright registration provides a public record of the copyright claim and is required if you plan to file an infringement suit for works that originate in the United States.

A good source of general information on intellectual property law can be found at the United States Patent and Trademark Office (USPTO), http://www.uspto.gov. This site also has some general information about international treaties that govern how copyright, patents, and trademarks are handled between countries. A general awareness of intellectual property issues is important because legal disputes can result in great cost to a company and in the worst case, result in the loss of critical technology.

Competitive analysis techniques apply to your competitors' sites, to other sites with similar functionality (whether they compete with you or not), and to previous versions of your own site. In addition to simply listing things your competitors have done, you can evaluate them for usability, through user testing or usability inspections, or by asking people to respond to the sites in interviews and focus groups. Evaluating the usability of competitors' sites identifies the problems you should avoid and establishes a benchmark for comparing the ease of use of your own site.

A competitive analysis is a way to establish a starting point in design, but don't give too much credit to competitors. You don't know if your competitors have tested their sites or what hidden influences may have played a role in their designs. Their site may look great, but they may be getting customer complaints left and right. More than anything, competitive analysis should be used for idea generation, but ideas you develop will need to be corroborated with feedback from users.

As a brief example, we compare the home pages of the Amazon and Borders Web sites in Fig. 2.1. Both are attempting to target mass-audience sales of books and other media. The Borders home page has a heavy emphasis on music, suggesting that this is a relatively high priority for them. In this comparison, we identify the main techniques, both good and bad, used on the pages. In a more complete analysis, we'd want to examine the site architectures and the steps necessary to find a product and complete a purchase.

Amazon.com

Pros

- Two-tiered menu at top shows structure hierarchy
- Search toward top of page
- Text-only option at top

Cons

- Too cluttered
- Layout unclear, not sure where to look
- Help not available if no images

Usability Issues

- Typography contributes to confusing layout

Borders.com

Pros

- Browsable navigation on side
- Good visual hierarchy
- Search toward top of page

Cons

- Icons are difficult to interpret
- Music dominates top of fold

Usability Issues

- Top navbar different from text navbar at bottom
- Light-brown links

FIGURE 2.1
Comparing two bookstore Web sites.

A competitive analysis is most useful in the following circumstances:

- When you're designing a product from scratch (When you're building a revision of your current system, feedback from your users will play a larger role.)
- When you have little experience in the target domain and need a source of good ideas
- When you're developing a transactional system, as opposed to a purely marketing site (In both the cases, some competitive analysis is useful, but transactional systems are more likely to have evolved in response to user demands and have unexpected features.)
- When the application is complex, so that good shortcuts and simplifying metaphors are crucial to discover
- When a competitor is threatening to take market share from your company and you need to understand your competition better

INTERVIEWS AND FOCUS GROUPS

Interviews and focus groups are useful for getting the subjective reactions to your designs and for finding out how people live and work and solve their problems. The main difference between the two methods is that interviews entail speaking to one individual at a time, whereas focus groups gather a group of people together to discuss issues that you raise.

The main advantage of an individual interview is that the individual is not biased by other people in the group. The advantage of a focus group is that if one person raises an idea, then another person can develop that idea, and you can delve into far greater detail on some issues by following up lines of thought that the interviewer might not have even known to pursue. However, you need to watch out for *groupthink* in focus groups, where people tend to conform to one another's views and are reluctant to disagree with the consensus view. A group can get sidetracked on a particular topic or point of view because it is easy or interesting to discuss rather than because it is an important topic. Table 2.2 summarizes the advantages of each method.

Conducting the Interview or Focus Group

Interviews and focus groups are best started by getting to know the interviewees. Many interviewees are nervous, and simple introductions can help encourage them to speak more freely. You should wear a name tag (first name only) so that the interviewees don't need to learn your name. At the beginning of a focus group, ask everyone to introduce themselves, which will help to get participants accustomed to participating in the discussion.

When interviewing people in a corporate setting, where they might feel their views could affect their job stability, it's a good idea to let people know that their participation will be anonymous and that they can review your notes if they are worried about what you may tell their boss.

Table 2.2 Interviews versus Focus Groups	
Advantages of Interviews	**Advantages of Focus Groups**
Interviewees do not influence one another's responses (no groupthink)	Group members can react to one another's ideas and can be prompted by another group member into considering an issue that the interviewer could not have anticipated
For the same level of confidence in the results, fewer people are required to sample a broad range of viewpoints	For the same number of interviewees, the time and cost are much smaller
In-depth exploration of individual tasks and problems is possible	Incorrect facts (that the interviewer may not know) can be corrected quickly
Each interview can refine the questions for following interviews	Noncontroversial issues are quickly resolved, and controversial issues are quickly identified

INCLUDING A SURVEY

You may want to begin or end the discussion with a written survey that addresses the basic information such as demographics and simple facts and preferences that won't affect the interview. A survey at the beginning is helpful if the interview might be interrupted prematurely. Usually, in a reasonably structured session, a survey is a good way to signal the end of the interview, and putting it at the end avoids biasing the interviewee about the intent of your interview.

STRUCTURED VERSUS UNSTRUCTURED INTERVIEWS

A structured interview is one that follows a fixed list of questions – essentially a survey conducted conversationally. An unstructured interview opens the floor to almost any kind of relevant discussion. The interviewer asks open-ended questions and follows them up by asking for more details as such details seem to be important. Most interviews fall somewhere between the two extremes. The structured interview gathers more consistent responses, permitting easier analysis, whereas the unstructured interview allows issues to be explored that could not have been anticipated by the interviewer.

USER NEEDS AND FUNCTIONALITY

Focus groups and interviews are really good for eliciting the user needs and functionality ideas. Ask people what they want from your Web site and why they would go there. Ask them how it fits into their lifestyle, and when and how they'd like to use it. Ask them what features they'd like and what they'd use; provide them with suggestions if they don't come up with anything on their own. While people can give you very accurate descriptions of how they currently do their work, hypotheticals are another story, and you should not rely too heavily on them. People are very poor at saying how likely they would be to use a feature that doesn't exist. However, their ideas for such features are a gold mine of possibilities you may not have considered.

REVIEWING MOCKUPS

Focus groups and interviews are also very good for exploring preferences, opinions, and subjective reactions. If you already have a Web site online or you have mockups available, ask people to look at the designs and tell you what they think. Reviewing alternative mockups with a set of users is a much more valid approach to choosing a design direction than reviewing them with management. A nice trick is to take your competitors' designs, brand them with your logo, and ask people which design they like best for your site. If your own design is among them, then you can verify whether your design is more effective than your competitors', and you can find out what aspects of your competitors' sites they like, while avoiding the bias of having them try to favor your own design.

As you review mockup alternatives and competitors' sites, ask people to respond to the layout, color, ease of use, and appeal of the site. If you've determined a specific feel that you want, ask them how well your designs fit your intention. For instance, you may want a site that is professional (vs. personal), traditional (vs. futuristic), objective (vs. subjective), and conservative (vs. daring). Your business has a certain image it wants to project, and you can ask whether that image makes sense and how well you've achieved it.

WALKTHROUGHS

If you already have a Web site or you've worked through the design so that you have several screens or a storyboard to review, you can also walk people through the design, asking them for their reactions as they go, performing an informal kind of user testing. This helps to identify labeling and placement problems early on. And unlike most user testing, you'll more easily get feedback on the look and the concept of the site. People may comment on text or layouts they don't like, inefficient tasks, concerns about privacy, and their own design tastes. This type of feedback is easier to get in an interview than in user testing, where you'll often miss out on more global issues because the users are focused on problem-solving and they're not as likely to mention odd aspects of the interface as long as they're able to get their task completed.

RECORDINGS

Audio recordings can capture what transpired in an interview and help you to fill in the holes from your notes when you fall behind. Get permission from anyone you're interviewing before recording them. Most people are quite comfortable with audio recordings if you keep them inconspicuous, but prepare for a mix of both recorded and nonrecorded sessions (when interviewees don't agree to being recorded).

Videotaping is typically so conspicuous that it makes people self-conscious about what they're saying, and rarely offers enough value to be worth the trouble. In focus groups, video cameras can be hidden in a corner or behind a mirror, which typically works out well. Video is useful for capturing gestures or drawings (which are rarely an important part of a focus group), for filling in your notes on what was said (but audio recordings are usually sufficient), or for presenting video clips later to the design team or the client. However, it is usually quite time-consuming to do the video editing.

Organizations

When developing intranet or extranet applications, the interview is an especially appropriate technique for uncovering complex organizational roles and relationships and understanding work processes (workflow). As an interviewer, you'll need to be especially sensitive to the politics of the situation and develop an empathy with each interviewee without appearing to take sides. In these settings, many people are concerned with how your work will affect theirs: will the new system create more work for them or threaten to eliminate their job role? Save sensitive questions until the end of an interview to develop as much empathy as possible before addressing them. Your letter of introduction may seem to ally you with a particular perspective, and, when possible, you may want to stress your status as an outside observer.

Look for where work practices vary from officially documented processes and explore why these exceptions take place. Do your best to discuss each job role with the person who fills that role rather than getting that information second-hand. Management will often have a different mental model of how work gets done than the people actually doing the work.

Preparing for an Interview or Focus Group

Most of the same issues apply in recruiting interviewees as in getting a sample for your survey or recruiting users for the user testing. Do your best to choose a representative sample of users. Selection is especially important because you can't get the quantity you would in surveys, and the types of opinions you collect require representative users. If you talk to people who aren't in the target market, you are likely to get uninformed and misleading ideas that are no more useful than guessing at the answers yourself.

Prepare all of your questions and materials ahead of time, even if you are planning an unstructured interview (see Form 2.4; download from http://www.mkp.com/uew/). Rehearse the interview or focus group with some of your colleagues, ensuring that your questions can be answered in a reasonable amount of time and that you're able to encourage a constructive dialogue. Practice taking notes and work out a shorthand so that you can take notes quickly and inconspicuously during the conversation. When possible, conduct team interviews with a primary interviewer and a note-taker, so that the primary interviewer can focus on the conversation and the note-taker can focus on capturing everything said.

FORM 2.4.
Focus Group Preparation Worksheet.

Focus Group Preparation Worksheet

Project _____

Dates and times _____

Location _____

Facilitator and other observers _____

Required demographic _____

Number of groups _____

Number of people (per group) _____

Payment (per person) _____

Food and refreshments _____

Videotaping and audiotaping: video / audio / none

Recruiting ad   *Where to place it?* _____

               Wording _____

               _____

Questions to ask:

_____

_____

_____

Materials
Check that you have each of the following, as needed, for your focus group.

❑ Consent form
❑ Demographic questionnaire
❑ Debriefing sheet
❑ Mockups
❑ Observer notes sheets
❑ List of participants
❑ Name tags
❑ Payment checks
❑ Audio and videotape
❑ Seating chart

A typical note-taking approach follows these guidelines:

- Mark every page of notes with the interviewer's name, the date, the project, and any other context that will help you remember the situation (location, interviewee code, etc.).
- Write down exact quotes in double quotes, write down paraphrases in single quotes, and write general conversation topics and opinions without any special marking.
- If you have any design ideas that were derived from the conversation, but that weren't explicitly discussed, write them down in square brackets.
- Put an asterisk (*) next to important issues you'll want to make sure you don't miss them during the analysis.
- In focus groups you may want to number each participant on a seating chart and number each comment you write down accordingly.
- Type your notes as soon as possible after the interview so that you remember as much as possible.

Focus Groups

Focus groups have some additional considerations not required for individual interviews. They are concerned primarily with deciding how to select and organize groups of people. Groups are more difficult to coordinate, and a facilitator is needed to help manage interpersonal interactions.

FACILITIES

Interviews can easily be conducted on the street or in someone's office, whereas focus groups need a good meeting place with a quiet, undistracting atmosphere, a way to display mockups to the participants (which can be mounted on boards and passed around or displayed on an overhead screen), a central table for participants to sit around, and an appropriate place for observers to sit. Many focus-group facilities have an observation room behind a one-way mirror for sets of observers to watch. If people are being surreptitiously observed, you need to tell them about it in advance, and usually it's not a problem. However, we usually find it's just as easy to have up to three observers sitting in the room who are introduced as assistants.

THE FACILITATOR

The primary person conducting the focus group is known as the *facilitator*. You can hire professional facilitators who are expert at encouraging discussion and getting everyone to participate. One of the goals of a focus group is to get people to respond to one another's input, and so you may even want to foster arguments – these lead to a lot of information about why people feel the ways they do and reveal the controversial issues. Of course, you'll want to prevent arguments from getting out of hand and hurting people's feelings. Generally, the idea is that one person's ideas can generate deeper analysis by a second person. The facilitator also encourages each person to participate, so no viewpoints get lost.

EDITOR'S NOTE: WHAT MAKES A GOOD FACILITATOR?

The skill of the facilitator is a key to a successful focus group. Skilled facilitators must (Krueger & Casey, 2000; Stewart, Shamdasani, & Rook, 2007):

- Balance empathy and sensitivity against objectivity and involvement
- Involve all the participants in the group
- Not speak too much or give away their particular feelings about the topics of the session
- Generate interest in the discussion topics and keep the focus group energized
- Be reasonably consistent in the way they ask questions
- Ensure that the participants are answering the target questions and not going off on a tangent
- Know enough about the topic to put answers in context and understand the comments of participants
- Keep dominant personalities from monopolizing the discussion
- Know when to follow a line of inquiry that isn't part of the plan
- Know when a line of questioning is not likely to lead to useful data
- Avoid giving away the expectations or concerns of the sponsors

NUMBER OF PEOPLE PER GROUP

Since not everyone shows up as scheduled, it's usually best to invite about two more people than your optimal number of participants. A focus group, generally, works well with six to 12 participants. We typically invite about 10 people, expecting anywhere from eight to 10. Ask people to show up 10 minutes early so you can start on time. Bring drinks (coffee, water, soft drinks) and possibly some simple snacks, and prepare for a break in the middle if you go over an hour. A good way to handle a break is to give participants a questionnaire or some other individual activity in the middle of the session. However, the risk in taking a break is that some people may never return from it, especially if you're conducting your session during work hours or in their workplace.

NUMBER OF GROUPS

You'll want to conduct more than one focus group, typically three to five. A single focus group may be heavily biased by the mix of people involved, and you would never even know there was a problem unless you'd conducted a second group. Two groups is a bare minimum to get a sense of how opinions vary, but, optimally, you'll continue recruiting groups until additional groups provide no substantial new information.

COMPOSITION OF GROUPS

What's a good mix of people in the group? In heterogeneous groups, you select a diverse set of people. Each group then contains a reasonably representative sample of your target audience. This is usually the preferred approach if you have a small number of groups. However, heterogeneous groups may comprise too wide a sample, bringing together people who have little in common and thus have little to respond to in what others say. In homogeneous groups, people of common demographics are selected, and you make sure each group samples a different demographic. This may lead to easier conversation, but each group tends to be more toward a single viewpoint so that more groups are necessary to sample a diversity of demographics.

When to Conduct Interviews and Focus Groups

Interviews and focus groups are a good way to understand work practices and obtain subjective reactions to your Web site. They're appropriate at almost any stage of design. Conducting them earlier will enable lessons learned to have a bigger impact on the final design. Conducting them later enables the interviewees to react in a more specific and concrete way to actual designs. As such, if you can only do them once, an optimal time is usually early in the design process when some mockups have already been created. They are sometimes not practical to conduct with inaccessible user populations, such as highly paid, busy professionals and business executives (doctors and movie producers). Focus groups are difficult to conduct for users who are geographically isolated and for highly specialized fields, where the target population is small (ambassadors and arctic explorers). These may be problems that can be solved: seek conferences they all attend and consider conducting online interviews.

INFORMED PROJECT OBJECTIVES

It's all too common for Internet businesses to be founded on *presumed* user needs and *presumed* market demand, only to discover that false assumptions about users won't support the financial needs of a business. These steps of user inquiry – surveys, interviews, and focus groups – involve nontrivial time and cost, but the information they provide aims a project in the right direction so that the Web site can actually fulfill the real needs. Many of the steps taken at this stage, such as listing the functional requirements or analyzing competitive sites, are undertaken for the sake of being methodical and complete. These steps establish the groundwork upon which the design is laid out.

TASK ANALYSIS

Once you've determined the initial requirements for your Web site, you need a way to analyze and optimize the procedures your users will follow while using your site. This forms a crucial part of the specifications for the Web site. From your requirements analysis, you should be able to build a profile of who your users are, what knowledge and abilities they come with, and the general goals you'd like them to be able to achieve while at your site. As a designer, you want to provide an efficient means for your users to achieve those goals. Task analysis is meant to specify how the information and functionality found in the requirements analysis will be used. In addition to codifying user procedures, task analysis can also be used as a design tool.

A *task* is the sequence of steps a user will follow to achieve a specific goal. Whether you're using Web technologies to automate a company's processes or you're providing information about your grandmother's favorite cookie recipes, there is always a set of goals in mind and a set of tasks for achieving those goals, even if they are somewhat implicit. The purpose of this chapter is to provide you with some simple, practical techniques for analyzing the tasks that will make your site development more efficient and make the user experience dramatically simpler. We describe the components of a task analysis, how it can be used in different situations, and how you can combine use cases with hierarchical task analysis within the Web site development process.

WHAT IS TASK ANALYSIS?

Task analysis refers to a family of techniques for describing various aspects of how people work. This can include procedural analysis, job analysis, workflow analysis, and error analysis. Procedural analysis is a set of techniques to analyze the procedures followed by people for an individual task. Job analysis is the identification of all tasks a person performs as part of a job role or to achieve some overall goals. Workflow analysis examines the flow of information and control that is necessary to complete a process that may include multiple people and multiple tasks. Error analysis determines where, when, and under what circumstances errors will occur.

The most crucial component of task analysis is gaining a deep understanding of the goals that people are trying to achieve. You can apply various task analytical techniques within your Web site development process to clarify and formalize the information from requirements gathering, and to design a process within your Web site that allows people to efficiently achieve their goals.

To illustrate how a task analysis might be used, consider the flowchart in Fig. 2.2, which maps out a sequence of screens a user might go through while purchasing a stuffed giraffe. Each thumbnail represents a screen in the buying process. The arrowed lines connecting the screens on the left represent a normal sequence of events. For instance, the user starts at the home page, goes to the Products page, goes to the Giraffe page, completes the billing information, verifies that he or she really wants to make the purchase, and receives a confirmation by the system that the stuffed giraffe has been ordered.

The lettered lines on the right side of the figure represent possible optimizations that can be found through a task analysis. For example, if the task analysis revealed that a significant number of users came to the site to buy giraffes, the company might place a giraffe link on the home page that would take users directly to the Giraffe page (line A). This could save users a significant amount of time by bypassing the Products page. As indicated by line B, the company could also place a Buy Giraffe button on the home page that would take users directly to the Billing page, bypassing two unnecessary screens. If the company

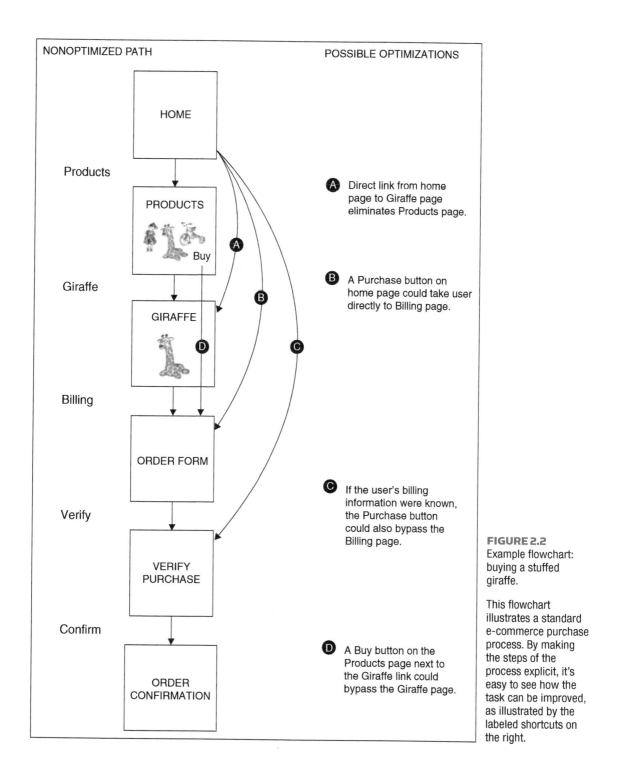

NONOPTIMIZED PATH

POSSIBLE OPTIMIZATIONS

Products

HOME

PRODUCTS

Buy

Giraffe

GIRAFFE

Billing

ORDER FORM

Verify

VERIFY PURCHASE

Confirm

ORDER CONFIRMATION

A Direct link from home page to Giraffe page eliminates Products page.

B A Purchase button on home page could take user directly to Billing page.

C If the user's billing information were known, the Purchase button could also bypass the Billing page.

D A Buy button on the Products page next to the Giraffe link could bypass the Giraffe page.

FIGURE 2.2
Example flowchart: buying a stuffed giraffe.

This flowchart illustrates a standard e-commerce purchase process. By making the steps of the process explicit, it's easy to see how the task can be improved, as illustrated by the labeled shortcuts on the right.

had customer billing and shipping information stored from a previous visit, it could also bypass the Billing page, saving customers even more time (line C). Likewise, there are other optimizations that could occur within the process, such as placing Buy links on the Products page to bypass individual product pages (line D). In addition, there may be ways to eliminate screens, perhaps by combining the purchase confirmation with another page, thus saving the user even more time and effort. There are many different optimizations that might be made, and making the process explicit through a task analysis allows the designers to make rational choices regarding them.

Task analysis can help improve the consistency and coherence of the procedures required to use your Web site. Because it makes explicit the procedural knowledge expected from your users, it also clarifies learning requirements and can provide the basis for training materials. Furthermore, since the procedures are clearly spelled out, a task analysis can be used to provide a context-based help system for your users. Task analysis is critical to providing a system that is efficient to use and easy to learn while not exceeding human limitations. In addition, the high-level goals specified in the task analysis make explicit the functionality that you are building into the system. Thus, there is little confusion about the intended purpose of the site.

Task analysis is used throughout the design process because it acts as a road map for the entire design team. In each portion of the design, the task analysis is used as a guide to answer the question, "Does this design support the task?" For example, an information architecture is useful only if it supports the task. The same goes for writing and graphic design. No stage of design can be done in a vacuum. Likewise, when performing quality assurance testing and user testing, the task analysis tells the team what to focus on, how important each element is, and how to determine whether the overall design is successful.

TASK ANALYSIS FOR WEB SITE DESIGN

If we only look at a single Web page, the procedures for using it are typically trivial. So why go to the extra effort of conducting a task analysis? The answer, of course, is that Web sites are not made up of just one page, and the interactions between users and Web pages are not necessarily trivial. We need to consider at least three distinct levels when conducting a task analysis.

1. We need to look at the big picture. Who are the user groups that will be using the site, and how do they interact with the other users of the site in the course of their overall job responsibilities?
2. We need to consider the pages that a single user will navigate to accomplish his or her goals.
3. We need to address the procedures that a user will utilize within each of the pages.

If we address only one of the levels, we may make the procedures within each of the pages very simple, but might neglect the possibility that some of the pages may be altogether unnecessary. We may also fail to see additional improvements that could be made to the overall workflow.

One way to specify the necessary information at each of the levels is to combine *use case analysis* with *hierarchical task analysis*. Use cases document the interactions between different user groups and are used as a first pass at high-level design. The following sections describe use cases, hierarchical task analysis, and their combination into a powerful analysis technique.

USE CASES

Use cases were developed by Jacobson (1987) and Jacobson, Christerson, Jonsson, and Övergaard (1992) as a way to analyze software development from the perspective of how a user would typically interact with the system. Use cases combine a simple way of capturing user scenarios (i.e., instances of how a user might perform a procedure) in a text document and diagramming how different user groups interact while using the system. They start with the users or *actors* of a system and describe the activities the actors engage in while using the system. Actors can be users, databases, other companies, or anything else that interacts with your system. A scenario is the set of steps or actions that an actor must accomplish to achieve a particular goal. Use cases include the typical, or primary, scenario that the user will go through to accomplish a particular goal and can also include a set of alternative scenarios that the user may go through in atypical situations. An example use case is shown in Fig. 2.3.

Use cases are easy to work with because most of the necessary information for building a system can be specified in a standard format. The interaction between different actors in a system can then be captured using use case diagrams. Use case diagrams provide a standard means for viewing an entire transaction in a single view.

Although use cases are a very powerful tool for system development, they have some weaknesses in the design of usable systems. For instance, a use case won't necessarily tell us if a procedure (scenario) is inefficient. It also won't tell us whether our procedures are within the possibilities of human performance or how much training would be required for a person to perform them. These weaknesses exist because the use cases were developed as a software development tool. They are neither rooted in human psychology nor are they intended for that purpose. For many projects, such attention to detail may not be necessary. For mission-critical or safety-critical tasks, ensuring efficient, error-free performance becomes much more important. For these types of tasks, we turn to hierarchical task analysis.

FIGURE 2.3
This use case shows how a customer would use the system to buy a book. The specification identifies the name and description of the use case, the actors involved, and the step-by-step process. In addition, exceptional circumstances, such as Alternative 1, can be spelled out.

Use Case: "Buy a Book"
Description: Customer orders a book using the book's ISBN
Actors: Customer, System
Additional Use Cases Needed: "Complete Order" use case

1. Customer locates the search field.
2. Customer enters the ISBN into the search field.
3. Customer presses the Search button.
4. System displays the Description page for the book.
5. Customer verifies that the book is correct and presses the Order button.
6. Customer completes the order (follow a "Complete Order" use case).

Alternative 1: ISBN incorrectly entered
At step 5 the customer realizes that the book displayed is not the desired book.
5a. Customer sees wrong book displayed.
5b. Customer locates search field and returns to step 2.

FIGURE 2.4
An example use case diagram.

This diagram shows the actors and use cases involved in a simplified process for selling a book to a customer.

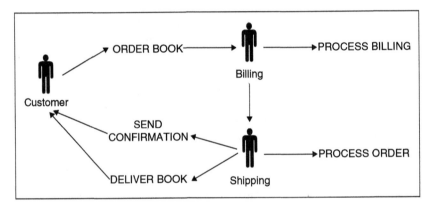

HIERARCHICAL TASK ANALYSIS

Hierarchical task analysis is a means of systematically defining a task from the user's perspective. We can look at task procedures on three levels: user level, platform level, and application level.

User-Level Goals and Procedures

At the top level, task procedures are generic descriptions of the goals that users will accomplish, like buying a book. These descriptions can be viewed as generic because we can accomplish the goal of buying a book through many means, both electronic and physical.

Platform-Level Goals and Procedures

At the bottom level, task procedures are those imposed by the interface. If we are buying books online, we will probably be using a Web browser and will be utilizing common Web browser interaction techniques such as pointing, clicking, and using pull-down menus and text-edit fields. Alternatively, if we are buying our book from the local bookstore, we will probably employ different interaction techniques, which might include driving a car, searching bookshelves, and completing a transaction with a clerk. This level is also generic in that many different high-level goals can be accomplished using various combinations of low-level procedures.

Application-Level Goals and Procedures

In between the high and low levels, task procedures at the middle level specify how users will accomplish their top-level goals using the low-level interface procedures required by your system's platform. This is the level where, as designers, we can often have the greatest impact. High-level goals are driven by the user needs and marketing decisions that are often a fixed requirement given to the design team. Likewise, low-level procedures are often determined by the underlying hardware and software, and also cannot be changed. What we can easily change is how the low-level procedures are used to accomplish the higher-level goals. We can affect how many and what kind of steps the users must perform. We can determine what information is shown on their screens, and we can determine how many pages they have to navigate. This is true of noncomputer interaction as well. For instance, we could change the procedure by which customers bought books in our bookstore example by having employees personally find books for customers and suggest related books for them. This would minimize the time customers spend searching for books, but doing this for every customer would be very expensive and might have undesired side effects like reducing impulse buying.

Understanding the Tasks and Their Context

The biggest challenge in performing a task analysis is accurately capturing the essence of the user's job. Simply asking users what they do and how they do it is not enough because users don't think about the steps they go through. A typical response to "How do you do this?" is "I don't know. I've been doing it this way for 20 years and it's the only way I know." Describing procedural knowledge is notoriously difficult for many people. The most direct method is to start by finding any written documentation on how users are supposed to be doing their job, and observing them in action to see how their behavior differs from the "official" instructions. If no written procedures exist, then analysts must observe users as they perform typical task scenarios. Formal methods exist for understanding the context of people's tasks, such as *contextual inquiry.* For a comprehensive treatment of contextual inquiry and contextual design, see Beyer and Holtzblatt (1998). Use cases provide a good starting point for organizing this information. For other techniques, see "Techniques for Understanding Tasks."

A potential pitfall when interviewing users is putting too much emphasis on their design suggestions. Although user participation is critical in the design process, caution should be exercised because users don't always know how to design what they want or need. For instance, it is common for some users to assume that an aesthetically pleasing site is more productive. Likewise when considering task performance time, users' perceptions of their productivity do not always reflect their actual efficiency. Their opinions about interface quality are always valuable, but they are not always correct.

Hierarchical Task Analysis for Web Site Design

Applying hierarchical task analysis to Web site design is a direct and systematic approach to characterizing the knowledge required by a typical person to use your site. As the name implies, it involves organizing the tasks in a hierarchy and decomposing the procedures to an adequate level. The process of decomposing the user's tasks is iterative and involves the following steps:

1. Identify the primary user goals.
2. List the steps that a user must perform to accomplish the goals.
3. Improve the procedure.

After the task is described at a sufficient level of detail, the procedures can then be improved to minimize the number of steps, improve consistency among similar procedures, reduce user errors, or make any other adjustments that may be critical to your site's goals.

Often, as a procedure is listed, it will be revealed that the steps to accomplish a goal are actually a collection of other, smaller subgoals. For instance, filling out a form involves filling out a series of text fields, radio buttons, checkboxes, and so forth. Instead of listing out each individual action for each form element, we can just say "Complete the address text field" or "Select a country from the pop-up menu." Each of those steps is actually a low-level interface goal involving a number of user actions. For example, to accomplish the goal "Select a country from the pop-up menu," the user must do the following:

1. Locate the pop-up menu named "Country".
2. Move the cursor to the menu.
3. Press the mouse button.
4. Locate the appropriate country from the list.
5. Move the cursor to the country name.
6. Press the mouse button.

This type of generic procedure may be used many times in an interface by just changing the name of the menu and the menu item to be selected. Do we need to list this out every time? No, it is only necessary to specify it once, knowing that it is simply a generic procedure, much like a computer program. Change the input data (e.g., the menu name) and the same procedure can apply anywhere there is a pop-up menu. Furthermore, there is an additional incentive to optimize such routines because if you optimize one generic routine, the benefits are seen every time the routine is used, potentially a much greater payoff than optimizing a procedure that is used only once.

TECHNIQUES FOR UNDERSTANDING TASKS

In developing Web-based tasks, we'd like to understand how people currently perform their tasks without the Web. This is especially useful when building Web sites that will support people's job tasks. Gathering task data is a natural extension to techniques such as interviews and observations. We need to understand how domain experts currently do their jobs, how they think about the tasks that are necessary to their jobs, and consider how their lives might be improved by optimizing those tasks and creating better user interfaces to support them. There are several techniques to start collecting such data. Typically, they are used in combination.

Training Materials

Existing training materials illustrate how the designers of a system think the job should be done. Such materials are often a good place to start because they help to build an initial framework for the roles and tasks involved in the job.

Standard Operating Procedures

Manuals of standard operating procedures specify how management expects tasks to be performed. Manuals can clarify the interaction between roles, establish responsibilities for individuals, establish performance criteria, and identify risks inherent to the tasks.

Observation

Users can be observed or videotaped while performing the task of interest. This is a relatively unobtrusive way to get information about people's observable actions. However, it's not possible to observe how decisions are made or how thought processes unfold.

Interviews and Focus Groups

Interviews and focus groups can be conducted with other techniques (such as observation) to uncover the thought processes behind people's actions. However, inaccurate recollection, groupthink, and other limitations of interviews apply here as well.

Think-Aloud Protocol

In the think-aloud protocol, users explain their actions as they perform their tasks. It is more obtrusive than observation and thus has a greater likelihood of changing how the task is performed. For example, talking through the task as they perform it may help people recall certain things they need to remember for the task, or it may make them forget. Despite this caveat, the think-aloud protocol is, in general, helpful for determining why users behave in the manner observed. It's especially helpful when users act in unexpected ways.

EDITOR'S NOTE: THINKING ALOUD AND TASK PERFORMANCE

The evidence is mixed on the impact of thinking aloud on task performance (Dumas, 2003). Rhenius and Deffner (1990) found that thinking aloud increased task times for participants. Wright and Converse (1992) compared participants who were asked to think aloud with participants who did not think aloud. The results of their study showed that participants who thought aloud were quicker and committed fewer errors than their silent counterparts. Berry and Broadbent (1990) found that participants who thought aloud as they worked on a task were nine percent faster than participants who did not think aloud.

Instrumented Browsers

Certain browsers can be used that record users' actions as they browse. Collecting keystrokes, mouse clicks, and other user actions automatically is an unobtrusive way to collect accurate data on user behavior. On the downside, it suffers from the same disadvantages as observation. These browsers can also provide a massive amount of data that may be difficult to decipher.

EVENT LOGS VERSUS WEB SERVER LOGS

Web server logs generally provide information about the interactions across Web pages and performance data. For example, many servers provide data about: dates and times, entry and exit pages, browser types, requested pages, files downloaded, IP addresses, level of Web server activity, and the number of page views (the number of times a user requests a certain page). Web server logs often need filtering since they collect all transfer requests between servers and browsers.

Event logs provide a detailed time-stamped view of user interactions within a software system. The term, event log, is a general term that has been around the user-centered design (UCD) community for decades. In the Web context, an event log would track what links, fields, or controls a person uses, what options are chosen, what errors occur, and often, what characters are entered into specific fields. An event log can be thought of as a more granular description of what happens for a particular Web server interaction. For example, a Web server log might show that a person has moved from one page in a checkout process to another; the event log would describe what happens on each page in detail (like what type of shipping the person requested and how much his or her order was for). So both Web server and event logs can provide useful usability input, but event logs yield more detail about what happens on a page.

Contextual Inquiry

The goal of this technique is to understand the context in which a task is being performed. In contextual inquiry, the usability specialist actually becomes involved in the users' tasks, experiencing them in the same manner, under the same risks and performance criteria, as the users themselves. A successful way of conducting such a study is to establish a master–apprentice relationship with a domain expert. In this way, the domain expert (master) teaches the usability specialist (apprentice) how to do the job. Such studies can be time-consuming and expensive, but they are effective when the cost can be justified.

How Far Down Should You Decompose a Procedure?

Tasks should only be decomposed to a granularity that you have any control over or that will affect your decisions on interface design choices. The point is that task decomposition should only be done as long as there is a potential gain from the analysis. For example, it may not be necessary to list out the steps to select an item from a pop-up menu because there may be nothing you can do to change it. If the system dictates that only a limited set of interface elements can be used, then a deeper analysis is pointless. However, if you need to choose between two interface elements that can produce the same result, it may be useful to see what is required from the user's point of view.

A typical stopping point for decomposition is the level of observable user actions, such as keystrokes and mouse movements. However, designers should not neglect the mental effort that users must exert while performing a task. For example, each new screen presented to the user will require at least several seconds to understand (i.e., time to establish a gestalt). It is also important to consider items that users must remember between screens and complex decisions that users must make, as these are a prime source for errors. For guidelines on how to assess the mental actions that users must perform during a task, see Kieras's "A Guide to GOMS Model Usability Evaluation Using NGOMSL" (Kieras, 1997) or Raskin's *The Humane Interface* (Raskin, 2000).

A good benchmark for determining an appropriate stopping point is whether a person can perform the task properly using your procedures. The task procedures should be general enough to apply to any set of input data, but include enough specific information that a person could perform the task. For more information on this type of task analysis, see the "GOMS Analysis".

GOMS ANALYSIS

GOMS analysis is a powerful, formal technique for conducting a task analysis. GOMS is a family of techniques developed by Card, Moran, and Newell (1983) and others, for modeling and describing human task performance. GOMS is an acronym that stands for Goals, Operators, Methods, and Selection Rules, the components of which are used as the building blocks for a GOMS model. Goals represent what a user is trying to accomplish, usually specified in a hierarchical manner. Operators are the set of atomic-level operations with which a user composes a solution to achieve a goal. Methods represent sequences of operators, grouped together to accomplish a single goal. Selection rules are used to decide which method to use for solving a goal when several are applicable. One reason GOMS is so powerful is that it is rooted in cognitive psychology. This makes it relatively straightforward to optimize procedures, check for consistency, and detect procedures that users may have difficulty performing.

Uses of GOMS

From a research standpoint, GOMS provides a framework for modeling aspects of human performance and cognition. From an applied perspective, GOMS provides a rich set of techniques for evaluating human performance on any system where people interact with machines. GOMS analysis can provide much insight into a system's usability, such as task execution time, task learning time, operator sequencing, functional coverage, functional consistency, and aspects of error tolerance. Some type of GOMS analysis can be conducted at almost any stage of system development, from design and allocation of function to prototype design, detailed design, and training and documentation for operation and maintenance. Such analysis is possible for both the new designs and redesigns of the existing systems.

For More Information

Bonnie John's article "Why GOMS" (John, 1995) provides a very nice introduction to GOMS. "Using GOMS for User Interface Design and Evaluation: Which Technique?" (John and Kieras, 1996a) provides guidance for choosing a GOMS technique using a series of case studies for illustration. "The GOMS Family of User Interface Analysis Techniques: Comparison and Contrast" (John and Kieras, 1996b) compares and contrasts the predominant GOMS techniques according to their basic assumptions and constraints. It uses a single task example as a comparison vehicle.

A HYBRID APPROACH TO TASK ANALYSIS

We favor a hybrid approach to task analysis that combines both the high-level interactions of users and other actors with the depth and psychological grounding of hierarchical procedure decomposition. The general steps are (1) start with use cases, (2) decompose tasks hierarchically, and (3) determine appropriate technologies.

Start with Use Cases

Determine the actors by asking who will be using the system and what parts of the system they will be interacting with. For example, in a simple business-to-business commerce Web site, actors might include a set of office personnel from each department responsible for keeping office supplies in stock. Also from the customer's company, purchasing agents might need to negotiate prices and confirm orders over a certain dollar value. Users from accounts payable would need to review monthly bills from the seller and issue checks. Actors from the seller's side might include customer account representatives who would need to monitor customer buying patterns, credit representatives who would need to approve high-value orders, and shipping agents who would handle customer deliveries.

Next, build user profiles by determining the background of the users, their knowledge, skill level, motivation, and any other relevant background information.

Obviously the backgrounds of the actors described will vary greatly from financial experts to office administrative staff to delivery staff. Their possible motivations will be likewise varied. For instance, the motivation of the office staff might be to make sure no one in their department runs out of essential supplies. Users from the purchasing department, however, might be tasked with ensuring that departments don't go over the budget. The seller's account representatives would be motivated by sales amounts and would instead try to maximize the sales.

The next step is to develop typical scenarios by asking: "What are the users' goals? What are the typical things they will try to accomplish?" Do this for each user group identified. For instance, one scenario for the customer's office staff might describe placing a regular monthly order for pens, paper, and printer cartridges. Another scenario might describe someone from the customer's company purchasing a special onetime item like a microwave oven.

From your scenarios and user profiles, determine the necessary functionality by asking what additional functionality the system must provide to support the users. In the first example scenario just described, the customer needs a way to see the previous month's order for office supplies and modify it for the current month. On placing the order, the customer would need to complete the transaction and verify any billing information required. In the second example, the customer would need a means for quickly performing a keyword search from an online catalog, comparing costs and features for all of the microwaves sold, and seeing which models were available. As in the first case, the users in this example would also need to complete the transaction.

Finally, you need to organize the scenarios. Based on common functionality within user groups, what are the high-level tasks? In both of the examples given, the users needed to place orders, confirm transactions, and verify billing information. Although not specified, they also probably needed to log in at the beginning and obtain written confirmation at the end. Each of these subgoals requires a specific task procedure that will allow users to accomplish their goals and complete their tasks.

Decompose Tasks Hierarchically

In this phase, your first task is to prioritize and determine the frequency of tasks. Start with high-priority, high-frequency tasks. After looking at all of the scenarios for all of the actors, the designer in our example might determine that the monthly purchase task would occur with the highest frequency and would be classified as such. Given the importance of the task – the dollar value of the combined instances in any given month and the potential cost of making mistakes within an entire month's purchases – it might also be classified as high priority, perhaps warranting additional analysis and testing.

Next, decompose the high-level tasks down to page- or mid-level procedures. For example, the monthly purchase task might be decomposed into the following subtasks: (1) log in, (2) view previous month's order, (3) modify previous order with current needs, (4) confirm order, and (5) get receipt.

Evaluate at each level of decomposition and repeat the process as necessary. For example, if we saw that several of the high-frequency tasks also included the login task, we would know that logging in was a high-frequency subtask that warranted additional optimization. If it was also known that users operated from secure computers, some or all of the login information could be stored on their computers. This would allow the login procedure to be simplified by requiring the user to enter less information during login.

Determine Appropriate Technologies

This phase begins with mapping out server requests and dataflow. For example, the monthly purchase task might translate to the following steps:

1. Get customer ID from login.
2. Determine the department.
3. Access the account.
4. Get the previous month's purchase.
5. Look up item descriptions from item numbers on the purchase.
6. Generate a new order form.
7. Format and display for the customer.

Next, create low-level, generic system procedures. For instance, looking up item descriptions could become a generic, building-block procedure that could be used in the monthly purchase task, and any other task that required the information.

Finally, map these into the application level. Combinations of system procedures can then be formed into application-level user tasks. For example, getting the customer ID, department, and account information could be combined into an account view for the customer.

PERFORMANCE IMPROVEMENTS

The goal of a task analysis is to improve the user's performance, productivity, and, ultimately, his or her experience. Used with other design techniques, task analysis can be a very powerful tool that can improve procedure consistency and clarity, reduce task execution and learning time, and reduce the number and types of errors that can occur.

Consistency

Interface consistency means that a system behaves in ways the users expect. It means that users can transfer the knowledge they gained in some previous experience to the current situation, and that their prior experience will in some way enhance their current performance. That is, if users have already learned one method for doing something, their performance will be better if they don't have to learn another means for doing the same thing with your system. For example, nonstandard use of blue or underlined text that is not a link often confuses users and results in increased errors and slower performance time.

Consistency also applies to the design of procedures. Although there are times when consistency itself can be confusing, such as when users mistake one procedure for another, it is generally a good idea to make procedures as consistent as possible. An example of inconsistent procedures can be seen in the JC Penney Web site shown in Fig. 2.5. Here there are two paths by which a person can purchase the sweater featured on the home page. By clicking on the thumbnail image, the user is presented with the screen shown in Fig. 2.6. There is a numbered sequence of steps that leads the user through selecting size, color, and quantity. If instead, the user enters the catalog number for the sweater in the field at the top of Fig. 2.5, the user is presented with a different method for selecting the desired sweater (Fig. 2.7). In this case, all of the colors and sizes are listed in a single pull-down menu at the bottom of the page.

Figure 2.5 is the JC Penney site (http://www.jcpenney.com) allows two ways to purchase products. Customers can either click on a product shown or enter the catalog item number in the text entry field at the top. Although both actions allow the user to purchase a sweater, there are separate procedures for selecting size, color, and quantity. See Figs. 2.6 and 2.7 for detail.

Both procedures seem to be adequate for selecting a sweater, but why are they different? At first glance it might seem that the designers have given extra effort just to make the procedures inconsistent. In reality, there is probably a technological or business-related reason for it: perhaps the two business functions of selling catalog items through the Internet and selling promotional items on the company Web site were designed by different development teams. But users don't care why. It may not even bother users enough that they would consciously notice that the procedures were different. But it might add a few extra seconds of confusion, and it might make users misremember where they had bought a previous item if the procedure is not the same. Furthermore, it might leave them with a feeling that things just aren't right. In general, you should strive to be consistent unless there is a good reason not to be. Technological issues alone should not dictate your users' experiences.

EDITOR'S NOTE: THE CASE AGAINST USER INTERFACE CONSISTENCY

Consistency is not always a good thing. There are times when consistency should be traded off against efficiency, memorability, or other user experience attributes. For additional background on the issues with user interface consistency, see the classic article by Jonathon Grudin (Grudin, 1989), "The Case Against User Interface Consistency" and the short article, "The Consistency Conundrum" by Chauncey Wilson at http://www.dux.typepad.com.

FIGURE 2.5
A problem with task
consistency.

FIGURE 2.6

One form of the sweater selection task.

Clicking the image link takes the user through a series of numbered steps (and screens) for selecting the size and color of a sweater.

FIGURE 2.7

Another form of the sweater selection task.

If instead the user enters the catalog item number, a different procedure for selecting size and color is required. In this case, the user selects sweater style from a single pull-down menu that combines size and color based on what's available.

Brevity and Clarity

Task analysis can also help to clarify and shorten your procedures. What may seem like an acceptable process for users to perform can sometimes prove much more convoluted when seen on paper. The task analysis makes your user interface procedures visible, showing both their good and bad aspects. It is the best way to find problems before user testing. There are two rules of thumb when considering procedure clarity. First, procedures should be relatively short, not more than 15–20 steps, although 10–15 is better. People have trouble with long procedures unless there are memory aids provided on paper or by the system. The second rule of thumb is that if a procedure is difficult to describe on paper, it is probably difficult for users to perform.

Combined Functionality and Fewer Server Requests

Another goal of task analysis should be to combine functionality when possible. Each screen a user must view probably adds at least 30 seconds to a procedure (very complex pages can add significantly more time). Combining functionality means minimizing the amount of effort users must exert to accomplish the same goal, commonly by minimizing the screens users must navigate. A task analysis can be used to determine where such combined functionality might make sense. For instance, when the analysis shows that users do the same task multiple times, it might make sense to allow them to make multiple entries at the same time.

The catalog ordering system seen at the JC Penney Web site (Fig. 2.5) is an example of where such combined functionality might be useful. The site is designed to allow the customers to order only one item at a time. However, the paper catalog on which the Web site was based contains an order form that allows multiple items to be ordered at once. This encourages customers to purchase multiple items per order. Since the Web site design doesn't duplicate the functionality of the old paper-based system, ordering multiple items online is painfully slow. Purchasing multiple items per visit is therefore discouraged by the design. When designing technological replacements for manual systems, the new process should always be at least as good as the old process.

Example: Inefficient Tasks

Another suitable occasion to combine functionality is when little new information is given on a new screen. For example, a pattern that has emerged in some Web applications, especially those driven by database requests, is that of Search-List-Detail. Search denotes the screen on which some database query is generated; List is the set of items returned by the search; and Detail is the item from the list that contains the necessary information for the task. This pattern is common because development tools easily support it. However, it sometimes results in tasks with extraneous and nonfunctional steps that the user must perform. In many cases, screens can be combined to reduce the number of server requests, the number of screens, and, as a result, the overall task time.

Consider, for example, the train schedule shown in Fig. 2.8a (http://www.amtrak.com). It shows the normal schedule for all trains from Chicago to Ann Arbor. To find the current status of a particular train, the user must select that train by clicking on a radio button, and then pressing the Show Train Status button.

The system responds to the status request with the Train Arrival page shown in Fig. 2.8b. One way to optimize this procedure would be to replace the Choice buttons on the Schedule page with links or graphic buttons. This would eliminate the need for the Show Train Status button and save the user a couple of actions. A more fundamental change could be made by adding the status information to the Schedule page. This would eliminate both the selection actions and the need to load another page. Such systems are often designed in this way because the information sources are held in different databases (and possibly in different physical locations). To simplify the

database queries for the Web-application programmers, only one query is made per page. However,
this type of technology-driven design is often incon-
venient for the end user.

HUMAN-ERROR-TOLERANT DESIGN

Designing systems that are tolerant of human error
becomes crucial when any task has potentially dangerous and costly consequences, or when the outcome is not easily reversible. Financial and medical
Web applications are prime examples of sites where
reducing the human error is especially important. A
central theme in designing for human error is to build a multilayered defense.
Designing for human error effectively requires addressing several aspects of error
management, including the following:

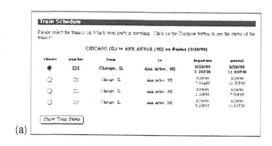

(a)

(b)

FIGURE 2.8
Example of an
inefficient task.

(a) The Schedule page
shows the published
schedules for each
train on a route. To
get the true status
for a train, the user
must select a train
and press the button
at the bottom of the
page. (b) The Status
page adds actual
status to the schedule
for each train. The
user's task could be
optimized by including
the status information
on the Schedule page.

> Prevention: Eliminate the potential for error to occur by changing key
> features of the task or interface. This is always the preferred and the most
> effective method for error management.
>
> Reduction: Reduce the likelihood that the user will get into an error state
> when prevention is not possible by ensuring the user is aware of action
> consequences and by training users on both normal and error-recovery
> procedures.
>
> Detection and identification: Ensure that if the user does err, the system
> makes it easy for the user to detect and identify the error.
>
> Recovery: Following error detection and identification, ensure that the
> system facilitates rapid correction, task resumption, and movement to a
> stable system state.
>
> Mitigation: Minimize the damage or consequences of errors if they cannot
> be recovered from. Even when all the other error management steps have
> been taken, errors will still be made, so systems should be designed such
> that catastrophic outcomes from human error are not possible.

Example: Error Recovery

The issues for error recovery are detection, identification, correction, and resump-
tion. For the user the questions are simple: What happened? What do I do now?
Electronic commerce is a prime domain for error-recovery design flaws that
can adversely affect usability. Consider, for example, the order form in Fig. 2.9a
(slightly modified from http://www.netopia.com). Here, the form indicates that
certain asterisked fields are required. The credit card selection menu is not indicated as a required field and is easy to miss (the card type is not really necessary
and can be derived from the card number). Also note the instructions at the bottom of the form telling the user not to use the Stop or Back buttons. These instructions help prevent users from accidentally performing multiple transactions or

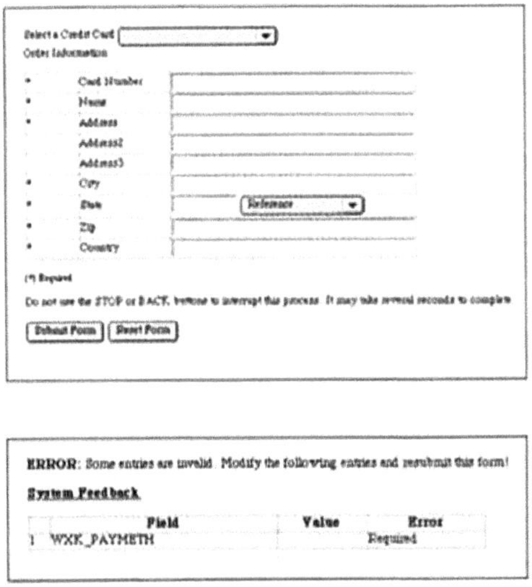

FIGURE 2.9
An error prevention and recovery problem.

(a) The form indicates that asterisked fields are required. It does not indicate that selecting the credit card type from the pull-down menu is also required. (b) The error page indicates that an error has happened, but doesn't clearly identify the error. It also doesn't provide the user with adequate navigation instructions to correct the error.

from mistakenly believing that a transaction was canceled when it was not. The problem is that this error-management measure hinders recovery from other error types. If the user forgets to select the credit card type from the pull-down menu, the commerce server indicates an error by displaying the screen shown in Fig. 2.9b.

The user detects that an error has occurred from the message heading. The system even identifies the error as an invalid entry in "WXK_PAYMETH" field. Unfortunately, that field name is only clear to the system and its programmers. Most users would not know from this that the problem is an incorrect entry for the payment method. In fact, the credit card menu is not strictly a field and does not really reflect an entry as the message suggests. This would likely cause more confusion. Even if the error is deduced by the user, correction is hindered by the message on the original order form that said, "Do not use the STOP or BACK button." There is no other navigation on the error page, so using the Back button is, in fact, the only option.

A better way to handle incorrect data entries is to return the user to a facsimile of the order form, with the missing or erroneous data fields highlighted in red (or indicated in some other salient way). Examples of correct entries can also be helpful. Minimally, error pages should identify errors in a way that users can understand and provide clear recovery paths when possible.

Simple, practical techniques, when applied consistently, can dramatically improve the Web site development process. More significantly, these fundamental task analysis methodologies please the ultimate critic: the user.

CHAPTER 3
Card Sorting

Catherine Courage and Kathy Baxter

EDITOR'S COMMENTS

Card sorting is a method for classifying or categorizing content, names, icons, objects, ideas, problems, tasks, or other items by putting them into actual or virtual piles that are similar in some way. While card sorting is a common name for this method in user experience design, it goes by other names as well, including "pile sorting" (cultural anthropology), "free grouping," and "partitioning" (mathematics and statistics). Card sorting is a powerful tool for shaping information architecture in Web sites and software applications.

Card sorting can be done individually by researchers as a way to organize some data (personal sorting – the kind you might do to help you organize a report), by a group of participants trying to come to consensus about how to organize many items (group card sorting), or by multiple participants whose independent sorts are combined and analyzed for common themes or patterns. In this chapter, the primary focus is on "open sorting," where piles are created without explicit categories and then given names that reflect the contents of the piles. The authors of this chapter take you through the entire process of planning, conducting, analyzing, and communicating the results of your card sorting. Tips and tricks are shared that can make your card sorting sessions both efficient and effective.

INTRODUCTION

Creating a product that has a logical information architecture is critical to the success of your product. Information architecture refers to the organization of a product's structure and content, the labeling and categorizing of information, and the design of navigation and search systems. A good architecture helps users find information and accomplish their tasks with ease. Card sorting is one method that can help you understand how users think the information and navigation should be organized within your product.

This method involves writing objects that are in – or proposed to be in – your product (e.g., hotel reservation, rental car agreement) on cards and asking users to sort the cards into meaningful groups. The objects are pieces of information or tasks that are – or will be – in your product. You want to understand how the users think those objects should be organized. You then strive to replicate these groupings in your product. By doing so, users will be able to easily find what they are looking for when using your product.

In this chapter, we discuss uses for card sorting, how to prepare for and conduct a card sort, and how to analyze and present the information. Several modifications are presented at the end to help you customize the method to your particular needs. Finally, a case study by Redish & Associates, Inc. is offered so that you may see how an industry icon has used card sorting with success.

WHEN SHOULD YOU CONDUCT A CARD SORT?

Card sorting is excellent for situations where you want the users' mental model to drive the information architecture of the product. You should use a card sort anytime you need feedback about the content, terminology, and organization of your product.

Unfortunately, many developers design products to conform to their own mental model of a domain. They may base their decisions about the information architecture or a product's layout on the underlying technology (e.g., the database). In the case of designing a Web site, some companies mirror their organizational or departmental hierarchy. Users are rarely aware of the developer's point of view, the underlying technology, or the company's departmental organization. As a result, they will have difficulty using a product design based on those considerations. There have been cases where it has taken us a month of working with the development team to get a list of objects within the product and definitions that everyone can agree upon. This happens when the product is not well defined or each person on the team has a different understanding of the product. The exercise of identifying objects and defining them can be eye-opening for the development team and demonstrate the need for a card sort as well as other usability activities.

You can do a card sort for entire sets of information (e.g., a Web site's entire information architecture) or for subsets of information (e.g., the information within a specific Web page). In a large product, different sections have different users. In this case, you will likely want to conduct a card sort on each section by users most likely to use it. Additionally, you can compare novice versus expert mental models.

There are several types of information that you can obtain with a card sort:

- Overall organization of the content or tasks in your product
- Terminology employed by users

- Labels users apply to different categories of information or tasks
- Missing objects
- Unnecessary objects

THINGS TO BE AWARE OF WHEN CONDUCTING A CARD SORT

Users may not always have optimal mental models (Nielsen & Sano, 1994). Designing a system based on flawed user mental models can clearly hamper user performance. For this reason, you should avoid including users in your card sort with no or little experience in the domain of concern. Obviously, if a user does not understand a domain well and have experience in it, that person's mental model will not be as efficient or even correct as that of others who do.

GROUP OR INDIVIDUAL CARD SORT?

You need to decide whether to conduct your card sort with several participants at once or one at a time. We conduct these sessions with several participants simultaneously because this allows us to collect large samples of data in a short period. You can conduct a card sort with as many people at a time as you physically have room for. Even though we have a group of participants in the same room at the same time, they are not working together – they are each working individually.

The disadvantage with running several participants simultaneously is that you cannot collect think-aloud data, so you do not know why the users grouped the data the way they did. Although think-aloud data are helpful, participants typically provide enough information in their description of each group so that the need to collect data quickly and from large samples outweighs the benefit of having think-aloud data.

Some people dislike running a group card sort because they feel that the participants turn it into a race. In our experience, this has not been a problem. We encourage people to take their time because we will be there for as long as they need to sort the cards.

If you have the time, a hybrid approach works quite well. After collecting data from a group of participants, run one or two individual card sorts to collect think-aloud data. This additional data can help you better understand the groupings.

PREPARING TO CONDUCT A CARD SORT

ARE YOU READY?

Before you begin any user requirements activity, there are a number of things that you must be familiar with. Because these elements are common to all user requirements activities, now is a good time to double-check the list.

1. Introduction to user requirements
   - Get stakeholder buy-in for your activity
2. Before you choose an activity
   - Learn about your product
   - Learn about your users
3. Ethical and legal considerations
   - Create consent forms
   - Create confidential disclosure agreements
4. Setting up facilities for your user requirements activity
   - Create or acquire a facility for your activity
5. Preparing for your user requirements activity
   - Develop an activity proposal
   - Determine the time of day and duration of your session
   - Recruit participants
   - Develop an activity protocol
   - Pilot your activity
6. During your user requirements activity
   - Welcoming participants
   - Dealing with late and absent participants
   - Warm-up your participants
   - Successfully moderate your activity

Now that we have presented when and why to conduct a card sort, we will discuss how to prepare for one.

Preparation Timeline

The timeline in Table 3.1 covers in detail the sequence and timing of events to prepare for a card sort. These are *approximate* times based on our personal experience and should be used only as a guide. It could take longer or less time for each step depending on a variety of factors, such as responsiveness of the development team, access to users, and resources available. It can take as long as a month or as little as two days to identify the objects for the sort and develop clear definitions. The time it takes to create the cards depends on the number of cards and participants needed; but on average, it can take about three and a half hours to create enough cards for 60 objects and 10 participants.

Identify Objects and Definitions for Sorting

There are several ways to obtain your objects (i.e., pieces of information or tasks) and definitions for sorting. The first and most frequent method is to work with the development team to identify the objects and then develop clear definitions. The creation of definitions can be surprisingly time consuming since the development team may define things in terms of the way the back-end or technical components of the product works. It is your job to make sure the definitions

Table 3.1	Preparation Timeline for a Card Sort	
When to Complete	**Approximate Time to Complete**	**Activity**
As soon as possible	1–2 weeks	Meet with team to identify and define objects
		Meet with team to develop user profile
After identification of objects and profile	3 hours	Create and distribute proposal
After the proposal has been agreed to by all stakeholders	2 weeks	Identify and recruit users
		Prepare materials
		Assign roles for the activity (e.g., moderator)
		Acquire location
		Acquire incentives
		Prepare documentation (e.g., the non-disclosure agreement [NDA], informed consent form)
		Order food (optional)
1 week before activity	2 days	Conduct pilot
		Make necessary changes to cards and procedure based on pilot
Day before card sort	1 hour	Call and confirm with participant(s)
Day of card sort	3 hours	Create and place "Welcome" sign in lobby
		Set up location with all materials necessary
		Pick-up food (optional)

are clear and easy for participants to understand. Without those definitions, you cannot be sure that you and the participants are on the same page, speaking the same language.

In cases when your product is still in the conceptual stage, you may not have a list of contents or tasks for the product. While still working with the development team, you may need to supplement your knowledge with input from the marketing department or a competitive analysis. You may find it beneficial to do a wants and needs (W&N) analysis to learn about the information or tasks you would like to have in your product. You will need to ensure that, during the brainstorming portion of the W&N analysis, you clearly understand what each idea means so that you can write complete definitions for your card sort.

If a version of the product already exists and your goal is to rearchitect the product, you and the team can together identify the possible areas to rearchitect. Once you have done this, you can make a list of all the objects contained within these areas. If there are objects that will be omitted in the next release, you should omit these from the card sort. Conversely, if there are new objects that the product team intends to add to the product, you should certainly include these.

Finally, you can also obtain objects for a card sort by asking participants to free-list all the items associated with a given domain (i.e., participants write down every phrase or word associated with a particular topic, domain, etc.). This is a brainstorming activity similar to a W&N analysis and can be done either individually or as a group. The difference is that, in free-listing, you are asking participants to name every "item" they can think of that is associated with a domain – not just the ones they want for a given product or system. Using our travel example from other chapters, we might want to ask participants to name every piece of information they can think of that is associated with making travel reservations. Some responses might be plane ticket, car rental, hotel room, confirmation number, and frequent-flyer miles.

How many participants are needed for this kind of free-listing activity? The answer is, "It depends." The best way to determine the appropriate number is to conduct the activity with five or six participants, tally the results to see the number of participants identifying each object, and then see how those results change by adding one or two new participants. If the results are stable, no further participants are needed.

EDITOR'S NOTE: EXAMPLES OF FREE-LISTING QUESTIONS

- List all the things you would want to know about the movies at local theaters.
- List and describe all the tasks that you perform in your job during a week.
- List all the things you have done with travel sites on the Web.
- List and describe all the tools that you use in your work.
- List all the forms and documents that you use in your work.
- List all the functions that you use in [product name].
- List all the things about [product name] that frustrate or irritate you.

Free-listing questions can be asked in questionnaires, during individual or group interviews, in focus groups, and in e-mail, listservs, wikis, and other online techniques. You can do a free-listing exercise with large groups in a manner of minutes and gather large amounts of data. For example, you might ask the question, "What usability methods do you use in your job?" to attendees at your conference presentation and ask people to write the answers on a notecard. You can get hundreds of answers in a few minutes. Free-listing is easy, doesn't require expertise in moderation, and allows you to collect information from an individual, small group, or large group.

For more information on free-listing see "Beyond cardsorting: Free-listing methods to explore user categorizations" at http://www.boxesandarrows.com/view/beyond_cardsorting_free_listing_methods_to_explore_user_categorizations (Sinha, 2003a).

The benefit of both the W&N analysis and free-listing is that you obtain information about the users' terminology because they are offering their ideas in their own language.

We have found that it is best to limit the number of objects to be sorted at 90 or less, because participants cannot keep more than that in their mind at one time. However, there are studies where more cards have been used. One study was found to use 500 cards (Tullis, 1985)! We would not recommend this. Keep in mind that the more cards there are to sort, the longer it will take for the participants to sort and the more you will fatigue and overwhelm them. In addition, sorts with large numbers of cards will take considerably longer to analyze.

Although it may seem unnecessary to run a pilot session for a card sort, it helps to have several individuals review the objects and definitions on the cards. A fresh set of eyes can find typos or identify confusing definitions and terms. In addition, a pilot can help you get a sense of how long it will take for participants to complete the sort and determine whether you missed any objects.

TIP
If you plan to use a computer program to analyze the data, check for any limit to the number of cards or users it can handle. There often is a limit. Sometimes this information is buried in the "Release Notes" or "Known Bugs."

Activity Materials

You will need the following materials for a card sort:

- 3 × 5 inch index cards (different colored cards are optional)
- Printer labels (optional)
- Stapler
- Rubber bands
- Envelopes
- Plenty of workspace for a participant to spread out the cards

To create the cards, type the name of the object, a blank space, and the definition of the object on a sticky printer label (see Fig. 3.1). You can also add an example of the object, if you feel it will help users understand the object. Make sure that you use at least a 12-point font. It is easy to create a file of the objects and then

Attributes of the Hotel Room	Vacation Packages
The various benefits or accommodations of the hotel room. Some examples include: non-smoking, mini bar, king size bed, ocean view.	Travel packages that typically include air travel, hotel and rental cars often for a discounted price.
Destinations	Customer Reviews
A list of places where you can arrange to travel to.	Reviews of a product or service written by customers who have used it.

FIGURE 3.1
Replication of several cards used in card sorting exercise (reduced size).

TIP
To save time during data collection, card sorts can be conducted as a group. If you are running the sort as a group, you will need three different colors of index cards. When participants are sitting next to each other, it is easy for cards to get mixed up. You don't want to hear participants ask, "Are those my cards or yours?" Alternate the colors of the cards between users sitting next to or across from each other.

print out several sheets. You can then quickly stick labels on the cards. Alternatively, you could buy sheets of punch-out index cards and print directly onto the sheets; however, we have found them only in white.

The number of index cards needed (C) can be computed by multiplying the number of objects in the sort (O) by the number of participants you intend to recruit (P):

$$C = O \times P$$

So, if you have 50 objects and 10 participants, you will need 500 index cards. We recommend providing about 20 blank cards per participant for labeling their groups.

Additional Data Collected in a Card Sort

Of course, the main type of data you will collect in a card sort relates to the information architecture, but you can collect additional information. There are five types of changes participants can make to the cards you provide:

- Delete an object
- Add a new object
- Rename an object
- Change a definition
- Place an object in multiple groups

Any of the changes that participants make to the cards must be analyzed manually. Often, the additional information that you obtain by allowing participants to make these changes justifies the additional work. However, it is a decision for you to make.

DELETE AN OBJECT

If a participant does not think an object belongs in the domain, he or she can remove it. For example, if you have the object "school bus" in a card sort for your travel Web site, a participant may want to remove it because in that person's experience, school buses are never provided as an option on travel Web sites. Additionally, you may allow participants to delete a card if they do not use the object in real life.

Allowing participants to remove cards reveals whether you are providing users with content or tasks that are unnecessary – which represent "noise" for the user to deal with. It can also reveal whether you (or the development team) have an incorrect perception of the domain (e.g., providing school buses on a travel Web site). However, you may have a product where all your features must be included for business reasons. If this is the case, you would not want to allow participants to create a "discard" pile.

ADD A NEW OBJECT

As participants read through the cards, they begin to understand the depth and breadth of information or tasks your product supports. They may realize that certain information or tasks are missing from the sort and therefore from your product. Using our travel example, a participant may notice that "airport code" is missing from the sort and add it in. Perhaps this was left out because the development team thought that the full name of the airport was more helpful and the airport code is unnecessary. Allowing participants to add cards points out information or tasks that users expect to have in your product. You should also ask users to define any objects they add and state why they are adding them.

RENAME OBJECTS

As we mentioned at the beginning of the chapter, you can collect information about terminology in a card sort. You might present participants with an object they are familiar with, but in their opinion, the name of the object and definition do not match up. Sometimes differences exist between companies or different parts of the country, or there is an industry standard term that you were not aware of. Technical jargon or abbreviations that we are not aware of are sometimes used in the workplace, or users may simply have another term for the object in their workplace. By allowing participants to change the names of your objects, you collect information about terminology that you may not have had before.

CHANGE A DEFINITION

Providing a definition for each term ensures that everyone is on the same page. This is critical when asking participants to organize information. If everyone has a different understanding of the objects they are sorting, there will be no consensus in the organization of the cards. Sometimes, the definitions provided are incomplete or not quite right, so allow participants to make additions, deletions, or word changes to the definitions. For example, you may have defined a certain object as "standard" or "best practice" but the participants point out that the object is just one of many practices and not necessarily the best practice or even the standard. This is important for you to know.

PLACE AN OBJECT IN MULTIPLE GROUPS

Sometimes participants tell you that a single object belongs in multiple locations. To do this, a participant would need to create a duplicate card. This adds some complexity to the data analysis, but you may want to collect this information. You want to understand where an object *best* fits, so ask participants to place the card provided in the best group. Then, ask them to create as many duplicate cards as necessary and place them in the additional locations.

Players in Your Activity

Of course, you will need end users to take part, but you will also require other people to help conduct the activity. In this section, we discuss the details of all the players involved in a card sort session.

THE PARTICIPANTS

A study recently conducted with 168 participants found that a card sort with only 20–30 participants can yield an average correlation coefficient of well over 0.9 (Tullis & Wood, 2004). Beyond 30 participants, you get diminishing returns. We typically run one or two group sessions with 10–12 participants of the same user type. If you are short on time and resources, however, run six or eight participants and analyze the data. Add an additional couple of participants and see whether the addition of each new user changes the groupings (this is a good time to collect think-aloud data). If the results are stable and the major groups do not change, there is no need to run additional participants.

All participants should meet the same user profile. If you wish to compare user types (e.g., novice versus expert), we recommend using the analysis technique above (i.e., run six or eight of each type, analyze the data, add a couple more, see how the groups change, determine whether more participants are needed). It is not advisable to mix user types. If different user types sort information differently, you may need to create a different interface for each user type. Mixing the user types in the same sort washes out those differences and could result in an interface that no one can use.

Preparing to Conduct a Card Sort

THE FACILITATOR

Only one facilitator is needed for the activity, whether it is conducted as a group or individually. If you run a group, it helps to have a coworker as an extra pair of hands, but that is optional. The job of the facilitator is to provide initial instructions, distribute the materials, answer any questions along the way, and then collect the materials. If run as a group, the majority of the session is spent sitting quietly, answering any questions, and making sure people are not comparing their sorts. If run individually, the facilitator must be familiar with the think-aloud protocol and how to instruct participants in it. The facilitator will also need to take notes of what a participant is thinking, and it is advisable to record the session in case you miss something.

THE VIDEOGRAPHER

If you are conducting the card sort as a group, there is no discussion to video-tape, but if conducting the sort individually, it is beneficial to record so that you can capture the think-aloud data. If you plan to record, make sure that someone takes responsibility for this task. It is ideal if you can have someone monitor the video equipment during the session in case something goes wrong; but if that is not possible, set up the shot, hit "record," and hope that nothing goes wrong.

Inviting Observers

If you are conducting the card sort as a group, there is nothing for an observer to see except a room full of people silently grouping cards. If the session is conducted individually, stakeholders will find it interesting to hear why people group objects the way they do.

CONDUCTING A CARD SORT

You have prepared for the card sort and now you need to actually conduct the session (see Fig. 3.2). Whether conducted with a group or individually, the steps are the same. Some minor differences in instructions are noted below.

FIGURE 3.2
The action! As you can see, participants do not need a lot of space.

Table 3.2	Timeline for Conducting a Card Sort
Approximate Duration	**Procedure**
3 minutes	Welcome participants (introductions, forms)
5 minutes	Conduct a card sort practice
3 minutes	Instructions
30–100 minutes	Card sorting
5 minutes	Wrap-up (distribute incentives, thank participants, escort them out)

Activity Timeline

The timeline in Table 3.2 shows the sequence and timing of events to conduct a card sort. These are *approximate* times based on our personal experience and should be used only as a guide. The overall length of the session will obviously depend on the number of cards to be sorted. As we mentioned earlier, participants can typically sort 50–70 cards in a one-hour session.

Welcome the Participants

This is the time during which you greet your participants, allow them to eat some snacks, ask them to fill out paperwork, and get them warmed-up.

Practice

Upon their arrival, explain to the participant(s) that the purpose of the activity is to gain an understanding of how people group a set of concepts. We then begin with a practice exercise so that they understand exactly what we will be doing. We typically write about 12–15 types of zoo animals on a flip chart or whiteboard (e.g., grizzly bear, ape, polar bear, monkey). We then ask participants to call out animals that they think belong in the same group (e.g., polar bear and grizzly bear). We circle the items and then ask them to name that group (e.g., bears). See Fig. 3.3 for an example.

Card Review and Sorting

Once everyone is comfortable with the concept, distribute the cards and provide some instructions. You can use the following sample script:

We are currently designing <*insert product description*> and we need to understand how to best organize the <*information or tasks*> in the product. This will help users of the product find what they are looking for more easily.

On each of the cards we have written a <*piece of information or task*> in our proposed product, along with a description of it. Please read through all of the cards and make sure both the terms and definitions make sense. If the

FIGURE 3.3
A card sort
demonstration
exercise.

terms or definitions do not make sense, please make corrections directly on the cards. Use the blank line to rename the object to something that makes more sense to you. In addition, please let me know what changes you are making so I can be sure that I understand what you are writing.

Once you have reviewed all the cards, you may begin sorting them into groups that belong together. There are no right or wrong answers. Although there may be multiple ways you can group these concepts, please provide us with the groupings that you feel make the most sense. When you are sorting, you may place any cards that do not belong (or that you do not use, do not understand, etc.) in a discard pile, and you may use the blank cards to add any objects that are missing. If you feel that a particular card belongs in more than one location, please place the card provided in the *best* location you believe it fits. Use the blank cards to create as many duplicate cards as necessary and place those in the secondary groups.

When you have completed your sort, use the blank cards to name each of your piles.

If this is a group card sort, add, "Please do not work with your neighbor on this. We want to understand how *you* think these cards should be grouped. We do not want a group effort – so please don't look at your neighbors' cards." If this is an individual sort, state, "I would like for you to think-aloud as you work. Tell me what you are thinking as you are grouping the cards. If you go quiet, I will prompt you for feedback."

Whenever participants make a change to a card, we strongly encourage them to tell us about it. It helps us to understand why they are making the change. In a group session, it offers us the opportunity to discuss the change with the group. We typically ask questions like

> John just made a good point. He refers to a "travel reservation" as a "travel booking." Does anyone else call it that?

or

> Jane noticed that "couples-only resorts" is missing. Does anyone else book "couples-only resorts?"

If anyone nods in agreement, we ask him/her to discuss the issue. We then ask all the participants who agree to make the same change to their card(s). Participants may not think to make a change until it is brought to their attention, otherwise they may believe they are the only ones who feel a certain way and do not want to be "different." Encouraging the discussion helps us to decide whether an issue is pervasive or limited to only one individual.

Participants typically make terminology and definition changes while they are reviewing the cards. They may also notice objects that do not belong and remove them during the review process. Most often, adding missing cards and deleting cards that do not belong are not done until the sorting stage – as participants begin to organize the information.

TIP
We prefer to staple the groups together because we do not want cards falling out. If your cards get mixed with others, your data will be ruined; so make sure your groups are secured and that each participant's groups remain separate! We mark each envelope with the participant's number and seal it until it is time to analyze the data. This prevents cards from being confused between participants.

Labeling Groups

Once the sorting is complete, the participants need to name each of the groups. Give the following instructions:

> Now I would like for you to name each of your groups. How would you describe the cards in each of these piles? You can use a single word, phrase, or sentence. Please write the name of each group on one of the blank cards and place it on top of the group. Once you have finished, please staple each group together, or if it is too large to staple, use a rubber band. Finally, place all of your bound groups in the envelope provided.

DATA ANALYSIS AND INTERPRETATION

There are several ways to analyze the plethora of data you will collect in a card sort exercise. We describe here how to analyze the data via programs designed specifically for card sort analysis as well as with statistical packages (e.g., SPSS, SAS, STATISTICA™) and spreadsheets. We also show how to analyze data that computer programs cannot handle. Finally, we walk you through an example to demonstrate how to interpret the results of your study.

When testing a small number of participants (four or less) and a limited number of cards, some evaluators simply "eyeball" the card groupings. This is not precise and can quickly become unmanageable when the number of participants increases. Cluster analysis allows you to quantify the data by calculating the strength of the perceived relationships between pairs of cards, based on the frequency with which members of each possible pair appear together. In other words, how frequently did participants pair two cards together in the same group? The results are usually presented in a tree diagram or dendrogram (see Figs 3.4 and 3.5 for two examples). This presents the distance between pairs of objects, with 0.00 being closest and 1.00 being the maximum distance. A distance of 1.00 means that none of the participants paired the two particular cards together; whereas 0.00 means that every participant paired those two cards together.

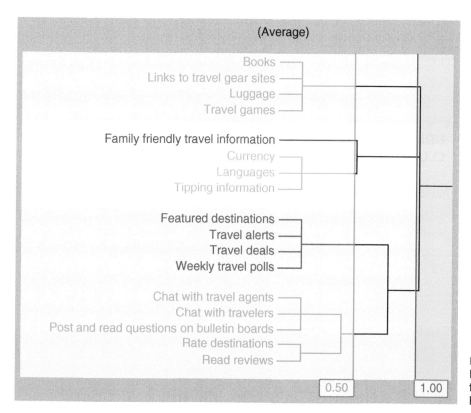

FIGURE 3.4
Dendrogram for our travel Web site using EZCalc.

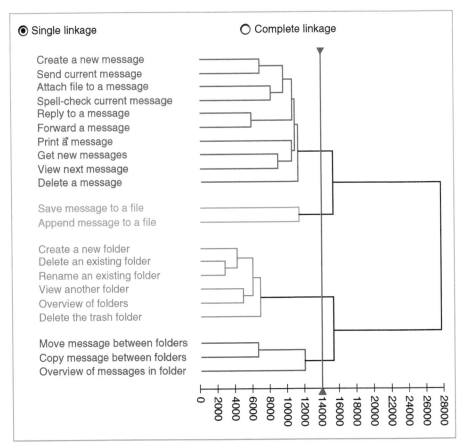

FIGURE 3.5
Tree diagram of
WebCAT data analysis
for an e-mail system.

BRIEF DESCRIPTION OF HOW PROGRAMS CLUSTER ITEMS

Cluster analysis can be complex, but we can describe it only briefly here. To learn more about it, refer to Aldenderfer and Blashfield (1984), Lewis (1991), or Romesburg (1984).

The actual math behind cluster analysis can vary a bit, but the technique used in most computer programs is called the "amalgamation" method. Clustering begins with every item being its own single-item cluster. Let's continue with our travel example. Below are eight items from a card sort:

Hotel reservation	Airplane ticket	Rental auto	Rental drop-off point
Frequent-guest credit	Frequent-flyer miles	Rental pick-up point	Featured destinations

Participants sort the items into groups. Then every item's difference score with every other item is computed (i.e., considered pair-by-pair). Those with the closest (smallest) difference scores are then joined. The more participants who paired two items together, the shorter the distance. However, not all the items are necessarily paired at this step. It is entirely possible (and in fact most probable) that some or many items will not be joined with anything until a later "round" or more than two items may be joined. So after Round 1, you may have the following:

- Hotel reservation and frequent-guest credit
- Airplane ticket and frequent-flyer miles
- Rental auto, pick-up point, and drop-off point
- Featured destinations

Now that you have several groups comprised of items, the question is "How do you continue to join clusters?" There are several different amalgamation (or linkage) rules available to decide how groups should next be clustered, and some programs allow you to choose the rule used. Below is a description of three common rules.

Single Linkage

If any members of the groups are very similar (i.e., small distance score because many participants have sorted them together), the groups will be joined. So if "frequent-guest credit" and "frequent-flyer miles" are extremely similar, it does not matter how different "hotel reservation" is from "airplane ticket" (see Round 1 groupings above); they will be grouped in Round 2.

This method is commonly called the "nearest neighbor" method, because it takes only two near neighbors to join both groups. Single linkage is useful for producing long strings of loosely related clusters. It focuses on the similarities among groups.

Complete Linkage

This is effectively the opposite of single linkage. Complete linkage considers the most dissimilar pair of items when determining whether to join groups. Therefore, it doesn't matter how extremely similar "frequent-guest credit" and "frequent-flyer miles" are; if "hotel reservation" and "airplane ticket" are extremely dissimilar (because few participants sorted them together), they will *not* be joined into the same cluster at this stage (see "Round 1" groupings above).

Not surprisingly, this method is commonly called the "furthest neighbor" method, because the joining rule considers the difference score of the most dissimilar (i.e., largest difference) pairs. Complete linkage is useful for producing very tightly related groups.

Average Linkage

This method attempts to balance the two methods above by taking the average of the difference scores for all the pairs when deciding whether groups should be joined. So the difference in score between "frequent-guest credit" and "frequent-flyer miles" may be low (very similar), and the difference score of "hotel reservation" and "airplane ticket" may be high but, when averaged, the overall difference score will be somewhere in the middle (see Round 1 groupings above). Now the program will look at the averaged score to decide whether "hotel reservation" and "frequent-guest credit" should be joined with "airplane ticket" and "frequent-flyer miles" or whether the first group is closer to the third group, "rental auto" and "rental pick-up point."

SUGGESTED RESOURCES FOR ADDITIONAL READING

If you would like to learn more about cluster analysis, you can refer to:

- Aldenderfer, M. S. & Blashfield, R. K. (1984). *Cluster analysis.* Sage University paper series on quantitative applications in the social sciences, No. 07-044. Beverly Hills, (CA): Sage Publications.
- Lewis, S. (1991). Cluster analysis as a technique to guide interface design. *Journal of Man-Machine Studies, 10,* 267–280.
- Romesburg, C. H. (1984). *Cluster analysis for researchers.* Belmont, (CA): Lifetime Learning Publications (Wadsworth).

You can analyze the data from a card sort with a software program specifically designed for card sorting or with any standard statistics package. We will describe each of the programs available and why you would use it.

Analysis with a Card Sorting Program

- At the time of publication, there are at least four programs available on the Web that are designed specifically for analyzing card sort data: NIST's WebCAT® (http://zing.ncsl.nist.gov/WebTools/WebCAT/overview.html)
- WebSort (http://www.websort.net/)
- CardZort/CardCluster (http://condor.depaul.edu/~jtoro/cardzort/cardzort.htm)
- XSort (http://www.xsortapp.com/)
- UserZoom (http://www.userzoom.com/online-card-sorting-study)
- OptimalSort (http://www.optimalsort.com)

Data analysis using these tools has been found to be quicker and easier than using manual methods (Zavod, Rickert & Brown, 2002).

Analysis with a Statistics Package

Statistical packages like SAS, SPSS, and STATISTICA are not as easy to use as specialized card sort programs when analyzing card sort data; but when you have over 100 cards in a sort, some packages cannot be used. A program like SPSS is necessary, but any package that has cluster analysis capabilities will do.

Analysis with a Spreadsheet Package

Most card sort programs have a maximum number of cards that they can support. If you have a very large set of cards, a spreadsheet (e.g., Microsoft Excel) can be used for analysis. The discussion of how to accomplish this is complex and beyond the scope of this book. You can find an excellent, step-by-step description of analyzing the data with a spreadsheet tool at http://www.boxesandarrows.com/view/analyzing_card_sort_results_with_a_spreadsheet_template.

Data That Computer Programs Cannot Handle

Computer programs can be great, but they often do not do all the analysis for you. Below are some of the issues that we have encountered when using different electronic programs. Although the data analysis for these elements is a little awkward, we think the value that the data bring makes them worth collecting.

ADDING OR RENAMING OBJECTS

One of the basic requirements of cluster analysis is that all participants must have the exact set of cards in terms of name and number. If participants renamed any of the objects or if they added any cards, you will not be able to add this information into the program. You will need to record this information for each participant on a sheet of paper and analyze it separately. The number of cards added or changed tends to be very small but it is an extra step to take. Returning to our earlier example, you notice that Participant 1 added the object "airport code." Write this down and then tally the number of other participants who did the same thing. At the end, you will likely have a small list of added and renamed objects, along with the number of participants who made those changes. Based on the number of participants who added it, you can assess its importance.

GROUP NAMES

The group names that participants provide are not presented in the analysis. You will need to record the pile names that participants suggested and do your best to match them to the results. We typically write down the names of each group for each participant and look for similarities at the end. How many participants created an "Airline Travel" group? How many created a "Hotel" group? When examining the dendrogram, you will notice clusters of objects. See if there is a match between those clusters and the names of the groups that participants created.

DUPLICATE OBJECTS

As we discussed earlier, sometimes participants ask to place an item in multiple locations. Because the computer programs available do not allow you to enter the same card more than once and you must have the same number of cards for each participant, include the original card in the group the participant placed it. The duplicate cards placed in the secondary groups will have to be examined and noted manually.

DELETED OBJECTS

EZCalc is the only program we are aware of that can handle discards automatically, but IBM has pulled EZCalc off its main site. The only location for downloading *EZCalc* is http://www.tripledogs.com/ibm-usability/. Many computer programs cannot deal with deleted cards. For these programs, if you have allowed participants to create a discard or miscellaneous pile of cards that they do not believe belong in the sort, there is a workaround you need to do. You cannot enter this collection of discarded cards as a group into a computer program since the cluster analysis would treat these cards as a group of objects that participants believe are related. In reality, these cards are not related to any of the other cards. Place each rejected card in a group by itself to demonstrate that it is not related to any other card in the cluster analysis. For example, if participants placed "Frequent-Flyer Miles," "Companions," and "Meal Requests" in the discard pile, you should enter "Frequent-Flyer Miles" in one group, "Companions" in a second group, and "Meal Requests" in a third group.

Interpreting the Results

You now have a collection of rich data. The dendrogram displays groups of objects that the majority of participants believe belong together.

Changes that participants make to cards can make interpretation of the results tricky. When a deleted object is repeatedly placed in a group by itself (or left out, in the case of *EZCalc*), you may see it on a branch by itself or loosely attached to a group that it really doesn't belong with. Additionally, if participants place an object in multiple groups, they may not have agreed on the "best" location to place it. Consequently, you may find the object is living on a branch by itself or loosely attached to a group that it really doesn't belong with. You must use your knowledge of the domain or product to make adjustments when ambiguity exists. Use the additional data you collected like new objects, group names, changed terminology, and think-aloud data to help interpret the data.

Let's walk through our travel example and interpret the results of our dendrogram shown earlier in Fig. 3.4. Using our domain knowledge and the group labels participants provided in the card sort, we have named each of the clusters in the dendrogram (see Fig. 3.6). We appear to have four clear groups: "Products," "Resources," "News," and "Opinions."

It is important to note that the card sort methodology will not provide you with information about the *type* of architecture you should use (e.g., tabs, menus). This decision must be made by a design professional. Instead, the tree diagram demonstrates how participants expect to find information grouped. In the case of a Web-based application with tabs, the tree may present the recommended name of the tab and the elements that should be contained within that particular tab.

Now, you should examine the list of changes that participants made (e.g., renamed cards, additional cards) to discover whether there is high agreement among participants.

- What objects did participants feel you were missing?
- What objects did participants feel did not belong?
- What are all the terminology changes participants made?
- What definitions did participants change?
- What items did users want in multiple locations?

Use this information to determine whether your product needs to add or remove information or tasks to be useful to participants. You may recommend

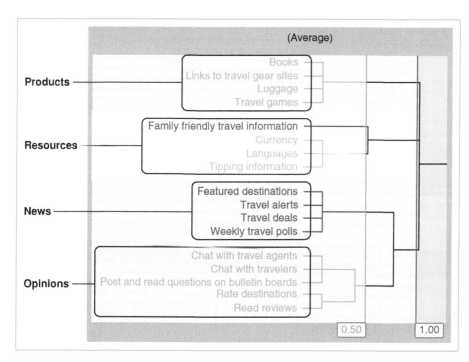

FIGURE 3.6
Dendrogram of a travel Web site card sort with group names added.

to the team that they conduct a competitive analysis (if they haven't already) to discover whether other products support such functionality. Similarly, use the information about deleted objects to recommend the team to examine whether specific information or tasks are unnecessary.

Terminology can be specific to a company, area of the country, or individual. With each terminology change, you will need to investigate whether it is a "standard" – and therefore needs to be incorporated – or whether there are several different possible terms. When several terms exist, you will want to use the most common term but allow your product to be customized so that it is clear to all your users.

Finally, examine the definition changes. Were the changes minor – simply an issue of clarification? If so, there isn't anything to change in your product. If, however, there were many changes, you have an issue. This may mean that the product development team does not have a good grasp of the domain or that there is disagreement within the team about what certain features of the product do.

COMMUNICATE THE FINDINGS
Preparing to Communicate Your Findings
The specific data that you communicate to product teams can vary depending upon the activity you conducted, but some elements of *how* you communicate the results are the same regardless of the method.

Tab name	Objects to be located within the tab
Resources	Tipping information Languages Currency Family friendly travel information
News	Travel deals Travel alerts Featured destinations Weekly travel polls
Opinions	Read reviews Post and read questions on bulletin boards Chat with travel agents Rate destinations
Products	Travel games Luggage Books Links to travel gear sites

FIGURE 3.7
Travel card sort table
of recommendations.

When we present the results of a card sort analysis to executives or teams, we present the actual dendrogram generated by the application (as in Fig. 3.6) and a simple table to review (see Fig. 3.7). We also present a table of changes that participants made to the cards (added objects, deleted objects, terminology changes, and definition changes) and any sketches the designers may have produced to illustrate the recommendations.

As with all the other user requirement methodologies, the card sort is a valuable addition to your software requirement documentation. These results can be incorporated into documentation such as the Detailed Design Document. Ideally, additional user requirement techniques should be used along the way to capture new requirements and verify your current requirements.

MODIFICATIONS

Below are a few modifications on the card sorting technique we have presented. You can limit the number of groups users can create, use computerized tools for the sort instead of physical cards, provide the groups for users to place the cards in, ask users to describe the items they would find in a particular category, or physically place groups that are related closer to each other.

Limit the Number of Groups

You may need to limit the number of groups a participant can create. For example, if you are designing a Web site and your company has a standard of no more than seven tabs, you can ask participants to create seven or fewer groups. Alternatively, you can initially allow participants to group the cards as they see fit; then, if they create more than seven groups, ask them to regroup their cards into higher-level groups. In the second case, you should staple all the lower-level groups together and then bind the higher-level groups together with a rubber band. This will allow you to see and analyze both levels of groupings.

Electronic Card Sorting

There are tools available that allow users to sort the cards electronically rather than using physical cards (e.g., *OptimalSort, WebSort, xSort,* and *CardZort*). Electronic card sorting can save you time during the data analysis phase because the sorts are automatically saved in the computer. Another advantage is that, depending on the number of cards, users can see all the cards available for sorting at the same time. Unless you have a very large work surface for users to spread their physical cards on, this is not possible for manual card sorts. Electronic sorting has the disadvantage that, if you run a group session, you will need a separate computer for each participant. This means money and potential technical issues. In addition, you need to provide a brief training session to explain how to use the software. Even with training, the user interface may be difficult for users to get the hang of.

Some tools support remote testing, which allows you to gather data from users anywhere. However, users may have a more difficult time without a facilitator in the room to answer questions.

Unfortunately, none of the computer-based programs provides a definition with the objects. Also, they do not allow users to add, delete, or rename the objects. In our opinion, this is a serious shortcoming of the tools and the reason why we do not use them.

SUGGESTED RESOURCES FOR ADDITIONAL READING

The article below provides a nice comparison of some of the automated card sorting tools available (at the time of publication) if electronic card sorting is of interest to you:

- Zavod, M. J., Rickert, D. E. & Brown, S. H. (2002). The automated card-sort as an interface design tool: A comparison of products. In: *Proceedings of the human factors and ergonomics society 46th annual meeting*, Baltimore, MD, 30 September–4 October, pp. 646–650.

Prename the Groups

You may already know the buckets that the objects being sorted must fit into. Going back to our Web site example, if you cannot completely redesign your site, you may want to provide participants with the names of each tab, section, or page of your site. Provide participants with a "placemat" for each group. The placemat should state the name of the group and provide a clear description of it. Participants would then be tasked with determining what objects fit into the predetermined groups.

To go one step further, you may have the structure for your entire application already laid out and simply want to find out whether you are correct.

EDITOR'S NOTE: CLOSED AND REVERSE CARD SORTING

The last example where you provide users with the names of categories and then put items into those categories is called closed card sorting. Closed sorting is useful when you are verifying an existing hierarchy or structure (e.g., the main menu of an application or Web site) or adding new items to an existing structure. Closed sorting can be a follow-up to open sorting and be used to validate the categories that emerged from the open sorting.

Reverse card sorting is similar to closed sorting. In reverse card sorting, participants are asked to place cards that represent navigation items onto a diagram of a hierarchy (or other structure) and optionally, rate how certain they are that they are putting the card into the "right" place on the hierarchy. The average percentage of cards that are sorted into the correct place in the hierarchy would indicate how well your users understand the structure. This method is useful for validating changes to Web site navigation or task structures. Human Factors International, for example, used reverse card sorting to compare an old design with a new design of a Web site. In their study, "… 96 percent of the users understood the new site's categorizations and task groupings, compared with only 45 percent on the old design" (Human Factors International, ND, http://www.humanfactors.com/about/arinc.asp).

LESSONS LEARNED

The first time we used *EZSort* (IBM's predecessor to *USort/EZCalc*), we did not know that the program would choke if given over 90 cards. We prepared the material, ran the study, and then entered the data for 12 participants and 92 cards. When we press the button to compute the results, it blew up. There was no warning and nothing to prevent us from making the mistake. It took extensive investigation to determine the cause of the problem, including contacting the creators of *EZSort*. By that point, there wasn't much we could do. We were forced to divide the data, enter it in chunks, and compute it. This had to be done several times so that the data overlapped. This was a painful lesson to learn. Rest assured that we never use a free program now without thoroughly reviewing the "Release Notes" and Web site from where we downloaded the program. We also look for other documents such as "Known Bugs."

PULLING IT ALL TOGETHER

In this chapter, we have discussed what a card sort is, when you should conduct one, and things to be aware of. We also discussed how to prepare for and conduct a card sort, along with several modifications. Finally, we have demonstrated

Case Study

Ginny Redish conducted a card sort for the National Cancer Institute's Division of Cancer Prevention. Since she does not work for the National Cancer Institute, she describes how she worked as a consultant with the development team and gained the domain knowledge necessary to conduct the card sort. She describes in wonderful detail the process of understanding the user profile, identifying the objects for sorting, creating the materials, and recruiting the participants. She provides a unique perspective because she conducted the sort individually with think-aloud protocol and opted not to use cluster analysis software.

various ways to analyze the data and used our travel example to show you how to interpret and present the results.

Below, Ginny Redish presents a case study to share with readers how she recently employed a card sort to build the information architecture for a government Web site.

HOW CARD SORTING CHANGED A WEB SITE TEAM'S VIEW OF HOW THE SITE SHOULD BE ORGANIZED

Janice (Ginny) Redish

Redish & Associates, Inc.

This case study is about the Web site of the U.S. National Cancer Institute's Division of Cancer Prevention. When the study began, the division's Web site focused on its mission and internal organization (see Fig. 3.8).

Our Approach

I was brought in as a consultant to help the division's Web project team revise the site. They knew it needed to change, and the division's new Communications Manager, Kara Smigel-Croker, understood that it did not have the public focus that it needed.

We began by having me facilitate a two-hour meeting of the division's Web project team at which we discussed and listed the purposes of the site and the many user groups the site must serve.

Although the site, at that time, reflected the organization of the division and the research that it funds, the project team agreed that the mission of the Web site was to be the primary place that people come to for information on preventing cancer.

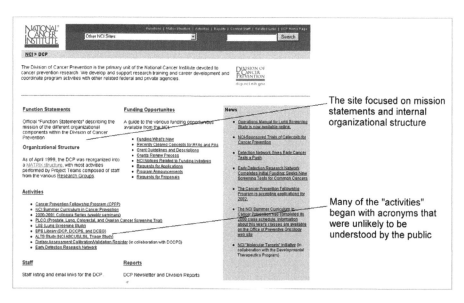

The site focused on mission statements and internal organizational structure

Many of the "activities" began with acronyms that were unlikely to be understood by the public

FIGURE 3.8
The Web site before card sorting.

When we listed audiences, we found many potential users – from the public to medical professionals to researchers to students – and, of course, realized that there would be a wide range of knowledge and experience within each of these audiences.

In addition to listing purposes and audiences, the third activity in our initial meeting was to understand the scenarios that users would bring to the site. I handed out index cards, and each member of the project team wrote a sample scenario. The most interesting and exciting result was that after just our brief discussions of purposes and audiences, 17 of 18 members of the project team wrote a scenario about a member of the public coming for information about preventing cancer, even though, at that time, there was almost no information on the site for the general public! (The eighteenth scenario was about a graduate student seeking a postdoctoral fellowship – a very legitimate scenario for the Web site.)

The stage was now set for card sorting. The project team agreed that card sorting was the way to find out how members of the public and medical professionals would look for information on the site.

Planning and Preparing for the Card Sorting

Members of the project team wrote cards for topics. In addition to the topics from each research group and from the office that handles fellowships, we added cards for types of cancer and for articles that existed elsewhere in the many National Cancer Institute Web sites to which we could link.

HOW MANY CARDS?

We ended up with 300 cards – many more than we could expect users to sort in an hour. How did we winnow them down? We used examples rather than having a card for every possible instance of a type of topic or type of document.

For example, although there are many types of cancer, we limited the cards to about 10 types. For each type of cancer, you might have information about prevention, screening, clinical trials, etc. Instead of having a card for each of these for each type of cancer, we had these cards for only two types of cancer – and our card sorters quickly got the point that the final Web site would have comparable entries for each type of cancer. Instead of having a card for every research study, we had examples of research studies.

Even with the winnowing, we had about 100 cards – and that was still a lot for some of our users. An ideal card sorting set seems to be about 40–60 cards.

WHAT DID THE CARDS LOOK LIKE?

Figure 3.9 shows examples of the cards. Each topic went on a separate 3 × 5 inch. white index card. We typed the topics in the template of a page of stick-on labels, printed the topics on label paper, and stuck them onto the cards – one topic per card. We created two "decks" of cards so that we could have back-to-back sessions.

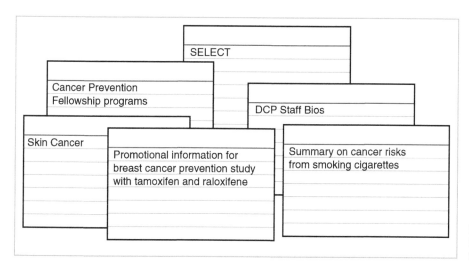

FIGURE 3.9
Examples of the cards used.

We also numbered the topics, putting the appropriate number on the back of each card. Numbering is for ease of analysis and for being able to have back-to-back sessions. Here's how it worked. In hour 1, Participant 1 sorted Deck 1. In hour 2, Participant 2 sorted Deck 2 while someone copied down what Participant 1 did, using the numbers on the back of the cards to quickly write down what topics Participant 1 put into the same pile. Deck 1 was then reshuffled for use in hour 3 by Participant 3, and so on.

With stick-on labels and numbers for the topics, you can make several decks of the cards and have sessions going simultaneously as well as consecutively.

RECRUITING USERS FOR THE CARD SORTING

We had two groups of users:

- Eight people from outside who came one at a time for an hour each
- About 12 people from inside – from the project team – who came either singly or in pairs for an hour each; pairs worked together, sorting one set of cards while discussing what they were doing – like codiscovery in usability testing

The National Cancer Institute worked with a recruiting firm to bring in cancer patients/survivors, family members of cancer patients/survivors, members of the public interested in cancer, doctors, and other health professionals. Our eight external users included people from each of these categories. The external people were paid for their time.

CONDUCTING THE CARD SORTING SESSIONS

The only real logistic need for card sorting is a large table so that the participant can spread out the cards. We held sessions in an empty office with a large desk, in a conference room, and on a round conference table in another office. The conference room table worked best; one participant especially liked the chair on wheels so he could roll up and down next to the table looking at his groupings. Other participants sorted the cards standing up so they could reach along the table to work with the cards they had already put out.

In addition to the deck of cards with topics on them, we also had:

- Extra white cards for adding topics
- Sticky notes for indicating cross-links (when participants wanted a topic to be in two places, we asked them to put it in the primary place and write a sticky note to indicate what other group should have a link to it)
- Cards in a color for putting names on the groups at the end
- Rubber bands for keeping each group of cards together at the end
- Pens for writing new topics, cross-links, and group names

The instructions for card sorting are very simple. You put the first card on the table. You then look at the second card and decide whether it goes into the same group as the first or not. If yes, you put the two cards together. If no, you start a second pile. And so on. Participants had no difficulty understanding what to do.

We also explained that we were building the home page and navigation for a Web site. This gave participants a sense of about how many piles (groups) it would make sense to end up with.

Participants were also told that they could:

- Rearrange the cards and groups as they went – that's why the topics are on separate cards
- Reject a card – put it aside or throw it on the floor – if they did not know what it meant or if they did not think that it belonged on the site
- Write a card if they thought a topic was missing
- Write a sticky note if they would put the card in one group but also have a link to it from another group

We encouraged the participants to think-aloud, and we took notes. However, we found that the notes we have from think-aloud in card sorting are not nearly as rich as those we have from usability testing and that the card sorts themselves hold the rich data. Therefore, we have done card sorting studies for other projects in which we have run simultaneous sessions without a note-taker in each – and thus without anyone listening to a think-aloud. (We did not tape these sessions.) In these other projects, several sorters worked at the same time, but each worked independently, in different rooms, with the facilitator just checking in with each card sorter from time to time and doing a debrief interview as each person finished.

When the participants had sorted all the cards, we gave them the colored cards and asked them to name each of their groups. We also asked them to place the groups on the table in the approximate configuration that they would expect to find the groups on the home page of a Web site.

The Analysis

In this study, we found that we did not need to do a formal analysis of the data to meet our goals of understanding at a high level what categories people wanted on the home page, where on the home page they would put each category, and the general type of information (topics) that they would expect in each category. We did not do a formal analysis with complex cluster analysis software for at least four reasons:

- This was a very small study – eight users.
- We were looking only at the top level of an information architecture. Our interest was the home-page categories with names and placement on the page for those categories and a general sense for the types of information that would go in each category. We were not doing an entire information architecture or putting every underlying piece of content into a category.
- This was just one step in an iterative process. Our goal was to get input for a prototype that we would take to usability testing. The project continued through several rounds of prototypes and usability testing.
- It was obvious as soon as the sessions were over that there was incredibly high agreement among the users on the categories, names, and placements.

If any of these four had not been the case, a formal analysis with one of the available software tools would have been imperative.

We put each person's results on a separate piece of paper – with the group (category) names in the place they would put it (see Fig. 3.10).

We spread these pages out on a conference room table and looked them over for similarities and differences. The similarities were very striking, so we took that as input to a first prototype of a new Web site, which we then refined during iterative usability testing.

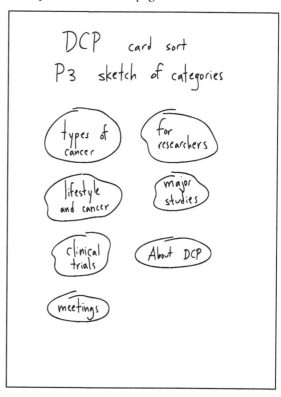

FIGURE 3.10
Example sketch of one user's placement and names for categories.

Main Findings

ACHIEVING CONSENSUS

Card sorting can produce a high degree of consensus about what a home page should look like. In this case, looking just at the eight external card sorters' topics for the home page:

- Seven had types of cancer or some variant – and they put it in the upper left corner of the page.
- Six participants had prevention or lifestyle or some variant. This category included topics such as exercise, tobacco cessation, nutrition, eating habits, as well as general information about preventing cancer.
- Five participants had clinical trials or some variant. They wanted a main entry to all the clinical trials as well as a link to each from the relevant type of cancer.
- Six participants had *About NCI DCP* or *Administration.* This category included the mission statement, organization chart, directory, etc. Although two of the eight participants also wanted a very brief mission statement with a link in the upper left corner of the home page, all six put the *About NCI DCP* category in the lower right of the page.

OPENING INTERNAL USERS' EYES

The technique itself can open the eyes of internal users to the problems with the way the site is currently designed.

The participants from the Web project team (the internal users) all started by sorting cards into their organizational groups, creating once again the old Web site. However, after five to 10 minutes (and sometimes with a bit of prodding to "think about the users and scenarios you wrote in the meeting"), they made comments like this: "How would someone from the public know that you have to look under [this specific research group] to find out about that?"; "The public would want to look up a specific type of cancer."; "The public would want to look up information about diet or nutrition."

In the end, each of the internal users came to very similar groupings as the public. They also realized on their own that information about the organization would not be the most important reason people came to the site. Like the public users, they put the *About NCI DCP* category in the lower right of the page.

If you think of internal users as "developers," you may wonder whether it was wise to let them do the card sorting. Of course, you do not want to have the developers (or internal users) be the only card sorters. The primary audience for the site must be the primary participants in any card sorting study.

In this case, however, the internal users were very curious about the technique. They wanted to try it, too. If we could have set up the card sorting sessions with the project team as observers (as we typically do for a usability test), that might have satisfied their curiosity. However, we did not have the facilities for observation for this particular study, so we decided to let them try the card sorting for themselves.

The danger, of course, was that they would remain in their own frame and not get beyond creating once again the site they knew. Just a little prodding to "think about the users," however, made these internal project team members realize for themselves both that they could put themselves into the users' frame and that, once in that frame, they could see how the users would want the site to be organized. Letting the internal people also do the card sorting might not always be wise; but in this case, for many of them, it was a "lightbulb moment" that made them empathize even more with the external users.

DISCOVERING GAPS IN UNDERSTANDING

With card sorting, you can find out about words that users do not know. All the external card sorters ended up with some cards in a pile of "I can't sort this because I don't know what it means."

The most common cards in that pile were ones with acronyms like ALTS, STAR, SELECT. Others were words like "biomarkers" and "chemoprevention." This was a huge surprise to many of the NCI researchers. It was a critical learning for them; the acronyms refer to clinical trials that the division is funding. Information about these clinical trials is one of the great values of the site, but people will not find the information if it is hidden under an acronym that they do not recognize.

GETTING A BETTER UNDERSTANDING OF CARD SORTING

Card sorting is like usability testing in that you have to be concerned about recruiting representative users, but it is logistically easier than usability testing. You need only a conference table, cards, someone to get the user going and – if you are running consecutive sessions – someone to record what each participant has done and reshuffle the cards for another participant. The difficult part of card sorting is deciding on the topics to include and limiting the number of cards by choosing good exemplars of lower-level content rather than including every single article that might be on the site.

What Happened to the Web site?

Figure 3.11 is the "after" version that was launched in the summer of 2001. (The current site at http://www.cancer.gov/prevention is a later update following NCI's adoption of new look and feel standards.)

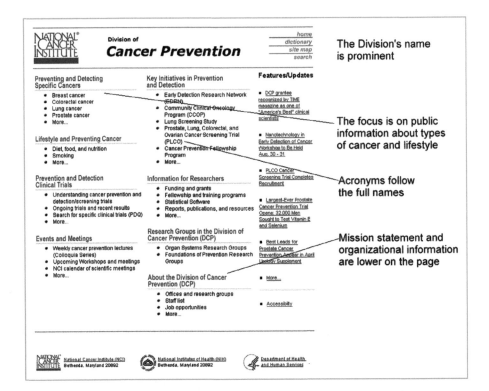

FIGURE 3.11
The Web site after card sorting, prototyping, and iterative usability testing.

ACKNOWLEDGMENTS

My time as a consultant to the NCI Division of Cancer Prevention (DCP) came through my work with the NCI Communication Technologies Branch (CTB) in the NCI Office of Communication. NCI is part of the U.S. National Institutes of Health, Department of Health and Human Services. I thank Kara Smigel-Croker (DCP Communications Manager) for leading this project and Madhu Joshi (who was a CTB Technology Transfer Fellow at the time) for handling all logistics and support.

PART 2
Generating Ideas

CHAPTER 4

Brainstorming

Chauncey Wilson

EDITOR'S COMMENTS

Nearly every organization engages in "brainstorming," but few do it effectively. There is a belief (you might call it a myth) that brainstorming is easy; but in fact, good brainstorming is a complex social activity where there is evaluation apprehension, behaviors that can block the production of ideas, and the reality that only one person can present an idea while the other 10 people are trying to remember their ideas. This chapter describes how to plan and conduct good group brainstorming sessions. You will find dozens of tips, guidelines, and ground rules that will increase the quantity of ideas that emerge from your brainstorming sessions. Good brainstorming!

INTRODUCTION

Brainstorming is an individual or group method for generating ideas, increasing creative efficacy, or finding solutions to problems. This chapter focuses on group brainstorming where participants generate ideas on a particular topic or problem in a nonjudgmental environment following a set of ground rules. The basic procedure for group brainstorming involves the following:

1. Selecting a group of three to 10 participants with different backgrounds
2. Posing a clear problem, question, or topic to the group
3. Asking the group to generate solutions or ideas with no criticism or attempts to limit the type and number of ideas

4. Discussing, critiquing, and possibly prioritizing the brainstorming results for subsequent action (this last step is often called the "convergent" phase where there is a winnowing of all the ideas into the ones that are judged as most applicable to a problem)

Variations on this group brainstorming procedure can be used to gather ideas from large groups, geographically dispersed individuals, or participants who are inhibited by their personality, the social environment, or cultural norms. These variations are described later in this chapter.

Alex Osborn, an advertising executive, is generally credited with developing modern organizational brainstorming procedures in the 1940s and 1950s (Osborn, 1963). Osborn's brainstorming process (originally called "thinking up") is described in his classic book, *Applied Imagination: Principles and Procedures of Creative Problem-Solving.*

EDITOR'S NOTE: "BRAIN STORMS" AS MENTAL DISEASE AND FORTUNATE THOUGHTS

In the early part of the twentieth century, "brain storm" referred to violent bouts of temper or bouts of lethargy and depression. Toward the middle of the twentieth century, the usage of "brainstorm" changed to mean "sudden and fortunate thoughts" (OED, n.d.). Alex Osborn, the "father of brainstorming" used the term "brain storm session" in the mid-1950s to describe his method of generating solutions to problems (Osborn, 1963).

There are three fundamental principles for group brainstorming:

1. *Aim for sheer quantity.* Quantity, not quality, is the sole goal of brainstorming. The only criterion for the success of brainstorming is the sheer number of ideas that are generated. Anything that limits the number of ideas is contrary to the intent of brainstorming. For example, brainstorming participants should not be taking their own notes because that reduces their cognitive resources available for generating ideas. Participants should not be monitoring e-mail (so easy now with wireless connections) or reading reports during brainstorming. All the resources of the participants should be focused on generating as many ideas as possible. The principle that "more is always better" is generally supported in the research literature although there are issues with defining exactly what quality means in brainstorming.

2. *Defer judgment about the quality of ideas.* Do not criticize the ideas of others either implicitly (for example, through facial expressions or other nonverbal behaviors) or explicitly (for example, saying "Wow! That is a crazy idea!"). While the rule about criticism is well known, another more subtle rule is to avoid praise, just as you avoid criticism. Praising an idea is attaching a judgment to the idea, which means that lack of praise can be construed as tacit criticism. So, it is best to avoid both praise and criticism.

3. *Encourage wild ideas and new ideas formed by synthesizing ideas, stretching ideas (bigger, faster, smaller), applying metaphors, or improving on existing ideas.* Wild ideas that may not be directly applicable to a brainstorming topic can serve as triggers for ideas that are potentially useful. Ideas from science fiction stories or movies, for example, might seem odd but many existing products are filled with concepts like teleportation, invisibility, and the ability to travel back in time (Freeman & Gelernter, 1996).

The apparent simplicity of these principles leads many people to assume that successful brainstorming is easy and can be done by anyone. However, this is an assumption that is not always warranted. Good brainstorming is rare, and in many cases what people consider "good brainstorming" is often seriously deficient.

Osborn's "structured brainstorming" approach with clear ground rules and procedures contrasts with "unstructured brainstorming," in which a group gets together to generate ideas without a facilitator and clear ground rules. Ideas that emerge from unstructured brainstorming are often criticized as they are generated and loud or dominant individuals can exert inordinate influence on the quiet participants, thus limiting the number of ideas that participants are willing to express. This chapter will focus on structured brainstorming where there is generally a facilitator and a set of explicit rules for participants.

EDITOR'S NOTE: DON'T BELIEVE ALL THAT YOU READ ON THE WEB: GROUP BRAINSTORMING ISN'T SIMPLE!

Although group brainstorming seems simple, there are many social issues like status differences, shyness, informal relationships, ego, and cultural factors that can affect the quantity of ideas. Camacho and Paulus (1995) found, for example, that social anxiety had a significant effect on brainstorming productivity and suggested that "...interactive [group] brainstorming may be best suited for people who are low in social anxiety." (p. 1,078). A trained facilitator can mitigate some of these factors, but even a good facilitator won't have total insight into all the social forces and group dynamics that can influence productivity. Jared Sandberg (2006) summarizes some key requirements for successful group brainstorming:

> "In fact, great brainstorming sessions are possible, but they require the planning of a state dinner, plenty of rules, and the suspension of ego, ingratiation, and political railroading."

When Should You Use Brainstorming?

You can use brainstorming to:

- Generate ideas or requirements
- Find solutions to problems

- Support conceptual design
- Explore new design spaces
- Generate social cohesion among product teams by having them work on ideas and solutions together

Brainstorming is often used in the early to middle stages of product development; however, this method is applicable at any time when new ideas or solutions are required. If you have an unexpected and difficult problem just before you release a product, brainstorming would be an appropriate method for generating potential solutions.

Strengths of Brainstorming

- It has name recognition. Most people have some sense of what a brainstorming session is like.
- It helps identify ideas that could lead to solutions for the problems.
- It provides many ideas quickly.
- It requires few material resources. Paper, pens, sticky notes, and tape are all that you require unless you are doing remote brainstorming.
- It is a useful way to get over design blocks that are holding up a project.
- It is a democratic way of generating ideas (assuming that particular individuals don't dominate and you have a good facilitator).
- It provides social interaction – people like to work together in groups to solve problems.

Weaknesses of Brainstorming

- The focus on the quantity of ideas can be derailed easily by criticism or poor facilitation.
- It requires an experienced facilitator who is sensitive to group dynamics and social pressures.
- It is sometimes less effective than having the same number of participants generating ideas individually. The quantity of ideas can suffer when one person in the brainstorming group blocks the production of ideas by other participants by telling "war stories" or whispering to a colleague and distracting the rest of the group.
- It can be chaotic and intimidating to the quiet or shy individual.
- It can reduce individual recognition for good ideas (though you can compensate for this by being known as a "good brainstormer" and creative contributor).
- It may be difficult in some countries or cultures where "wild ideas" may be viewed as inappropriate because those ideas are contrary to those of more senior colleagues, corporate initiatives, or cultural norms.
- The status or experience differences among participants can reduce brainstorming effectiveness. Mixing senior and junior colleagues can result in the junior people deferring to their more senior colleagues.

Procedures and Practical Advice on Brainstorming

PLANNING THE BRAINSTORMING SESSION

1. *Decide if group brainstorming is the best method for generating ideas or solutions for your particular question.* Other idea generation methods like brainwriting, free listing, or the nominal group technique (NGT) might be more appropriate for some contexts. For example, if you have some quiet people who might feel intimidated because their managers are part of the brainstorming session, you might try a less public method like brainwriting.

2. *Develop the question or topic that will be the focus of the brainstorming session.* The topic should be neither overly broad ("What can we do to make consumer products better?") nor so narrow ("What color should we use for the background of the horizontal navigation bar in our Web site?") that creativity is stifled.

3. *Choose a facilitator who has some experience conducting brainstorming sessions or similar activities like focus groups or design reviews.* If you have a contentious group with some overpowering participants, consider a facilitator with formal training. Brainstorming sessions are enhanced by experienced facilitators who can focus on eliciting as many ideas as possible.

4. *Decide on the size and composition of the group.* A group of three to 10 participants is recommended although if you have a large group, you might consider a variation called the "buzz group" or "buzz session" (described later in this chapter) where you split a large group into smaller groups of three to six participants. These buzz groups each conduct their own short brainstorming sessions and report the results to everyone (Brahm & Kleiner, 1996). Then all the ideas are combined into a single list. If there are a mix of managers and employees, the managers can brainstorm in their own group so that they don't intimidate those who work for them.

    It is advantageous to have a somewhat diverse group to explore ideas from different perspectives, but be careful about the mix of participants. Try to invite participants who are about the same rank in the organization. If you invite outsiders – people who are not known to the main group – introduce them with a bit of background and do some warm-up exercises before you get started with the official brainstorming topic. Some 10–15 minute warm-up exercises that you might consider are as follows:

    a. Have pairs of colleagues tell each other about their favorite vacation place or street and then have each person take a minute or two and relate what they heard from their partner.

    b. Hold up an item like a brick or paper clip, or show a photo of a common object and ask people to brainstorm as many ways to use the object as possible. A brick for example, could be used as a paperweight, prototype, weapon, chicken-flattener, door stop, or hammer.

c. Give people a word like "apple" or "strong" and ask the group to list as many associations with the word as possible (for example, with "apple" you might get gravity, Fuji, computer company, pie, doctor, health, crisp, record, Beatles, California, juice, fritter, and jack).

EDITOR'S NOTE: DIVERSITY CAN BE GOOD OR BAD

Diversity is important, but group comfort and cohesion is also important for successful brainstorming sessions (Milliken & Martins, 1996). The brainstorming guidelines and best practices often call for diversity in the backgrounds of group members on the assumption that the more diversity among individuals, the more diversity in the ideas that are generated. This is true to a point, but diversity can also create problems for brainstorming.

The relationship between diversity and creativity is complex; sometimes diversity in groups can lead to discomfort (Milliken, Bartel, & Kurtzberg, 2003). For example, having several senior managers and strangers from other parts of a company join you for a brainstorming session might increase the diversity, but also make the junior participants feel awkward or anxious about voicing "bad" or "wild" or "politically incorrect" ideas in front of other managers or strangers.

---

5. Choose a location that is comfortable and has flipcharts and space on the walls for posting ideas: Try to get a room other than the room where you meet every day to talk about boring topics like the daily bug reports or changes to the project plan (Berkun, 2004). If this is a critical session, you might want to get your participants out of their building and away from possible interruptions (any interruptions will reduce the quantity of ideas). In larger cities, there are companies that will often rent out rooms in half-day increments. Convince your participants not to bring their laptops and to put their mobile phones in silent mode. You do not want participants answering calls, checking e-mails, whispering to each other, or doing other work during brainstorming. Each interruption takes time away from idea generation and blocks the production of new ideas.

6. Develop a short introduction (several minutes is often enough) that describes the brainstorming process and your goals for the session:
   A checklist of items for the introduction would include the following:
   - Introduce yourself and your role.
   - Describe the goal of the session.
   - Lay out the timeline for the session.
   - Describe the process.
   - Describe the ground rules and how they will be enforced.
   - Describe what you will do with the data.
   - Conduct a brief warm-up.

7. Develop an explicit set of rules for the brainstorming session and go over them during your introduction. Paulus and Brown (2003, p. 130)

proposed some rules for productive brainstorming sessions. These rules include the following:

- Set high goals for the number of ideas you want from a session: Paulus and Dzindolet (1993), for example, conducted a study where participants were given goals that were about twice those of a "typical performance." The groups that were given high goals increased their performance by about 40 percent. In addition to setting goals, you can urge people to get to the next level by exhorting participants with statements like, "We have 90 ideas, let's try for 100 or more!"
- Number all the ideas (Kelley, 2001): Having a number on all the items makes it easier for the facilitator or participants to refer to a particular idea during the brainstorming session or later when the ideas are being evaluated. Additionally, knowing that you have 90 ideas might be strong incentive to break the 100-idea barrier.
- Ask the participants to listen carefully to the ideas of others since those ideas may trigger creative associations: A common (and often ignored) rule in brainstorming is that only one person speaks at a time. The "one-person-speaks" rule should be firmly enforced.
- Do not allow side conversations: A primary responsibility of the facilitator is to suppress side conversations because they will distract the group and block the production of new ideas.
- Avoid "filler conversations": Filler conversations occur when a participant states an idea and then goes on to explain or elaborate excessively on the idea or "tells a war story." Filler material wastes time that could be used to generate new ideas and can block the production of ideas by others who have to attend to their colleague's unneeded verbosity. Group brainstorming is more effective when filler material is kept to a minimum (Dugosh, Paulus, Roland & Yang, 2000).
- Focus on one major topic or one aspect of a problem at a time: Nijstad, Diehl, and Stroebe (2003) recommend breaking large problems or topics into several pieces to keep the level of productivity high throughout the session. Spreng (2007) recommended that facilitators choose narrow brainstorming tasks or break complex problems into separate and simpler problems and brainstorm on those separately. The introduction of new pieces of a problem or a new topic will lead to increased motivation and idea generation, and will postpone the feeling that ideas have run out.
- Include short breaks (five to 10 minutes) during a brainstorming session to stimulate different approaches to a problem or to overcome mental blocks: Schedule short breaks every 20–30 minutes if you have a long brainstorming session or multiple topics to cover. Brainstorming is an intense activity and short breaks will keep the ideas flowing. Give the participants cards or sticky notes to write down any thoughts they have during the breaks.

8. Ensure that all the ideas generated during brainstorming are visible to all participants: The facilitator or a designated notetaker should be writing the ideas down on large sheets of paper or large sticky notes so that everyone can see all the ideas. Write the ideas large enough and legibly enough for the person furthest away in the room to read them easily. Avoid typing ideas into a computer and displaying them to the participants unless you are doing sessions with colleagues at different sites. Even with high-resolution displays, only a small subset of ideas will generally be visible, which reduces the likelihood of early ideas triggering later ideas.

9. Decide if there is some "homework" for the brainstorming session that prime the participants and encourage more ideas: You might expose your colleagues to stimuli related to your brainstorming topic. Kelley (2001), for example, describes a warm-up "experiment" for a brainstorming session on toy design that involved different types of homework. One group of designers did no preparation for the session; a second group read books related to the design of toys and listened to a lecture; the third group took a field trip to a toy store. Each group then engaged in a brainstorming exercise. According to Kelley, the group that actually went to the toy store generated more and better ideas than the other two groups. If your brainstorming session dealt with how users could find a single item in a huge list, you could ask your participants to spend some time looking at visualization methods or metaphors related to the topic.

10. Plan how you will record, track, and decide which brainstorming items to pursue further: In most cases, you will probably type the ideas into a spreadsheet or database for later use. A common complaint from brainstorming participants is that they often don't know how the ideas were eventually used. Keep in mind that ideas from one session might be useful a year later. You might consider keeping an online catalog of ideas that are searchable or an "idea book" where you organize ideas that might be reusable.

CONDUCTING A BRAINSTORMING SESSION

1. Schedule time before the brainstorming session to prepare the room.
   a. Arrive early to assess the brainstorming facilities.
   b. Make sure that you have paper, tape, sticky notes, markers, and other materials ready for quick access during the session. If you have to fumble with materials during the session, then you are wasting time and blocking the production of ideas by others. A subtle quality of good brainstorming is that of "smooth flow" where the disruptive actions (like taking a few minutes to tape more paper on the wall) are minimized.
   c. Tape paper to the wall and have extra sheets ready for the ideas.
   d. Set up any remote connections if you have distant participants. Remote brainstorming requires somewhat different rules since it is harder to know when the remote participants want to contribute an idea.

EDITOR'S NOTE: IDEAS FOR GETTING INPUT FROM REMOTE PARTICIPANTS

Many companies are using Internet collaboration tools to conduct business and exchange ideas with geographically dispersed teams. Remote brainstorming using these tools is difficult because it is hard to know when someone at a different site has an idea to contribute. Several possibilities for engaging the remote participants include the following:

- Using electronic brainstorming tools with the remote meeting tool so that your distant colleagues can see all the ideas.
- Asking the remote participants to type their ideas into chat windows where they can be read off to everyone and added to a physical or electronic list of ideas. You could have someone assigned to type the local ideas into chat so that the remote colleagues can have the benefit of seeing as well as hearing all the items.
- Asking groups at different locations to each use a column in Google Spreadsheet and have someone type their ideas into their designated column in the spreadsheet (site A using column A, site B, column B, and so on. Since Google Spreadsheet shows everyone what is in a cell when you move to a new cell, all the ideas will be visible to all the remote groups. This works quite well and since people are typing things in at the same time, you can see which group is generating the most ideas and try to match them.
- Instituting a rule for switching to a remote site and getting their input periodically. For example, you could explicitly ask your remote colleagues to list their ideas on paper, and then about every three minutes or so ask for their ideas to ensure that they aren't forgotten. The problem with explicit switching between the local and remote sites is that you will lose some time (and thus ideas) because of the lag between asking for remote input and getting feedback.

   e. Arrange the seats so that everyone can see the ideas that are generated. If you are going to an unfamiliar location for brainstorming it is worthwhile asking for a diagram of the room early so you can plan the best layout for the session.

   f. Spread candy and healthy snacks around the room to increase the energy level and show that you care for your participants.

2. *Introduce the facilitator and also ask the participants to introduce themselves if they do not know each other.* Introductions are important and you might want to do something creative for the introductions, but don't let the session extend too long or allow people to talk past your general guideline – say one minute per person. You could make the introductions into a warm-up exercise as noted earlier in this chapter.

3. *Describe the topic of interest and how long the session will last.* Display the topic or question for the session prominently by writing it in large clear text on a board or poster (or computer projection) so that it is visible to all participants. This is important for keeping the meeting focused.

4. *Describe the brainstorming process to the group and explain the key principles and ground rules of your brainstorming session.* Write these principles and other ground rules on the board or create a playful poster or handout as a constant reminder about what will make the session successful. One of your rules could be that you will explicitly note when someone breaks a rule ("John, you are telling a war story"). Some specific principles that you need to point out, every time you conduct a brainstorming session include the following:

    a. *No criticism or discussion of any ideas (other than to explain something like an acronym or unfamiliar idea or phrase).* This can include verbal disparagement ("What a dumb idea!") or nonverbal behaviors (facial expressions or body language that indicate disapproval). Although most organizers of brainstorming sessions stress the cardinal rule of "no criticism," it is important that the facilitator be aware of subtle verbal and nonverbal behaviors as well as blatant attempts to criticize participants.

    b. *Quantity is the sole measure of brainstorming effectiveness.* Stress that the only metric for brainstorming is the sheer number of ideas that the group can generate and anything that gets in the way of quantity is bad.

    c. *Ideas can be totally new, modifications of existing ideas, or ideas that come from combining other ideas.* Explain that there is no shame in expressing an idea that is an extension or modification of another idea or combinations of several ideas. If you were brainstorming breakfast foods you participants might come up with "pancakes" and "eggs" which could be combined into a "pankegg" – an egg cooked inside a pancake (which, by the way, is quite a tasty breakfast item).

    d. *Duplicates are OK.* Trying to determine if something is a duplicate of an earlier item wastes time, especially when you have a few hundred ideas. Just list an item and combine the duplicate item later during grouping and prioritization activities.

5. *Designate one or more notetakers for the brainstorming session.* For many sessions, the facilitator can write the ideas on the work surface. For longer (and larger) sessions, you might consider multiple notetakers who alternate recording the ideas so writing delays don't interfere with the brainstorming. If you have two notetakers, one person could write the items on a board while the other notetaker writes them on sticky notes for later grouping and prioritization. If you use multiple notetakers, work out the basic rules for who writes what, and when. For example, one rule could be to divide the room or table, where people are sitting, into two areas and have each notetaker write down the ideas from one side of the table. Remember, there is no harm in having duplicates.

6. *Describe what you will do with the brainstorming items that the group decides to examine further.* Failure to inform people about how the ideas will be used may lead to skepticism about the value of brainstorming.

7. *Consider a warm-up for your brainstorming.* This warm-up could be a short practice run on a fun topic that you do just before your planned brainstorming session. This warm-up should take only a few minutes, but can help loosen inhibitions and put participants in a positive mood. Positive mood has been linked to increases in individual creativity (Grawitch, Munz, Elliott & Mathis, 2003; Isen, 2000) so taking some time to set up the brainstorming session as a positive, fun, and creative activity is a worthwhile investment (spreading small plates of candy, grapes, or nuts on the table could be part of your mood enhancement).

8. *Review the topic, problem, or question that is the focus of the brainstorming session and remind the participants of the brainstorming rules.* Let the participants know that if they violate the rules, the facilitator will provide gentle reminders. Ask if there are any questions and if not, begin the brainstorming.

9. *Invite participants to shout their ideas so that everyone can hear, one idea at a time, as quickly as possible.* Do not let participants:
   a. Interrupt one another
   b. Start elaborating on ideas beyond what is needed to understand the ideas
   c. Engage in distracting side conversations, phone calls, texting, or other activities
   d. Worry about quality

EDITOR'S NOTE: WHAT DO YOU DO WHEN THE RATE OF IDEA GENERATION SLOWS DOWN?

During a brainstorming session, the rate at which ideas are generated will vary from fast and furious to slow and awkward. If there is a lull in idea generation, take a short break or try a different approach. For example, the facilitator might focus on one idea and ask for variations on that idea rather than press for completely new ideas. You could also try using analogies, random words, or other creativity techniques to stimulate some additional ideas (Higgins, 2005; Infinite Innovations, n.d.). There are numerous techniques for stimulating idea generation and it is useful to have a small repertoire of the methods that you can call on when the rate of ideas slows down.

10. *Ensure that each idea is understood and adequately captured before accepting the next idea.* Allow for brief questions to clarify an idea.

11. *Review the items with the group.* At the end of a session, clarify any unclear or ambiguous items so that you know what each item means – even days or weeks later. Eliminate or combine duplicate items. Consider grouping related items and prioritizing the items immediately or make explicit plans to prioritize them later. After the brainstorming session:
   a. Designate a specific person or team to handle all the data after the session.
   b. Capture all the ideas and record which ideas will be considered further. Catalog the ideas, preferably in a database so ideas that were not

considered important at first, may become important later. Your ideas could be useful two years from now or help another group who had a similar problem with a different product.

c. Develop a plan for investigating the important items in more detail. You might, for example, create a matrix of potential solutions and look at the costs and benefits of each and then narrow the list of ideas to the ones that seem feasible under your current constraints. Some of the general approaches for making decisions about what ideas or solutions to consider further are as follows (Borchers, 1999):

- Private rankings or ratings: Participants in the brainstorming session privately rate the brainstorming items and the highest rated items are considered further. You might, for example, rate each idea on a simple 1 (low priority) to 3 (high priority) scale and then take the average value of the ratings for each idea. You could, after the ranking/rating exercise, choose the top 10 for further consideration. Private ratings are at the core of the NGT, the Delphi method, and other brainstorming variations. Private rankings or ratings are useful for mitigating the influence of managers and loud, influential, domineering, or high-status colleagues.

- Majority vote: Participants vote on which ideas to consider and the majority rules. In some brainstorming sessions, there can be too many ideas to consider a majority vote on every idea, so you can do a preliminary elimination based on technical feasibility, resources, schedule, or other important attributes.

- Consensus: Consensus is an accord reached by a group as a whole. The brainstorming participants or the people designated to choose ideas must all agree on the "best" ideas through discussion and debate. Achieving true consensus on what ideas to consider can be difficult and require time outside the actual brainstorming session.

- Compromise: Participants come to agreement about what ideas to consider further by giving up some of their individual demands.

- Decision by a "leader": The final decision is made by a designated leader (who may or may not be the facilitator for the session). For example, the engineering manager, who controls the development resources and has to make other trade-offs of time, features, and quality, could make the final decision. In some companies, the product managers, who often define the requirements for products, might decide what ideas should be considered further.

- Arbitration: Another person or group makes a decision for the brainstorming participants. For example, a usability team might brainstorm solutions for a user interface problem surfaced by developers, but the development manager and the product managers would be the final arbiters who make the final decision about which solutions to consider.

- Criteria-based prioritization: This is discussed in the data analysis section, but briefly, this approach would rate each idea against explicit criteria like feasibility, cost, and time. The highest rated items across the criteria are chosen for further consideration.

    d. Consider a method for tracking which ideas are used during the product development process: Assign ownership and due dates to the ideas and solutions so that they are not just left open.

    e. Collect feedback on the brainstorming process: You might ask participants to fill out a short survey or you might conduct a short "plus/delta" session where everyone is asked to discuss what worked well (the "plusses") and what could work better (the "deltas"). Apply good suggestions about the process to future brainstorming sessions.

Variations and Extensions to Brainstorming

BUZZ SESSIONS (ALSO KNOWN AS THE PHILIPS 66 TECHNIQUE)

The buzz session, or Philips 66 technique, is a way to generate ideas when you have groups that are too large for traditional brainstorming, like a college class or group of colleagues at a professional conference. The buzz session divides a large group (say more than 12 people) into several smaller groups (four to six people). The small groups are given a topic, a set of brief rules, and then asked to brainstorm for a period of time (six people for six minutes in the Philips 66 technique). At the end of six minutes, the groups report on the results of their brainstorming (or other activity like prioritizing ideas). The idea here is that you might have a large group for a short period of time that could provide valuable input to a question or problem. The major benefit of this brainstorming variation is that it gives more people a chance to speak. A major disadvantage is that you have to coordinate multiple groups and decide how to report and combine the results (Brahm & Kleiner, 1996). You might also have some initial inertia to overcome if the people in the short-lived groups don't know each other.

Free Listing

Free listing (Sinha, 2003a) involves asking individual participants or a group to list as many ideas or items as possible, on a specific topic or question, in a short period of time, often just a few minutes.

Some examples of free listing questions for user-centered design are as follows:

- List all the ideas you have for solving a problem.
- List and describe all the tasks that you perform in the course of a week.
- List and describe all the tools that you use in your work.
- List all the forms and documents that you use in your work.
- List all the functions that you use in (product name).
- List all the things about (product name) that frustrate or irritate you.

Free listing is a research technique used by cognitive anthropologists to uncover how different cultural groups classify concepts (Trotter & Schensul, 1998). For example, you might ask members of a particular cultural group to, "List all the foods they eat." Trotter (1981), for example, asked 378 Mexican Americans (1) what home remedies for illnesses they knew and (2) what illness was treated by which remedy. From these two questions, he was able to compare response frequencies by gender, age, place of birth, and other factors. The results of free listing can be used to rank order the words or phrases by frequency or other dimensions (Bernard, 2006; Sinha, 2003a).

Free listing can be used to understand terminology, concepts, behaviors, and beliefs (Trotter & Schensul, 1998). In the domain of user-centered design, free listing can be used to gather ideas and complement brainstorming and other idea-generation methods. However, you can also use free listing as cultural anthropologists do, to understand the cultural and cognitive domains of users and other stakeholders. Sinha (2003a) recommends free listing as a method for understanding a domain or mental model by examining the frequency and the order of answers to the free listing question. If there is statistical consistency across participants in the frequency and position of many items in a list, the researcher would have a "coherent domain"; if there is little consistency in the set of free listing items, the domain may not be too coherent.

Free listing questions can be asked in questionnaires, during individual or group interviews, in focus groups, in e-mail, listservs, wikis, and other online techniques. If you are using this information to study a particular group, you may want to conduct face-to-face free listing so that you can use probes to increase recall (Bernard, 2006). Brewer, Garrett & Rinaldi (2002) compared two types of probes for increasing the number of items in a list:

- Alphabetic probes: Asking participants after a free listing activity if they knew any more items starting with successive letters of the alphabet. So after a person does a free listing session about usability methods, you might say, "Think of all the usability or user-centered methods that begin with the letter 'A' and tell me any new ones that you haven't already said." This might prompt a person to remember "affinity diagramming" and "A/B Testing." You would do this for each letter in the alphabet.
- Semantic probes: Asking participants to go through the lists they generated earlier and use those items as cues for additional ones. Here you would ask something like, "Try to remember the usability or user-centered design methods that are similar to or like [the first item listed by the participants]." For example, if a person had listed "cognitive walkthrough," you could ask, "Are there any other methods that are like a cognitive walkthrough?" to which the person might remember that she had once used a "structured heuristic walkthrough." You would do this for each item in the original list.

The benefits of free listing are as follows:

- It is simple, but powerful.
- You can administer the free listing method to large groups as well as individual participants.
- Free listing can be done face to face or remotely using the phone and a variety of electronic methods like chat or wikis.
- It is a quick way to gather information about a domain, product, or process.

The drawbacks of free listing are:

- Participants may forget items.
- Participants may not understand that they should generate an exhaustive list.
- Answers may require some interpretation. For example, if you asked participants to list all the attributes that are associated with user-friendly products, they might combine two separate attributes in a compound phrase ("quick and easy to learn"). You might also have people use idiosyncratic phrases that require interpretation like "a kernel that keeps on going" or close synonyms like "credible" and "trustworthy" where you might have to decide if they were similar enough to be a single item.
- The basic data analysis is simple, but it can also get complex and involve cluster analysis, multidimensional scaling, and other sophisticated analyses.

THE NOMINAL GROUP TECHNIQUE

The nominal group technique (NGT) (Delbecq, Van deVen & Gustafson, 1975; Higgins, 2005; McGraw & Harbison, 1997; Stasser & Birchmeier, 2003; VanGundy, 1984) is designed to reduce the social anxiety associated with face-to-face group brainstorming. In the NGT, participants are given a problem or topic and are asked to write ideas privately for a specified period of time. Then all the ideas are listed on a board by having each participant read out one idea at a time. If a participant doesn't have an idea, he or she can pass for that round. No criticism is allowed when the ideas are read out. When all ideas are listed publicly, the facilitator reviews each idea to see if any further clarification is needed. If clarification is needed, the person who proposed the idea has 10–30 seconds to explain (but not defend, refute, or sell the idea).

After everyone understands all the ideas, the participants vote on or rank the ideas using a secret ballot. The ideas with the most votes or highest average ranks are chosen for further consideration. If there are too many ideas after the first voting session, a second round of voting can be conducted.

EDITOR'S NOTE: USING ANONYMOUS IDEA CARDS IN THE NGT

To reduce the anxiety of participants in the NGT even further, you could present the topic or question and then ask everyone to spend a few minutes writing ideas on 3 × 5 cards or sticky notes (Teaching Effectiveness Program, n.d.). When the time is up, you can collect the cards and then redistribute them randomly to the group. Then ask the participants to read aloud what is on each card as they place them on the brainstorming surface. Participants can ask for clarification on the items. Then you can conduct the secret ballot on the ideas. This approach separates people from ideas and is meant to reduce the anxiety associated with the creation of ideas and voting on the best ideas.

The benefits of the NGT are as follows:

- A reduction of the social inhibitions and anxieties that might occur in traditional brainstorming.
- A highly efficient method for generating ideas.
- A better chance for equal participation. Quiet, shy, or fearful participants have a chance to state their ideas.
- A separation of ideas from the personalities of the originators (especially if you use the anonymous card approach mentioned in the sidebar).
- A reduction in the evaluation apprehension that group members may feel if there are status differences among the participants (for example, your boss or vice president is in the group).
- A sense of closure since private voting is a specific step in the procedure (it may or may not be in traditional group brainstorming).

The drawbacks of the NGT are as follows:

- Limited interaction among the group members
- The relative obscurity of the method (it is not a well-known variation on traditional group brainstorming)
- A lack of synergy because all the ideas are generated privately
- A possible lack of convergence on what the best ideas are during the prioritization or voting (for example, many ideas each get a few votes with no clear "winner")

For details on how to conduct a nominal group session see *Group Techniques for Program Planning: A Guide to Nominal Group and Delphi Processes*, (Delbecq, Van deVen & Gustafson, 1975).

REVERSE (NEGATIVE) BRAINSTORMING

This is a variation on brainstorming where you ask the participants to first brainstorm negative aspects of a topic and then, with the list of negative aspects visible, brainstorm positive items for related clusters of comments. (CreatingMinds. org, n.d.; MindTools, n.d.; VanGundy, 1984).

The basic procedure for reverse brainstorming is to:

1. Brainstorm on a negative topic: For example, instead of asking, "How can we improve customer satisfaction?"; you might ask, "What can we do to make customers dissatisfied?" or "How can we cause customers to be dissatisfied?" or "How can we make customers mad?" You could also ask "What is everyone else NOT doing?" rather than list what they are doing to improve product satisfaction.
2. Group the related comments: Arrange the related items in groups to simplify the next step.
3. Generate the positive statements for the negative groups of items. In Table 4.1, negative statements about customer support for an

Table 4.1	Negative Items from Reverse Brainstorming and Their Positive Counterparts	
Negative Statements	**Positive Statements**
■ Keep people from returning items – it is really expensive	■ Put the link at the top of the page for returns
■ Hide the link for returns to the company	■ Highlight the liberal return policy in a clear block above the fold
■ Avoid telling customers how much the shipping will cost	■ Provide for a simple feature for estimating the cost of shipping for customers before they have to fill out a lot of information
	■ Provide rough estimates in a table that shows the various ways to ship
■ Hide the phone number for calling our company directly ■ "Virtual" companies shouldn't tell people where they are located or how to call	■ Provide a customer support phone number in the contacts area and also in the check-out process
■ Don't tell people that their passwords are case sensitive	■ Provide a short tip on password formats
■ Don't make it easy to retrieve passwords	■ Ignore case (but require at least one number)
■ Don't tell people that their password is their e-mail	■ Provide an easy way to retrieve lost passwords

e-commerce site are listed in the left column and positive statements on the right.

4. Evaluate the positive statements for potential solutions:

Topic: What can we do to make our customers dissatisfied?

The philosophy behind reverse brainstorming is that it is easier to find fault first, then use the faults as input on how to improve some aspect of a Web site, product, or service. You might also use this approach when:

- You have a very judgmental group and traditional group brainstorming is difficult.
- You are working on a product or service that is complex to implement (Mycoted, 2006).

SWOT ANALYSIS

Strengths, weaknesses, opportunities, and threats (SWOT) is a strategic planning method where an organization or group within an organization tries to analyze its competitive advantages and disadvantages. Managers can examine where strengths can be used to take advantage of opportunities and fend off threats.

SWOT uses structured brainstorming and focuses on four major topics: strengths, weaknesses, opportunities, and threats. In the SWOT method, you create a table with four cells and brainstorm strengths, weaknesses, opportunities, and threats related to a particular issue and examine how strengths can be used to counteract threats and take advantage of opportunities and how weaknesses can be overcome (Kyle, 2003).

Strengths and weaknesses are internal resources and capabilities. Examples of general strengths and weaknesses that might be considered in SWOT analyses include the following (NetMBA, 2006; Wikipedia, n.d.):

- Expertise of designers and developers
- Financial resources of the organization
- Availability of key personnel
- Patents and other intellectual property
- Position in the marketplace
- Maturity of the software development process
- Flexibility of existing code
- Customer service
- Good reputation for settling customer complaints
- Quality
- Ability to change quickly
- Competitive advantages

Opportunities and threats are external forces that can impact your company, team, or product. For example, the impact of high fuel prices or bad economic conditions are examples of an external forces that would affect online travel sites or car sales. Similarly, a competitor that significantly improves the user experience of a product would be a threat to your company, but perhaps an opportunity to expand your user-centered design (UCD) team to counteract that threat. Examples of general opportunities and threats include the following:

- Competitors' actions in the marketplace
- Market factors
- New technologies
- Economic conditions
- New to the marketplace; no strong reputation yet
- Social changes
- Political and regulatory issues (for example, laws and regulation regarding disabilities)
- Press regarding your company's products

A common representation of a SWOT session is Table 4.2, which contains the results of brainstorming on the strengths, weaknesses, opportunities, and threats to a user-centered product development process in a corporate setting.

Disadvantages of the SWOT method include the following (NetMBA, n.d.; Wikipedia, n.d.):

- The SWOT analysis could oversimplify what is, in reality, a complex situation.

Table 4.2	The Four Cells of a SWOT Table Used to Examine Strategic Issues Facing a User-Centered Design Team	

Strengths	Weaknesses
■ Voice of the customer is taken seriously here	■ No dedicated usability lab
■ A few very good senior people	■ Junior UCD colleagues have limited commercial experience
■ Included in manager's meetings	■ No clear metrics of success
■ Strong manager who publicizes our work	■ Access to customers requires several levels of permission
■ Good travel budget	■ No dedicated recruiter
■ The team collaborates with other groups	■ NDA process is very complex
	■ No good UCD infrastructure for templates, reports, and other artifacts

Opportunities	Threats
■ Good press on the usability of the last product that we worked on	■ Pressure to move to Agile development where usability isn't a priority
■ Product sales are increasing, but complaints about usability of some key features	■ Team is being asked to do too much
■ Senior management referred to usability as key for the future	■ The user interface toolkit used by development does not support a flexible architecture
■ Main competitor got high marks on usability on their new product	■ The team is now expected to write gigantic user interface specs, which consume vast amounts of time
■ The UCD team is being asked to work on the design of new features	

- Some factors, like corporate culture, could be seen as both strengths and weaknesses in a SWOT analysis.
- A SWOT analysis requires perspectives from multiple stakeholders, not just a single analyst. A SWOT analysis should have input from internal staff, customers, business partners, support personnel, industry consultants, and others.

For examples of the use of SWOT in user-centered design see the following:

- Nieters, J. & Dworman, G. (2007). Comparing UXD Business Models. http://www.uxmatters.com/MT/archives/000206.php
- Väyrynen, S., Röning, J. & Alakärppä, I. (2006). User-centered development of video telephony for servicing mainly older users: Review and evaluation of an approach applied for 10 years. *Human Technology*. Vol. 2(1), April 2006, 8–37.

DELPHI METHOD

The Delphi method was developed at the Research and Development (RAND) institute in the 1960s (Brown, 1968) to study the opinions of experts without having face-to-face meetings where the psychological factors such as dominant personalities, status, or approval, can strongly influence the outcome of the meetings.

The Delphi method involves a coordinator and a group of experts who are given a problem and a questionnaire that asks for ideas on how to solve the problem, and general questions related to the problem (Delbecq, Van deVen & Gustafson, 1975). The experts are asked to provide reasons for their opinions and the reasons are then critiqued by the rest of the experts. After the experts fill out the initial questionnaire, the results are collated and summarized by the coordinator and sent back to the panel of experts with no names attached to the ideas. A second questionnaire asks more specific questions (based on the earlier results) and once again the anonymous results are sent around to the experts who are asked to evaluate the ideas from the last round and to add any new ideas.

The coordinator repeats the process of summarizing the results and sending out new questionnaires until there is convergence on the best ideas for solving the problem. The selection of the best ideas can emerge as a result of consensus of the experts or the final set of ideas can be ranked or rated anonymously. The Delphi method is most often applied to complex problems with relatively large groups of experts. Given the complexity of modern software development where requirements must be multinational and design is done by multiple groups across many time zones, the Delphi method has a place in the repertoire of UCD professionals.

EDITOR'S NOTE: DELPHI STUDIES BY E-MAIL

Early Delphi studies relied on traditional paper mail. The exchange of questionnaires and responses between the coordinator and the team of experts could consume many weeks. With e-mail and other software, this delay can be reduced considerably. The Delphi method is powerful, but the coordinators can spend many hours creating the succession of questionnaires and feedback forms necessary for converging on the best ideas.

For details on the origins and early examples of forecasting studies using the Delphi method, go to the RAND Web site (http://www.rand.org). For current examples of the use of Delphi method, see Harrison, Back, and Tatar (2006) who employed a version of the Delphi method for project planning of design projects and Francis, Firth, and Mellor (2005) who used the Delphi method to examine user-centered design of assistive technologies with autistic users.

REMOTE BRAINSTORMING

Remote brainstorming can be accomplished with synchronous and asynchronous communication technologies. Here are some general approaches for remote brainstorming:

- Online chat and instant messaging (IM): You can assemble a distributed team to brainstorm topics using chat or IM software. Members of the brainstorming team are sent instructions beforehand with the topic of interest and rules for the session. The session is recorded and the ideas that are generated can be prioritized later. One of the problems with using chat or IM is that ideas can scroll out of view so you lose the ability to see everything which is important for encouraging variations on ideas that were listed earlier.
- Electronic whiteboards: Electronic whiteboards allow distributed teams to post ideas in real time. You can use whiteboards and conference calling systems to run remote brainstorming sessions.
- E-mail: Participants can do individual brainstorming and send items to an e-mail address where they are combined and then listed on a Web site or other type of archive.
- Listserv software: Remote participants can submit ideas that are circulated to everyone on the brainstorming team. The facilitator compiles the items and makes them available to the group for prioritization or further review.
- Blogs and wikis: Remote participants can add comments on a specific topic or question to a blog or wiki for a designated period of time.
- Specialized online brainstorming software: A search of the Web using search phrases like "online brainstorming" or "brainstorming software" will reveal commercial online brainstorming tools and services with specialized features like threaded idea generation, features for organizing ideas, facilitator prompts, polls for rating ideas, and decision matrices where each idea is rated against a set of criteria.

Dennis & Williams (2003) compared electronic brainstorming to verbal (face-to-face) and nominal brainstorming methods. Their research revealed that electronic brainstorming can be an efficient complement to verbal or nominal group brainstorming especially for large groups. Electronic brainstorming allows some synergy between members while mitigating process losses in the number of ideas from production blocking and social anxiety.

One caution – the first time you use a remote approach for a method like brainstorming, conduct a pilot test on a small group of remote participants and colleagues to work out the ground rules and best practices.

Major Issues in the Use of Brainstorming

WHAT IS "QUALITY" IN BRAINSTORMING

A mantra of brainstorming is that quantity begets quality, but just what is this "quality"? Quality in brainstorming research is, generally, measured by considering the novelty or originality of an idea and the feasibility or appropriateness of the idea to the problem at hand. So a quality idea might be considered as something that others haven't thought of before that can be reasonably implemented with the resources available. One way to examine the quality of ideas from brainstorming sessions is to have several experts rate ideas for their novelty and appropriateness. Other criteria used in research to evaluate the outcomes of brainstorming sessions include the following (Isaksen, 1998):

- Satisfaction with the ideas generated
- Flexibility of the ideas
- Generality of the ideas

The often-repeated statement that quality comes from quantity is generally supported in the research literature. Diehl & Stroebe (1987), for example, found a high correlation ($r = 0.82$) between the quantity of ideas generated and the number of "quality" ideas. One open issue regarding the value of brainstorming is the overall impact of good brainstorming ideas on product success. What is the return on investment (ROI) associated with brainstorming and the ideas that are applied from the brainstorming? There doesn't seem to be a good answer for that yet.

HOW MANY PARTICIPANTS SHOULD I HAVE IN BRAINSTORMING SESSIONS?

Earlier in this chapter, the recommended number of participants for effective group brainstorming fell in the range of three to 10 people with some diversity in background. The optimal size of a group is determined, in part, by the factors that influence production gains (larger groups may have more synergy and more persistence) and production losses (social anxiety, evaluation apprehension, production blocking, and cognitive interference, where old ideas start popping up and people have to think if the idea is new or old). Diversity, for example, can result in idea production gains, but also result in losses if the diverse participants use a different language or have a different perspective that results in communication problems (Nijstad, Diehl & Stroebe, 2003).

There are many variables to consider when assessing what size groups should be in a particular context, but there is some discussion in the research literature that relatively small groups of three to five participants work well. Heller and Hollabaugh (1992), for example, recommend small groups that do not exceed three people. While small groups may be very effective at generating ideas, brainstorming with a small group may be seen as relegating the non-participants to an "out-group".

SOCIAL ISSUES THAT COULD AFFECT IDEA GENERATION IN GROUP BRAINSTORMING

Brainstorming involves a number of social issues that can impair creativity (Paulus & Nijstad, 2003). These social issues include the following:

- Fear of evaluation by other members of the group: Evaluation apprehension, the fear or being evaluated or tested, is a serious issue for group brainstorming (Camacho & Paulus, 1995; Rosenberg, 1969). Participants may not want to put forth wild ideas if they are afraid of losing credibility, having their idea rejected, or being humiliated. Facilitators can reduce evaluation apprehension by:

- Not inviting someone that the group fears. Avoid inviting managers who are tyrannical.
- Stressing that the quantity of ideas is the sole criterion for brainstorming success
- Reminding participants that all ideas are welcome
- Pointing out that the participants will not be judged on the quality of ideas. The worst thing that any facilitator or manager could do to stifle brainstorming would be to hint (or publicly state) that the results of brainstorming will be used as input to employees' performance reviews.
- Competition for speaking time: Facilitators should encourage participants to:
  - Respond crisply.
  - Not belabor an idea once it is understood.
  - Avoid criticism.
  - Watch for cues that someone is struggling to get his/her ideas out. While everyone should have a chance to speak, forcing people to speak or "going around the table" for input from everyone is, generally, not recommended.
  - Avoid "war stories" that steal time away from idea generation. War stories are "filler conversations" and all they do is reduce the time others have to generate ideas. Facilitators should prevent participants from telling their favorite war stories. It is hard to attend to a war story and also be creative.
- Motivating participants: Facilitators can influence participants' motivation by describing the importance of the task and providing feedback about past brainstorming sessions ("In the last sessions, we generated 103 ideas in just 30 minutes").

COMPETITIVE BRAINSTORMING CAN INCREASE THE QUANTITY OF IDEAS

Coskun (2000), Paulus & Dzindolet (1993) and others who study the brainstorming process have found that setting high expectations ("We would like to get at least 70 ideas during this session!") or providing brainstorming teams with feedback about what constitutes poor or good performance (regarding the number of ideas, not the quality of ideas) can increase the number of ideas generated by the group. If you are doing electronic brainstorming, you could indicate the average number of ideas being generated per person (though never identify anyone by name). As a general rule, the expectations for group performance should be set reasonably high (Paulus & Brown, 2003).

ADDITIONAL TECHNIQUES FOR INCREASING THE NUMBER OF IDEAS

Osborn (1963) provided a checklist of techniques for changing and expanding ideas during a brainstorming session. This venerable, but still relevant, checklist includes the following techniques:

- Adapt: Is there something like this idea that might be worth emulating? Could you adapt a concept from physics or psychology or cooking to expand on an idea?
- Modify: Can you change something about the idea? What would happen if you changed color, materials, shape, motion, visual style, orientation, texture, or who the users are?
- Magnify: What happens if you add things to your idea or change some properties? What could you do to make it larger, faster, heavier, taller, wider, or sexier? What if you accentuated various properties like saturation or brightness? What if two people could use something that is currently a single person system?
- Minify: Can you subtract things from an idea? Can you make it smaller, shorter, lighter, or more condensed? Can you subtract features? Can you reduce complexity? Can you eliminate features? Can you shrink something in a single dimension?
- Put to other uses: Can you put your idea to some other use? What else could you do with the idea beyond the immediate use? For example, what nonstandard uses could you come up with for a set of features in a graphics program?
- Substitute: Can you interchange components, methods, techniques, ingredients, people, language, perspective, or something else? For example, you might take the perspective of someone who was 80 years old with arthritis, poor vision from macular degeneration, and hearing problems.
- Rearrange: Can you use a different organization, layout, sequence, or arrangement? Can you move things around? Can you invert or reverse the order of controls in a user interface?

Berkun (2004) proposes several other "tricks" for stimulating new ideas during the brainstorming sessions.

- Use random theme generators: Here you might have a list of random words, attributes, colors, shapes, or other stimuli that you use for design brainstorming. You would pull out random sets of words and ask how you would design something with these attributes.
- Eliminate constraints: Explicitly remove common barriers like cost, current technology, schedule, safety features, and expertise and see what ideas emerge when people are not operating with assumptions about everyday constraints. What could you do if you removed some of the things that the development team said "the development kit doesn't support"?

- Add constraints: Here you might impose constraints and generate ideas that fall within those constraints. For example, you might add a constraint that the product must work "under water," "in bright desert sun," or "in a hurricane." If you add the constraint that the product (and user) will sometimes be subject to intense vibration, you might come up with ideas for using a product in vehicles or while riding a bicycle.
- "Rotate": Berkun suggests adding a bit of physicality to brainstorming by asking people to get up and move one chair to the right or left. The rationale for rotating seating position is that a surprise physical action might loosen up the participants and inject a bit of levity and energy into the session. Rotating is potentially risky if your colleagues lack a sense of play in the workplace. Before trying actions that are clearly unusual like rotating seats, consider your audience carefully.

If you will be called on to facilitate brainstorming sessions or focus groups, keep a list of these methods with brief instructions on how to apply them if a brainstorming session starts to lose energy. These creativity stimulation techniques take practice, so try out some of them on a small and friendly group first. You can find other techniques for idea generation in books on creativity and design. Books by Epstein, (1996), Higgins, (2005), Michalko, (2006a,b) contain creativity techniques and tips for facilitators.

Data Analysis for Brainstorming

TYPES OF DATA

Types of data that can be collected during brainstorming include the following:

- A list of ideas generated by the participants
- Groupings of ideas into categories at the end of brainstorming sessions using the affinity diagramming method
- Elaborations and explanations of ideas during the review process
- A list of prioritized ideas
- Ratings of the ideas on one or more criteria
- Feedback about the brainstorming process itself

ANALYSIS TECHNIQUES

Listing Ideas

All the ideas from a brainstorming session can be listed in a spreadsheet, word processor, or specialized tools like PathMaker® or Inspiration. If you have numbered the items sequentially as they were generated, your list would be chronological. To facilitate recall days, weeks, or even months later when you look through this list, you can annotate the list with clarifications and brief explanation of any unusual terms or abbreviations.

Grouping Ideas from Brainstorming

Affinity diagramming, a method for organizing data by similarity, can be used to reveal groups of related items. The number of groups that emerge from an affinity diagramming is sometimes used as a measure in brainstorming research.

Voting on Brainstorming Ideas

A group can vote on which brainstorming items should be considered further by placing adhesive dots or ink marks on the items, by removing the items from the master list, or voting online using tools like Excel, Google Spreadsheet, or SurveyMonkey.

Criteria-Based Evaluation

Criteria-based evaluation uses a decision matrix to choose the top ideas from brainstorming. The people charged with choosing which ideas will be considered further rate or rank each idea against a list of criteria like cost, ease of programming, novelty, and generality. The ratings/rankings for each idea are averaged, the ideas are sorted by the average value, and the top rated/ranked ideas are chosen for consideration (see Table 4.3). Criteria-based evaluation can be done with online survey tools if you want to expand the process of choosing the top ideas beyond the brainstorming participants.

What Do You Need for Brainstorming?

PERSONNEL, PARTICIPANTS, AND TRAINING

You need a small, diverse group of three to 10 people for a brainstorming session and a facilitator who will explain the process and keep the brainstorming session going efficiently. An experienced facilitator is important for successful brainstorming. Key attributes of a good facilitator for brainstorming would include the following:

- An ability to keep the participants from engaging in the critical analysis of ideas too soon
- Sufficient energy to keep the ideas flowing
- A focus on the quantity of ideas rather than the quality (quality assessment comes later)
- Acceptance of radical ideas

| **Table 4.3** | A Decision Matrix for a Criterion-Based Approach to Choosing the Best Ideas from Brainstorming |

	Criterion 1	Criterion 2	Criterion 3	...	Criterion N	Sum	Mean Rating/ Ranking	Top Ideas
Idea 1								
Idea 2								
Idea 3								
Idea 4								
Idea	...	...	...	... ...		...	...	
Idea N								

Training requirements for the brainstorming facilitator are moderate. Research into methods for generating ideas (Paulus & Brown, 2003) highlights the need for experienced facilitators who are trained in procedures for effective group interaction (Paulus & Brown, 2003). Facilitators should be trained to:

- Apply the brainstorming rules consistently.
- Motivate participants using a variety of prompts.
- Ensure that no one dominates the session.
- Keep the focus on one issue, question, or topic, at a time.
- Notice when people are becoming fatigued.
- Be aware of best practices for ensuring an effective group interaction.
- Deal with the occasional silent period (sometimes participants will need to think a bit so the facilitator should not panic at momentary lulls in the conversation).

Training requirements for participants are relatively low. A short introduction to the brainstorming method and a clear statement of the rules for the process are basic requirements. The most difficult training issues for participants are probably those of minimizing verbal and nonverbal criticism and keeping filler conversations and war stories to a minimum. Smith (1993) found that groups with just five minutes of training on the effects of criticism of ideas produced more ideas than groups with no training. Examples of verbal criticism and other behaviors that will result in production blocking and fewer ideas should be a standard part of training for brainstorming.

HARDWARE AND SOFTWARE

No special hardware or software is required for brainstorming. Brainstorming can be done by writing ideas on a board or using sticky notes that you can affix to a board, wall, or other large surface. If you plan to organize ideas, using sticky notes makes grouping simple, but may slow down the brainstorming process (you may want two notetakers to write down items). You could also have someone type in ideas on a computer and project them to the brainstorming group (this is useful for remote brainstorming with distributed groups).

You can use software like Word and Excel to capture ideas from brainstorming sessions, but these business applications make it somewhat hard to move items around quickly and easily. Software tools like Inspiration and MindManager can be used to capture ideas quickly and then move and categorize those ideas.

DOCUMENTS AND MATERIALS

The key documents for group brainstorming include the following:

- A checklist with all the activities that you need to prepare and conduct the brainstorming session
- A statement of the problem or topic for brainstorming (this statement should be given to all the participants or posted in the location that is visible during the brainstorming session.)

- A set of brainstorming ground rules
- A list of the ideas generated during the session
- A list of the ideas that are chosen for further consideration (through ratings, rankings, or other forms of prioritization)
- An action statement or plan that describes who is responsible for following up on brainstorming ideas

The only materials that you need for face-to-face group brainstorming are sheets of paper, pens or markers, easels with poster paper, and some way to attach the pages of brainstorming to a wall or other surface that can serve as a temporary idea display.

Recommended Readings

Higgins, J. M. (2005). *101 Creative problem solving techniques: The handbook of new ideas for business (Rev. ed.)*. Winter, Park, FL: The New Management Publishing Company. Higgins' book is a compendium of problem-solving techniques. This book describes methods at a high level and provides practitioners who have used some traditional methods like face-to-face group brainstorming with variations for special cases (very large groups).

Osborn, A. F. (1963). *Applied imagination: Principles and procedures of creative problem-solving (Third Revised Edition)*. New York, NY: Charles Scribner's Sons. This is considered a classic book on modern brainstorming. Alex Osborn, who began his writings on brainstorming in the 1940s, wanted a meeting process that would reduce the inhibitions that block the generation of creative ideas. Many of the classic rules for modern brainstorming originated with Osborn. This book is out of print, but a worthwhile read if you can locate it. There are a number of versions of this book, each incorporating new ideas from Osborn. The 1963 version is the most-often cited. Used copies are generally available and reprints can be found at http://www.creativeeducationfoundation.org/press.shtml#imagination.

Paulus, P. B., & Nijstad, B. A. (Eds.), *Group creativity: Innovation through collaboration*. Oxford, UK: Oxford University Press. Paulus and Nijstad have edited a book that captures a wide range of research into group creativity. Much of the book deals with brainstorming and related methods for generating ideas and solutions to problems. Although the book is loaded with research and theory, most chapters have a set of practical implications for group creativity methods like brainstorming and brainwriting. The book discusses both face-to-face and electronic methods and their respective strengths and weaknesses. The book highlights how social inhibitors can affect creative productivity and provides some research-based tips on how to overcome these inhibitors.

CHAPTER 5

Sketching: A Key to Good Design

135

Bill Buxton

> Buxton's view, sketching can still be a useful tool requirements elicitation, brainstorming, workflow analysis, and conceptual design. Let this chapter be a source of insight and inspiration about the mysterious thing called "design" and its primary activity – sketching.

Societies do not evolve because their members simply grow old, but rather because their mutual relations are transformed.

Ilya Prigogine

THE QUESTION OF DESIGN

If design is so important yet neglected, and if we should be taking steps to remedy that situation, then perhaps it makes sense to clarify what we mean by "design."

Here is where the trouble starts. Take any room of professionals and ask them if they know what design is or what a designer is. Almost everyone will answer in the affirmative and yet practically everyone's definition will be different. That is to say, people's definitions are so broad that almost every act of creation, from writing code, building a deck, making a business plan, and so on, can be considered design. If one goes to the literature instead of one's colleagues, the result will be pretty much the same.

The problem is, when a word means almost anything or everything, it actually means nothing. It is not precise enough to be useful. Take your typical company trying to develop a new product, for example. If those creating the business plan, planning the sales and marketing campaign, writing the software, performing usability studies, etc. are all doing "design," then how can I be arguing that we need to incorporate design into the process? By that definition of design, it is already there at every level of the organization and every stage of the process.

Now I could be wrong about this. For example, the well-known writer and psychologist Don Norman has stated in an epilogue to his most recent book (Norman, 2004):

We are all designers.

I have the highest degree of respect for Don, but in my opinion, this is nonsense!

Yes, we all choose colors for our walls or the layout of furniture in our living rooms. But this no more makes us all designers than our ability to count our change at the grocery store makes us all mathematicians. Of course, there is a way that both are true, but only in the most banal sense. Reducing things to such a level trivializes the hard-won and highly developed skills of the professional designer (and mathematician).

If you are a nurse or paramedic, you can legitimately refer to yourself as a medical practitioner but not a doctor. None of this is intended to discount the skills or professionalism of those who have medical skills but are not MDs. To the contrary, their skills may well save a life. In fact, the more we understand and appreciate the nature of their specific skills, the more they help us understand and appreciate the specific skills that a doctor, or a specialist, brings to the table. And it is exactly this kind of awareness, in terms of the skills of the design professional, that I see as lacking in so many of those who profess to speak for the importance of design or their own affinity or capacity in design.

I think that I do understand what people like Don Norman are trying to express when they say, "We are all designers." I accept that it is well intentioned. But statements like this tend to result in the talents, education, and insights of professional designers being discounted or distinguished from everyday design decisions.

Perhaps the whole thing could be cleared up through a bit more precision in our use of language. Just as the term "medical practitioner" is more general than "doctor," we might distinguish between "design practitioner" and "designer." Or, perhaps we just need two distinct but related words, analogous to *arithmetic* compared with *mathematics*.

Regardless, in the sense that I use the term, everyone is distinctly not a designer, and a large part of this book is dedicated to explaining the importance of including a design specialist in the process of developing both things and processes, what their role is, and what skills they bring. But if now you are expecting me to give you a clear definition of design as I use the term, I am afraid that I am going to disappoint you. Smarter people than I have tried and failed. This is a slippery slope on which I do not want to get trapped.

What I mean by the term "design" is what someone who went to an art college and studied industrial design would recognize as design. At least this vague characterization helps narrow our interpretation of the term somewhat. Some recent work in cognitive science (Gedenryd, 1998; Goel, 1995) helps distinguish it further. It suggests that a designer's approach to creative problem solving is very different from how computer scientists, for example, solve puzzles. That is, design can be distinguished by a particular cognitive style. Gedenryd, in particular, makes it clear that sketching is fundamental to the design process. Furthermore, related work by Suwa and Tversky (2002) and Tversky (2002) shows that besides the ability to make sketches, a designer's use of them is a distinct skill that develops with practice and is fundamental to their cognitive style.

I can also say what I do not mean by design, in particular, in the context of this book. I do not mean the highly stylized aesthetic pristine material that we see in glossy magazines advertising expensive things and environments. This is fashion or style that projects a lie, or more generously, a myth – a myth that can never be real. By "design," I don't mean the photographs of interiors of rooms where nobody could live, of clothes that nobody could wear, or of highly stylized computers or other appliances whose presentation suggests that they were "designed" as if they don't need cables and that they are to exist on perfectly clear desks without even a human around to mar their carefully styled aesthetics.

No, the type of design that I want to talk about in this book gets down and dirty. It is design for the real world – the world that we live in, which is messy and constantly changing, and where once a product is released, the designer, manufacturer, and vendor have virtually no control or influence over how or where it is used. Once sold, it leaves the perfect world of the glossy advertising photos. In short, I am talking about design for the wild. Carrying on our bicycle theme, contrast the renderings of the two mountain bikes illustrated in Fig. 5.1 with that shown in Fig. 5.2. Hopefully, this helps make my point. The "design" that I want to talk about goes beyond the object and cannot be thought of independent of the larger physical, emotional, social, and experiential ecology within which it exists. (To further pursue other notions of "the wild," see, e.g., Attfield, 2000 or Hutchins, 1995).

I can offer another approach, one that makes an end-run around the whole dilemma. This option takes a lead from Fällman (2003a,b). Rather than pursue the question, "What is design?" (which probably none of us will agree on anyhow), let us ask a different (and perhaps better) question: "What is the archetypal activity of design?"

FIGURE 5.1
Two renderings of a mountain bike. The above view is expository. It shows the design in an objective way. In the one on the facing page, it was decided to render the bike in a stance that was less neutral – one that started to project some character (for me at least), a kind of embedded playfulness. Now contrast these representations to that in the following figure!

Images: Trek Bicycles.

FIGURE 5.2
Down and dirty (and wet) in the wild. The real test comes not where the rubber meets the road, but the mud, rocks, sticks, and yes, the water. Even though the images in Fig. 5.1 have value, this is a rendering of what a mountain biker really buys. It is the aspiration (and hopefully the reality) of the experience. And despite being the best representation of what one gets with the product, unlike the preceding renderings, the bike is hardly visible. This is the wild!
Images: Trek Bicycles.

For Jones (1992), the answer would be drawing

> ...the one common action of designers of all kinds (p. 4)

Fällman's answer is similar, but just a little more specific – it would be sketching. In agreeing with him, I am not alone. Others, such as Goel (1995), Gedenryd (1998), and Suwa and Tversky (1996), have come to the same conclusion.

In saying this, it is important to emphasize that I am not asserting that the activity of sketching is design. Rather, I am just making the point that any place that I have seen design, in the sense that I want to discuss it in this book, it has been accompanied by sketching. So, even if we can't (or won't) define design, we can perhaps still gain some insights into its nature and practice by taking some time to delve into the nature of sketching.

WE ARE NOT ALL DESIGNERS

I can feel the hackles of some of my colleagues rising when I make such a dogmatic statement as, "We are not all designers," especially some of those from Scandinavia. The reason is that there is an approach to design called "participatory design" (Clement & Van den Besselaar, 1993; Greenbaum & Kyng, 1991; Muller, 2003) in which the layperson is an active and essential participant in the design process. Rather than following the "Designer as God" model, where products come from "on high" like manna from heaven created by "The Designer," participatory design adheres to an ethic of "Designer as Facilitator." In this case, the role of the design professional is to work with the users/customers as a kind of combination coach/trainer to help them come to an appropriate design solution themselves.

In the world of participatory design, therefore, we are all potential participants in the design process. However, a careful reading of my preceding words will show that there is no contradiction here. Yes, the layperson can play a critical role in the design process. But if we are all designers, then why is a design professional required in participatory design? Why don't the laypeople just do it on their own?

My words are far less controversial if you grant me one small concession: that design as a profession is as rich as math or medicine. We have no problem accepting that although medicine is distinct from math, it is still rich enough to encompass disciplines as diverse as neurology, cardiology, podiatry, and so on. Likewise, mathematics embraces a diverse range of specialties. As we shall soon see, my dogma does not apply to some narrow definition of design. The view of design that I am discussing in this book is broad enough to encompass participatory design, among other approaches to design practice. I see the discipline as that rich. But by the same token, as with math and medicine, I do not see that as implying that "we are all designers" or that there is not a distinct profession called "design."

So, when I speak of design, I do mean something distinct from engineering, marketing, sales, or finance, for example. However, in so doing, by no means do I mean to take away from, or downplay, the value or importance of the other creative activities that are part and parcel of any of these other functions. I am just not referring to these activities when I use the term "design."

THE ANATOMY OF SKETCHING

The only true voyage of discovery is not to go to new places, but to have other eyes.

Marcel Proust

Both sketching and design emerged in the late medieval period, and this was no accident. From this period on, the trend was toward a separation of design from the process of making (Heskett, 1980). With that came the need to find the means whereby the designer could explore and communicate ideas. Sketching, as a distinct form of drawing, provided such a vehicle.

The first examples of sketching, as we think of it today, come from Siena, from Mariano di Jacobi detto Taccola (McGee, 2004). In the first half of the fifteenth century, he embarked on a four-volume set of books on civil and military technology called *De Ingenisis*. In a manner not unlike George Lucas and *Star Wars*, he completed volumes 3 and 4 first and delivered them to the emperor in 1433. Volumes 1 and 2 were never completed. Rather, he went on to work on another project, *De Machinis*, which he completed in 1449.

This might seem like a little too much arcane detail, but you rather need to know it to understand the following excerpt from a recent book about Taccola's work:

> What is significant for our purposes is that Taccola worked out many of the ideas he presented in *De Machinis* by filling the unfinished pages of Books 1 and 2 of *De Ingenisis* with hundreds of rough sketches, turning them into a sort of notebook. Examining these sketches and comparing them to the drawings in *De Machinis* we are able to follow a person actually working out technical ideas for the first time in history.
>
> **(McGee, 2004; p. 73)**

That is, Taccola's sketches, such as those seen in Fig. 5.3, are the first examples of the use of sketching as a means of working through a design – sketching as an aid to thought.

For a discussion of the figure, we turn again to McGee:

> Here we see that Taccola has sketched three different kinds of protected attack boats: one with a stone dropper, one with a ram, and one with a large hook or "grappler" on the side. We immediately see that his technique has enabled him to quickly generate three alternatives. Using paper, he is able to store them. Stored, they can be compared. In short, Taccola's style provided him with a graphic means of technical exploration.
>
> **(McGee, 2004; p. 76)**

Now let us move from the Renaissance to the present. For the sake of argument, let us assume that design and sketching are related. Furthermore, let us assume that we can gain insights about design by way of cultivating a better understanding of sketching. Doing so is not too much of a stretch. For example, museums such as Boijmans Van Beuningen in Rotterdam exhibit sketches, models, and prototypes in their own right as a means to inform us about the process of product design.

> In the past few years within the profession of industrial design there has been increasing attention on the story behind the object, in which sketches, design drawings, models and prototypes play a prominent role. They make possible a reconstruction of the interesting history of their origin. Above all they make visible the designer's contribution, which is often very different to what one might expect.
>
> **(te Duits, 2003; p. 4)**

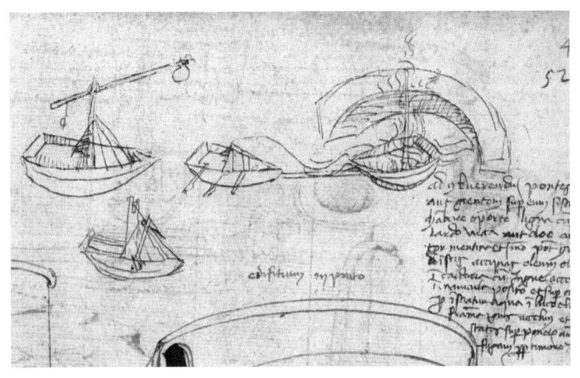

FIGURE 5.3
Details from Taccola's notebook. Several sketches of ships are shown exhibiting different types of protective shields, and one with a "grappler." These are the first known examples of using sketching as a tool of thought.
Source: McGee (2004); Detail of Munich, Bayerische Staatsbibliothek. Codex Latinus Monacensis 197 Part 2, fol. 52.

In this spirit, I want to introduce a number of sketches that were generated in the course of realizing a product, in this case a time-trial racing bicycle designed for Lance Armstrong for the Tour de France (Figs. 5.4–5.8). The first four images are in chronological order. The first three take us from sketch to engineering drawing. The visual vocabulary of all the figures is different, and it is important to keep in mind that these variations are not random. Rather, they are the consequence of matching the appropriate visual language to the intended purpose of the rendering. The conscious effort of the designer in doing so is perhaps most reflected in Fig. 5.7, where the designer has gone to extra effort to "dumb down" the rendering to ensure that it did not convey a degree of completion that was not intended.

In looking at the drawings, keep in mind that they follow only one of the many concepts explored – the one that was eventually built. Early in the design process it would not be unusual for a designer to generate 30 or more sketches a day. Each might explore a different concept. The figures used are intended to show different styles of visual representation of just one of these, not to show the breadth of ideas considered.

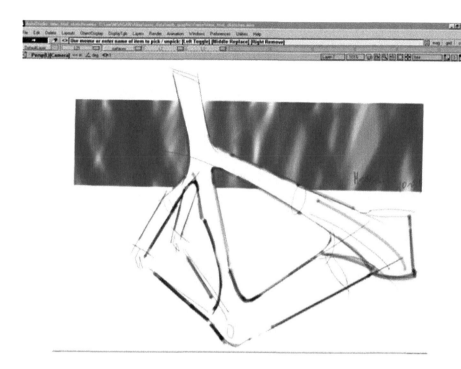

FIGURE 5.4
Early three-quarter view sketch of time-trial bike. Although done on a computer, this is a freehand sketch. Notice that the representation is tentative. What tells you this? Contrast this to the representation in Fig. 5.6.

Credit: Michael Sagan, Trek Bicycles.

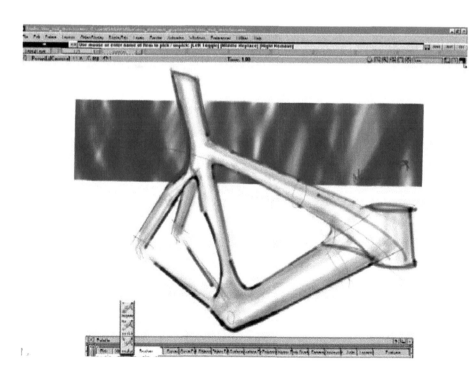

FIGURE 5.5
Shaded three-quarter view sketch of time-trial bike. This is a refinement of the sketch seen in Fig. 5.4. Through the use of shading, the sketch communicates more about the 3D form of the concept. Notice that despite this refinement, lines still extend through the "hard points."

Credit: Michael Sagan, Trek Bicycles.

FIGURE 5.6
Side view of 3D-shaded model of time-trial bike. This is a side view of the same bike seen in the previous two figures. Contrast this representation to that in Fig. 5.5. Both are shaded to highlight the form. Ignoring the addition of the graphics for the moment, is it obvious, is it clear which of the two is more refined, closer to "final," which took the most effort to create, and which will take the most effort to redo in the event of a change or suggestion? This image is clearly not a sketch.

Credit: Michael Sagan, Trek Bicycles.

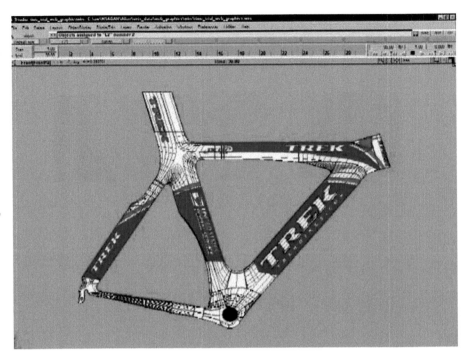

FIGURE 5.7
Accurate 3D-shaded model superimposed over three-quarter view sketch. This image is perhaps the most interesting. It is a composite of a three-quarter view of the 3D model seen in Fig. 5.6 superimposed over the sketch seen in Fig. 5.4. Given what we have seen thus far, ask yourself why the designer would do this.

Credit: Michael Sagan, Trek Bicycles.

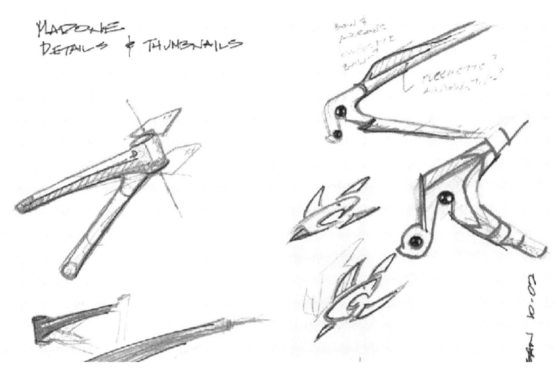

FIGURE 5.8
Thumbnail sketches, scanned from sketchbook. In what century were these made? Yesterday? During the Renaissance? You can't tell from the form, only from the content.

Credit: Michael Sagan, Trek Bicycles.

Looking at them individually, we see that Fig. 5.4 is clearly a sketch. Its visual vocabulary suggests that it was hand drawn, quickly and effortlessly, by a skilled artist. It says that it does not represent a refined proposal, but rather simply suggests a tentative concept. But what is it in the vocabulary that tells us all this? Largely, it is the freedom, energy, abandon, and looseness of the lines. It is the fact that the lines continue on past their natural endpoints. It tells us no rulers were used.

Even if the designer labored for hours (or even days) over this rendering, and used all kinds of rulers and other drafting tools, it does not matter. The rendering style is intended to convey the opposite, because the designer made this sketch with the clear intention of inviting suggestions, criticisms, and changes. By conveying the message that it was knocked off in a matter of minutes, if not seconds, the sketch says, "I am disposable, so don't worry about telling me what you really think, especially since I am not sure about this myself."

Figure 5.5 is a refinement of the previous sketch. It has all the sketch-like properties of Fig. 5.4, but includes rough shading to tell the viewer more about the detailed 3D form of the concept being pursued. As in the previous sketch, it would look at home on the wall of a drawing class. It says, "I'm thinking seriously about this form, but the ideas are still tentative. But as I am getting more serious; tell me now what you think."

Figure 5.6 is not a sketch. This is a "serious" piece of work. Because of the wireframe mesh on the surface, the precision of the lines, and the quality of the corporate graphics, this rendering says that it took a lot of care and work and that it was done on a computer. It is a 2D rendering of an accurate 3D model of the entire frame. Compared with the previous two drawings, it says "expensive" and "refined" (although the retention of the wireframe mesh in the rendering also says "but not finished"). It says, "We have made some decisions and are seriously considering this path."

Let me put it this way: of the dozens of concepts worked up to the level of the first two sketches, very few would be taken to this stage. To any literate reader of drawings, this is implicit in the style of rendering itself. The funnel is converging.

Now, we move to my favorite rendering, Fig. 5.7.

This is a hybrid. What the designer has done is make a photorealistic three-quarter view rendering of the 3D model previously seen in Fig. 5.6. He has then made a composite with it and the hand-drawn sketch seen in Fig. 5.4. But why would he do this? He was working to a tight deadline. He had no time to spare, and this took extra work. He already had done the 3D model. He just could have used the photorealistic three-quarter view rendering on its own. The answer is in the figure itself. The extra effort was undertaken to imbue the resulting image with the quality of a sketch, to make it look all the more effortless, to say, "This isn't finished," and to invite suggestions and communicate that the design was still open to change.

Now look at Fig. 5.8. By this stage, it is clear that these are examples of sketches. These types of sketches are actually among the first ones done in a project.

Michael Sagan, the designer, describes his process and use of such thumbnail sketches as follows:

> Typically I do very loose thumbnails to capture a gesture or a theme to start out. Often I will jot down words or phrases that I use as a semantic guide. As a design review step I will have another designer evaluate my 3D work...checking back against my thumbnails and semantic guide-words. If the designer hits any of the words I count that as a success. In the case of this sheet that I included here...one designer picked out almost all of the words...much to his surprise when I showed him these images.

Finally, note the following: First, these thumbnail sketches were made in the course of designing what, at the time, was probably the most technologically advanced bicycle ever built. Second, stylistically speaking, they are completely in keeping with, and would be perfectly at home in, the sketchbooks of Taccola.

Sketching is not only the archetypal activity of design, it has been thus for centuries.

Having come this far, what I would like to do now is step back and try to use what we have seen in these examples as a means to come to some characterization of sketches in general. What I am after here is an abstraction of sketches and sketching. What I want is to go meta and identify a set of characteristics whose presence or absence would let us determine if something is, or is not, a sketch – at least in the way that I would like to use the term.

Here is my best attempt at capturing the relevant attributes of what we have seen and discussed. Sketches are:

- Quick: A sketch is quick to make or at least gives that impression.
- Timely: A sketch can be provided when needed.
- Inexpensive: A sketch is cheap. Cost must not inhibit the ability to explore a concept, especially early in the design process.
- Disposable: If you can't afford to throw it away when done, it is probably not a sketch. The investment with a sketch is in the concept, not in the execution. By the way, this doesn't mean that they have no value or that you always dispose of them. Rather, their value largely depends on their disposability.
- Plentiful: Sketches tend not to exist in isolation. Their meaning or relevance is generally in the context of a collection or series, not as an isolated rendering.
- Clear vocabulary: The style in which a sketch is rendered follows certain conventions that distinguish it from other types of renderings. The style, or form, signals that it is a sketch. The way that lines extend through endpoints is an example of such a convention, or style.
- Distinct gesture: There is a fluidity to sketches that gives them a sense of openness and freedom. They are not tight and precise, in the sense that an engineering drawing would be, for example.
- Minimal detail: Include only what is required to render the intended purpose or concept. Lawson (1997, p. 242) puts it this way, "…it is usually helpful if the drawing does not show or suggest answers to questions which are not being asked at the time." Superfluous detail is almost always distracting, at best, no matter how attractive or well rendered. Going beyond "good enough" is a negative, not a positive (Fig. 5.9).
- Appropriate degree of refinement: By its resolution or style, a sketch should not suggest a level of refinement beyond that of the project being depicted. As Lawson expresses it, "…it seems helpful if the drawing suggests only a level of precision which corresponds to the level of certainty in the designer's mind at the time."
- Suggest and explore rather than confirm: More on this later, but sketches don't "tell," they "suggest." Their value lies not in the artifact of the sketch itself but in its ability to provide a catalyst to the desired and appropriate behaviors, conversations, and interactions.
- Ambiguity: Sketches are intentionally ambiguous, and much of their value derives from their being able to be interpreted in different ways, and new relationships seen within them, even by the person who drew them.

FIGURE 5.9
Designing a performance. The outcome of any design process is a desired effect. Sketches have to be understood as steps in this process. Although the beauty or clarity of each individual drawing might be appealing to the designer, ultimately the goal is to attain the performance declared at the beginning of the design process. This awareness is what differentiates a dexterous designer from a proficient renderer.

Credit: Trek Bicycles.

In the preceding section, the notions of visual vocabulary, resolution, and refinement are really significant and interdependent. Sketches need to be seen as distinct from other types of renderings, such as presentation drawings. Their form should define their purpose. Any ambiguity should be in the interpretation of their content, not in terms of the question, "Is this an early concept or the final design?"

...a sketch is incomplete, somewhat vague, a low-fidelity representation. The degree of fidelity needs to match its purpose, a sketch should have "just enough" fidelity for the current stage in argument building....Too little fidelity and the argument is unclear. Too much fidelity and the argument appears to be over – done; decided; completely worked out...

(Hugh Dubberly of Dubberly Design Office; private communication)

Some of the most serious problems occur if various parties – managers and/or customers and/or marketing – begin to view the early prototypes [read sketches] they see as the final product.

(Hix & Hartson, 1993; p. 260)

Finally, in its own way, our list is more than not like a sketch itself. It is tentative, rough, and has room for improvement and refinement. And also like a sketch, these same values may very well contribute to, rather than reduce, its usefulness.

FROM THINKING ON TO ACTING ON

...we are in danger of surrendering to a mathematically extrapolated future which at best can be nothing more than an extension of what existed before. Thus we are in danger of losing one of the most important concepts of mankind, that the future is what we make it.

Edmund Bacon

Now, we change gears.

In this section, we are going to look at the work – and more particularly, the working methods – of very good designers, from established professionals to talented students (see Fig. 5.10). This approach serves five important functions:

- To illuminate what I perceive as best practices
- To help those who work with the design team (including managers and the executive team) to understand these practices and their output
- To foster a shared literacy among the design team of some of the relevant "classic" examples from our diverse traditions
- To show exemplary student work side by side with that of those who pioneered the field to show that what I am advocating is attainable
- To give a sense of some of the basic competencies that I would expect in an interaction/experience design team, and hence in the educational programs that train them

When I speak of "best practices," I am referring to a repertoire of techniques and methods with which I would expect any experience design team to have a reasonable degree of fluency. This is not a "How to design a great product" manual or a treatise on "How to be creative," but it does stake out part of that turf, namely a subset of design primarily relating to ideation and sketching. There is a good chance that someone who reads this section will be familiar with some of what I discuss, but I suspect that there will be few for whom there is not something new. And, even with familiar material, I hope that I am able to bring a sufficiently fresh perspective to contribute new insights.

FIGURE 5.10
Workshopping ideas. One of the best ways to draw out the best from people, designers, and users alike.
Photo: Brooks Stevens Design.

As for the second point, before product managers or executives dismiss the material in this section as being irrelevant to them, they might want to recall Alan Kay's quote that I mentioned earlier:

> It takes almost as much creativity to understand a good idea, as to have it in the first place.

One of the best steps toward fostering a common culture of creativity among a diverse team is to become as fluent as possible in each other's languages. I have tried to make this book as accessible to the businessperson as the designer because I think that the designer's efforts will be for naught if the executive and product manager don't understand the how and what of the designer's potential contribution to the organization. Just think back to the case of Jonathan Ive at Apple. Do you want to squander the potential of your design team, as was largely the case until Steve Jobs came back to Apple, or do you want to improve your ability to exploit it the way that Steve did? Simply stated, the sooner you understand a great idea, the more lead time you have to do your part in executing it. That is why you need to read this section. Not to become a designer, but so that together with your design team (which you are paying for anyhow!), *and with the rest of your organization,* you can make design a more effective differentiator in your company.

As to the third point, I confess to being captivated by history – of my profession and of almost everything I am interested in. To me, history is both interesting and part of basic literacy. I think that it is important to the effective practice of our craft. The problem is, the experience design team of today involves people from many different traditions, each with its own history. I would hope that those from each tradition would know their own history, but I would never assume that they know each other. For example, industrial designers will likely know about Christopher Dresser (Whiteway, 2001), Norman Bel Geddes (Bel Geddes, 1932), Dreyfus (1955), or Raymond Loewy (Tretiack, 1999), and why they are important. But more often than not, these names will draw a blank when given to a user interface designer who has a computer science or psychology background. By the same token, names such as Doug Engelbart (Bardini, 2000), Ivan Sutherland (Sutherland, 1963), and J.C.R. Licklider (Waldrop, 2001), which should be familiar to the user interface designer, are most likely unknown to those from the tradition of industrial design.

Yet, the histories of each of our various disciplines, including marketing, have the potential to lead to more informed design. Knowing each other's histories lays the foundation for shared references and the common ground that it creates. So, whenever appropriate, I have chosen to mix key historical examples from various traditions into what follows. Although it is not a history lesson per se, hopefully it will make some contribution toward building a shared literacy and tradition among the emerging culture of experience design.

Fourth, while familiarity with some of the classic examples from our history is important, it can also be intimidating. By relying on such examples, am I setting the bar too high? Is this standard attainable by a student or is this too much to ask from someone that you are thinking of hiring? I think not. I have consciously also incorporated examples from the work of students from around the world to convince you of this point. For me, meeting these students and being exposed to their work was one of the most encouraging and enjoyable parts of researching this book.

Finally, a new approach to design implies a new approach to design education. Let's say that what I talk about makes sense and that by some miracle executives all over the world say, "Yes! Let's incorporate something like this in our company." Who are they going to hire? Where are the people going to come from? What kind of skills and experience should one be looking for? This section provides the basis for a partial answer. But I need to add, yet again, a cautionary note: this is not a comprehensive manual on product design. I am only trying to fill a gap in the literature, not cover the whole space. There are other books on topics such as participatory design, user-centered design, usability, industrial design, ethnography, marketing, and so on. We do not have to start from scratch. Second, no individual will or can have equal competence in all the requisite skills. So, the second thing to keep in mind is that we need coverage of the larger skill set distributed among a heterogeneous team, not the individual. But, and this is the important "but," for that team to function well, the players must have at least basic literacy in each other's specialties, if not a high level of competence.

Is this section going to be technical? On the one hand, yes, we are going to dive into the design funnel and talk about what goes on inside. On the other hand, it is not going to be any harder to follow than what we have already discussed. And I certainly hope that it is as interesting and relevant. It is definitely not going to take the form of some academic analysis of formal design theory or methodology. Why bother? As Chris Jones says in his book, *Design Methods*:

> There seem to be as many kinds of design process as there are writers about it. [There is] little support to the idea that designing is the same under all circumstances, and...the methods proposed by design theorists are just as diverse as are their descriptions of the design process.
> **(Jones, 1992; p. 4)**

In many ways, we wouldn't be in our current situation if formal design theories and methodologies worked as advertised, with their many boxes and arrows that map out the process. Gedenryd (1998) makes this argument pretty well. Speaking about architecture, Snodgrass and Coyne (2006) say:

> Contemporary architecture theory now largely ignore the vast literature on systems theory and design methods....(p. 24)

And in his book, *How Designers Think*, Bryan Lawson remarks:

> Well, unfortunately none of the writers...offer any evidence that designers actually follow their maps, so we need to be cautious.
>
> These maps, then, tend to be both theoretical and prescriptive. They seem to have been derived more by thinking about design than by experimentally observing it, and characteristically they are logical and systematic. There is a danger with this approach, since writers on design methodology do not necessarily always make the best designers. It seems reasonable to suppose that our best designers are more likely to spend their time designing than writing about methodology. If this is true then it would be much more interesting to know how very good designers actually work than to know what a design methodologist thinks they should do!
> **(Lawson, 1997; p. 39)**

Whenever possible, I have video clips that compliment what I say with words and pictures. These can be accessed from the companion Web site: http://www.mkp.com/sketching.

I have structured this section in a kind of musical "E-A-B-C-D" form. Perhaps this is my earlier life as a composer coming out. I am going to start with a few rich examples that foreshadow where we are going, then pull back to a simpler world. From there I will build back up toward where we started, laying more of a foundation in the process. And just as a warning, somewhere in the middle, I am going to insert an interlude where I can add some metacomments and examples.

But when I talk about richness or space, what is the scale on which my A, B, C, and so on lie? I am going to draw on a tangentially related field, experiential learning (see, e.g., Kolb, 1984). In this literature, Gibbons and Hopkins (1980) developed a *Scale of Experience*, illustrated in Fig. 5.11. With it, they attempt to establish a kind of taxonomy of levels of experience. Although a legitimate target for debate, it can serve our purpose.

At the lower levels are things where one is at the receptive end of experience. The notion is that although you can experience seeing a train or a bear in a movie, there is a higher level of experience seeing it live. Likewise, there is a deeper level still if you get to play with the train or (hopefully teddy) bear, rather than just see it. The argument made is that as one goes up the scale, one moves through different modes, from receptive through analytic and eventually through to what they call psychosocial mode.

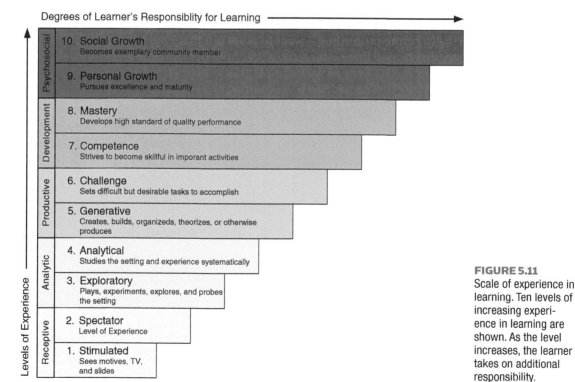

FIGURE 5.11
Scale of experience in learning. Ten levels of increasing experience in learning are shown. As the level increases, the learner takes on additional responsibility.

If we push too hard on this, its relevance to our work diminishes. After all, the scale was developed for a different purpose – education rather than design. There are really only three things that I want to draw out of it.

First, when I say that I am going to organize this section on an E-A-B-C-D structure, I am going to start with a few examples from the high end of a scale analogous to that of Gibbons & Hopkins. I will then drop back to examples and techniques that are at the lower, receptive, level of the scale, and work my way back up.

Second, Gibbons & Hopkins argue that higher levels of experiential learning imply a higher level of responsibility on the part of the learner for what they learn (the autodidact). This is represented by the horizontal axis in Fig. 5.11. Likewise, from the design perspective, our renderings (be they sketches or prototypes) afford richer and richer experience as we go up the scale. However, reaping the potential benefit of the design knowledge, or learning, that can be extracted from these renderings also depends on assuming the responsibility for using them appropriately.

Third, going a step further from the previous point, keep in mind that the level or type of experience that one can get out of renderings at the lower levels should not necessarily be considered impoverished. Seeing something live is not necessarily better than seeing it in a movie – it is just different. There are different types and levels of experience. Knowing how to use them appropriately in design is where the artistry and technique come in.

Finally, before proceeding, I want to point out that I did notice the "Those who can, design, and those who can't, write about design" aspect of the earlier quote by Lawson. The irony of including it, much less Lawson's writing it in the first place, is not lost on me. I have tried to keep its message in mind in what I write. Second, I think that there are times that design goes through transitions due to new demands that are made on it. In such times, thought and writing about design can provide a useful role in helping us get through those transitions with minimal problems. I view us as being in the midst of just such a transition, hence my sticking my neck out and taking up my proverbial pen.

CHAPTER 6

Persona Conception and Gestation

John Pruitt and Tamara Adlin

EDITOR'S COMMENTS

The concept of a persona, a fictional person who represents the typical attributes and behaviors of a group of users – was introduced to user-centered design by Alan Cooper (1999) in his provocative book, *The Inmates are Running the Asylum: Why High Tech Products Drive Us Crazy and How to Restore the Sanity*. Although the book described what a persona is and how it might affect influence the design of a product, it did not provide much in the way of a process for creating and using personas. Cooper and his colleagues provided more details about the persona process in *About Face 2.0* (Cooper & Reimann, 2003) and *About Face 3.0* (Cooper, Reimann, & Cronin, 2007), but even those efforts fell short. John Pruitt and Tamara Adlin extended and enhanced the work by Cooper and others in their comprehensive book *The Persona Lifecycle: Keeping People in Mind throughout Product Design* (2006). The life cycle metaphor covers personas from conception through end of life. At each stage of persona development there are processes, tools, and tips on how to make personas useful, usable, and engaging. This chapter focuses on how to start and nurture new personas and establish an environment where personas will have a positive impact on the design of Web sites, products, or services.

SETTING THE SCENE: WHAT'S GOING ON IN YOUR ORGANIZATION NOW?

The best time to start the persona conception and gestation phase is when your last product is fully out the door and your product team is poised to begin a new development effort. There's no solid direction for the new product yet, so competing visions, misinformation, rumors, and team-wide anxiety may exist.

False starts are likely to occur as the product strategy and vision settle into place. Anyone involved in the early stages of planning would clearly benefit from the data you have amassed about users, customers, and the broader market. Typical activities during this phase of product development include the following:

- The executive staff wants to provide high-level direction, a vision, for the entire team. They will be interested in market trends, emerging technologies, and the competitive landscape. They are eager to get the ball rolling.
- Product and project managers are trying to figure out what to build into the next product, working with lists of cut features from the last cycle or investigating what customers are saying about their current products.
- The development team at large is still supporting the previous release – fixing bugs, training support engineers, or cleaning up unfinished code for a point release. But they are eager to be done with the old stuff. Some may be exploring new technologies or working on pet projects.
- Like the development team, the QA team is recovering from the previous effort.
- Usability specialists, technical writers, and information, interaction, and UI designers are likely to be working with the product and project managers, brainstorming features and new ideas.
- The marketing team is still fully engaged with the release of the last product.

WHAT IS CONCEPTION AND GESTATION FOR PERSONAS?

Conception and gestation is the phase of the persona life cycle in which you actually create your personas. It is the phase in which you use data to create engaging representations of individual users that your team can use for planning, design, and development. During this phase, you will face the tricky question of how many personas to create and how to prioritize them. You will process the data and/or assumptions you have collected (by prioritizing, filtering, and organizing) to discover information about your users. Using this information, you and your core team will create bulleted persona "skeletons" that key stakeholders can prioritize according to business goals. You will develop your prioritized skeletons into complete personas that are then ready to be introduced to your organization in the birth and maturation phase.

The Six-Step Conception and Gestation Process

Persona creation is largely a serial and straightforward process in which you summarize, cluster, and analyze the data to discover themes (see Fig. 6.2). You use these themes to generate rough persona "skeletons." You then cull and prioritize the skeletons to focus only the most important, most appropriate, targets. Finally, you enrich skeletons into full personas by making the details concrete and adding personality and a story line. [For comparison, see the creation methods of Baxley in *Making the Web Work* (Baxley, 2003), Cooper and Reimann in *About Face 2.0* (Cooper & Reimann, 2003), Kuniavsky in *Observing the User Experience* (Kuniavsky, 2003), and Wodtke in *Information Architecture* (Wodtke, 2002).]

As shown in Figs. 6.1 and 6.2, we recommend a six-step persona conception and gestation process that includes the following activities.

CONCEPTION

- Step 1: Identify important categories of users. If you can, identify categories of users that are important to your business and product domain. Identifying these categories now (even if they are based solely on assumptions) will help you structure your data processing and build a bridge between the ways people think of users today and the data-driven personas you will create.
- Step 2: Process the data. Process your raw data to extract information relevant to your user and product domains and then identify themes and relationships. We suggest that you do this by conducting a collaborative "data assimilation" activity.
- Step 3: Identify and create skeletons. Evaluate your processed data to verify the categories of users and to identify subcategories of users. Create skeletons that are very brief (typically bulleted) lists of distinguishing data points for each subcategory identified.

GESTATION

- Step 4: Prioritize the skeletons. Once you have a set of skeletons, it is time to get feedback from all stakeholders. You will evaluate the importance of each skeleton to your business and product strategy and prioritize the skeletons accordingly. Your goal is to identify a subset of skeletons to develop into personas.

○ Discuss categories of users
○ Process data
○ Identify and create skeletons
○ Evaluate and prioritize skeletons
○ Develop skeletons into personas
○ Validate the personas

FIGURE 6.1
The six-step persona creation process.

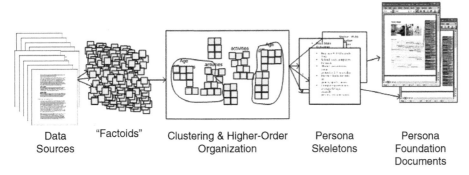

| Data Sources | "Factoids" | Clustering & Higher-Order Organization | Persona Skeletons | Persona Foundation Documents |

FIGURE 6.2
This diagram illustrates the activities described in Steps 2 through 5 of our conception and gestation process. The conception and gestation phase starts with raw data reports, which you will analyze and filter into factoids and organize into "information" to form categories of users. From these categories, you can create terse "skeletons," which you can then evaluate and prioritize. You can develop the prioritized skeletons into rich representations of target users; that is, into personas.

- Step 5: Develop selected skeletons into personas. Enrich the selected skeletons to create personas by adding data, concrete and individualized details, and some storytelling elements to give them personality and context.
- Step 6: Validate your personas. Once you have added details, it is important to double-check to make sure your final personas still reflect your data.

We know that many of you have short windows of opportunity to create personas that will be available and useful throughout product design. Many of you are also probably wondering how many personas you will need to create for your product. We address these important questions before describing the six-step conception and gestation process in detail.

How Long Does Conception and Gestation Take?

The amount of time you spend on conception and gestation activities will depend on your project schedule, the amount of data you have, and your goals for the persona effort. You can create useful assumption-based personas in less than a day, or you could take months to fully analyze mountains of data and create personas that link every detail back to a data source. In most cases, you and your team will compromise between these extremes and create useful data-driven personas in about one to two weeks.

To help determine (or justify) the amount of time you will spend creating personas, consider the length of time you will be using them. On some occasions, we have seen persona sets stay useful for several years. For example, personas for long-term projects at Microsoft have been used for five or more years. Personas for service of this length might be built, for example, to describe call center employees or office personnel whose job functions and goals don't change significantly from year to year. Personas can prove to be useful through several product versions or release cycles. In cases such as these, your time up front should be considered a long-term investment.

In many cases, product life cycles are much shorter (some Web sites are updated once every month or so), and taking months to create personas is simply not possible. It is also possible that your product life cycle is long but is already underway and you feel you have to quickly "catch up" and create the personas very quickly for them to be used. In these situations, it is helpful to plan for all six of the conception and gestation steps but to (sometimes radically) shorten the time allotted for each.

Your efforts toward personas are a direct trade-off with other user-centered design (UCD) activities or with more direct product development work. You will need to balance the time you spend on your personas with the demands of other UCD activities that are planned. As you plan these trade-offs, remember that the conception and gestation steps will help you fully understand your user data, which is helpful regardless of which UCD methods you choose.

Because most of us work in schedule-driven organizations, we have to work backward from a planned design-complete date to build our persona schedules. As you work on your schedule, try to plan time for the entire core team to get together often during the data analysis part of the project. It is important to build and keep momentum so that you can find and act on information that emerges from your data. In addition, schedule your persona evaluation meetings with stakeholders as early as possible. Make sure stakeholders are aware that you are going to need their attention to help with assessing appropriateness and priority across your developing target personas.

IF YOU ONLY HAVE A WEEK OR TWO: LOW-BUDGET APPROACHES

Personas don't necessarily need to be highly detailed to be effective. Even personas created in just a few hours can be useful. If you only have a week or two (or perhaps only a few days) to create your personas, you have a couple of options, discussed in the following sections.

Create Assumption Personas

Assumption personas communicate and align the assumptions that already exist in your company. During the conception and gestation phase, you can assimilate the assumptions using the same techniques we recommend for assimilating data. If you decide to create and use assumption personas, an overview of your process during conception and gestation work might look as follows (note that we include detailed instructions for each of these processes in the analogous section for data-driven personas, below).

EDITOR'S NOTE: WHAT ARE ASSUMPTION PERSONAS?

Assumption personas are brief sketches that reflect the assumptions about users that are held by internal stakeholders such as product management, development, and senior management. Assumption personas can be useful for making underlying assumptions explicit and improving communication with the product team about who the target users are. You might find, for example, that management or development considers PhD statisticians the primary user group. Armed with this assumption, you can then use existing user research or design new timely research to validate that assumption before you go too far designing a product for the wrong audience. In their book, Pruitt and Adlin (2006) note that the creation of assumption personas can uncover "dirty laundry" and expose researchers to some political jeopardy. If you find yourself in jeopardy, you might follow the advice of Pruitt and Adlin to create your personas only from primary data sources rather than internal sources who might feel threatened.

- Step 1 (2–4 hours): Assimilate assumptions (assumptions you have already collected or collect and assimilate at the same time). In a meeting with the persona core team and product stakeholders, identify important categories and subcategories of users.

- Step 2 (1–2 hours): Create skeleton personas with your core team. Create a skeleton persona for each category and subcategory of user.
- Step 3 (2–4 hours): Have your stakeholders review the skeletons that emerged from your assumption exercise. Continue to develop those that are important. Add concrete details and personal facts to make them resemble real people.

Create Quick Data-Driven Personas

If you have had time to collect data, but need to create and introduce personas on a tight schedule, you should spend as much time as possible understanding and assimilating your data to create meaningful and relevant skeletons (there is always time to add more detail after the personas are introduced). If you decide to create quick, data-driven personas, your process during the conception and gestation phase might run as follows.

- Step 1 (1/2–1 hour): Meet with your core team and product stakeholders to identify categories of users that are important to your business and product domain.
- Step 2 (2–4 hours): Process the data. The core team should thoroughly read the data sources, identify important factoids, and complete an affinity diagramming exercise to cluster the factoids around the categories of users.

EDITOR'S NOTE: AFFINITY DIAGRAMMING

Affinity diagramming is a group activity for organizing large sets of data. A team moves items on cards or adhesive notes into related groups or clusters and then generates names for each of those clusters. The items for affinity diagramming can be generated in many ways including brainstorming, field studies, and open-ended data from questionnaires and interviews. In the persona process, you would take the assumptions and any data you've collected, break that data into information chunks (factoids), and then conduct the affinity exercise. For more information on affinity diagramming, see Courage and Baxter (2005) and Holtzblatt, Wendell, and Wood (2005).

- Step 3 (2–4 hours): Identify and create skeletons (either in a meeting with your core team or independently). Evaluate your processed data to verify the categories of users and to identify subcategories of users. Create skeletons from the key data points for each subcategory you have identified.
- Step 4 (2–4 hours): With your core team and product stakeholders, prioritize the skeleton personas. Add concrete details and personal facts to enrich and personalize the skeletons. If you need to speed up the conception and gestation process, spend your time making sure that the skeletons you create the sketches from reflect the assimilated data and your conclusions about the resulting categories.

If you do need to create your personas quickly, be aware that the stakeholder review and prioritization can be an unpredictable and time-consuming process. To get these done quickly, you will have to be well organized and very proactive. For example, you will need to provide clear goals, explicit instructions, and time lines to your stakeholders.

IF YOU HAVE SEVERAL WEEKS OR MORE: GETTING THE MOST OUT OF YOUR DATA

If you have a lot of data, or if you can only eke a few hours out of every week to work on personas, allot more calendar time for conception and gestation. Identify a few particularly important data sources and explain how your persona effort will help the development team fully understand and benefit from the information the personas contain.

The majority of your time during the conception and gestation phase will be taken up with understanding and organizing your data sources. The remaining steps (creating and prioritizing the skeletons, building and enriching final personas, and validating the personas you created) don't have to take a long time, but they do require core team collaboration.

How Many Personas Should You Create?

We have found that roughly three to five personas is a good number to target. However, we believe that although you may choose to communicate just a few personas to the development team, your businesses' goals and your data should

Story from the Field

A Quick but Effective Persona-Building Process

—Colin Hynes,
Director of Usability, Staples.com

When I was ready to create personas, I began by blocking off my calendar for two days. Then, I wrote out one defining sentence on each persona. For example, "Comes to the Web site to research so she can buy in our store." While writing the descriptions, I recalled vividly the experiences I had while visiting offices during our extensive contextual inquiry studies and when listening to customer phone calls through customer service representatives. I used this information to build the persona descriptions, which were then reviewed with members of the usability team.

As a team, we filled in color about the personas' motivations, goals, up-sell potential, defining quote, onsite conversion potential, and other key factors that created the whole of each persona. We started with nine personas and then cut it back to six when there seemed to be too much overlap. Even though the process wasn't as rigorous as some, it was incredibly useful to "get the personas down on paper" so that I would have something for stakeholders to react to.

drive the number of personas you create. During the conception and gestation phase, your goal is to create a set of personas that are:

- Relevant to your product and your business goals
- Based on data and/or clearly identified assumptions
- Engaging, enlightening, and even inspiring to your organization

Note that your goal is not to describe every possible user or user type, nor to detail every aspect of your target users' lives. Your personas will aid decision making by both narrowing the field of possible targets and highlighting user data that is important and highly related to the product you are creating. This chapter will help you analyze your data sources, decide how many personas to create, and determine what (and how much) information to include in each persona and which personas to prioritize.

THE ARGUMENT FOR A SINGLE PRIMARY PERSONA

In their book *About Face 2.0*, Alan Cooper and Robert Reimann (2003) include an axiom that states, "Design each interface for a single, primary persona." Cooper argues that you must prioritize your personas to determine which single persona should be the primary design target for any given interface. We have noticed that many people assume that this means there should only be one primary persona for the entire product. We believe this is a misinterpretation of Cooper's axiom. Yes, there should be one primary persona per interface, but many products have several interfaces (e.g., the interface you use when you read e-mail is quite different from the interface used by the administrator who maintains the e-mail server, but both interfaces are part of the same product). There are also secondary personas – perhaps those that use the product less often or use a particular interface as a peripheral aspect of their job.

Cooper recommends that we start by creating a "cast of characters." We should then identify primary (preferably one) and secondary (probably several) personas within that cast. By definition, each primary persona will require a unique interface [because to be primary, the persona must be satisfied and it cannot be satisfied by any other persona's interface (Cooper and Riemann, 2003, p. 137)]. If you must create more than three primary personas (and therefore three interfaces), Cooper argues that the scope of the project is probably too broad.

Cooper's insistence on clearly identified primary personas is the cornerstone of his approach, for good reason. One of the benefits of personas is that they focus and clarify communication around the qualities and needs of target users. Of course, personas are only clarifying if they are actually used by the product team. If people don't remember who the personas are and don't use them in their everyday communication, the focus and clarity will be lost. Thus, your personas need to be visibly representative of the customer base and unfalteringly credible to your product team.

Strictly limiting the number of personas also forces stakeholders to make difficult and important decisions very early in the design process. Your work will be a forcing factor for clarifying business goals as early as possible, and the earlier you understand clear business goals the easier it is to build a product to suit those goals.

CREATING THE ONE PERSON TO DESIGN FOR: GREAT IN THEORY; COMPLICATED IN PRACTICE

In many cases, you, your core team, the product team, and/or business stakeholders will not accept a single primary persona. This might be because focusing so specifically may simply not feel right. It is difficult to convince an executive team that all design efforts should target a single person because the thought of building a product that "will only appeal to one person" is sometimes too difficult to combat. Top-down buy-in for your persona effort is important. If people (especially stakeholders) are uncomfortable with your cast of personas, they will not support or use them.

Even if you do have a go-ahead from the executive team to create one primary persona per product interface, you may not know how many unique interfaces (and therefore how many primary personas) you should create. Many find themselves facing a chicken-and-egg dilemma: should you decide how many unique interfaces your product needs and then create personas or should you create the personas first and then create user interfaces accordingly?

In addition, if it is so important to create a single primary persona for each unique interface (or for the entire product), why create secondary personas at all? And if you do create secondary personas, how should you use them to enhance but not interfere with the design process?

Because each project, product, and team is different, there is no "right" number of personas to create. However, saying "it depends on your project" is certainly not very helpful. The type of product you are building, the nature of your target audience, the information you discover in your data, and the particulars of your business goals should help you answer the following questions.

- How many personas do I need?
- Which personas do I need?
- Which personas should be primary or secondary?
- How do I use secondary personas without designing "for everyone"?

We believe that the best way to answer these questions is to analyze user goals, user roles, and user segments to identify important categories and subcategories of users of your product. For each category and subcategory, you will create at least one skeleton persona.

You can prioritize your skeletons according to business and product objectives. Finally, you will enrich your prioritized skeletons to create personas.

Your final personas will each include details about that persona's goals, role or roles, and segment. Because of this, we believe you can define categories of users according to whichever makes the most sense for your business and your product. Rönkkö, Hellman, Kilander, and Dittrich (2004) describe the process as follows.

> [Our] personas were not conventional creations in the original sense of persona. Personas are defined by their goals, at the same time as the goals are defined by their personas. Hence, personas and goals are discovered at the same time in the initial investigation of the problem domain. The three personas developed were not derived from a strict process of identifying groups which share the same goal; instead the process combined finding similar goals, trends, age groups, sex, professions and interests and relating these in a creative way to possible usages of mobile smart artifacts.
>
> **(Rönkkö, et al., 2004; p. 115)**

In Step 1 of material to follow, we describe how to identify your categories of users (if possible, before you process your data). In Step 3, we tell you how to use your processed data to identify subcategories of users, prioritize the categories and subcategories, and prepare to create at least one persona for each.

WHEN SHOULD I DETERMINE HOW MANY PERSONAS TO CREATE?

We believe you should identify categories of users as early as possible. If you know that stakeholders in your company are already attached to thinking about your target users in a particular way, use this information to define the categories of users before you begin your data assimilation. After you have completed your data assimilation exercise, you will be able to validate the categories, identify subcategories, and make final decisions on how many (and which) personas to create. The final decision occurs in Step 4 of our process.

Story from the Field

Developing Personas and Organizational Archetypes

Tammy Snow, Robin Martin Emerson, Leslie Scott, Trinh Vo Yetzer, and Dawn Baron, Windows Server, Microsoft Corporation

This case study describes our approach to developing personas to meet the needs of the Windows Server product and development team. In 2 years of work, we have modified the persona process by first describing a set of fictional businesses and then describing the IT Pro personas associated with each business. As a result of this process, we have developed over 30 personas spread across four fictional companies representing small, medium, and large organizations. We don't propose that what we describe is the best or most appropriate use of personas but rather provide a description of why we chose this particular approach and how it has affected our product team and the work they are doing. The primary goal of persona development was to help our product team identify and understand its target audience.

Brief Overview of the Windows Server Product and Development Team

Microsoft Windows Server is the operating system that enables organizations to build and operate their IT infrastructure. The Server operating system has evolved from

Windows NT to Windows 2000 Server with Active Directory, to the current version, Windows Server 2003. The product team is now working on the next version of Windows Server code named "Longhorn." There are over 12 different development teams and over 3,000 people working on Windows Server. Most of the teams work on specific server functionality that is used and managed by unique individuals in the IT organization. That being the case, we have a significant challenge in helping each of these teams identify and design for its target users. This case study describes an approach we chose to take in helping our product teams understand their customers.

The Problem

Historically, the Windows Server product team has relied on market research data and intuition in understanding who their customers are and what they need. Over the past few years, it has become increasingly clear to the leadership for Windows Server that to better meet our customers' needs we need to understand who they really are. Because personas had been developed by other teams at Microsoft (including Windows Client and Office), and because those personas were gaining exposure and credibility, it became apparent that there needed to be personas developed for Windows Server.

Early in development, we determined that we could not take a traditional approach to developing server personas. The problem was two-fold: (1) servers are about providing IT infrastructure for companies and organizations rather than for individuals and (2) often IT tasks are done by multiple individuals at different times across multiple computers (servers and desktops). In addition, we had reason to believe that IT organizations and IT pros differed in establishments of different sizes.

The Solution

As a solution, we decided that we would start by developing models to describe fictional companies that use our server technology. We called these models archetypes, for short, though they are really organizational archetypes. We would then define personas within each archetype and describe the work practice and work flow involved in deploying and managing server technologies. In addition, we would define the overall IT organization, IT budgets, the IT purchase decision model, and any relevant information related to purchasing and using Microsoft Server products. We determined that by taking this approach we could provide rich context about IT organizations and how server tasks are often completed by a number of server administrators working together.

The first step in the process of developing archetypes was determining what we would base our model companies on. We knew from the outset that there were often discussions among the product team about how organizations of various sizes purchased, deployed, and managed our solutions, so we decided to use organization size as the key determinant for the archetypes we would develop. We believed that the context of organization size would be a key to helping us understand what different IT organizations look like and how this influences work practice – what administrators do and how they do it.

We developed archetypes to represent four distinct business sizes defined by number of PCs and number of servers. Our work focused on one small business archetype, two medium business archetypes, and one large business. Because the medium business is one we felt we knew least about, we determined a need to look at medium-size organizations at both the small and large end of this category. The table shown in Fig. 6.3 outlines key characteristics for each of our archetypes.

Archetype	Range of Servers	Range of PCs	Avg. # of IT pros.
Small orgs.	1–3	1–24	0.6
Core medium orgs.	4–15	24–249	3
Upper medium orgs.	16–99	250–499	8
Large orgs.	100+	500+	56

FIGURE 6.3
Key characteristics of our Windows Server organizational archetypes.

Developing the Archetypes and Personas

We started our work by reviewing all existing usability and Microsoft-sponsored market research data related to each size of organization we were targeting. We analyzed these data sets looking for trends toward generalizing and developing a data-informed framework describing each of the four sizes of organization. Each archetype described a representative company, including size, type of business, number of office locations, and so on. In addition, we included any information we had about needs, pains, and issues related to our technology. It is important to note that we reviewed data from many types of organizations because we were not interested in creating vertically specific archetypes.

Once we had reviewed existing data, we started conducting original research to validate what we had learned from our initial analysis and to fill in gaps not covered by existing data. Our research was qualitative in nature and involved interviews with over 100 IT professionals. Information from these interviews was analyzed, again looking for trends that could be generalized. These generalized findings were then added to the archetypes and used to develop our first set of personas for each archetype.

The Outcome

Once we had completed the first version of our archetypes and personas, we had 32 unique IT-related personas. The large-organization archetype incorporated 23 total personas, including personas specific to Microsoft Windows Server and related products, to UNIX administration, and to mainframe systems. The small-organization archetype had a single IT-related persona, and the medium-size archetypes had two (for core medium organizations) and seven (for upper medium organizations) personas.

As initially suspected, we found some clear distinctions in the way IT pros organize themselves and perform their jobs based on company size. In large organizations, there is a high degree of specialization for IT pros (i.e., an individual is responsible for working on a specific type of technology, such as messaging or databases). In addition, large IT organizations tend to have well-defined processes for purchasing, deploying, and managing technology. As organizations become smaller, the level of technology-specific generalization goes down and you see a minimal process for purchasing, deploying, and managing technology.

Dealing with Many Personas

One of the more frequent questions we hear from people is, "How do you deal with 32 unique personas?" Clearly, we can't expect people to know about and remember all 32 personas! Fortunately, no one team in the Windows Server division would ever deal with more than four or five personas in developing their features. The challenge is working with the various teams to help them identify their target personas and then make use of those personas in defining, designing, and developing their features.

PERSONA CONCEPTION: STEPS 1, 2, AND 3

Step 1: Identify Important Categories of Users

Categories of users are usually defined as sets of characteristics that groups of users share. The sets of characteristics you found are probably highly related to the business goals of your product. Identifying these categories now (even if they are based solely on assumptions) will help you structure your data processing and build a bridge between the ways your organization thinks about users today and the data-driven personas you will create.

If you find that your company or team does not currently think or talk about users at all, we believe you should try to define major categories of users before you begin processing your data. If you conducted your own user research as part of the family planning phase, you likely already defined user categories as you recruited participants.

You can articulate or define large categories of users by describing common user roles, user goals, or user segments that are important to your business and product. Note that identifying important categories of users does not mean identifying every possible way of grouping your users. In our experience, major categories of users tend to stand out.

Even if they don't reveal themselves easily, we recommend that you simply put forth a proposed set of user categories as high-level conceptual targets. Either way, your data will establish the appropriateness of these categories during the analysis process.

WHY SHOULD I TRY TO IDENTIFY CATEGORIES OF USERS BEFORE I LOOK AT THE DATA?

There are two reasons to identify categories of users before you look at the data. The primary reason is to ensure that your data assimilation exercise produces results that are relatively easy to create personas from. The second is to establish a clear connection to the existing language used to describe users.

The data assimilation process is typically a bottom-up deductive process in which you find important relationships between and among the data sources. Using high-level categories to provide structure to assimilation adds a layer of top-down inductive analysis. The use of categories ensures that you will be able to express the information you find in the clusters of data as personas. Without categories, your clustered data will yield interesting information, but you might have a difficult time using this information to form personas.

When you are ready to communicate and use your personas, you will find it much easier to do so if you can describe them in language that is already familiar – even in the case where your data suggests that the initial categories should be replaced by different ones. In the next three sections, we describe three differences between target users that can be used to discover and define the categories important to your business and product: differences in user roles, user goals, and user segments. Each of these is accompanied by an example scenario. All the scenarios describe the same company (a bank) and project (an online banking system). In the example scenarios, we show you how differences in roles, goals, or segments can be used to create high-level categories of users depending on business objectives and the existing corporate environment.

In our banking examples, no matter which personas the team ends up creating, all of them should be traceable back to the categories of users. When people ask, "Why did you create these particular personas?" (and this question will come up) the answer will be something similar to the following: "We created at least one persona for each major category of user. We create these categories for one of the following reasons:

- Stakeholders identified user roles our product had to support to be successful.
- Stakeholders identified user goals we had to satisfy to have a successful product.
- Stakeholders identified user segments we had to satisfy to have a successful product."

No matter how you initially categorize your users, all of your completed personas will include information related to that persona's role, goals, and segment. In other words, it is completely acceptable to create categories of users based on existing assumptions if you think that will help people understand and accept the personas you end up creating. Your data will validate and enrich the categories or will provide solid information to show that the existing categories are inappropriate. It will also allow you to define important subcategories of users that should also be expressed in personas.

> **HANDY DETAIL**
>
> **Roles Are Not Always the Best Choice. Beware of Automating the Misery**
>
> If you are working on a redesign of an existing product or process, be very cautious about creating personas based on existing roles. Remember that your redesign might automate some tedious chores, enable some advanced activities, and so forth. If you create personas based solely on existing roles, tasks, and activities, you will miss the opportunity for revolutionary change in your product.

THINKING ABOUT USER ROLES, USER GOALS, AND USER SEGMENTS

The sections that follow explore processes for thinking about user roles, goals, and segments.

User Roles

When you describe a person according to sets of tasks, job descriptions, responsibilities, or other external factors related to his or her interaction with your product, you are describing the user in terms of his or her role. For the purpose of software development, a user role is often defined with regard to the relationship between the user and a system. Specific roles don't necessarily map to specific users. Individual users might find themselves in any of these roles at different times. Roles are generally related to business, work, and productivity. In fact, sometimes they are directly related to job type, position, or responsibilities. However, they may also be related to an activity that defines a person as a type of consumer (e.g., the "shopper," the "browser," the "agent," or the "assistant").

Scenario 1: Create categories based on user roles. Your bank is large and offers many services for many different tiers of customers. Everyone at the company knows that the bank's Web site is going to continue to evolve over the next few years and will eventually support the specific needs of many types of customers. However, for now you have to figure out what features you need to build first. That is, which will give the bank the most bang for the buck as they try to attract more customers and reduce their current customer support costs. You decide to create your categories of users based on various user roles. In this scenario, it would be appropriate to describe the following role-based categories of users.

- The new account shoppers
- The existing account holders
- The borrowers
- The investors

User Goals

When you describe a user in terms of what he or she is trying to achieve – in his or her own terms – you are describing the user's goals. Individuals have general goals that apply to many things they do in their lives, including the way they approach products. People also have specific goals that relate to tasks. Goals have a timelessness that roles do not. Whether or not you use goals as your primary differentiator, communicating your personas' goals will be critical during the birth and maturation and adulthood phases.

Scenario 2: Create categories based on user goals. Your group has been assigned to create an online banking experience to help the bank catch up with its main competitor. You also need to satisfy some of the customer requests that have been coming in for online access to account information and management tools. Your bank has been working hard to build a reputation as a trustworthy, solid financial institution, and you know that the online banking application needs to reflect this reputation. Your research shows that many people are dissatisfied with current online banking options because they are not sure the Internet is completely safe and reliable. You decide to create your categories of users based on different user goals. In this scenario, it would be appropriate to describe the following goal-based categories of users.

- Users who "want my financial life to be simpler"
- Users who "want my money to work for me"
- Users who "want to feel like my money gets as much attention as a millionaire's money"
- Users who "want to feel safe when I'm banking online"

User Segments

When you describe a user in terms of characteristics he or she shares with many other users, you are describing the user in terms of a segment. Segments are defined according to shared demographics, psychographics, attitudes, and/or behaviors. In marketing, segments are often used to create targeted messaging and advertising to increase product sales. Marketing teams, product planners, and/or business development groups often define their objectives in terms of segments they have built to reflect the existing market and opportunities for innovation and new sales.

Segments can be rigorously defined through quantitative analysis of data, but they can also evolve through casual references to groups of users or customers (which, by the way, are sometimes referred to as "user classes"). Because segments are often used as shorthand when business stakeholders are talking about users and customers, they exist (are embedded) in the culture and lingo of many companies regardless of how rigorously they are defined. If segments already exist in your company's vocabulary, they will influence your persona project.

Scenario 3: Create categories based on user segments. The bank executives have been walking around for weeks talking about critically underserved markets for your bank's service and their desire to fulfill some of these unmet needs through the new online banking services. The executive team asked the marketing team to identify segments of consumers who would be likely to sign up for a new online banking service. The marketing team did some research and identified three main segments, which they described as enthusiasts, ostriches, and neophytes. You know that if your personas don't fit within these segments, your executive staff will reject them. You decide to use the segments (as they are currently defined by market research) to describe the following categories of users.

HANDY DETAIL

Segments Can Be Conceptually Simple

Some companies describe market segments in fairly simple terms (e.g., "current customers," "potential customers" (no one's customers), and "customers of our competitor"). Figure 6.4 shows an example of one way Hewlett-Packard publicly describes its user base. In the right-hand column of their home page, they present the following five major customer groups.

- Home and home office
- Small and medium business
- Large enterprise business
- Government and education
- Partners and developers

Categories such as these tend to be strategic business divisions, and though they might have strict definitions (e.g., small business = companies with 10 or fewer employees), they are conceptually simple. They are likely not quantitatively derived segments based on customer/market research, and their definition might not include anything specific to users and/or consumers. Either way, if such segments have a long tradition of use in your organization, they may be an appropriate and politically acceptable starting point for creating personas. You will be doing your organization a huge favor by putting quantitative and qualitative data, along with engaging and memorable stories, behind the existing terms.

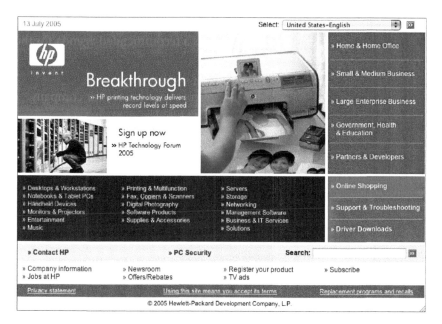

FIGURE 6.4
HP.com has five customer groups presented as navigational elements on the right-hand side of their main home page. These might serve as the starting point for five or more personas.

- Financial enthusiasts: 35–65 years old, urban or suburban, professional, college educated, yearly household income of $50K–250K, make decisions related to finances and review all account balances and activity at least once a month, aware and wary of Internet security issues, and careful researcher and informed consumer of financial services
- Financial ostriches: 25–40 years old, urban or suburban, professional, college educated, have children, yearly household income of $35K–90K, busy with life and work, seldom balances checkbook, seldom reviews financial decisions, have several accounts at various financial institutions (including individual retirement accounts [IRAs] from old jobs), not entirely sure what they have at any given time, and feel overwhelmed whenever they think of organizing finances
- Financial neophytes: 18–25 years old, some college, yearly household income of $10K–60K (with potential for considerable income growth), newly financially independent, tend to be interested and motivated but nervous, aware of current financial status, tend to have debt and credit concerns, and think of money in terms of "what I can afford today."

HOLD A MEETING TO DETERMINE CATEGORIES OF USERS

If these categories of users are not clear from your work in the family planning phase, hold a meeting with your stakeholders to make this notion explicit. Plan to meet for about an hour to discuss preexisting categories of users used in your company, as well as roles, goals, and segments to determine the best strategic target groups for your product. The following is a recommended agenda for the user categories' meeting.

1. Describe the goals, rules, and outcome of the meeting.
2. Discuss preexisting language for customers and users at your company.
3. Discuss the concept of roles, goals, and segments.
4. Brainstorm on your company's most appropriate categorization scheme or consider generating assumption personas.
5. Generate the proposed high-level groups or categories of users.
6. Get consensus on the high-level target groups before closing (you will want roughly three to five groups).

BRIGHT IDEA

Assimilate Assumptions to Define Categories of Users

As we discussed in regard to family planning, it is sometimes necessary, and almost always valuable, to create assumption personas. You can do this to identify assumptions about categories of users if they have not been made explicit. While we describe the assimilation process in detail in the next section (for processing your data), the following are a few ideas specific to assimilating assumptions. The following is a recommended meeting agenda for assimilating assumptions.

1. Describe the goal and intended outcome of the assumption exercise. It is espe-cially important to be clear about your goals when creating assumption personas (e.g., "our goal is to create a temporary set of target personas that will be used for initial planning discussions but validated later with research"; "the outcome of this meeting will be that each of the stakeholders has a clear and agreed-upon vision of our most strategic customer targets"). Make sure that everyone involved knows why you are doing this exercise and why you believe it is worthwhile.
2. Solicit assumptions and record them on sticky notes. Ask everyone to write their assumptions about users' roles, goals, and/or segments on sticky notes. Sticky notes might say things like "fourth grade boy who hates homework but loves com-puters," "involved mom who isn't tech-savvy and worries about her kid online," "good student looking for information about an assignment," and "social preteen who wants to chat with friends." What are their important characteristics: physical attributes, skills, behaviors, activities, goals, needs, preferences, and opinions? Ask everyone to record each idea on its own sticky note.
3. Assimilate the sticky notes. See Step 2 in the next section for detailed instructions for assimilation.
4. Create higher-order categories of users and persona sketches. Identify the major categories or classes of users the groups of assumptions relate to. Then sketch out individual profiles for each category, providing specific and concrete values for important characteristics to the extent possible (e.g., preteen should be specified as "in fifth grade," 8 to 11 years old, or even exactly 9 years old).

Step 2: Process the Data

During the family planning phase, you collected and reviewed many data sources, including research reports containing summaries, highlights, and significant details extracted from raw data of some sort. Your next task is to process these research findings, pulling out the bits and pieces that are relevant to your team and product domain. Once you have isolated these relevant factoids, you and your core team will process them (through an assimilation exercise) using the user categories you agreed upon in Step 1.

DATA PROCESSING METHODS

There are many ways you can go about processing your data to create personas, and we strongly recommend a specific approach: affinity diagramming (which we and others often refer to as "assimilation"). We use the assimilation method because it is quick, easily understood, and overtly collaborative. It also works across a variety of data types and formats.

As an alternative, you might consider doing quantitative analysis (such as factor analysis, cluster analysis, or some other multivariate statistical procedure) or qualitative analysis (with a tool such as Atlas.ti, HyperQual2, HyperRESEARCH, NUDIST, or Xsight, a trimmed-down version of NUDIST). These tools are quite useful for extracting the underlying themes from any type of data, as you possibly did with raw data during the family planning phase. For example, Rashmi Sinha describes a persona creation process using principal components analysis to identify the critical underlying dimensions (Sinha, 2003). Her analysis uncovered independent clusters of needs (very similar to goals), which were then used in combination with other information as the basis for creating distinct personas. Such an approach is similar to cluster analysis and other statistical techniques typically used in the creation of quantitative market segments. Although we believe that analyses such as these can be a great starting point, we recommend that you also conduct a data assimilation exercise as the primary method of persona creation, particularly when combining data from a variety of sources.

Story from the Field

Rapid User Mental Modeling (RUMM)

Rashmi Sinha,
Founder and principal, Uzanto Consulting

User-centered information architecture (IA) requires understanding of how users tacitly group, sort, and label tasks and content. Although personas have gained popularity, it remains difficult for information architects to incorporate them into their design process. For information-rich domains, personas need to incorporate input about the ways in which people think about the domain and their information needs and mental models. The cast of personas chosen should reflect the types of information needs.

In the course of our work, we have developed RUMM. This is a three-stage persona-creation and mental modeling tool set for interaction designers. The RUMM process begins with open-ended exploration (Stage 1: Explore); progresses toward a more detailed understanding of user needs, mental models, and personas (Stage 2: Understand); and ends with a verification and test of preliminary IA (Stage 3: Verify and Refine). RUMM produces reliable and repeatable results by basing personas and mental models on data.

RUMM also offers a specific series of steps for using personas to drive IA design. In addition, both mental modeling and personas can draw from the same set of user research, reducing time and effort and reducing the risk that personas and mental modeling will drive the design in different directions.

In this case study, we describe how we used the RUMM methodology to redesign the IA for a complex Web site with a varied user base. The site was an online travel site that offered the ability to make reservations (air, hotel, car rental, cruises) and contained a great deal of online content (about visas, day trips, sight-seeing, and so on). In that the site had such varied content, organizing the content was a major challenge. The company had recently forged a partnership with a travel content provider and wanted to add a lot of new information to the site. The old IA could not accommodate this new content.

RUMM Stage 1: Explore the Information Domain

Our first step was to understand the scope and boundaries of the domain in users' minds. We used a free listing exercise (targeting both current and prospective users) and asked participants to list all the types of information they might look for when planning for a trip (e.g., passport requirements, weather, accommodations, car rental, food, tourist spots). They were also asked to list the factors they consider while planning a trip (e.g., price, travel time, taxes, penalty for late changes, and so on). The exercise was conducted (via an online survey) with various types of users, including business and leisure travelers of various ages.

As you can imagine, we got a wide and varied assortment of responses, so we sifted through that data to get the most frequently mentioned types of content (e.g., cancellation policies).

We also met with executives at the company and got them to identify which pieces of content they felt were critical

to the business success of the company. Combining these two lists, we were able to arrive at a list of content topics that although not exhaustive represented the most critical content on the site.

RUMM Stage 2: Understand Users' Needs and Mental Models

In the second stage, we took the list of critical content that had been generated in Stage 1 and asked 55 respondents to rate the subjective importance of types of travel content and factors they considered while purchasing airline tickets.

Through statistical analysis (principal components analysis), we were able to identify clusters of users. One group of users had an extremely narrow focus of interest: they were only interested in one destination, they were not overtly interested in price-comparison features, and they were not interested in destination details (e.g., sight-seeing information, day trips, or restaurant ratings).

Another group of users found much of the travel-related content to be of interest (e.g., tourist information, restaurant information, accommodations, and passport and currency information). They were also interested in price/destination comparison and were much more interested in destination details. We used this information (in conjunction with other qualitative information) to craft a primary and a secondary persona for the site.

Primary Persona: Irene the Comparison Shopper

Irene (62) used to work as a secretary at Greenfield Community College. Bill, her husband for 30 years, just retired from his job running a small pet store. They had always wanted to travel after their retirement and saved carefully so that they would be able to afford to do so. The first year after retirement, they joined a group tour of the Italian countryside. This left them wanting more. This year, they want to go to Italy again (but this time on their own). Last year's trip cost too much and they want to keep costs down.

Their son has been telling them about the cheap fares one can get on the Internet if one looks hard. Irene has been spending a lot of time looking on travel sites, trying to find tickets to fly to Rome and hotels to stay in once they get there. They want to visit some vineyards and go to the Vatican for a day.

Irene is an amateur painter and is interested in visiting sites associated with art. She is also fond of Italian food, but not all the time. She likes to stay in tourist areas so that she can easily get American food when she wants.

When she searches travel sites, she looks for cheap fares. She is flexible about dates. While looking for airline tickets, she also looks for hotels. In planning her itinerary, she looks for travel information about the various cities she is thinking of visiting. She does not mind if it ends up taking a little time to find what she wants, but she gets very frustrated when the system does not give her all the information she is looking for. For example, she likes to know exactly how much time the flight will take, how much the tax will be, and what the fee will be for changing or canceling a ticket. She does not like to click on numerous links to obtain each piece of information.

Secondary Persona: Mark "All Business, All the Time"

Mark (36) is a sales professional for SOP, an enterprise software firm headquartered in the Bay Area. He travels a lot for work. He is married and has two kids. His wife works at the same firm (in the marketing department). They live comfortably, but much of their income is spent on the mortgage for their suburban house and on child care.

Because of recent cutbacks, for the first time in his career, Mark is responsible for making his own travel arrangements. He finds this very frustrating and wants to spend the least amount of time possible on the task (after he books the ticket, he can go home for the day). He prefers staying at hotels near the airport, renting a car, and driving to where he needs to. He does not care about price information because he is not spending his own money. However, he favors one particular airline so that his travel miles don't get spread between multiple accounts. He has so many travel miles that he is often able to upgrade his seat or room and still has plenty of miles left over for his personal travel.

He does not like the recent airline strategy of not offering meals any longer, though he generally ends up purchasing a meal. He likes to sit near the exit rows so that he gets more space. He wants to book a hotel, car, and plane ticket with no cancellation penalties because his plans often change.

In addition, he likes a travel agency to have good phone support because he often needs to make changes when he is away from his computer. He would really like the ability to enter a detailed profile with all of his preferences so that he could find suitable tickets faster.

The next step was to understand user mental models. We had run an online card-sorting exercise at the same time as the online survey. Users were given the list of items we developed in Stage 1 and were asked to put them into categories and provide a label for each category. We then used cluster analysis to create hierarchical models representing how users think about the domain of online travel information. We generated a generic hierarchical model from the entire population and models from the two subpopulations we had identified (business and leisure travelers).

To craft an initial cut of the IA, we took the hierarchical model from the population from which the primary persona (Irene) was derived. We then verified that the limited content the secondary persona (Mark) would be interested in had entry points that made sense from the perspective of his hierarchical model.

RUMM Stage 3: Verify Preliminary IA

In Stage 3, we tested our proposed IA on a larger population (120 respondents) of the site through an (online) closed card-sort study. We made sure that our survey included participants from a variety of backgrounds, including business travelers and leisure travelers.

The closed card-sorting study was used to examine the suitability of the hybrid IA we designed in Stage 2. Any items that were frequently placed in different categories, or were placed in the "other" category by a large number of users, were revisited in the design. In this way, the closed card sort served as an early usability test for the IA.

Summary

Over the three stages of the RUMM process, we gained an understanding of (1) the scope of current and planned content/functionality, (2) the hierarchical structure of user mental models for the content/functionality, and (3) which content matters to which users. We used this information to craft personas and used those personas to design an IA that served as a basis for the successful site redesign.

COLLABORATIVE ASSIMILATION HAS SIDE BENEFITS

Because the entire core team is involved in the assimilation exercise, everyone has an opportunity to see the factoids from all data sources. By the time the assimilation exercise is complete, everyone on the core team will have been exposed to the data and to the inherent patterns, themes, and relationships in the data. This shared understanding is priceless. As a side benefit, through your assimilation exercise, you create a core team that is fully cognizant of a huge amount of data from a wide variety of sources. Armed with your clustered and labeled data, you and your team are perfectly prepared for the next step: identifying and creating skeletons.

ASSIMILATION WORKS WELL, BUT IT DOES HAVE A FEW DRAWBACKS

Assimilation does have a couple of drawbacks you should be aware of before you begin.

- During an assimilation exercise, you and your team will group factoids that have been extracted from their original contexts. Factoids that are unrelated when you read them in context may seem related (and end up grouped) after they have been extracted from their sources and copied onto sticky notes. This opens the possibility for misrepresenting the original data in your final personas.
- Identifying relationships between factoids is a subjective exercise. Two different teams might group factoids in different ways and end up with different conclusions.

Because affinity diagramming does open the door to misrepresentations of your data, we encourage you to schedule enough time to validate your personas after you have created them. However, it is also important to remember that personas can never fully express or represent the data in the same way it is expressed in the original sources and that this is not the point of the personas. Rather, personas will help you communicate the essential and helpful information the data contains. The danger that some aspects of the personas may misrepresent some aspects of the data is outweighed by the guarantee that the personas will convey important and data-driven information to your product team.

HANDY DETAIL

What to Do If You Are Drowning in Data

If you have collected a lot of data during the family planning phase, you might find it difficult to get started with your data analysis. Staring at a huge stack of printouts can be incredibly intimidating. If you are having a difficult time getting started, try sorting your printouts into three stacks: very relevant (to your product domain and intended users), moderately relevant, and not very relevant. Conduct an assimilation exercise with only the very relevant documents and see what types of clusters you get. After you run your first assimilation exercise – even if it is just with a subset of the data resources collected – you will find that it is easier and much quicker to identify interesting factoids in future exercises. If you are then still dissatisfied with the depth of insights revealed initially, and have the time, you can continue assimilating with less relevant data.

Plan Your Assimilation Meeting

An assimilation meeting typically lasts two to four hours. It should include all members of your persona core team. These meetings work best in medium to large rooms that have plenty of wall space (or floor space). Before the meeting, make sure you have plenty of sticky notes, markers, tape, and large sheets of paper on hand.

If you have a relatively small to medium amount of data, you should be able to assimilate all of it in a single meeting. If you have a large amount of data, consider distributing the data sources and request that your colleagues identify relevant factoids before the meeting. Alternatively, simply schedule multiple meetings that focus independently on each identified user category. If you do the latter, make sure to have a final meeting in which the assimilation results for all user categories are reviewed together. Generally, the agenda for an assimilation meeting should be as follows:

1. Describe the rules, goal, and outcome of the meeting.
2. Identify key data points (factoids) in the data sources.
3. Transfer key data points (factoids) to sticky notes.
4. Post user category labels in various locations in the room.
5. Assimilate the key factoids.
6. Label groups (and do some higher-order organization).

Describe the Goal and Outcome of the Meeting

Your goals for this meeting are fairly simple.

- Filter and prioritize the data down to the most important and relevant bits of information, or factoids, for your specific product and team.
- Organize these factoids into meaningful, related groups, paying attention to the user categories you identified in Step 1.

These groups of factoids will serve as the core content and structure for creating personas, but note that when this meeting is over, you will not have personas in hand.

Identify Key Data Points (Factoids) in the Data Sources

The first step in processing the data is to review and filter the information in each of the research reports. You do this because not every data point in a given study/report is relevant to the definition of your target audience or to the design of your product. Whether it is done before or during the meeting, ask your core team members to highlight findings they think are key in understanding your target audience or that are highly insightful toward defining aspects of your product. In other words, you want them to look for findings that are relevant to your market, industry, or domain. Highlight any facts that seem important to your product's audience or to the product itself. The case study following shows examples of highlighting in two different data documents: a qualitative site visit report and a quantitative market research report.

Determining what pieces of information are important may seem daunting at first. Don't fret too much over this until you have tried it. When in doubt, be inclusive. It is better to start with too many factoids than too few. You might be tempted to develop criteria ahead of time (e.g., criteria for factoids that are irrelevant, too detailed, too broad, or otherwise not very helpful). We recommend that you do not. In our experience, such criteria are not easy to come by and are difficult to apply. Attempting to generate them consumes valuable time that could be used more directly with the data. In fact, because your core team consists of key individuals across your organization and from different disciplines, each person will have different insights and perspectives on what is important. This is good. You will find that agreement on the importance of any individual piece of data actually happens through the assimilation process.

In the end, even your full personas will not include or reference all the data you find and cluster. If you find yourself drowning in data or your team stuck in "analysis paralysis," just force yourself to move on to the next step and trust that the process will still work. Be willing to try things out, and plan to use your time on iteration (not initial perfection).

Transfer Factoids to Sticky Notes

After everyone has had a chance to comb through their assigned research documents, it is time to go back through the items they highlighted, reevaluate their importance, and then transfer them to another medium to enable assimilation. Each important factoid should be copied or cut out of the original document. We prefer to do the factoid assimilation using sticky notes (as shown in the following case study), though larger sheets of paper (e.g., 8-1/2 × 11 or easel sheets) can be useful for readability and easier collaboration. It may be more practical to simply physically cut the data points out of the research document with scissors and then glue/paste them onto 3 × 5 index cards. (You could also use printable sticky notes or 3 × 5 cards and have someone type them in and print them during the meeting.) Either way, remember to note the source and page number on each factoid.

Post User Category Labels Around the Room

Before starting your assimilation exercise, it is important to "seed" the room with the user category labels you identified in Step 1. If your categories are based on quantitatively derived segments, include the major defining characteristics of the segments as well. These labels will serve to direct your initial placement and high-level organization of the factoids. We recommend that you do this with larger sheets of paper instead of sticky notes to ensure that they are salient and visible (see Fig. 6.5).

Be sure to leave room between and underneath each label for the multitude of sticky note factoids that will be placed in relation to them. Your assimilation and prioritization activities, detailed in the following, will revolve around these predefined categories, so make sure everyone in the room is intimately familiar with them.

Assimilate the Factoids

Now the interaction (and fun) begins. To do the assimilation, everyone will get up (at the same time) and place their factoids around the room, positioning related factoids near each other to form groups or clusters. Ask everyone to review their factoids and start putting them on the wall or floor in relation to other people's factoids (and in relation to the predefined categories).

FIGURE 6.5
Seed the walls with your user category labels.
Photograph courtesy of Jonathan Hayes.

For example, if one person has a factoid about children's Internet use behaviors after school, and another has a factoid about children's daily entertainment activities in the home, these two factoids might be placed near each other. As everyone adds their factoids, similar or related factoids will cluster, and factoids that are not related will end up far apart. Figure 6.6 shows an assimilation exercise in progress.

During your assimilation exercise, you might find "factoid islands" of sticky notes that turn out to be difficult to cluster. If you find factoids that cause extended arguments or that you feel you have to force into a cluster, put them aside and return to them later. You won't use every factoid you have created and clustered in your finished personas.

You might also find that a single factoid fits well in more than one location. Make copies of the factoid and put it everywhere it belongs. As the assimilation progresses, you will find that your opinions on how to cluster factoids evolves. Your team will probably want to redistribute factoids and even move entire clusters as the exercise progresses, and you should encourage them to do so until they feel that the clusters make sense.

Look for "puddles" of sticky notes: If you see more than five to 10 sticky notes clustered closely together (in a "puddle"), try to find additional distinctions between the factoids on those sticky notes. Instead of a single large cluster, try to create several smaller clusters that reflect these distinctions.

FIGURE 6.6
An assimilation exercise in progress. In this case, the factoids are written on larger sheets of paper to facilitate collaboration. Photograph courtesy of Jonathan Hayes.

Label the Clusters of Factoids

As the clusters of factoids (and/or assumptions) become stable, begin labeling the clusters with sticky notes. Be sure to use a different color for the labels. Remember that assimilation is given structure by the categories you initially identified, but at its core, the resulting clusters are determined by the data (i.e., it is a bottom-up process). Not all of your clustered factoids have to fit cleanly into your defined categories. When you label your clusters, you will identify supporting data related to your categories, distinctions in categories (subcategories), and new information about your targeted users.

> **HANDY DETAIL**
>
> **You Can Include Collected Assumptions in Your Assimilation Exercise**
>
> If you collected assumptions during family planning (or to help you identify categories of users), you can assimilate these along with the factoids. Assign one sticky note color to indicate assumptions so that you don't confuse them with factoids. Assimilating assumptions along with your factoids allows you to easily see which assumptions are supported by data (those that end up clustered with factoids) and which are not (those that end up alone or in small clusters with other assumptions).
>
> Assimilating assumptions in with your factoids can produce some very interesting results. For example, you can create your categories, assimilate your assumptions (perhaps using yellow sticky notes), and then assimilate your factoids (using blue sticky notes). After your assimilation is complete and you have labeled all of your clusters of factoids (see material following), you will probably find that some clusters include only blue stickies (factoids) or only yellow stickies (assumptions). This is helpful information. If a cluster includes only factoids, it could mean the following:
>
> - Your organization doesn't have any assumptions about this topic.
> - Your organization does have assumptions about the topic but you have not surfaced these assumptions yet.
>
> To find out, you can ask your stakeholders to tell you their assumptions about the topic in question. If a cluster includes only assumptions, it could mean the following:
>
> - The data does not support the assumptions.
> - You did not find and use the data related to these assumptions in your exercise.
>
> If you find a cluster with only assumptions, look for more data to either support or specifically contradict the assumptions. You know that the assumptions exist and therefore could exert influence on the design of your product. It is worth looking for data now.

DATA TENDS TO CLUSTER IN EXPECTED AND UNEXPECTED WAYS

The data you have assimilated had many different authors with many different purposes. It is not possible to determine before you assimilate it what truly insightful and compelling relationships in information you will find. Factoids will not all naturally cluster in ways that seem immediately relevant to your

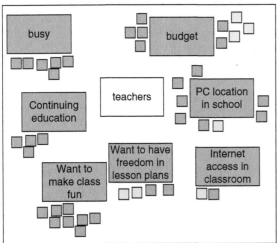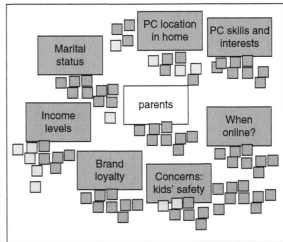

FIGURE 6.7
Categories of users (white), cluster labels (pink), factoids (blue), and assumptions (yellow) after assimilation exercise. In this illustration, we show the labels (pink) much larger than the sticky note clusters. This is simply so that you can read the cluster labels. We recommend that you use sticky notes to label the clusters of factoids (in this example, blue stickies) and assumptions (in this example, yellow stickies) you find during your assimilation exercise because this facilitates moving and changing the labels as needed.

persona effort (see Fig. 6.7). This information may not map neatly to user types or goals, but it may contain domain-related insights that prove invaluable to your effort. If you find "odd" clusters developing, don't try to force them to fit. Examine them for insights into your user base.

KNOW WHEN TO STOP

Continue the assimilation and labeling exercise until:

- Everyone has placed their set of factoids on the floor or wall in relation to other factoids.
- The groups or clusters have started to settle.

Note that you may have to just force yourself to stop, as the organization of factoids, labeling, and reorganization can go on for a long time. One way to force the issue is simply to stop once every group has a label (even if you don't have agreement on the current organization and labeling).

Step 3: Identify Subcategories of Users and Create Skeletons

During Step 3, you will evaluate your assimilated data to confirm the original categories of users you started with and to identify interesting subcategories of users. You should plan to create one skeleton persona per unique category or subcategory. This will ensure that you have a set of skeletons that reflect and cover the data you have collected. Once you have created your skeletons, you (and your stakeholders) can prioritize them. Using this process, you may create a relatively large set of skeleton personas, but this does not mean that you will communicate all these possible target personas outside your core team during the birth and maturation and adulthood phases of your project.

IDENTIFY SUBCATEGORIES OF USERS

When you created your categories of users in Step 1, you thought about the differences in user roles, user goals, and user segments between groups of your target users. To identify subcategories of users, you will now think about these differences within each of your categories based on key findings across the clusters. For example, if you created categories of users defined primarily by differences between user roles, you can now examine each of those categories for important differences in user goals and user segments. You may also find that there are specific subroles that form subcategories. You should create a subcategory to describe any product-significant differences you find within your categories that seem important and are clearly indicated in the assimilated data.

Clusters Identify Groups of Facts; Subcategories Identify Groups of People

Look at the data clustered under each of your user categories. As a team, evaluate and discuss the possibility that each category should be divided into two or more subcategories. Consider roles, goals, and segments in this assessment. As you identify subcategories, you can write them on a whiteboard. You might also find it helpful to transfer the subcategory names onto sticky notes and place them appropriately in your assimilated data. In doing this exercise, you are simply exploring the possible groups of users that have emerged from your data.

When Does a Difference Merit a Subcategory?

The most difficult part of this process is determining whether a difference is meaningful and useful. Step back and see if subcategories are "bubbling up" out of your assimilated data.

Your goal is to express what Robert Barlow-Busch, Director of Product Design at Primal Fusion, calls "the differences that make a difference" between the types of people described in your data sources. As your core team discusses the results of your assimilation, consider the following questions in determining which merit the creation of subcategories.

- Does this subcategory represent a group of users important to the design of our product? Does this subcategory likely require different features from other subcategories and different ways of interacting with our product?
- Does this subcategory represent a group of users important to our business? Does this subcategory produce revenue, bring mind share, or influence other people regarding your product?
- Is this subcategory clearly unique compared with the other subcategories? Is the subcategory different enough to warrant a separate and distinct persona?

What If We End Up Creating a Lot of Categories and Subcategories?

As long as you feel you can distinguish the categories and subcategories you discover in the data, it is fine (and often a good idea) to create subcategories. Create as many categories and subcategories as it takes to capture your data. You will not necessarily create personas for all of them. The product design and development team will likely not be able to embrace more than about five to seven personas effectively. In the next section, we describe how to prioritize your categories and subcategories of users generated after first turning them into skeleton profiles.

CREATE SKELETONS

Once you have identified and agreed upon the categories and subcategories of users, you are ready to create skeletons. Skeletons are very brief, typically bulleted, lists of distinguishing data ranges for each subcategory of user. Skeletons help your core team transition from thinking about categories of users to focusing on specific details. They also allow your team to present the key findings of the assimilation exercise to stakeholders.

Create one skeleton for each of the subcategories you identified. On each skeleton, list the cluster labels that relate to that subcategory. These cluster labels will become headings in your skeleton. Because you will be comparing and prioritizing skeletons against each other, it is important that each contains at least somewhat comparable information. Consider including common characteristics or headings across all of your skeletons. If you do this, you may find that you are missing information for some skeletons. In these cases, either leave that information blank, perhaps marking it as "need data," or make an informed estimation about what it might be. If you do the latter, be sure to indicate that it is an assumption to be followed up on.

Under each heading, create a bulleted summary of the information you found in the data. You are not exhaustively including every aspect of the associated

<hr />

Story from the Field

Identifying Your Most Demanding Users

George Olsen,
Principal, Interaction by Design

Personas are commonly built around the "neediest" users. That is, if you can solve a design problem for them, you will likely solve it for all of your other users as well. But it can also be useful to look at your most demanding users – those most vocal. Although this runs the risk of tilting toward power users, it is not uncommon for consumer-facing products

to have a minority of customers account for a majority of profits. It therefore makes sense to highlight their needs. (It might also be the case that noncustomers, who the company hopes to attract, want more out of the product than it currently delivers.) But the principle is the same as designing for the neediest users: see if by satisfying a design problem for the most demanding users you can satisfy a much larger group of users. Thus, this can be valuable complementary approach, but just use it with care.

Skeleton

> **Boy, age 10–13**
> **Computer use at school**
> • Has access to a shared computer in his classroom or a computer "lab" shared by the whole school
> • Has at least one computer-related assignment a week
> • Finds computer use at school "boring"
> **Internet use at home**
> • Shares a home computer with family
> • Uses Internet to play games and (sometimes) do school work
> **Interests/Activities**
> • Likes to talk about games with friends
> • Likes video games more than computer games
> • Participates in multiple organized sports

Sketch

> **Danny**
> Danny is 12 and he just started sixth grade, which is very cool. He has computer lab once a week and he likes it a lot. He usually spends recess in the computer lab looking for info about the Lakers and for new games to try. He thinks he's a computer pro; his mom's been coming to him for help with silly stuff for years now.

FIGURE 6.8
A skeleton versus a sketch persona. Note that the skeleton includes headings derived from cluster labels (from the assimilation exercise) and data points. For now, avoid any narrative details that might distract stakeholders as they try to prioritize the skeletons.

factoids. Try to identify the key points that capture the essence of the subcategory. Do not give the skeletons names or other personal details that make them feel like people (which may relate to, but are not specific to the data). As shown in Fig. 6.8, skeletons are not sketch personas; they are selected facts that define and distinguish your subcategories of users.

HOW MANY SKELETONS SHOULD I CREATE?

We recommend that you create skeletons only for subcategories of users you believe are interesting or important to your product. If you create a large number of skeletons, you can use the prioritization exercise following to narrow in on the few you will evolve into personas. However, it is much easier for stakeholders to prioritize fewer skeletons. Use the criteria listed previously under "When does a difference merit a subcategory?" to discuss each skeleton as you create it and to combine, augment, or discard skeletons.

HANDY DETAIL
Think About Your Users

Earlier in this book, we reminded you to think about the users of your own work products.

Skeletons are a perfect example of the importance of this. Skeletons are documents you use to communicate with your business stakeholders. You will ask these stakeholders to prioritize the skeletons in accordance with business objectives. This is precisely why you do not want to include fictional details (such as a name, favorite color, or favorite activity). Any information in the skeleton document that is not obviously derived directly from data will distract the stakeholders and invite debate on details – and this is not the appropriate time for that debate.

HANDY DETAIL

What If You Find "Scary" Information in the Data?

What if you have some data that makes you create a persona that inherently will not like your product? For example, maybe you are building a product for television and the data says that people in a key set of target users are too busy to watch TV. What do you do? If you run into this type of problem, you can:

- Escalate the data you have found to the stakeholders so that they can reevaluate the strategy for the product. If they push back, show them the data that led to your conclusions.
- Reevaluate your data sources to consider whether they are really in line with the existing strategy with respect to target users.
- Build this information, and the related design challenges, into the personas you create. Given that your targets don't like to watch TV currently, and that you cannot change the delivery medium, how do you get these people to change their behavior and turn on the TV to access your product? How do you build a specific product that will appeal to them, given their needs and goals?

PERSONA GESTATION: STEPS 4, 5, AND 6

Once you have a set of skeletons, it is time to get feedback from your stakeholders. You will evaluate the importance of each skeleton to your business and product strategy and prioritize the skeletons accordingly. During gestation, you will identify a subset of skeletons to develop into personas.

Step 4: Prioritize the Skeletons

It is time to prioritize your skeletons. To do this, schedule a meeting with members of your persona core team who understand the data you have collected and stakeholders empowered to make decisions about the strategic focus of the company. If stakeholders are not aware of the data and general process that led to these skeletons, present that information before introducing the skeletons to them. It is important to carefully plan and manage your prioritization meeting. Before you get started, remind everyone of the goals of the meeting and the impact their decisions will have on the project.

- These skeletons were derived from data and should map fairly clearly to the user types (categories and subcategories) you already reviewed together.
- Prioritization should focus on immediate goals or low-hanging fruit. Remind the team that the goal is to reduce the possible set of targets to just those that are critical to your current product cycle. Remember that you can prioritize the skeletons differently for subsequent versions of this product or for derivative or sibling products.
- Prioritizing does not mean abandoning the interests of the lower-priority skeletons. It simply means deciding that in the case of feature or

functionality debates the interests of the persona derived from the most important category or subcategory of users should be considered before anyone else's. If the stakeholders insist that all the skeletons are critical, ask them to consider which would be most useful to the development staff. For example, have them do a Q-sort in which they can place a particular number of items in each of three priorities (high, medium, and low) and then have them sort within each category for one more gradation. You can always provide a slightly different set of personas to those teams who might benefit most from them (e.g., provide your marketing team with the set of personas closest to purchase decisions).

■ Prioritizing should be relatively easy if the business and strategic goals for the product are clear. If prioritizing is difficult, it may mean that the stakeholders have some more work to do on their own. The skeletons and the detailed category and subcategory distinctions may be able to help them in this work.

It is important to reach consensus on the importance of the various skeletons, but it is not often easy to do so. When you ask your stakeholders to rank the skeletons you identified, they will probably respond in one of the following ways:

■ "These three [or some subset] are the ones we really need to target."
■ "They are all great."
■ "They are all great, but we need to add X, Y, and Z customers to this list," or "You are omitting many of our major customer groups."
■ "None of these are good."
■ "I can't tell you which ones are the right ones."
■ "Wow, we need to do some (more) customer research," or "We really need to know X about our users."

Although getting the first answer is the best, all these answers are actually okay.

They provide useful, actionable information. Of course, you could get a completely different response from each stakeholder. If that happens, know that it is useful information and take note of it.

Some of your stakeholders' answers may point to problems in your organization – problems in business strategy or lack of real knowledge about your customers. If this is your first time doing personas, we can pretty much guarantee that there will be difficulty and indecision. You are asking difficult questions that your stakeholders may not have been asked before or probably have not been asked this early in the product cycle.

STRUCTURE THE DISCUSSION

It is helpful to provide some structure to the prioritization exercise. The first step is simply to have them rank order the skeletons by perceived importance. There will likely be some disagreement as they sort the list. That is okay at this point.

Once you have a rough order in place, we suggest assigning each skeleton one or more values that can more closely be tied to data.

- Frequency of use: How often would each skeleton use your product? Daily users would likely be more important regarding design decisions than those that only use your product once a month.
- Size of market: Roughly how many people does each skeleton represent? Larger markets are usually more important than smaller ones. Do you plan to aim your new product at a new market? In that case, you might consider the importance of a small market with growth potential.
- Historic or potential revenue: How much purchasing power does each skeleton encompass? If this is a new product, you may have to estimate this amount (e.g., through trade journals, market trends, market research, and understanding spending behaviors in related markets). In many cases, users might not directly make the purchase. Someone else buys such products for them. Still, they may influence those purchase decisions.
- Strategic importance: Decide who is your most strategically important audience. Is it those who make the most support calls, those who rely on your product for critical activities, those who use your competitor's product, or those who don't use yours or anyone's product yet? Are you trying to expand or grow your market? If that is your primary goal, do your skeletons include nonusers, technology pioneers, or trend setters? Which target audiences will help your team innovate or stretch?

You might derive other attributes that are more directly related to your line of business. Either way, you can use just one of these attributes or some combination of them to more accurately prioritize the skeletons. If time is critical for your stakeholders (which is usually the case), consider generating the values for these attributes yourself, and even doing the prioritization, prior to the meeting. To help your leadership team through the review process and toward a conclusion, remind the stakeholders that validation work can and will happen later in the process to ensure that the current decisions and resulting personas are on track.

Finally, you will want to ask your stakeholders if there are any missing skeletons (i.e., categories or subcategories of users) that are truly important to your company. If the answer is yes, have the stakeholders create those skeletons based on their collective knowledge and assumptions. You should include those additional "assumption skeletons" in the prioritization process.

BRIGHT IDEA

If You Are Stuck, Create Anti-personas

Consider preparing skeletons of clear nontargets for your stakeholder review meeting. These are audiences that no one would refute as being outside your product's audience. Cooper refers to these as negative personas in *The Inmates are Running the Asylum* (Cooper, 1999, p. 136). These are usually quite obvious once described, but it is helpful to make it clear that your product is not for everyone in the known universe. For example, if you are developing an e-commerce Web site, your target audience probably shouldn't include people who are non-PC users, people without Internet connectivity, or (more ridiculously) infants and toddlers.

This is particularly useful if your team members see themselves as the target audience. It is also useful if there is a well-known audience or well-liked audience that is not a good business target. For example, anti-personas might include:

- Extreme novices ("my mom can't use this")
- The seasoned expert or guru ("macros and shortcut keys are critical!")
- The domain enthusiast (an obvious audience that might actually be very small in size and thus not a good target for the business)

IDENTIFY PRIMARY AND SECONDARY TARGETS

It is important that you identify the primary and secondary user targets for your product and eliminate any skeletons that are not critical to the success of the current development cycle. In the next steps, you will create personas based on the prioritization decisions you make here with your skeletons. If there are too many primary targets for your product, the personas will lose some of their strength and utility. Therefore, even if the differences in priority are small, you must clearly define which skeletons are going to be focused on and which will not (for now). Select the top three to five skeletons by priority values to be enriched into complete personas.

Why insist on what could result in some difficult discussions or even arguments? Because the alternative is to invite difficult discussions and arguments later in the development process, personas must be able to end arguments. To do this, they must narrow the design space to something that is manageable.

Story from the Field

In the End, the Choice of Targets Is a Management Decision

Matthew Lee,
Usability Engineer, InfoSpace, Inc.

At a financial services company I worked for, management did not agree that one person could be an identifier for an entire segment (over one million people). The segment in question included a huge portion of the population (lower-income people who rent their homes). This segment included many types of people, from single mothers with kids, to older retired people living on Social Security, to people living paycheck to paycheck. Management didn't believe that one person could represent all these people in a meaningful manner and insisted we create three personas to represent the segment.

BRIGHT IDEA

Got a Lot of Possible Users? Plot Them by Critical Dimensions

Len Conte, BMC Software

Are you creating a product that will have many users? Not sure how to approach creating personas that will be useful? We suggest plotting large groups of users according to the critical dimensions of technical and domain expertise and looking for clusters of users (see Fig. 6.9).

For example, for an online media player, you could collect a large group of assumption personas or sketch personas and cluster them according to their domain knowledge (how much expertise do they have with respect to media?) and technical expertise (how facile are they with computers and the Internet?).

Wherever you find a group of dots, that's where you need a persona. This can be a great tool for a reality check on assumptions. Perhaps one or more of the executives assumes that the target market is largely in the top right quadrant (perhaps highly technical music enthusiasts), but your data shows that most potential users of your product cluster in other quadrants.

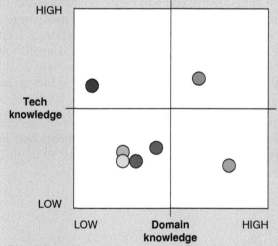

FIGURE 6.9
A plot of technical expertise and domain knowledge. Each colored dot represents a large group of current or target users. You'll need at least one persona wherever you see a cluster of dots.

Step 5: Develop Selected Skeletons into Personas

You now have a reduced set of basic skeletons your stakeholders helped select. Your task at this point is to enrich these skeletons to become personas by adding data as well as concrete and individualized details to give them personality and context. You will also include some storytelling elements and photos to make the personas come to life.

As you build on your skeletons, all the details of your personas will be encapsulated in a foundation document. Depending on the available time and the needs of your product, you might create full personas for just the small set of primary personas you defined or you can create full personas for a larger set of primary and secondary personas. We have found that it is time and resource effective to first fully develop the high-priority primary skeletons and then to enrich, but not exhaustively complete, the nonprimary skeletons into sketch personas.

WHAT IS A PERSONA FOUNDATION DOCUMENT?

We use the term foundation document to describe whatever you use as a storehouse for all of your information, descriptions, and data related to a single persona. The foundation document contains the information that will motivate and justify design decisions and generate scenarios that will appear in feature specs, vision documents, storyboards, and so forth.

Foundation documents contain the complete definition of a given persona, but they do not have to be long or difficult to create. Depending on your goals and the needs of your team, your foundation document could range from a single page to a long document. Creating a foundation document for each persona will provide you and your team with a single resource you can harvest as necessary as you create your persona communication materials. At the very least, complete personas must include core information essential to defining the persona: the goals, roles, behaviors, segment, environment, and typical activities that make the persona solid, rich, and unique (and, more importantly, relevant to the design of your product). If you have time, your completed foundation documents should contain the following:

- Abundant links to factoids
- Copious footnotes or comments on specific data
- Links to the original research reports that support and explain the personas' characteristics
- Indications of which supporting characteristics are from data and which characteristics are fictitious or based on assumptions.

As your foundation document grows, it is helpful to add headings and a table of contents. Consider creating your foundation documents as an HTML page for each persona. This will allow you to add links and keep your materials organized while providing access to your various core team members and stakeholders during its development.

The more details you include now the easier you will find the birth and maturation and adulthood life cycle phases. Complete multipage foundation documents can contain a tremendous amount of information and take considerable effort to create. It is up to you and your team to decide how rich your foundation documents need to be and how you will collaborate on or divide the work required to create them.

If you are extremely time and resource constrained, you can start with brief one-page description or resume-style foundation documents. Then, as you find the

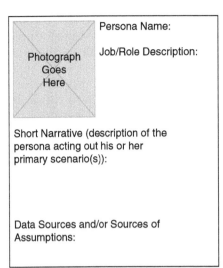
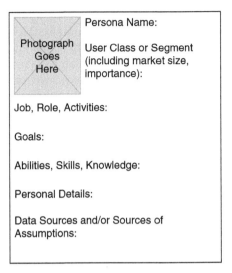

FIGURE 6.10
One-page (left) and resume-style (right) foundation document templates. These are the shortest possible foundation documents, and in most cases (unless you are extremely time and resource constrained), your foundation documents will include considerably more detail. Note that it is a good idea to develop your own template before you dive into creating your foundation documents. The templates help organize your work as you add and look for data to include in the document.

time, you can always come back and add to the information in these short foundation documents. Figure 6.10 shows one-page and resume-style outlines for these brief foundation documents.

CHOOSE PERSONA CHARACTERISTICS TO INCLUDE IN THE FOUNDATION DOCUMENT

Your assimilated data as well as your product and team needs will dictate what content to include in your foundation documents. When you created your skeletons, you were purposely selective in what information you included. Now you need to be more exhaustive. This means that you need to include all headings and information appropriate and useful to understanding your audience and developing your product. Different types of information will be relevant for different people on your team and will have different uses toward product development.

Your skeletons will serve as the starting point for the foundation documents. Each skeleton has a bulleted list of characteristics. Your next step is to add important content headings based on three things:

- The labels for the clusters that came out of the assimilation exercise
- Topics relevant to your product domain or business (e.g., if you are creating an Internet product, you probably need a section on Internet activities, equipment, and/or Internet connection environments)

- Some common headings in persona documents that help create a persona that is well rounded, realistic, useful, and complete

Regarding the second and third of the previous items, consider the following list of persona characteristics that you can use as a content "menu" and template for your foundation documents. When you are deciding which characteristics to include in your foundation documents, think about the types of information that will be most helpful to your core team and to the development team. We recommend that you include at least rudimentary information in each of the following categories of persona characteristics:

- Identifying details
  - Name, title, or short description
  - Age, gender
  - Identifying tag line
  - Quote (highlighting something essential to that persona, preferably related to the product)
  - Photograph or brief physical description
- Role(s) and tasks
  - Specific company or industry
  - Job title or role
  - Typical activities
  - Important atypical activities
  - Challenge areas or breakdowns, pain points
  - Responsibilities
  - Interactions with other personas, systems, products
- Goals
  - Short-term, long-term
  - Motivations
  - Work-related goals
  - Product-related goals
  - General (life) goals, aspirations
  - Stated and unstated desires for the product
- Segment
  - Market size and influence
  - International considerations
  - Accessibility considerations
  - General and domain-relevant demographics
    - Income and purchasing power
    - Region or city, state, country
    - Education level
    - Marital status
    - Cultural information
  - Skills and knowledge
  - General computer and/or Internet use
  - Frequently used products, product knowledge
  - Years of experience

- Domain knowledge
- Training
- Special skills
- Competitor awareness
- Context/environment
  - Equipment (Net connection, browser brand and version, operating system)
  - "A day in the life" description
    - Work styles
    - Time line of a typical day
  - Specific usage location(s)
  - General work, household, and leisure activities
  - Relationships to other personas
- Psychographics and personal details
- Personality traits
  - Values and attitudes (political opinions, religion)
  - Fears and obstacles, pet peeves
  - Personal artifacts (car, gadgets)

This list was partially adapted from Mike Kuniavsky's list of attributes in *Observing the User Experience* (Kuniavsky, 2003; pp. 136–143), where he provides detailed descriptions of these and other possible persona attributes.

To further help you think about what information you might want to include in your personas, we have included a brief content analysis from several personas we have collected over the last few years (see Fig. 6.11). These personas were created for a variety of products in several different industries (though all are for either software or Web site products or services). Our goal here is to show you what others have typically included and perhaps to inspire you to include certain information you had not considered previously.

Figure 6.11 shows the frequency of basic characteristics across many personas. There are 31 personas included in this analysis, each representing a different company and product. We have organized the characteristics by high-level category: Basic Details, Personal Information, Job/Work Information, Technology Access and Usage, and Other. Within these groups, we have ordered the characteristics by frequency of occurrence among the 31 sample personas.

Use the information in Fig. 6.11 as a guide. Your product needs will likely dictate that you use only a subset of these characteristics, or some that are not included here.

START A FOUNDATION DOCUMENT (TRANSFER FACTOIDS INTO YOUR SKELETONS)

Your skeleton documents are a template you can use to create a foundation document for each persona. Each skeleton should now have a similar set of headings. For each of those headings, transfer the appropriate factoids into the related sections (as shown in Fig. 6.12). It is likely that some sections will have a lot of factoids in them and others will be nearly empty.

Frequency of persona characteristics across 31 sample personas	
Basic Details	
Name	90%
Photograph/Illustration	71%
Tag Line ("essence" title)	39%
User Classification/Segment	32%
Personal Information	
Age	84%
Fears/Obstacles	75%
Motivations/Aspirations/Goals	67%
City/State/Country	61%
Marital/Family Status	55%
Hobbies/Leisure/SocialLife	55%
Educational Background	45%
Description of Environment/Home	42%
Other Personal? Responses: books, current state of mind for disability claimants, knowledge of SSA programs, context of use, i.e., working at home, in short sessions, using library or neighbors, computer, daily life style, symptoms, disabling condition, description of family, gender, relationships with others and their descriptions (e.g., brother)	42%
Personality Traits	32%
Car/Significant Personal Artifacts	23%
E-mail Address	13%
Social/Political Opinions	10%
Physical Description of person	10%
Other	
Relationship to your product/Attitudes and opinions towards your product	83%
Market Size, Spending/Buying & Influence (indicator of the importance/priority of your persona)	50%
Scenario(s)/Walk-throughs with your product or features of your product	45%
International Considerations	33%
Supporting Research/References	29%
Accessibility/Disability Considerations	25%
Other? Responses: Type of persona. We identify who's primary, secondary, and anti, how designing for one persona can influence/serve other audiences.	17%

Job Work Information	
Typical Activities	92%
Job Title	84%
Goals	81%
Job Description/Responsibilities	74%
Company/Industry	65%
Challenge Areas/Breakdowns	61%
Interaction with Colleagues	61%
Work Style	61%
Typical Workday/Time line of Day	58%
Core Competencies/Skills	58%
Professional Motivation	55%
Quote(s) about work	52%
Previous Work History/Experience	45%
Work place Description/Artifacts	32%
Opinion of Company	29%
Workspace Photo/Sketch	19%
Salary	10%
Other work related? Responses: Geographic area, traffic and workload in field office, type of clientele they service, whether they are a specialist or a generalist	3%
Technology Access and Usage	
Computer/Internet Use	58%
Applications/Languages Used	58%
Technology Opinions/Attitudes	68%
Hardware Spec/Equipment & Technologies Used	45%
ISP/Connection Speed	83%
Other Technology Related? Responses: Tools used in their job, domain expertise, time of day using Internet, competitive products used and why, types of gadgets used and why/how	50%

FIGURE 6.11

Frequency of persona characteristics across 31 sample personas used in a variety of companies to design a wide range of products.

Persona Skeleton:
Boy, age 10–13

Computer use at school
- Has access to a shared computer in his classroom or a computer "lab" shared by the whole school
  - Factoid
  - Factoid
  - Factoid

- Has at least one computer-related assignment a week
  - Factoid
  - Factoid

- Finds computer use at school "boring"
  - Factoid
  - …

FIGURE 6.12
Transfer factoids verbatim into your skeleton document. This document will evolve to become your persona foundation document, which will be the repository for all information on each persona.

GET SPECIFIC ABOUT EACH CORE CHARACTERISTIC

Once you have copied your factoids into your skeleton documents, evolving the skeleton into a more precise persona can be relatively easy. You will create a concrete fact, phrase, sentence, or paragraph to replace each factoid or set of factoids in the skeleton. To this point, you have likely been dealing largely with ranges of values (e.g., age = 25–35, parent, works full-time) instead of specific values. You purposely stayed at this abstract level when considering the few attributes of your skeletons to stay as close as possible to the actual data during the evaluation process. Now it is time to turn most of the characteristics in your skeleton personas into very specific and more concrete values. For example:

- "Works full-time" becomes a specific job, such as bank teller, department store manager, or high school teacher.
- "Parent" becomes mother or father.
- "Seventy percent female" becomes Laura, Dianne, Irene, and so on.
- "Lives in a major metropolitan city" becomes Chicago, Los Angeles, or Houston.

More specifically, from your skeleton (see Fig. 6.13, left), transform your headings and factoids into specific, concrete details in your foundation document (Fig. 6.13, right).

As you replace factoids with specific details to enrich your persona, copy the factoid or set of factoids into a comment or a footnote in your foundation document. A lofty but worthy goal is to have every statement in your foundation document supported by user data. You likely will not achieve this, but the attempt helps you to think critically about your details and highlights places where you might want to do further research. (In fact, when such research questions come up it is a good idea to make a note of them directly in the foundation document.) By the time you finish creating a description for each persona, you will have also created a very rich document that is full of direct references to data (as illustrated in Fig. 6.14).

MOVING TOWARD PRECISION MEANS MOVING AWAY FROM ACCURACY

In many cases, the accuracy of your data lies in its ranges (not just central tendencies but descriptors of variance, percentages, and skew). By selecting precise descriptors, you are going to lose some of that accuracy. For example, if a category includes males and females, you cannot create a single individual who

Parent (skeleton)

Demographics:
• People who make enough money to have two computers in their home tend to live in major metropolitan areas (source 3, p. 1).
• Etc.

Work:
• 85 percent of parents surveyed work full-time in white-collar professions (source 5, p. 2).
• Etc.

Goals, fears, aspirations of parents:
• Mothers are more concerned with their child's behavior online than fathers (source 2, p. 10).
• Etc.

Irene Pasquez, the involved parent (1)
(foundation document)

Overview:
Irene lives in a suburb of Houston (2) with Emanuel, her husband, and her one child: Preston, who just turned 5.

Even though Irene works full-time as a manager in a local branch of Bank of America (3), she is heavily involved with Preston's daily activities and has the opportunity to see him during the working day because... etc.

Data references
1. Mothers are more concerned with their child's behavior online than fathers (source 2, p. 10).
2. People who make enough money to have two computers in their home tend to live in major metropolitan areas (source 3, p. 1).
3. 85 percent of parents surveyed work full-time in white-collar professions (source 5, p. 2).

FIGURE 6.13
An example skeleton (left) being transformed into a foundation document (right).

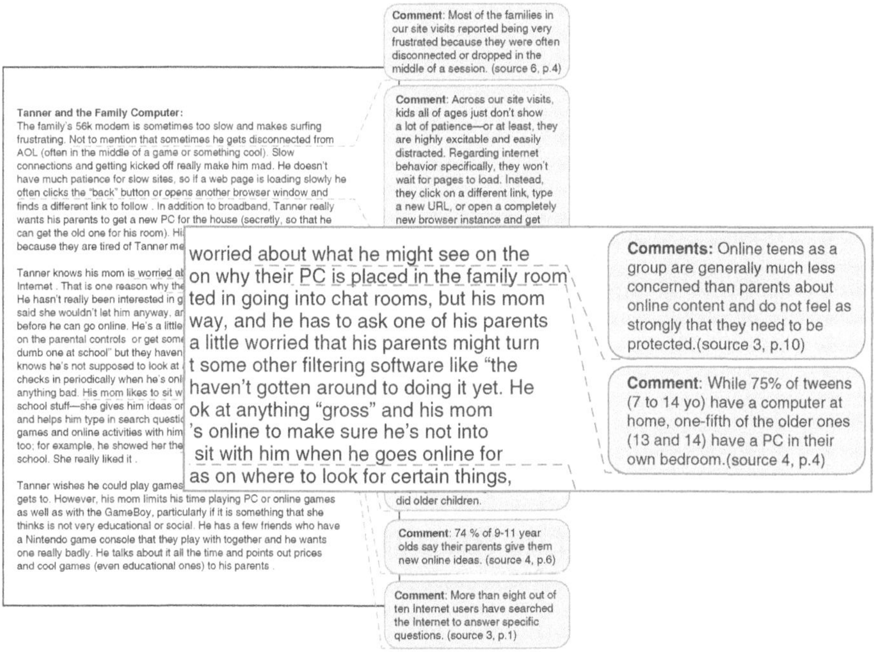

Comment: Most of the families in our site visits reported being very frustrated because they were often disconnected or dropped in the middle of a session. (source 6, p.4)

Comment: Across our site visits, kids all of ages just don't show a lot of patience—or at least, they are highly excitable and easily distracted. Regarding internet behavior specifically, they won't wait for pages to load. Instead, they click on a different link, type a new URL, or open a completely new browser instance and get

Tanner and the Family Computer:
The family's 56k modem is sometimes too slow and makes surfing frustrating. Not to mention that sometimes he gets disconnected from AOL (often in the middle of a game or something cool). Slow connections and getting kicked off really make him mad. He doesn't have much patience for slow sites, so if a web page is loading slowly he often clicks the "back" button or opens another browser window and finds a different link to follow . In addition to broadband, Tanner really wants his parents to get a new PC for the house (secretly, so that he can get the old one for his room). Hi... because they are tired of Tanner me... worried about what he might see on the

Tanner knows his mom is worried a... on why their PC is placed in the family room
Internet . That is one reason why the... ted in going into chat rooms, but his mom
He hasn't really been interested in g... way, and he has to ask one of his parents
said she wouldn't let him anyway, an... a little worried that his parents might turn
before he can go online. He's a littl... t some other filtering software like "the
on the parental controls or get som... haven't gotten around to doing it yet. He
dumb one at school" but they haven... ok at anything "gross" and his mom
knows he's not supposed to look at ... 's online to make sure he's not into
checks in periodically when he's onl... sit with him when he goes online for
anything bad. His mom likes to sit w... as on where to look for certain things,
school stuff—she gives him ideas or...
and helps him type in search questio... did older children.
games and online activities with him...
too; for example, he showed her the...
school. She really liked it .

Tanner wishes he could play games...
gets to. However, his mom limits his time playing PC or online games
as well as with the GameBoy, particularly if it is something that she
thinks is not very educational or social. He has a few friends who want
a Nintendo game console that they play with together and he wants
one really badly. He talks about it all the time and points out prices
and cool games (even educational ones) to his parents .

Comments: Online teens as a group are generally much less concerned than parents about online content and do not feel as strongly that they need to be protected.(source 3, p.10)

Comment: While 75% of tweens (7 to 14 yo) have a computer at home, one-fifth of the older ones (13 and 14) have a PC in their own bedroom.(source 4, p.4)

Comment: 74 % of 9-11 year olds say their parents give them new online ideas. (source 4, p.6)

Comment: More than eight out of ten internet users have searched the Internet to answer specific questions. (source 3, p.1)

FIGURE 6.14
An example of statements in a foundation document supported by factoids using the "insert/comment" feature in MS Word.

"represents" the entire category. Rather than trying to represent every nuance of the entire category, try to pick values that are reasonable, believable, and meaningful.

As you choose specific details to include in your personas, you are zooming in on a particular person. That is, you are transitioning from rough descriptions of categories and subcategories of users to precise values and detailed depictions of a particular persona. As you build these detailed depictions, you will be making educated guesses and adding fictional elements, some of which will be directly related to the data you have collected and some of which will not. (It is a good idea to document these assumptions and to consider them possible research questions that may need answering during the validation of your personas.)

HANDY DETAIL

There Are Many Ways of Including References in Your Foundation Documents

Many word processing programs and HTML editors allow you to add annotations, references, or even pop-up comments to your text. For example, in Microsoft Word, you can use the Comment feature to do this linking and annotation. To do so, highlight a word or phrase, select Insert/Comment, and type or paste your factoid into the comment field. This makes your links not just explicit but very salient to the reader (see Fig. 6.14). If you are creating HTML foundation documents, you can create hyperlinks directly to electronic versions of data or pop-up windows containing direct quotes or summarized data from your original sources.

If you use Microsoft Word to add comments in support of specific details, consider checking the options/security "hide personal info" so that the reader of the document will not see who inserted the comment:

- Select Tools > Options...
- In the Options dialogue box, select the User Information tab.
- Check the box to remove Personal Information from file properties on save.

This is a particularly good idea when multiple people are creating the foundation document. When you find yourself referencing a factoid from a data source, don't forget to include the bibliographic information for that source in the "References" area at the end of the document.

EDITOR'S NOTE: WHERE TO LOOK IN OFFICE WORD 2007

In Office Word 2007, the procedure for hiding personal information changed from earlier versions. The new procedure for hiding personal information is:

- Click the Microsoft Office Button in the upper left of the application.
- Select Prepare > Inspect Document.
- In the Document Inspector dialogue box, select the appropriate check boxes to choose the hidden content you want to inspect.
- Click Inspect, examine the output of the inspection, and click Remove All by the type of contents that you want to remove.

Think of your data, and your categories and subcategories of users, as describing neighborhoods of related users of your product. As you create your personas, you are describing a specific "resident" of each neighborhood. As in real life, each resident inhabits his or her neighborhood, but no one resident can represent all qualities of all people in the neighborhood.

No one who reads a persona description can understand all the intricacies of the data behind that persona. However, as design targets, personas can stand in for all data in your communications. Think of a town meeting. Each neighborhood might send a single representative who stands in for everyone else in the neighborhood, even though that one person cannot accurately communicate the particular demographics, attitudes, needs, and desires of every one of his or her neighbors. Instead, the representative communicates the essence of all of his or her neighbors' needs. Your personas will represent your data in the same way that a single neighbor can represent an entire neighborhood. (For additional discussion of this, see "Handy Detail: It depends on what you mean by 'represent'," by Diane Lye, earlier in this chapter.)

When in Doubt, Choose Details That Are Precise and Memorable

As you select specific characteristics for your personas, try to choose values that are clearly within the range and essence of the data and findings from which they came. You may choose to select values in the middle of the ranges described in your data, but you don't have to. Try to choose values that are reasonable, believable, and meaningful. As a rule, try to choose values that have face validity while not adding any extra "baggage." Your goal is to create personas who feel real and relevant, while being memorable and even interesting. If selecting an off-center value helps you make a more memorable persona, we would argue that it is good to do so.

Incorporate Narrative and Storytelling Elements

Enriching your terse skeletons into personas that are realistic and engaging requires some storytelling. To do this well, remember that you are trying to "tell the story" of the data in your foundation documents with narrative. What do your personas sound like and act like? What can they do or not do? Turn your factoids and specific details into a running story; that is, a sequence of actions and events with interaction and even a plot. Demonstrate their interactions with people, objects, and systems. Narratives in persona documents are typically written in third person, active voice. The following is an example of a descriptive overview a nine-year-old persona named Tanner written as a narrative.

Tanner is nine years old and is a fourth-grade student at Montgomery Elementary School, a public school. He lives with his mother and father (Laura and Shane Thompson) in a suburb of Chicago, Illinois. Tanner has been using computers at school since kindergarten and has had a family computer at home for two years. He has been using the Internet in his school's computer lab for some time but only recently got Internet access at his house (six months ago through his family's America Online® AOL account). Even though Tanner loves to be physically active (riding his skateboard and bike, playing in the yard and nearby creek, participating in organized sports, and so on), Tanner thinks computers are really fun and prefers the PC to the TV. He uses the PC mostly to play games and to surf the Web for "stuff" but occasionally does research for school projects. His favorite computer game of the moment is The Sims 2. His uncle gave it to him for his birthday (his mom and dad usually just buy him educational games). He also really likes Roller Coaster Tycoon 3. Because his dad likes computer sports games like NBA Live 2005, Tanner sometimes plays those with him. Tanner has a GameBoy Color and saves up his allowance to buy new games for it, but his parents say he can only play GameBoy for half an hour each day (they tell him "it will rot his brain").

Writing these stories can be difficult at first. This part of persona creation does take creativity and inspiration. If you have skilled writers on your persona core team, you should likely enlist them to do this part. Start writing your stories by simply expanding the bulleted factoids with context, adding situations, other characters, objects, actions, and events. If you feel blocked or awkward in writing narrative, look through the raw notes and observations from your field research and other qualitative data; that is, use anecdotes and incidents from those real people to enrich your personas.

> ### BRIGHT IDEA
>
> **Combine Validation and Data Collection to Help Finish Your Creation Process**
>
> If you did not have time to collect qualitative and quantitative data before you started creating the personas, or find that you need additional information to create good narratives for your personas, you can stop your persona creation efforts now and embark on your validation exercise before continuing (discussed in material following). As you do the footwork necessary to validate your developing personas, you can collect the "missing" qualitative information that will allow you to add narratives to your personas based on observations rather than assumptions.

Derive Specific Details and Stories from Real Observations

You will notice that we are now moving from the realm of hard, accurate data, observations, and facts to more subjective, "best guess" information and particulars (i.e., toward fiction). In other words, you are starting to include details that are not solidly derived from data. This step is generally uncomfortable, but it can be fun too. Like you had to do when you were determining what types of information (including the categories and headings) would go into your foundation document, you now have to make decisions about specific details that are based on the data, the needs of your team and product, and your knowledge of the world. Your personas need backgrounds and context to be real. Consider using specific, observed information from your site visits or other research as the exact values or characteristics of your profiles. Doing so can ease the burden of being creative, stop disagreements among your persona creation team, and add an aspect of credibility or authenticity to your resulting personas.

You Can Use Stereotypes, but Use Them with Care

You may be tempted to use stereotypes and common knowledge or cultural lore in your personas. If you do, do so carefully. For example, consider the following transition from abstract profile to specific details to stereotype/cultural phenomenon.

Yvonne Chandler lives in suburban Chicago with her husband, William, and their two kids, Colbi (age 7) and Austin (age 13). Yvonne works part-time now that the kids are in school, but she always arranges her work schedule to accommodate a fairly complex system of carpools and after-school activities (she has become a "soccer mom"). She feels tremendously busy but wants to make sure that her kids have a lot of opportunities and learning experiences. She also feels pressure to "keep up with the Joneses" in many aspects of her life, from the activities she involves her kids in to the entertaining she does at home. Before she had kids, Yvonne was known as the neighborhood "Martha Stewart" because of the dinner parties she would host. She would like to entertain more but right now she is just too busy with her kids.

If you are creating a persona of a user who happens to be a suburban mother, you may find yourself tempted to add details based on your own perceptions of a "typical soccer mom" or a "Martha Stewart type." In both cases, utilizing a stereotype or strong cultural icon can be dangerous. The "soccer mom" stereotype is very evocative, but perhaps in ways that work counter to the persona effort. For example, maybe there is someone in your organization who has a similar set of responsibilities, and recognizes herself in the persona, but is put off by the reference to "soccer mom" because she does not want to think of herself that way. Perhaps there are others in the organization who are scornful of "soccer moms" and the stereotypical suburban lifestyle. This distaste can get in the way when you ask your colleagues to use the personas in their everyday work. Similarly, Martha Stewart generally evokes a fairly strong image, at least for a North American audience – one that is either positive or fairly strongly negative.

Persona use brings sociopolitical issues to the surface. Each persona has a gender, age, race, ethnicity, family or cohabitation arrangement, socioeconomic background, and work and/or home environment (even if you don't include all of these directly in the persona description, the photos you use will imply decisions on these details). This provides an effective avenue for recognizing and perhaps changing your team's assumptions about users. Jonathan Grudin argues that stereotypes are very powerful influences that must be handled with caution because they can create a one-dimensional character – one that is not likely to be as rich and complex as most people naturally are (Grudin, 2006). Futhermore, Lene Nielsen argues that stereotypes are naturally formed by our teammates and can be difficult to work with in a design process (Nielsen, 2003b).

To overcome a stereotype, "It is necessary to get access to the users' feelings and knowledge as more than one dimension of the character is needed to raise sympathy" (Nielsen, 2003b, p. 4).

Beware Any Details That Can Evoke Strong Emotional Responses

Note that there are other types of information that can evoke strong responses. For example, if we say that Philip is a concerned dad who is recently divorced and battling for custody of his children, does this information get in the way of the more salient info about how he relates to his child as an online consumer? The information may be memorable and even be reflective of the data, but does it help your persona be effective as a design target?

So, be careful when evoking stereotypes or any information that could elicit a strong personal response. When in doubt, choose to include details that help others see your persona as a real person, with particular goals, needs, and interests that are understandable. Allow realism to win out over political correctness. Avoid casting strongly against expectations if it will undermine credibility. Break the mold if it helps get people on board with your effort. Alan Cooper addresses this issue by stating, "All things being equal, I will use people of different races, genders, nationalities, and colors" (Cooper, 1999, p. 128).

Story from the Field

The Villain in Us

Christina Wodtke,
author of *Information Architecture:*
Blueprints for the Web

When a group gets together to create personas, a funny phenomenon almost always occurs. They make a bad guy. It will start innocently enough, with a set of characteristics: a male in his 30s making six figures on the east coast. Then, as your team develops him into a persona – let's call him "Fred" – he only wears gray, has a gray BMW, and is a young securities trader who works 90-hour weeks. Then he's suddenly a jerk who doesn't have a girlfriend because he's too selfish, and he underpays his secretary and doesn't recycle. What happened?

Perhaps it is because we know people like this. Perhaps it is our human need to create villains. They are fascinating creatures from the wicked queen in Snow White to James Spader's amoral lawyer on *The Practice*. But the problem is that personas are not protagonists and antagonists; they

are design targets. You have to feel for them, or you won't be trying your best to make an interface that makes consumers happy: "Yeah, that jerk, he makes twice what I do. He can figure out the navigation himself."

The solution, interestingly enough, also comes from narrative: redemption. Except that in narrative, you usually wait until the end of the story to redeem your villain (if indeed you plan to do that rather than, say, drop him off a cliff). With personas, you have to redeem your villain with a bit of editing and a bit of back story before you begin your scenarios. In this example, we simply need to remove the fact that Fred underpays his secretary (it's probably the company's fault anyhow). Now, we need to get into the facelift.

"He only wears gray." This could be seen in a number of ways. Let's make him color-blind. Now he's afraid to wear color for fear of being unable to match his clothes. Fred knows that if he goes into work wearing green and orange, he will be mocked by his coworkers and his boss won't take him seriously. With this change, we have both made him more humane and given him a useful trait for our design work. When a designer makes an interface choice, he will remember that it needs to be high contrast with redundant channels of information for Fred, who is afraid of looking stupid at work. The designer cares because we have all been afraid of looking stupid at work.

Now, we can continue. Fred is a first-generation Chinese-American and is saving to purchase a house for his parents. He works long hours for that. He has a gray BMW, but it's a 202 and he works on it on weekends for fun. He is a 202

enthusiast and finds it easier to talk to other car geeks than to girls. But nothing would make him happier than a girl-friend, and his parents have started to bug him about it. Obviously, if this were a car site or a dating site, one aspect or another of the back story could be played up. But we now not only feel for him but understand what motivates him.

The villain is cool, seductive, and powerful – but he's not use-ful. Some may argue, "Some of our users are like that," but can you really do your best work designing to make a jerk happy? Redeem your personas, and redeem your design.

Don't overdo it.

Be sure to keep your stories to an appropriate length. You are not writing a novel. You will want to create interest and provide some background and context for your teammates, but keep your stories in check and don't include detail that is superfluous and highly irrelevant.

Some of the details you create will naturally be relevant to the design and devel-opment of your product, and others will seem completely irrelevant. That your persona "lives in Chicago" or "has been married for 10 years" may not inform any design decision. However, seemingly irrelevant details do have their place. Their purpose is to help make the personas into people – to make them believ-able and memorable. Think of this "irrelevant" content as you would salt and pepper or other spices used in cooking. You are adding flavor to your meal, but too much will ruin the taste. In regard to level of relevant and irrelevant detail, consider the following three examples written in narrative style:

- Too little detail—Tanner arrives home from school at 3:15 p.m. and calls his mom to let her know that he's there. He plays a computer game and watches TV until his mom arrives home.
- Just the right amount of detail—Tanner rides the bus home after school and arrives home at 3:15 p.m. Laura, his mom, is still at work, and per her requested routine, Tanner gives her a phone call to let her know that he made it safely home. Tanner throws his backpack on the floor in the entryway and immediately heads to the family room. He turns on both the TV and the family PC. Within minutes, he is watching his favorite after-school shows and instant messaging (IMing) two of his friends and playing an Internet game on his (currently) favorite site. He knows that he only has 45 minutes of "free" time before his mom arrives home.
- Too much detail—Tanner rides the bus home after school and arrives home at 3:15 p.m He likes his bus driver because he reminds him of the bus driver on the cartoon show *The Simpsons*. Laura, his mom, is still at work. Having a part-time job, she works until 4:00 p.m. three days a

week. She worries about Tanner being home alone after school – particularly regarding his trip home. She worries less once he is there, and so per her requested routine, Tanner gives her a phone call to let her know that he made it safely home. Tanner throws his backpack on the floor in the entryway, spilling some of its content on the floor, and immediately heads to the family room. He turns on both the TV (a nice but old 34-inch Sony Trinitron) and the family PC. Within minutes, he is watching his favorite after-school shows and IMing two of his friends and playing a flash-based Internet game on his (currently) favorite site. He makes the most of this play time, because he knows that he only has 45 minutes of "free" time before his mom arrives home. Laura arrives home a little late due to traffic, and gets a little irritated by the mess Tanner created in the entryway. She snaps at Tanner to get started on his homework.

Of course, part of your goal here is to make the persona memorable and engaging. It is possible that the detail that will make the personas stick in your organization will be something "irrelevant" with respect to the product. Try to find out what resonates for folks, what they all agree on, and what they love to debate and talk about. In one company, it was the persona's car that really made the persona seem real, tangible. Others have relied heavily on the tagline or user class. In the end, the most memorable part of any persona tends to be the name and the picture – and these are so useful in streamlining communication that it is worth adding any details that will secure the basics in the minds of your teammates.

Finally, it is important to note that not every section of your persona foundation document needs to be written as a story. Some sections are best left as bulleted lists, tables, or other summary formats. In our experience, narratives are especially useful in foundation documents for providing an overview, describing a "day in the life," and facilitating key usage scenarios including motivations, fears, and aspirations of the persona. Sections regarding goals, knowledge, skills, and equipment or environment might be best written as bulleted lists.

HANDY DETAIL

Determine Where Personas Stop and Scenarios Begin

A foundation document as we define it is a rich and detailed description of an individual, which may include stories about how he or she approaches work, gets things done, and interacts with colleagues and products (possibly yours). The stories you include in the personas should be there to help people deeply understand who that persona is. But this doesn't mean that your foundation document will contain all possible stories for that persona.

In this chapter, we discuss how additional stories, specific scenarios, design maps, and use cases can be created and used outside the foundation to help your team explore and define solutions to be built into your product. Scenarios, design maps, and use cases are typically much more specific and focused than the stories in foundation documents. They are stories designed to specifically describe a particular person interacting with a particular part of a product in a particular situation. Your personas will become the "particular people" (or "actors") in these additional stories.

Personas are generative in nature. That is, they can drive the creation of an almost endless set of possible scenarios. When defined appropriately, your personas serve as the motivational factor and grounding requirements for future scenarios – detailed scenarios in specific domains.

KNOW WHEN TO STOP

Once you start enriching your skeleton personas into full foundation documents, you might find it difficult to stop. You and your team will discover new data sources and will want to incorporate new information into the sketches. That is fine, but it should not get in the way of sharing and "birthing" the personas into your organization. At some point, you and your core team will have to decide that you have enough information in each persona and are ready to move on to the next phase. Remember that it is likely that no one outside your core team will ever read the entire foundation document. The document needs only to be complete enough to support your birth and maturation and adulthood activities to the extent that you are "ready." This does not mean that you cannot keep adding information. We recommend that you assign an owner to each persona. The owner can be responsible for keeping the persona up to date and integrating new data and information as appropriate.

ILLUSTRATE YOUR PERSONAS

Each persona needs a face, a photo or set of photos, to make them real. We believe photos or illustrations are critical. They help your team believe in the personas and understand that each persona describes a single person. The choice of what specific photos to use is difficult. These illustrations of your personas are extremely influential and can significantly affect how your personas are perceived.

A photo is more than just a face. The model's clothing, expression, activity, and general appearance – along with the setting and background – will communicate or dictate some of the characteristics of your persona. You can either take advantage of this fact or continually fight it. The sections that follow offer some suggestions to help you with this.

Don't Use Stock Photos

Stock photos can look too professional and slick, as the people in them tend to look like professional models (see Fig. 6.15).

With stock photos, you do not have control of the model's context, activity, or expression. There are also usually only one or two photos for a given model.

FIGURE 6.15
Stock photos can look too professional. The people look like models.

FIGURE 6.16
Photos of local people can look more real, more approachable.

It is useful to have a variety of shots of the same model. In addition, we have experienced situations in which a stock photo that was used for one team's persona was coincidentally used for a different persona for a different team in the same company. We have also seen stock photos for personas show up in magazines and on billboards. "Hey, isn't that our 'Dianna'?"

Instead of using stock photos, locate people who look the part and hold your own photo shoot. Photos of friends-of-friends will look approachable and real (see Fig. 6.16).

Using local, known people for your models means that you will likely be able to get additional photos at a later point if the need arises. If you choose to take your own photographs (which we highly recommend), you should start looking for models the moment you decide on the primary personas. The time-consuming part of this step is finding just the right faces. Each photo session takes about an hour.

If you can't locate your own models or do your own photo shoot for some reason, there are other options. We recommend Web sites such as stock.xchng (http://www.sxc.hu), which share photos by amateur photographers. If you find a photo you like, you can use it for free and can potentially contact the photographer to request more photos of the same subject. If all else fails, you can find good photos of people from pay-per-use online sources. Two good ones available at the time of this writing are http://www.gettyimages.com and http://www.istockphoto.com. There are also free images available from the Microsoft Design Gallery at http://dgl.microsoft.com and photos available at http://www.flickr.com/creativecommons have varying permissions for reuse associated with them.

HANDY DETAIL

Hold Your Own Photo Shoot

To do a photo shoot, start with stock photos that have the basic look you want. Then, ask your teammates and friends if they know anyone that resembles the models in the stock photos. Once you locate a few candidates, have them send a photo of themselves and have your core team evaluate which local model would work best. Then schedule 30 minutes to an hour with each model to do a quick photo shoot (preferably with a digital camera).

You will want your team to see different aspects of your personas. During your photo shoot, make sure you have the model pose in a variety of places – with different expressions and doing different things (talking on the phone, drinking a beverage, working at their desk, getting out of their car, and so on). Choose settings and activities that are core to each persona. Bring your own appropriate props to help make the right statement. Have the model bring a few changes of clothing. You can likely take 100 or more shots in an hour-long photo shoot. If possible, use a digital camera so that you get immediate review of your work. You will need about five to 10 good shots when you are done.

Consider paying your models with gift certificates or perhaps free products or services from your company. Finally, be sure to use an image release form with these models. This short form grants limited use of the images for internal, product development purposes. We recommend that you consult your company's legal representative before using this or any other legal form.

Note that it is critical that you review the details of the agreement on how these photos can be used. Ignoring the terms can get you into trouble. For example, there are collections of clip art (with photos) that say you cannot use more than 100 copies for a particular activity and/or that the use must be for educational purposes (such as passing out slides at a conference). These are normal conditions of the "fair use" clause under copyright law. It might be worth making a copy of the license for your records from whatever sources you use.

Illustrations Can Be an Interesting Alternative to Photos

Consider having an artist generate sketches to represent your personas. Although sketches feel less "real" and may detract from credibility, they do have their place. For example, sketches can keep your personas from being interpreted too literally. Further, you have a lot of control over what the sketches look like, what the personas are doing in the sketches, and so on.

BRIGHT IDEA

Collect Photos from Magazines

Whitney Quesenbery, Whitney Interactive Design, LLC

The photos of people in stock photography books often look too perfect to represent the personas I work with. Instead, I have a box of pictures I cut out of magazines. Family, health, cooking, and fitness publications often have good pictures of many diverse people: old and young and many ethnic backgrounds. They also use a wide variety of settings, including homes, neighborhoods, the outdoors, and work places. This is an easy way of collecting a lot of photographs to use for inspiration in giving your personas a face.

Note: Of course, these pictures cannot be reproduced (by any physical means) or disseminated (by any means, including passing around a folder). Any other use than private reference is illegal.

AUDITION THE PHOTOS AND/OR ILLUSTRATIONS

Hold auditions for proposed photos (or illustrations or models). Let a variety of teammates have a say in what photos or specific models are used for your personas. Doing so will obtain buy-in and should result in more broadly acceptable images. Generally, the selected models should be attractive; not supermodels, but people who have a look that is likeable, approachable, trustworthy, nice, and engaging. In addition, the facial expressions in the photos should be pleasant. These images will likely be around for a long time – perhaps several development cycles. Choose images that are easy to look at and that inspire your team to build great products.

NAME YOUR PERSONAS

The names you give to your personas are important, perhaps on par with the importance of the illustration. In many cases, the persona's name is the one detail that everyone will know and remember. Choose names carefully. There are several simple rules of thumb for selecting persona names:

- Don't use the name of anyone on your team or in your organization.
- Avoid using the names of famous people (such as Cher or Britney).
- Avoid using names that have any negative connotation.
- Do use names that are unique and distinctive.
- Consider building a mnemonic device into the persona names to help people remember them. For example, if you create personas for segments that are already named enthusiasts, ostriches, and neophytes, why not select names that share the first letter of each segment? For example, the enthusiast could be named Eddie, the ostrich Omar, and the neophyte Nanette.

If you need help in coming up with interesting and memorable names, you might look up one of the many baby name Web sites (there are many to choose from). If your personas are different ages, you can also look up popular names for the years each was born.

Consider getting your larger organization involved in the naming process. This serves the purpose of both getting good, agreeable names and getting your organization engaged early with your personas. If you decide to do this, we recommend that you select a set of names for each persona and allow everyone to vote during the birth activities.

CREATE NAME + TAGLINE COMBINATIONS

Generally, we recommend creating a name and tag line together, usually something alliterative. For example, you might have "Toby the Typical Teenager," "Abe the Active Administrator," or "Connie the Conscientious Consumer." Taglines make personas easier to remember and to differentiate. Along the same line, you might consider using a simple quote or job title to bring meaning to the name. You want to highlight a key differentiator/characteristic for each persona. However, be careful not to choose something potentially offensive (e.g., "filing goddess" or "obsessive organizer"). As a check, consider if it would bug you to be have these lines added to the end of your name.

Step 6: Validate Your Personas

You have just spent a lot of time crafting a persona to stand in for the users you researched. Your personas should now be looking and sounding great – full of solid information and complete with illustrative photos and meaningful names. Your stakeholders have reviewed them and you now seem to have the right set of target customers in your focus. But how can you be sure your personas embody the data you worked so hard to collect?

Your personas were likely created from a variety of data sources (primary and secondary sources; some older, some newer, some quantitative, some qualitative) all stitched together by educated guesses, assumptions, and business strategy.

Story from the Field

Descriptive Names and Alliteration Help People Remember Personas

Colin Hynes,
Director of Usability, Staples.com

In hindsight, the personas' staying power can be partially attributed to the naming of each. Although some experts caution against giving personas "cutesy" names such as Sally Sales-Sleuth, we found that it is was critical in keeping the personas in the lexicon over the long term. Many of the senior executives still reference the Sales-Sleuth even though they can't remember the name Sally (they replace Sally with any S-name they can think of, from Sammy to Suzy to Soupy). Although persona writers' feelings may be hurt that the names they spent time carefully crafting are being bastardized, the critical element of the persona is still maintained.

You have pieced together data points that may or may not actually fit together – some of which may not be directly comparable or inherently compatible.

Your goal during validation is to ensure that you did not stray too far away from your data when you made their characteristics specific and concrete and added elements of storytelling. Although it is true that personas cannot and do not need to be completely accurate, you do want to ensure that they reflect the essential information about your target users that you found in your data. If you built assumption personas, you want to ensure that the personas you created really do capture the assumptions in your organization. We discuss five approaches to validating your resulting personas (presented in order of increasing cost and rigor).

- Review your personas against the original data sources.
- Have experts (those closest to your users) review your personas.
- Have representative users of each persona review "their" persona.
- Conduct "reality check" site visits.
- Conduct large sample surveys or interviews.

These five approaches are not mutually exclusive nor are they the only means of validating your personas.

CHECK BACK IN WITH YOUR DATA

Now that you have enhanced your personas with details and narrative, schedule a short meeting with your persona core team. Ask everyone to skim back over the data sources from which the key factoids were derived. If you have transcripts or profiles from qualitative research, we suggest that you focus your review on these. As you skim the original data, ask each core team member to identify any ways in which the completed personas seem to contradict the data sources and decide together whether these contradictions are acceptable. Make appropriate revisions to your personas to ensure they are as representative of the data as possible.

HAVE SUBJECT-MATTER EXPERTS REVIEW YOUR PERSONAS

Consider taking your personas to people who know your target audience. Look for domain experts that have direct contact with your users (or proposed users) and who were not involved in the creation of your personas. These may be sales personnel, product support engineers, trainers or educators, or people who have directly conducted research with your audience (focus group moderators, usability engineers, ethnographers, and so on). If you built your personas to help redesign an existing product, you might have access to people in your company who are very close to your existing user base and can help you validate your personas. For example, you can show your personas to members of the sales and support teams, who should be able to tell you if your personas remind them of the customers they talk to every day. The marketing team can also help you validate your personas, though you should bear in mind that the marketing team's targets may be the purchasers of the product, not the users of the product.

Ask these experts to read the foundation documents and point out things that don't match their experience with these users. Again, make revisions as appropriate to the personas so that they best fit the original data and your experts' observations.

SHOW YOUR PERSONAS TO REAL USERS

Another simple but slightly more demanding way to validate your personas is to show them to the actual people they are designed to represent. For example, if you created a bank teller persona, show your persona to several bank tellers. Tell the real bank tellers that your goal was to create a profile of a typical bank teller and you would like to know if your persona "looks right" as such (see the following Story from the Field). You want to know what aspects of the persona resonate with real people that fall into that category of users.

In our experience, you only need to do this with a handful of people per persona. You will likely find that comments start to significantly overlap after the first three or four reviews. You might consider doing minor revisions after each review so that the next real person sees only the most "true" persona. As you do these reviews and revisions, make sure you are not violating your original data. If there are major conflicts, choose the characteristic you trust the most and note the need to do further research if the discrepancy falls in an area important to your product domain.

CONDUCT "REALITY CHECK" SITE VISITS

A more involved way of approaching persona validation (if you have the time and budget) is to visit people who are very similar to your personas and attempt to ascertain if your personas match your observations. The goal here is to visit users who match the personas on high-level characteristics to see how well they match on low-level characteristics. This goal is the same as with the previous validation technique, but here you are relying on your ability to see how real users actually are and how they behave, not just what they think about themselves and their reflection on their actions. We call these "reality check" site visits. To do this, you will take the steps described in the following sections.

CREATE PERSONA PROFILE SCREENERS

Work backward from your rich persona to a set of characteristics that are essential to that persona. The sketches you started from are likely to be useful here. From this set of characteristics, you will develop questions that can be used to evaluate whether or not any candidate participant is a good representative of one of your personas.

RECRUIT REPRESENTATIVE PEOPLE AND VISIT THEM

Using your new persona screeners, locate several people who are good representatives of each persona. Three to five people per persona should be adequate. Visit those people and conduct a brief observational study and interview in an attempt to determine how well the low-level and peripheral characteristics of your personas match these people. Alternatively, hold focus group sessions with groups of representatives of each persona. Use the outline of the foundation document as a rough script for your discussion sessions. In either of these cases, and in addition to your direct observations, you can also show them personas and get their feedback as you would, using the previous validation technique. With these observations and feedback, revise and refine your personas, being careful not to violate the original research findings that made up your personas. You will likely find that you are simply tweaking bits and pieces of the design-irrelevant details or fictional components of your personas to fit your validation findings.

CONDUCT LARGE SAMPLE SURVEYS OR INTERVIEWS

If you have even more time and resources, you can consider doing a more sophisticated validation effort. Using surveys, you can determine how pervasive your personas are in addition to the existence and coexistence of their attributes. To conduct this research, you will need to identify individual characteristics per persona and translate them into a form that real users can respond to as part of a questionnaire or survey. For example, you might generate a series of statements that respondents can rate (Examples A and B following) or check as appropriate (Example C).

Example A. Rate the following "After-school activity" statements regarding your own behaviors.
   a. I usually watch television after school. (strongly agree, agree, disagree, strongly disagree)
   b. I usually play computer video games after school. (strongly agree, agree, disagree, strongly disagree)
   c. I usually play outside at home after school. (strongly agree, agree, disagree, strongly disagree)
   d. I usually talk on the phone with friends after school. (strongly agree, agree, disagree, strongly disagree)

Example B. Indicate the frequency with which you engage in the following activities after school.
   a. Watching television (frequently, sometimes, never)
   b. Playing computer video games (frequently, sometimes, never)
   c. Playing outside at home (frequently, sometimes, never)
   d. Talking on the phone with friends (frequently, sometimes, never)

Example C. Indicate which of the following activities you engage in regularly after school (check all that apply).
   a. Watch television
   b. Play computer video games
   c. Play outside
   d. Talk on the phone with friends

Analysis of such data can take many forms and can be quite complicated. This can be similar to segmentation or cluster analysis, which you might have started your persona effort from, only now you have target profiles to evaluate the responses against. Your goal is to understand how the characteristics of a broad sample of users relate to the known (or proposed) characteristics of your personas. The details of doing such an analysis are beyond the scope of this book. We recommend that you do not undertake such a validation effort without the involvement of a trained statistician or researcher. Keep in mind, however, that this approach can be greatly simplified by focusing on only a few of the key attributes of your personas. The analysis for this simplified approach can be as basic as comparing a few descriptive statistics (e.g., averages or a series of frequency counts) or doing a correlation analysis. For an example of this, see the following sidebar by Colin Hynes regarding putting real values on your personas.

Story from the Field

Putting Real Values on Your Personas
Colin Hynes
Director of Usability, Staples.com

After a lot of effort went into creating meaningful and valid personas for our development team, and when our final personas were presented to the senior executives, our vice president of marketing commented, "I wish we knew how much each of these personas was worth in bottom-line dollars." This kicked off our "persona valuation project."

The main thrust of the persona valuation project was a joint effort between the usability and marketing teams. After several meetings between the two groups, we decided that data would be gathered through a survey with one simple question tied to the defining quote of each persona. This, of course, put much pressure on the defining quotes to fully encapsulate the essence of the persona. Our hope was that a user would read one of the quotes and immediately see himself/herself in the statement.

Then, we decided on the criteria for distributing the survey, which was simplified: people who had purchased from Staples (any channel) in the last six months, people who had visited Staples.com in the last six months, and people who had an e-mail address. We also decided to offer an incentive ($10 off) to participants, even though the survey was only going to be two questions. One requirement was that we had to be able to link responses to other info in the database for calculation of "value" regarding each respondent.

The invitation started with a subject line explaining, "Get $10 off your next purchase by filling out a quick survey." We sent the link out to 15,000 customers from our database. On the survey page, each respondent was presented with the seven defining quotes and an "Other" option for those who did not feel they bucketed neatly into any of the persona statements. After scrubbing the data, we ended up with 1,048 valid responses.

Upon our initial high-level analysis of the data, we were somewhat disappointed that respondents were fairly evenly distributed across the seven personas. There were some slightly heavier buckets, but all personas garnered between 10 and 20 percent of the overall distribution. The usability hypotheses that two particular personas would dominate the distribution were not supported. We feared that without one or two clear-cut "winners" we would be left trying to serve all personas. Our ultimate concern was that this would manifest itself in a Web site design that tried to be everything to everyone, instead of having focus.

One highly encouraging data point was that only eight of the more than 1,000 respondents bucketed themselves as "Other." This made us feel confident we had nailed the original persona descriptions.

Although the distribution did not give us the clarity we were hoping for, when we matched the responses against 12-month sales figures, the picture became crystal clear. We calculated the percentage of orders, sales, and margin generated for each persona. The figures were an aggregate of all purchases made through any channel. Strikingly, the data showed that two personas that made up a combined 36 percent of the distribution also made up 42 percent of the orders, 53 percent of sales, and 58 percent of the margin (see Fig. 6.17). Further, if we were to map the personas out in a Venn diagram to illustrate overlap in goals, these two personas would have the greatest overlap. Note: We tried to have as little overlap as possible overall in the personas. If we deemed that there was a significant overlap between personas, we combined the personas in the creation process.

It is difficult to overestimate the impact this data had on the future design direction of Staples.com. To ensure accuracy, we reanalyzed the data and obtained the same results. At that point, we knew we had lightning in a bottle. With the inclusive nature of the study and the airtight research design, the results were difficult to dispute.

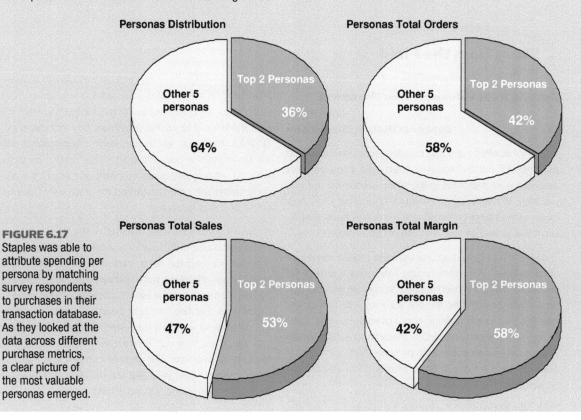

FIGURE 6.17
Staples was able to attribute spending per persona by matching survey respondents to purchases in their transaction database. As they looked at the data across different purchase metrics, a clear picture of the most valuable personas emerged.

VALIDATION IS AN OPPORTUNITY FOR DATA GATHERING

You may have created your personas based almost completely on existing data sources. If this is the case, you are probably missing some of the qualitative information that can inform the narrative surrounding your persona. If you utilized only qualitative information, you might need to understand aspects of your personas related to market size, spending, or other quantitative or domain-specific information. You can organize your validation efforts to serve two purposes: validate the persona details you have developed from your data sources and collect the additional information that will help complete the personas.

As you finished your assimilation exercises and moved on to create skeletons and full personas, you probably noticed some categories of information missing. For example, you may have collected tremendous amounts of data related to a teenager's schoolwork and entertainment interests, but may find yourself with virtually no information about typical family activities and concerns. When you create the narrative for your teen persona, you can:

- Fill in this information based on assumptions
- Return to your clusters, or even your original data sources, to see if there was relevant information you simply didn't use
- Take the opportunity to look for more details as you conduct your validation activities

Before you recruit people to survey or observe toward refining your personas, create a list of the types of information you still need, and use this additional data to inform targeted content areas or to create the narratives and storyline. It is perfectly reasonable to create the data-driven persona details and wait to build additional narrative until you have completed most of your validation activities.

COMPLETED PERSONAS DO NOT MARK THE END OF USER RESEARCH

At the point you finish the creation of your personas, you may be tempted to think that you do not need to further understand (do research) or involve real users in the development of your product. From our perspective, this couldn't be further from the truth. We believe personas are a great starting point for understanding and incorporating user information in the development cycle.

Personas can (among other things) be used to create excellent recruiting profiles for further testing and insight. User testing, focus groups, beta testing, and other methods of involving real users in the process should continue as possible throughout the entire development cycle. Personas can serve not only as recruiting targets for these activities but as a communication device and a repository for new findings. You may find that you need to update your completed personas every six months to a year as your target audience changes, though you must be thoughtful about how you approach this. In other words, even though other activities now take focus, the validation of your personas should continue throughout the persona life cycle.

Story from the Field

Adapting Personas to International Markets

Mina Gharb-Hamil, Sandra da Costa,
Neto Armando Pita
Window International, Microsoft Corporation

Many times, personas are created almost completely from information collected within the country that the development team exists in. Adding international information to personas can help ensure that products will delight customers worldwide. This case study shows how the Windows International Program Managers team (WI PMs) helped the USA-based Windows product development team adapt their target personas as they worked to design and develop a product to suit the global marketplace.

Why Consider Internationalization of Your Personas?

Anthropological, social, economic, cultural, and political uniqueness require a different approach for global markets.

Figure 6.18 presents an example of how PC activities vary among regions of the world. Note that the top activity in the United States, word processing, is not even present on the Latin American list. Consequently, the more attention we pay to these differences when designing products the more appealing the product will be for customers worldwide.

By not understanding how international customers use products, we are missing business opportunities. Look at mobile phones, for example – how can we satisfy our users if we don't consider how our international customers use their mobile phones? In some international markets, almost 100 percent of households have a cell phone versus 71 percent in the United States. Further, pagers were completely discontinued (for several years now) when the second layer of mobile phones started conquering the marketplace (about 1997/1998), whereas in the United States they are still a common means of communication. In international markets, the percentage of mobile phones with Internet access is almost three times higher than in the United States: 16 versus six percent.

For the WI PMs team, the need to adapt personas came from the fact that they were involved in the process of giving feedback to feature specifications for a new product. To test the scenarios against several international market segments, there were two options.

- Create new personas to represent different international markets, probably divided by region. This process would have generated a great variation of new personas from scratch, which would vary a lot depending on the world region with which they were associated. This would have consumed too much time, not to mention that the scenario evaluation would be very complex and the product development team would not have had the proper means of producing a better user profile adaptation for each world region involved.

Comparison of PC activities			
United States		Latin America	
Word processing	66%	Games	49%
Games	53%	School work	49%
Household records	46%	Graphic art and design	31%
Learning devices for children	30%	Household records	21%
School work	28%	Office work at home	21%

FIGURE 6.18
Statistics showing the differences in PC activities between the United States and Latin America.

■ Leverage the personas that already existed. To do this, it would have been necessary to adapt each persona's individual characteristics and habits to each country, consolidating it by ethnographic regions afterward. (An ethnographic region consists of all countries that share similar ethnic and linguistic origins. For example, Latin-speaking countries covered by the WI PM team are all countries in Latin America, as well as French Canada, Portugal, Spain, Italy, and France. Eastern Europe countries are Russia, Hungary, the Czech Republic, Poland, and so on.)

The Adaptation Process

WI PMs are based in Microsoft's international subsidiaries and are responsible for providing accurate and relevant information on local user needs, market requirements, and competitive situations. As natives of the countries they work in, they have the background to understand cultural, social, and political issues.

WI PMs collected the data from a variety of sources, including local market research; corporate customer visits; analysis of how their local friends, family, and colleagues interacted with their computers; and other local country data sources such as the subsidiaries' market intelligence reports and local associations. The process for integrating this data was as follows.

1. We studied the existing personas to have an in-depth knowledge of each. All related material was provided by the personas team, with which the WI PMs worked in very close cooperation.

2. We then selected the U.S. personas that represented the user scenarios they wanted to address, which meant all of those that were already common to international markets in accordance with known research data. Furthermore, special focus was given to the personas representing the Consumer and Enterprise segments.

3. Next, the U.S. personas were compared with the international market data to interpret activities and attributes for each international persona.

4. We then sketched the basic characteristics for each internationally adapted persona (which varied

according to country) and compiled the resulting data for each region.

5. The activities and attributes identified as important to each of the international countries' markets were used to assign a similarity rating. Ratings were assigned as follows: 5 = same as the United States, 4 = mainly similar to the United States, 3 = neutral, 2 = largely different, and 1 = completely different. For example, the similarity rating for the Europe, the Middle East, and Africa (EMEA) teenager persona for online shopping would be low because in most of the countries in that region, it would be illegal for him to shop on the Internet, as a consequence of citizen protection laws being much more strict in Europe than in the United States.

6. We then documented the similarity ratings, all the market data the ratings were based on, and references to the analysis of each country – highlighting all potential opportunities and risks so that everyone on the team could access the information according to their respective regional groups.

7. The resulting feedback was posted for each persona on the WI PMs Web site and incorporated in the Personas Foundation documents in the "International Considerations" section.

At the end of this process, for each U.S. persona, it was possible to identify a corresponding persona for each ethnographic region. One such persona was the EMEA Teenager, for whom there was a special "Overview" section (describing his main characteristics, habits, and daily activities) and a "Differences from the U.S. Persona Macro Analysis" section (containing all items rated largely or completely different from those of the U.S. persona).

Benefits of Using the Adapted Personas

When the development team uses our internationally adapted personas, they can detect which features are important to our international customers. For example, by understanding how the EMEA Teenager uses his mobile phone, the product team would recognize that a communication feature that allows him to send and receive messages to and from his mobile phone, and some Windows components would be very welcome. Or why not go even further and allow him to give instructions to his printer, fax, or any other hardware device via short message service (SMS) through his computer?

The personas can also help teams adapt existing features for upcoming versions of a product. For example, what type of privacy considerations are people around the world expecting from Microsoft? Let's assume that to register a new product, the customer will be asked to send personal information. In the United States, we expect this inquiry and will probably send the requested information. But if we analyze the social behavior of EMEA knowledge worker personas, we find that they are very concerned about privacy and would be upset with Microsoft for asking for their personal information. Conversely, the Latin American knowledge worker personas would gladly provide this information and would even develop a better perception of Microsoft if this data were used to foster a relationship with them.

Conclusions

With this information available to them, product teams should be thinking about how to offer software registration that will address the comfort levels in their various international markets. Writing software adapted to the international markets will surely increase worldwide customer satisfaction toward our products, as users will feel identified with them. This translates into a significant added value. Internationalizing our personas helped to fill this previously existing gap into the most variable user profiles.

HOW TO KNOW YOU ARE READY FOR BIRTH AND MATURATION

You should now have a set of rich, meaningful personas that have been validated against real users. Still, you may be tempted to keep refining your personas until they seem perfect. You may feel hesitant about putting them "out there" for people to see and use. How do you know when you are ready to begin introducing them to your broader team? There are signs that will indicate you are ready. You will notice that the amount of tweaking and reexamination slows down or stops. You may still have some open questions, but you shouldn't have any blank sections in your foundation document that are truly critical to your product domain. The personas will just feel right to you and your core team. In addition, your stakeholders should have signed off on your work. They now agree that no critical audience is missing and that the personas are robust, credible, and in line with your business objectives.

If your creation process took several weeks to several months, it may be that your product planning and design is now underway – or worse, that coding has begun. If so, it is likely that your broader team is becoming eager to obtain information about your target audience. They may be asking for you to deliver your personas ASAP. All these things tell you that you are ready to deliver – that the birth and maturation phase should start. Birth and maturation is the phase in which you not only introduce your personas to the team but begin a persona communication campaign. At this time, you introduce the persona method and other UCD techniques, many of which will directly employ your personas (possibly changing the team's design and development process forever).

SUMMARY

The conception and gestation phase of the persona life cycle involves a great deal of activity, teamwork, and decision making. You have become an alchemist, combining data, assumptions, and your understanding of what will and will not work in your company to create a rich set of design targets. You have translated raw data into information and that information into prioritized categories and subcategories of users. You have created a set of personas that combines fact and fiction to reflect your business priorities and convey the essential information about your target users you found in the data. As much as possible, you have with explicit links to the original data supported every important characteristic and statement found in your foundation documents. Last, you have done validation work before finalizing your personas.

As we have stated several times previously, we believe very strongly that personas should be based on data. Even the perception that the personas are not based on data can damage their credibility and utility. However, it is practically unavoidable that some elements of personas are generated from educated guesses or are simply made up. Your job in the conception and gestation phase is to make informed decisions about how much fiction and storytelling is needed to make your personas feel real and be truly engaging. Creating personas involves straightforward fact gathering, but there is also an art to it. Be inventive, but also be practical and stay as close to your data as possible. Even assumption-based personas can be highly valuable if they are agreed upon and visible targets.

Once your personas are complete, substantive, and stable, you have only just begun. You are now ready to begin the education process. Communicating your personas will take time and effort. You will have to be strategic, persistent, and patient. Once your personas are out there, they will need to actively participate in the design and development process (the adulthood phase of personas). Your personas are ready to be born. Labor can be painful.

HANDY DETAIL

Get Ready for the Birth and Maturation Phase by Cleaning Up

Once you have your personas fully created – pared down, prioritized, with perfect images in place, and details of profiles substantiated and revised with a quick user study – you probably need to do some cleanup work. Make sure you have solid, cleaned-up foundation documents before moving to the next phase (birth and maturation). Make sure you have copies of the reference research materials, including local copies of data you found on the Web (i.e., material that might move or otherwise disappear). Take notes about your specific process, including who did what, when, and how. You will want to have notes on the problems you encountered and the reasoning behind critical decisions made. You might even want to keep records of how long certain activities took. This could be useful for return-on-investment (ROI) measures in the final life cycle stage.

CHAPTER 7

Verify Prototype Assumptions and Requirements

Jonathan Arnowitz, Michael Arent, and Nevin Berger

EDITOR'S COMMENTS

In Chapter 5, Bill Buxton describes the importance of sketching for generating design ideas. Sketching is the beginning of a design funnel with many ideas at the start that get winnowed down to a smaller set of ideas as the product concept evolves. To understand the design issues that will affect the success of a product, you can use a variety of prototypes that include wire frames, storyboards, paper prototypes, interactive simulations, video prototypes, and coded prototypes. Each type of prototype allows you to examine different assumptions that you have about your product concept.

This chapter by Arnowitz, Arent, and Berger from *Effective Prototyping for Software Makers* (2007) outlines how you can use prototypes to validate and extract assumptions and requirements that exist among the product team. The overall goal of prototyping can be thought of as risk reduction. Poor requirements are often a major cause of late products with too many bugs and design flaws. An effective prototyping process can reduce costs and improve customer satisfaction and delight.

"My perspective is that the bulk of our industry is organized around the demonstrable myth that we know what we want at the start, and how to get it, and therefore build our process assuming that we will take an optimal, direct path to get there. Nonsense. The process must reflect that we don't know and acknowledge that the sooner we make errors and detect and fix them, the less (not more) the cost."

Bill Buxton

INTRODUCTION

This chapter focuses on transforming prototyping assumptions and requirements into a prototype design. Before you can effectively prototype, the first important activity is to review the balance of assumptions and requirements, including business/marketing, functional, technical, and usability ones. This review will help you determine whether you need more requirements before proceeding to build a prototype. It is also the point where you and your team can be clear about the assumptions (if any) being used as a basis for a software concept. Prototypes allow these assumptions and requirements to be validated, invalidated, modified, or substituted early in the software process, thus helping you avoid the risk and costs of making major modifications to your design after discovering that the design concept and usability are faulty during the software development stage.

Prototyping can track the assumptions and requirements of the software because of the continuous interplay of testing assumptions against documented requirements until all the assumptions are satisfied and requirements are validated. The nature of prototype iteration makes this interplay necessary. In one prototype iteration, some requirements are validated while new questions arise to be addressed in the next iteration. As often as we have seen only one prototype being produced in an entire software project, we have never seen that prototype provide all the answers. Indeed, the first prototype, as the first visualization of the software, invariably raises more questions about the requirements than it resolves. Similarly, we have also seen a prototype being received poorly, and see whole scale direction changes when only one or two of the key concepts needed changing. By charting both requirements and assumptions, you give your next iteration a basis for keeping what is good (what was validated) and discarding what was bad (what was invalidated).

The remainder of this chapter assumes that you have the basic knowledge of software requirements. It is outside the scope of a book on prototyping to go into the details of requirements gathering; there are plenty of books on this subject already. Refer to the sidebar on requirements gathering if you would like a brief review. The sidebar below is only a brief introduction to requirements; if you are interested in more in-depth coverage of the topic, we suggest Courage and Baxter (2005), Kuniavsky (2003), and Holtzblatt, Wendell, and Wood (2005). If you are also interested in using personas to help drive requirements or to help drive prototyping definition, we would recommend the most complete reference for practical use of personas, Pruitt and Adlin (2006). Chapter 6 in this book is an excerpt from Pruitt and Adlin and covers the creation and early nurturing of personas.

PROTOTYPING REQUIREMENTS ARE NOT SOFTWARE REQUIREMENTS

The basic prototyping strategy advocated in effective prototyping is the practice of basing your prototype design on a mixture of requirements and assumptions. You start with some requirement (even if it is only a vision) and prototype for this requirement based on assumptions. Some assumptions will be validated, others modified, and some others not evaluated. The results are documented, leading to firmer requirements for the next round of prototyping. (See the sidebar on categories of requirements for an example.) This iterative approach eventually leads to many firm requirements and few, if any, assumptions. The rest of this chapter assumes that your requirements come from some legitimate source in the software-making process; in our example, we also ask you to believe that when a requirement is referred to as established, it has been validated through user research, marketing research, technical investigation, or other legitimate means for establishing software requirements.

CATEGORIES OF REQUIREMENTS

In software creation, requirements arise from a number of different sources, such as businesses, market places, end users, customers, and technical opportunities. From the perspective of design and prototyping, requirements can be broken into four main categories: business/marketing, functional, technical, and usability.

Business/marketing requirements define the needs of business or the marketplace. They are generally derived from any combination of the following: market field research, market analysis, competitive analysis, domain expertise, sales force intelligence, and focus groups. The initial product vision is often embodied in these requirements. A typical source for business and marketing requirements is a standard document, usually called a marketing requirements document (MRD), business requirements document (BRD), or a product requirements document (PRD).

Functional requirements define the functionality necessary to support the business or marketing requirements. Similar to business/marketing requirements, functional requirements are generally derived from any combination of the following: field research (best in conjunction with user research), market analysis, competitive analysis, domain expertise, sales force intelligence, and focus groups. Usually, functional requirements are investigated and defined in parallel with business/marketing requirements. Functional requirements are also often identified as a result of user research and usability testing. Because product sales influence these requirements, they often include more functions (i.e., features) than those needed to satisfy the business requirements. For example, a business requirement may require form fill functionality. However, if the software is deployed internationally, it may require multiple language support in which form filling in the Roman alphabet can be functionally different from form filling in other languages, such as Asian languages based on ideograms. Functional requirements are usually found in a formal document, often called a functional requirements document or other functional specification document. Functional specifications are typically reflected in a prototype.

Technical requirements define the technology needed to implement the required functionality. Functionality can often be compromised by the immaturity, prohibitive costs, or unavailability of a required technology. Technical requirements are generally derived from any combination of the following: technology research, technical analysis, competitive analysis, technology expertise, sales force intelligence, and other similar means. Technical requirements are sometimes articulated in a formal specification, such as a technical definition document, but they can also be found in company-specific technology architecture documents or platform-specific guidelines, such as the Windows User Experience Guidelines or the Macintosh OS X Human Interface Guidelines.

Usability requirements define the user experience and usability requirements needed for user adoption of the software. They are generally derived from any combination of the following: user research, task analysis, competitive analysis, domain expertise, sales force intelligence, customer support intelligence, design and prototyping, usability testing, and other related means. Usability requirements, in conjunction with the other requirements described earlier, are transformed into user interface specifications, which are often embodied in high-fidelity interactive prototypes.

When prototyping, not all (or any) of the above-mentioned requirements may be available or in a form that is helpful for prototyping. Therefore, it is important to share the prototype with key requirements stakeholders to ensure complete coverage. For business requirements, it would be best to seek out product management and marketing as these stakeholders. For functional requirements, a domain specialist or anyone who has conducted user or market research can provide input. For technical requirements, either a lead architect or software engineer can provide critical input. Usability requirements can come from user research, task analysis, prior similar experience, and usability validation of your design. However, despite coming from individual experts, all these requirements still need to be validated holistically because software is never merely a sum of its requirements. Requirements may have unwanted side effects that, before creation of the final product, only a prototype can expose.

TRANSFORMATION OF ASSUMPTIONS TO REQUIREMENTS

To illustrate a typical course for converting assumptions into requirements through prototyping, we have outlined how requirements are first elicited as assumptions. These assumptions are then iteratively tested in a prototype. A prototype is completed in rounds of iterations until all the high-priority assumptions are validated into requirements. Per available time and resources, this is the process of validating prototype directions to the extent allowed by a given prototyping method that enables an iteration to proceed to the next step. The entire process is a repeatable series of three steps: gather, inventory, and prioritize.

To begin these three steps for transforming assumptions into requirements, you need to have the requirements necessary for proceeding with the development of the prototyping schema.

Step 1: Gather Requirements

(See sidebar on prior pages for some potential sources.)

The prototype team should not undertake an entire requirements-gathering process, which needs to be quite thorough; instead, it is assumed here that the software requirements-gathering process is occurring in parallel and is incomplete. So the gathering done here is just the current state of the requirements, as they are known at this moment. Depending on your stage in the requirements-gathering process, the list can be short and vague in the beginning to quite long and detailed at the end. After these requirements are gathered, enter them into Worksheet 7.1, which will look something like this.

WORKSHEET 7.1: Requirements

Project Name:

Project Date:

Product Name:

Current Phase: Design

Prototype Name:

Requirement Name (Examples)	Type	Priority	Validated? Y/N	Results	Requested Changes

This worksheet lists requirements for time-management software. The requirements are currently coming from two sources: an MRD and a presentation of a wireframe sketch to a group of stakeholders.

INFORMAL PROCESS TIP

There are formal processes for software product development in almost every software company. These processes guide you through the development process and help you determine at what stage (usually extremely early) you can change requirements and when they should be frozen (usually very early). By taking the inventory of requirements suggested in Step 1, you immediately discover how far you have progressed in the software development process. Are all the requirements known and worked out? Have they been validated? If so, you should be in the later stages of the process.

If the list remains short and vague, regardless of where the company believes they are in their own development roadmap, they are still in the early stages of the software-creation process. The more vague and general the requirements, the more they are open to interpretation and completion with nonvalidated assumptions. Too often in the software process, design and creation are crammed into the later stages when there is little time available for prototyping and validation, thus leading to high-risk software development.

As a general rule, the more you base software on assumptions, the higher the risk. Conversely, the greater degree that software is based on validated assumptions, the lower the exposure to risk.

Step 2: Inventory the Requirements and Assumptions

WORKSHEET 7.1: Requirements [Example]

Project Name: Time Out

Project Date: Dec 2007

Product Name: Time Out Time Management for All

Current Phase: Design

Prototype Name: T55

Requirement Name (Examples)	Type	Priority	Validated? Y/N	Results	Requested Changes
User must be able to enter time worked by week. MRD-Use Case 1.2	Functional		Y 31 DEC 2005	1207minutes.doc	Add ability to change project code for previous entries
User wants to optionally enter project Information	Usability		N		
User wants Excel interface	Usability		N		
Time summary reports for managers	Business		N		
Project reports for project managers	Business		N		
Time entry reports for employees' own data	Business		N		

List the state of each requirement. Make note of each requirement's origin (preferably linked to the related document). You can usually judge by its source whether a requirement is validated or just an assumption. If the requirement is validated, note when it was validated. As contradictory or complementary requirements arise later, it may become necessary to challenge old requirements that have fallen back into assumptions. You may, at any point, reclassify a requirement as an assumption if you believe that it has not been adequately validated or has been invalidated in light of newly introduced developments.

The sample worksheet lists a requirement already validated through an MRD for a time-management application and includes a link to the wireframe and the meeting minutes of the wireframe presentation. The validation also uncovered a new assumption that users may also need to enter project information. It is listed as a direction because the assumption came from a wireframe presentation, so it is a little firmer than just a mere assumption. We know there is a need to enter project information but have no idea yet as to how. If the analysis reveals that other assumptions are hidden in a requirement, they can be fleshed out in this worksheet. For example, the requirement states time entered by week. This requirement may have additional dimensions. Maybe time needs to be entered by a configurable time period? Or maybe just by week or month? The worksheet helps to list explicit new assumptions as well as the firm requirements. Finally, the worksheet shows an assumption that users want to use an Excel-like interface because the program they are currently using has a similar interface.

Step 3: Prioritize Requirements and Assumptions

The resulting worksheet from Step 2 is shown below. The last step in transforming assumptions into requirements is their prioritization. The priority refers to the priority for inclusion in the prototype, not priority for implementation in the software. Given that the first prototype is a storyboard, some requirements that are very important for the software are not the main concern of the prototype.

WORKSHEET 7.1: Requirements [Example]

Project Name: Time Out

Project Date: Dec 2007

Product Name: Time Out Time Management for All

Current Phase: Design

Prototype Name: T55

Requirement Name (Examples)	Type	Priority	Validated? Y/N	Results	Requested Changes
User must be able to enter time worked by week. MRD-Use Case 1.2	Functional	High	Y 31 DEC 2005	1207minutes.doc	Add ability to change project code for previous entries
User wants to optionally enter project information	Usability	High	Planned		
User wants Excel interface	Usability	Medium	N		
Time summary reports for managers	Business	High	Planned		
Project reports for project managers	Business	Medium	N		
Time entry reports for employees own data	Business	Medium	Planned		

REQUIREMENTS AND THE BIG PICTURE

Figure 7.1 shows how prototyping requirements all fit together holistically in the software creation process. We demonstrate how assumptions are essential to the prototyping process by tracing the diagram. Only when all the major assumptions are satisfied should the prototyping end.

ITERATION 1: FROM IDEA TO FIRST VISUALIZATION

In the first prototype iteration, the product (or the function or new addition to the existing product) is just an idea in a product manager's or business analyst's mind. Working interactively with a designer or by sketching the idea

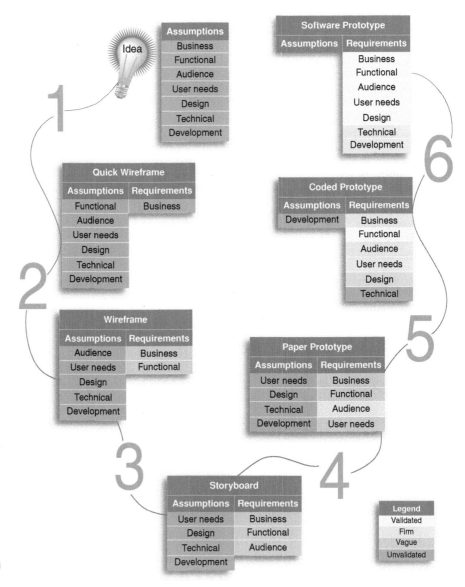

FIGURE 7.1
Step-by-step conversion of assumptions to validated requirements.
Note: The levels of gray show how refinement continues throughout the process; the darker the background, the less (if any) validation used.

out themselves, some of the assumptions can be visualized. This visualization provides a vague idea of the business value (i.e., is the idea worth pursuing?).

So even a quickly developed prototype can validate assumptions by providing visualizations to realize an idea. The visualization itself can communicate the value of proceeding to the next step in the process: working out the idea even further and validating its companion requirements. Figure 7.2 illustrates how a simple wireframe can be used to test assumptions and ideas about business, functional and other requirements and turn those assumptions into solid requirements. Also, through visualization some competing assumptions can make an idea less desirable, thereby invalidating the business requirement.

The travel and expenses reports example shown in Fig. 7.3 seems like a plausible idea to the stakeholders. Starting as just an idea for travel reporting, the visualization provided the product manager with the idea of a new assumption: adding normal expenses in addition to travel expenses. The visualization of this new assumption has not uncovered any undesirable effects, so the project proceeds to the next step: working out the wireframe depicted in Fig. 7.3 to make other assumptions clearer.

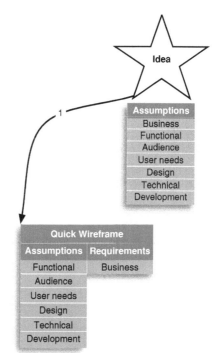

FIGURE 7.2
First iteration from idea to a quick prototype transforms business assumptions to firm requirements.

FIGURE 7.3
Quick wireframe for a travel and expense reporting software.

ITERATION 2: FROM QUICK WIREFRAME TO WIREFRAME

The second round of iterations is performed similar to the first prototype iteration. Assumptions and requirements are prototyped to either validate or invalidate them as shown in Fig. 7.4. Through this second round, the requirements worksheet becomes more complete and the direction of the product becomes clearer.

With the creation of the more refined wireframe shown in Fig. 7.5, the business case is not only a little clearer but also the functions needed to support this business case have become clearer and better reflected in the buttons and navigation visible in the wireframe.

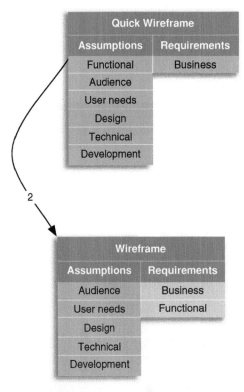

FIGURE 7.4
Second round of iterations verifies more requirements and makes other assumptions clearer.

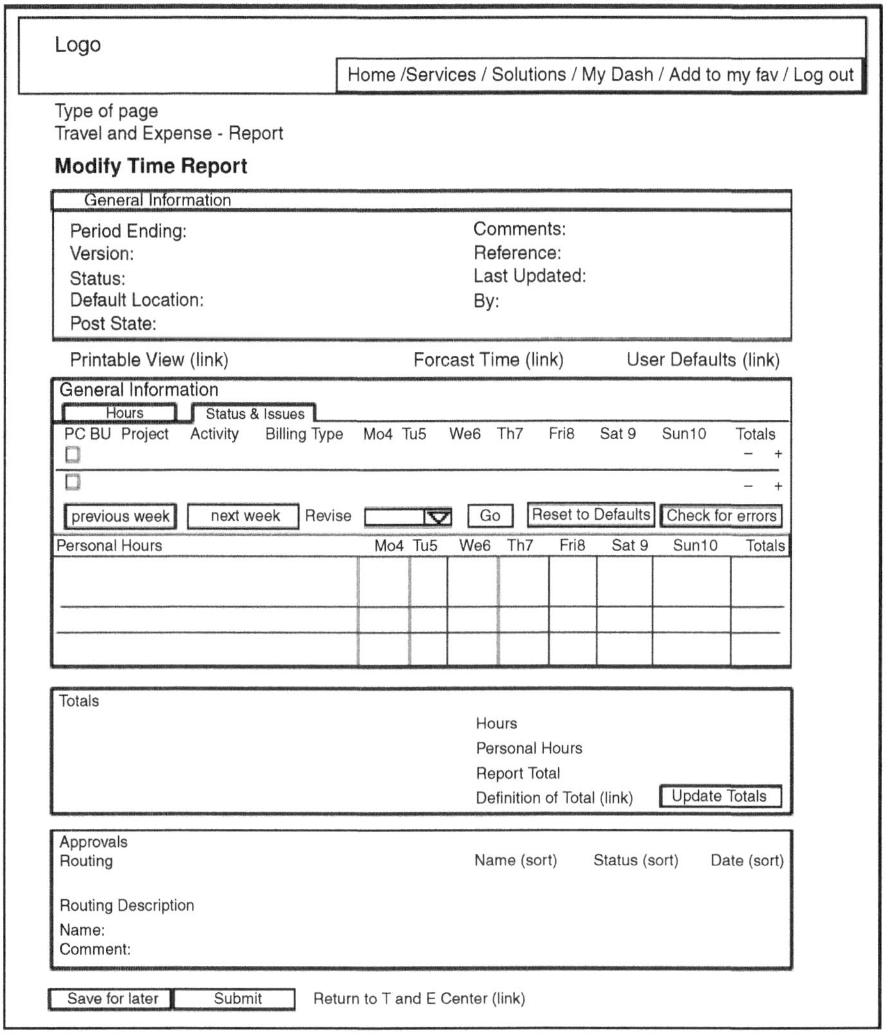

Logo

Home /Services / Solutions / My Dash / Add to my fav / Log out

Type of page
Travel and Expense - Report

Modify Time Report

General Information

Period Ending:	Comments:
Version:	Reference:
Status:	Last Updated:
Default Location:	By:
Post State:	

Printable View (link)   Forcast Time (link)   User Defaults (link)

General Information

Hours   Status & Issues

PC BU Project	Activity	Billing Type	Mo4	Tu5	We6	Th7	Fri8	Sat 9	Sun10	Totals
☐										− +
☐										− +

previous week | next week | Revise [▽] | Go | Reset to Defaults | Check for errors

Personal Hours	Mo4	Tu5	We6	Th7	Fri8	Sat 9	Sun10	Totals

Totals

Hours
Personal Hours
Report Total
Definition of Total (link)   Update Totals

Approvals
Routing

Name (sort)   Status (sort)   Date (sort)

Routing Description
Name:
Comment:

Save for later | Submit | Return to T and E Center (link)

FIGURE 7.5
A wireframe showing more functional assumptions of the product.

ITERATION 3: FROM WIREFRAME TO STORYBOARD

By using the recommended Worksheet 7.1, we see a definite increase in end-user-focused requirements when we get to the storyboard phase, which attempts to tell the story of the software in context. During this phase, new requirements will surface and other user requirements can be validated. For example, in the storyboard picture shown in Fig. 7.7, the end user does indeed need to track his project budget, validating not just optionally entering project data in the time report but also the need to have a project time report for the end user.

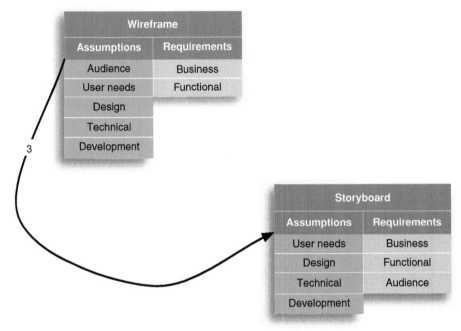

FIGURE 7.6
End-user's focus in requirements becomes visible as a result of a storyboard prototype.

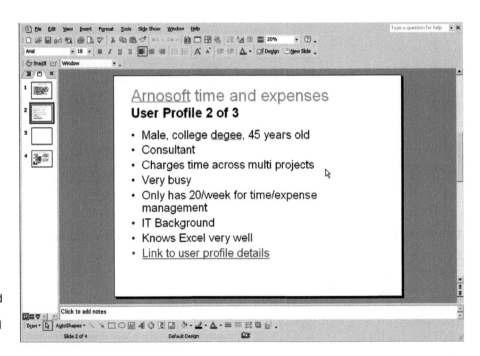

FIGURE 7.7
Storyboard showing validation of the need to enter project data for an archetypal end user.

ITERATION 4: FROM STORYBOARD TO PAPER PROTOTYPE

As the prototypes progress and the audience shifts from internal to external stakeholders, requirements start to be validated quickly, especially with direct user contact. Designer "requirements" about the audience suddenly become much clearer, and user needs becomes much more tangible as illustrated in Fig. 7.8. In the paper prototype shown in Fig. 7.9, the assumption is that an Excel-like interface failed miserably in usability testing. It invalidated an assumption of the end-user needs and replaced it with a new model that fits better but will still need verification (not pictured).

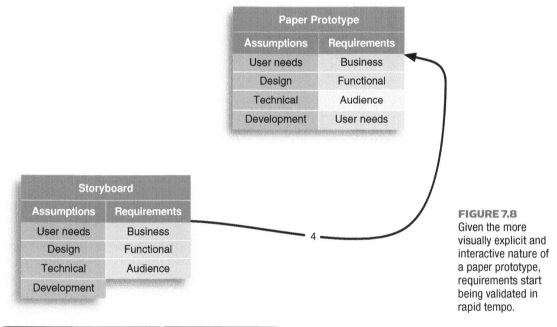

Paper Prototype	
Assumptions	**Requirements**
User needs	Business
Design	Functional
Technical	Audience
Development	User needs

Storyboard	
Assumptions	**Requirements**
User needs	Business
Design	Functional
Technical	Audience
Development	

4

FIGURE 7.8
Given the more visually explicit and interactive nature of a paper prototype, requirements start being validated in rapid tempo.

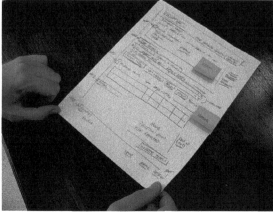

FIGURE 7.9
An interactive paper prototype.

ITERATION 5: FROM PAPER PROTOTYPE TO CODED PROTOTYPE

In the last stages of prototyping, many open design and technical questions can be answered. The required functionality, the audience, and the business case are already firm (see Fig. 7.10) and no longer the source of focus. Now, a high-fidelity prototype like the one shown in Fig. 7.11 is used to firm up the remaining requirements and design details.

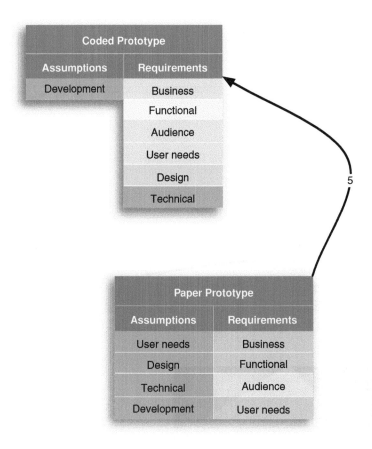

FIGURE 7.10
Late high-fidelity prototypes come closer to resembling a software product as well as the requirements.

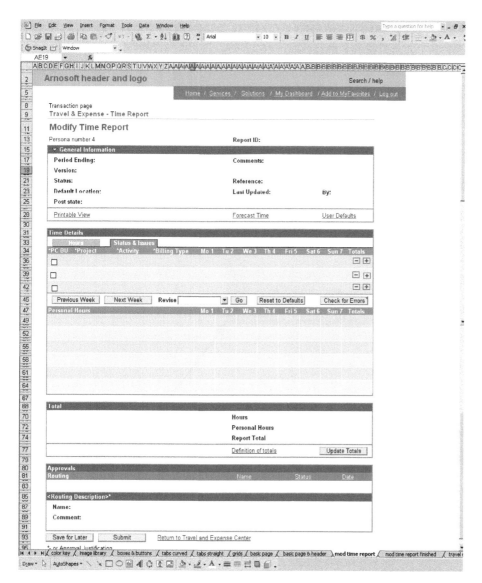

FIGURE 7.11

Late prototypes resemble the real software as the requirements become firmer, and more advanced prototype development can take place with greater confidence.

ITERATION 6: FROM CODED PROTOTYPE TO SOFTWARE REQUIREMENTS

In the last step, specifying the requirements from a late high-fidelity user-facing prototype (here in the form of a coded prototype) enables us to, finally, say that we have validated all the software requirements (see Fig. 7.12). The worksheet that was the basis for evaluating the prototype requirements could now almost double for a table of contents or central reference point for the software requirements. So the journey from the interplay of assumptions and requirements is now complete with the final product shown in Fig. 7.13 ready to ship; prototyping has been the primary aid in validating assumptions and transforming them into requirements. Although, it is important to note that prototyping has been an aid, not the sole source of requirements validation, such as focus groups, usability testing, market research, and competitive analysis.

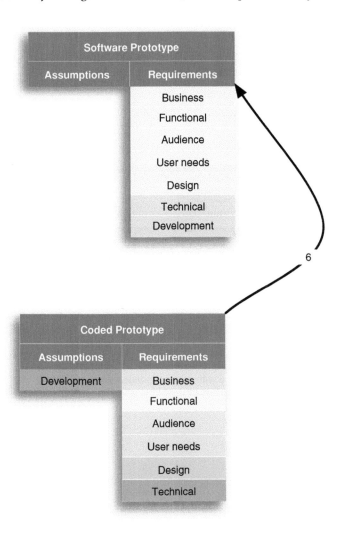

FIGURE 7.12
Only at the end of the prototyping process do the assumptions finally give way to concrete data to base the software creation and development.

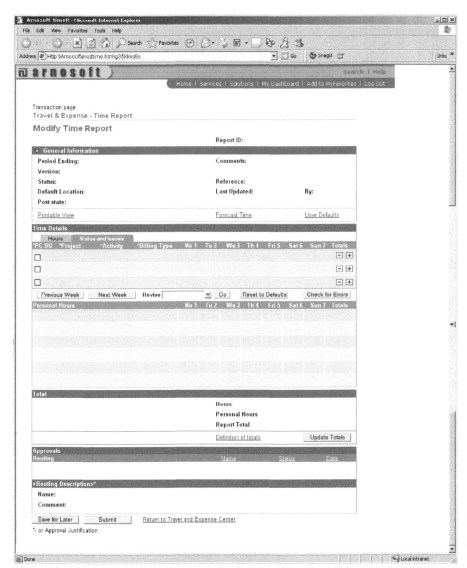

FIGURE 7.13
The final end product
for time entry at the
end of the project.

SUMMARY

We reviewed requirements setting for prototyping as the first step toward collecting prototype content. We have seen that prototyping requirements try to come as close as necessary to the actual business, functional, technical, and usability requirements. However, a prototype also has the flexibility to be based on assumptions. In fact, prototyping can be used to play with assumptions while being gradually turned into concrete validated requirements. For this validation, a worksheet template supports the three-step process:

Following this validation process and using the worksheet template, you can be assured that your prototype will address exactly the right assumptions and requirements your team judges to be important. The worksheet, with the prioritization of requirements and assumptions, also helps others understand what they should and should not be looking for when reviewing your prototype.

PART 3
Designing Your Site

CHAPTER 8

Designing for the Web

Debbie Stone, Caroline Jarrett, Mark Woodroffe, and Shailey Minocha

EDITOR'S COMMENTS

In the user experience world, design guidelines are recommendations about the look and feel of Web sites and applications that product teams are asked to follow. Guidelines are often combined with standards to create a style guide. One of the most common requests of user experience designers is to develop a set of guidelines and create a style guide for the following purposes:

- Improve consistency within and across products or services. A common assumption is that improved consistency will lead to better usability because users will learn an interaction style in one Web site and then leverage that learning across the other sites.
- Promote good design across the different product groups. A common scenario is that senior managers at companies get complaints that different sites or applications "look like they were built by different companies." Then there is a mandate to improve consistency through a style guide.
- Capture design knowledge to help new designers learn about prior design decisions when they join a group.
- Provide a common user interface language. Guidelines and style guides often define common labels and names for objects (for example, "radio button" versus "option button").
- Improve reuse within the design and development groups. A common goal for style guides is to reduce the cost of development by recommending common components and reducing the number of ways that teams do the same thing differently.

Guidelines and style guides are not effective unless they are accompanied by a process for publicizing and ensuring compliance, a difficult process that requires support by all levels of management.

This chapter provides core design principles and guidelines for the creation of Web site and detailed tips and examples on how to apply these principles and guidelines.

INTRODUCTION

Organizations and individuals around the world are developing Web sites. The good design of a Web site is essential for its success, as a user only needs to select the back button on the browser to leave the site – possibly never to return. Thus, as a designer, you need to create a site that is usable and useful, providing content and functionality that are of value to your users.

In this chapter, we look at five aspects of Web design.

- Design principles for Web sites: These are based around the mnemonic HOME-RUN, which stands for **H**igh-quality content, **O**ften updated, **M**inimal download time, **E**ase of use, **R**elevant to the user's needs, **U**nique to the online medium, and **N**et-centric corporate culture.
- Designing Web sites: We consider how to structure a site so that it is easy to navigate; users need to know where they are, where they have been, and where they can go.
- Designing home pages and interior pages: We consider the differing requirements of the home page and interior pages.
- Design issues for Web pages: We look in more detail at a variety of issues, including the layout of Web pages and designing for different screens and platforms.
- Writing the content of Web pages: In particular, we consider the inverted pyramid writing method that is used by journalists.

TIP
For more details of HOME-RUN, see Nielsen (2000).

At the time of the dot-com boom around the end of the 1990s/early 2000s, the Web was changing so fast that it seemed almost impossible to offer advice to people who were designing Web sites because it might be out of date in a day or two. Now we see a slightly slower pace of change. On e-commerce sites in the United States in 1998, there was little consistency: for example, you would have had to click on "order list" (http://www.qvc.com) or "shopping cart" (http://www.amazon.com) or hunt to a lower page (http://www.gateway.com) to see your purchases. Today, all these sites have a "shopping cart" linked directly from the home page – and most users expect to find a shopping cart or shopping basket when they are buying things online. Now that the pace of change is less rapid, we hope that the advice in this chapter will be helpful for some time to come.

In this chapter we include a progressive example based around the Web site for a hotel booking service. This only represents a single pass through the design process. In reality, you would iterate a number of times, involving the users throughout, using prototypes to check the developing design. We also include screen dumps from a variety of Web sites. These sites may have been redesigned if you visit them. This does not matter, as it is the design issues that count.

THE LOVELY ROOMS HOTEL BOOKING SERVICE

The Lovely Rooms hotel booking service is the example we have created for this chapter. You will find some gaps in the specification and you will need to make assumptions to fill the gaps.

Domain

The Lovely Rooms hotel booking service specializes in finding rooms in small, privately owned hotels in the East of England (Essex, Suffolk, Norfolk, Cambridge, Hertfordshire, and Bedfordshire). The hotel may be described as a bed and breakfast, an inn, or may be part of a pub, but we will call them all hotels for the moment. This is a semirural, somewhat old-fashioned part of England and the hotels are mostly in traditional buildings. Most of them only have two to five rooms to let, and the hotel owners do all the work in the hotel themselves including all the cleaning and cooking as well as the financial aspects and publicity.

Users

Lovely Rooms has identified three target groups of users:

- Vacationers planning to visit the East of England from overseas who want to find a uniquely British experience that they cannot get through a standard chain hotel
- UK residents who are visiting the area for an occasion such as a wedding or class reunion and want to take advantage of the lower rates offered by small hotels
- UK business travelers who are bored with the sameness of the big hotels and want the more personal experience offered by a small, privately owned hotel

All users will have a reasonable degree of computer literacy, otherwise they would not be surfing the Internet. However, they may be using the Internet in a relatively unsophisticated way, perhaps simply to find the telephone number of a hotel in the right area.

Tasks

Lovely Rooms would like the Web site to provide various services for customers, including the following:

- Recommend a choice of three hotels geographically nearest to a location specified by the user that have availability for the nights required ("Find a lovely room")
- Offer special rates and discount packages if the hotel chosen has one available ("Special offers")

- Allow the user to book the room online either through Lovely Rooms or by contacting the hotel's own Web site directly ("Online booking")

Environment

Because Lovely Rooms wants to appeal to busy business travelers, the booking service has specified that the site must be easy to use, even if the user is interrupted or in a noisy environment such as a busy open-plan office. Other than that, Lovely Rooms assumes that its users might be in any type of environment: home or office or even another hotel room.

Technology

Similarly, each user might have a different computer configuration. However, Lovely Rooms is assuming that some users, especially UK residents looking for a bargain, will have relatively low-specification PCs and will be using high-priced UK telephone lines and a slow modem. This means that the Web pages should be designed to download as quickly as possible.

Conceptual Design

The content diagram is based on a number of concrete use cases that are not included. It is only a small part of the conceptual design, focusing on the customer who wants to look at the details of hotels that are available. We have deliberately kept this simple so that the exercises do not take you too long.

- Primary task object: Hotel.
- Attributes: Hotel type (bed and breakfast, purpose-built hotel, converted older property, traditional inn or pub, restaurant with rooms); number of bedrooms; location; and special features.
- Actions: Browse through hotels; search for a hotel near a particular location.

Figure 8.1 illustrates a simplified section of the corresponding content diagram. The main container links to the sequences of containers that correspond to each of the primary tasks.

- Metaphors: To help users who are not very familiar with the geography of the region, results from a search will be shown on a map as well as in a list.

DESIGN PRINCIPLES FOR WEB SITES

Before we start looking at some more specific guidelines, you should be aware of a number of key principles. We have grouped these according to the HOME-RUN acronym defined in Nielsen (2000).

High-Quality Content

The content of your site is critical. If you do not provide the information or functionality that your target users want, they may never visit your site again. If your Web site sells, say, cars, and it does not include key information such

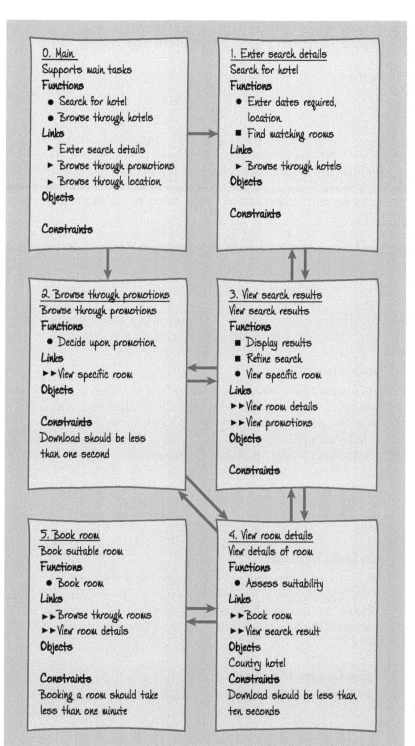

0. Main
Supports main tasks
Functions
- Search for hotel
- Browse through hotels
Links
▶ Enter search details
▶ Browse through promotions
▶ Browse through location
Objects

Constraints

1. Enter search details
Search for hotel
Functions
- Enter dates required, location
■ Find matching rooms
Links
▶ Browse through hotels
Objects

Constraints

2. Browse through promotions
Browse through promotions
Functions
- Decide upon promotion
Links
▶▶ View specific room
Objects

Constraints
Download should be less than one second

3. View search results
View search results
Functions
■ Display results
■ Refine search
- View specific room
Links
▶▶ View room details
▶▶ View promotions
Objects

Constraints

5. Book room
Book suitable room
Functions
- Book room
Links
▶▶ Browse through rooms
▶▶ View room details
Objects

Constraints
Booking a room should take less than one minute

4. View room details
View details of room
Functions
- Assess suitability
Links
▶▶ Book room
▶▶ View search result
Objects
Country hotel
Constraints
Download should be less than ten seconds

FIGURE 8.1
A section of the content diagram for the Lovely Rooms hotel booking service.

as current prices, availability, optional extras that can be selected, and delivery times, potential car purchasers may be disappointed and shop elsewhere.

Often Updated

Most sites need to be updated regularly. The frequency of the update will vary according to the nature of the site.

- A news site will probably need to be updated several times each day.
- A site selling washing machines will only need to be updated when there is a price change or a new model is added to the range, making a weekly update sufficient.
- A personal site will be updated when the owner feels that a change is necessary.
- An archival site, such as the records of meetings of a town council, will be added to (when the next meeting is held), but the older pages will need to stay as they are or at least keep the same addresses (URLs).

The importance of the updating process to the users varies according to the site. For example, the content of an online encyclopedia is likely to remain relatively unchanged, and updates will not be the main reason for most users to visit the site. In contrast, a news site will be visited because it is up to date.

Minimal Download Time

We will be talking about download time in more detail later in this chapter. However, most of us have experienced frustration at slow-to-download Web pages that contain large and unnecessary graphics or irritating animations. Such sites are likely to be unpopular with users, particularly those using slower dial-up connections or trying to connect from mobile devices.

Ease of Use

Users need to be able to find the information or services they need quickly and easily.

Relevant to User's Needs

In addition to having good content, your site must allow the users to carry out the tasks they want to perform. For example, if a user is choosing a car, it should be easy to compare the features of different cars on the same screen. You should be imaginative about the way in which the users will want to use the information on your site.

Unique to the Online Medium

Why use a Web site? Most companies have some expertise in developing publicity leaflets. If this is all you are using your Web site for, maybe you should just use a leaflet. Web sites should provide some additional benefits.

Net-centric Corporate Culture

The company behind the Web site needs to put the site first in most aspects of its operation. It is not enough to pay lip service to the technology. With the competitive international environment that currently exists, a good Web site could be the difference between success and failure.

DESIGNING WEB SITES

We are going to look at three specific areas of designing a Web site

- How the Web pages are structured in relation to the tasks the users want to carry out and the natural organization of the information
- How to tell users where they are
- How to help users navigate around the site

Designing the Web Site Structure

You are probably studying this book in a linear manner. An alternative approach would be to study the book in a nonlinear manner, jumping around the text.

The concept of nonlinearity has been implemented in many software systems.

It is usually referred to as *hypertext*. Hypertext is a network of nodes (often implemented as separate screens containing text, images, and other screen components) that are linked together. The Web is a hypertext system made up of a huge number of pages that are linked together in a very complex way. This means that you can surf the Web in different ways, visiting sites, and then moving on to new ones as you wish.

> ### EDITOR'S NOTE: WEB SITES MIX HYPERTEXT AND APPLICATION FEATURES
>
> Web sites are often a mix of hypertext and application functions. You can click on a link that takes you to an application within the Web site. Software as a service (SaaS), for example, can combine traditional hypertext models with application features like in-place editing, drag and drop, carousels, and dynamic querying. When you are designing these hybrid sites with embedded applications, see some useful design studies by Fowler & Stanwick (2004), Scott & Neil (2009), Shklar & Rosen (2009), and Vora (2009).

For more information on hypertext, see Nielsen (1990).

This approach is extremely flexible, but can be confusing for the user. Some Web sites are made up of hundreds or thousands of pages. Such sites may have developed over a number of years in a chaotic and unplanned manner. This can make it difficult for users to form a mental model of the site structure; hence, it is easy for them to lose track of where they are and become disoriented. For this reason, it is important for the site to be clearly structured. The most common site structure is some form of hierarchy, with the home page as the root node.

Some corporate Web sites are organized around the structure of the organization. This can be useful if you work for the company; thus, it can be suitable for intranets, but it can be confusing for an outsider.

The site structure should always support the tasks that the target users will want to complete. This can be difficult to achieve because, however good your requirements gathering is, it is difficult to anticipate every user requirement. For this reason, it is important to make the process of accessing the site as flexible as possible. That is why many Web sites allow you to search the site as well as to follow the links.

When you are designing the structure of a site, it can help to look first at the natural organization of the information. For example, Fig. 8.2 represents a fairly standard approach to classifying books. This classification can be useful for structuring a Web site to sell books. In fact, you could create a Web page for each node in this classification. However, it is often not this simple, as you need to consider the following points.

- *How deep and how wide should the hierarchy be?* As Web pages can be slow to download, it is irritating to have to move through too many pages to find the information you want. It is often better to have a structure that is broad rather than deep. If we were to translate every node in Fig. 8.2 into a Web page, this would produce a deep structure. However, if we were to have a very shallow structure, with every book linked to from the home page, then the home page would be extremely long. Thus, we need to achieve a compromise.
- *Is it better to divide a block of information into several short pages or leave it as one long page?* The advantage of having a single page is that the user does not need to keep waiting for pages to download. However, the original download will take longer. Longer pages also allow the user to read (or print out) the whole page, which can be more convenient than having to jump around. A general rule of thumb is this: if the Web page is less than two ordinary printed pages long, then it is probably better to leave it undivided. In a bookselling Web site, it is unlikely that the readers would want the details of a particular book to be spread over several Web pages, as these details naturally belong together and the readers may want to print them out.
- *Can several Web pages be combined into one larger one?* This is the complement of the previous issue. In a bookselling Web site, it would be possible to put the details of several

FIGURE 8.2
Organizing the book information.

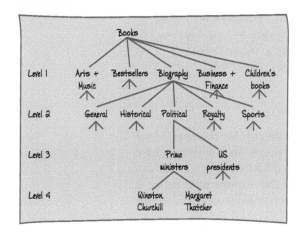

books on a single Web page. For example, the details of all the biographies of Winston Churchill could be on a single page, the details of all the biographies of Margaret Thatcher on another, and so on. This would remove the need for one layer in the hierarchy. It would also mean that the reader could browse through all the biographies of a particular person more easily.

- *Does the structure of the site reflect the structure of the tasks the users want to carry out?* For example, a user who just wants to see what is available will probably want to browse, whereas a user who knows what he or she wants will probably want to carry out a search. For browsing, the structure of the data will need to be reflected in the structure of the site, but this is not necessary if the users know precisely what they want. For example, if the users of a bookselling site knew precisely which book they wanted, then it would be possible to just have search facilities on the home page and no explicit hierarchy. In reality, such sites would probably want to cater for both browsers and searchers, so both approaches would be used.

- *How should the site content be grouped?* We have already discussed the natural organization of the site content, but this is not enough. In the bookselling example, as well as pages about books, we will need a page providing information about the company, another set of pages for book reviews, and so on. One way of deciding how to organize these pages in a meaningful way is to use card sorting (see Chapter 3 in this book).

Figure 8.3 illustrates one way of structuring the pages in a bookselling Web site. In Fig. 8.3 there is one page for each of the level-one categories from Fig. 8.2. These pages contain brief summaries about the level-four categories. These summaries then link to the corresponding detailed descriptions. For example, the biography page would contain a list of all the people whose biographies are available. These details would link to the detailed descriptions of the biographies of the particular person. Thus, the structure in Fig. 8.3 omits levels two and three of the book hierarchy. We are assuming that the number of level-four categories is quite small, otherwise the level-one category pages would become very long. If there were lots of level-four categories, then we might do better to keep all the layers shown in Fig. 8.2.

FIGURE 8.3
A possible structure for a bookselling Web site.

It is common to have additional links, such as links that are related by topic within the hierarchy. For example, the Winston Churchill page could be linked to the Margaret Thatcher page, as they were both prime ministers of the United Kingdom. This means that a reader who is generally interested in biographies, but more particularly interested in the biographies of former prime ministers, can browse through them more easily. We have chosen not to illustrate such links, because

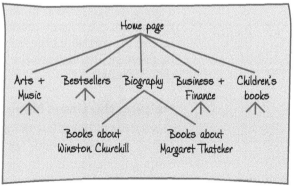

the structure can quickly become complex and rather confusing. However, you should be aware of the need to have a flexible navigational strategy. It is rarely adequate to only be able to move around the hierarchy level by level.

RECOMMENDED READING

Developing an information hierarchy, or "information architecture" for a large site is outside the scope of this book. We recommend Morville & Rosenfeld (2006).

The hierarchical structure of Web sites often breaks down when the user is booking or purchasing something. At this point it is common for the user to be stepped through a linear sequence of pages that collect all the necessary information. On a bookselling site, these pages typically request information about the delivery address, method of payment, and so on. The same design issues arise here: should all the information be requested on a single Web page, or should it be divided into several? In what order should the questions be asked? As ever, the design should reflect the requirements of the user. For example, if the user enters most of the information and then discovers that he does not have the appropriate credit card, he is likely to be very frustrated – it would have been better to warn him about the acceptable cards earlier in the interaction.

Helping the Users Know Where They Are

It is quite common for users to jump directly to a page within a Web site without passing through the home page. How are they supposed to know where they are? The answer is that you have to tell them by clearly labeling each page. The most common way of doing this is by including the organization's logo in the top-left corner, along with the name of the site.

Even moving within a Web site can be confusing. Have you left the site, moved to a subsite within the same organization but with a different subbrand, or moved to a linked site from another organization? For legal or branding reasons, some organizations have strict rules about how they handle this. For example, some sites insist on opening other sites in new browser windows. Other sites rely on a small disclaimer near to any external links. Some, especially blogs, make no mention of the move to another site but rely on branding of the target site to inform the user about the change. Table 8.1 lists techniques for informing users that they are leaving your site and some of the advantages and disadvantages of each technique.

Helping the Users Navigate around the Site

Three types of link allow the user to navigate around a site: *structural navigation links*, *associative links*, and *"See Also" links*.

- Structural navigation links: These form the underlying structure of the site. They point to other Web pages within the site.

Table 8.1	Advantages and Disadvantages of Ways of Informing Users That They are Leaving Your Site	
Technique	**Advantages**	**Disadvantages**
Opening a new window	Clearly shows that it is a different site Preserves the user's location in the originating site	User cannot use the Back button to return to the originating site. May disorient users who are using accessibility options such as screen readers or enlargers
Putting a disclaimer near the external link	Doesn't mess up the use of the Back button Warns users that they are going to the external site but does not force them to locate a new window	Some users may fail to see the disclaimer. Text of the disclaimer takes up space. Negative wording of the disclaimer may undermine confidence in the originating site.
Relying on branding of the destination site	Minimizes the disturbance to the user: the Back button continues to work and users do not have to locate a new window.	Users may not notice that the destination site has new branding or is from a different organization, so they may be confused about where they are.

- Associative links: When a page is particularly long, it is common practice to have associative links that connect to fixed places on the page. For example, there may be a contents list at the start of the page, with each list item being an associative link that points to the corresponding section further down the page.
- "See Also" links: These point to the other Web sites. They are often of particular value to users as they enable them to explore related sites. This can be useful if your site is not quite what the user was looking for. Links of this sort also provide an endorsement for the site being pointed to, so you have to be careful which sites you choose for your "See Also" links: an inappropriate link may reflect badly on your site.

Text is often used to represent links. You should consider the following questions when you use text links:

- *What color should text links be?* At one time, most sites stuck to the convention of saturated blue underlined text like this for links. The color then changed to purple or red after the link had been selected. Now we have learned that Web sites that look good are also more trusted and are perceived as easier to use, so many designers use a variety of cues to indicate a clickable link that they consider to fit within the overall impression of the Web site. When choosing your colors and styles for links, make sure that your choices are distinctive and consistent so that users can tell where the links are ("Provide consistent clickability cues," Guideline 10.8, http://www.usability.gov/pdfs/chapter10.pdfs, 2009), and make sure that the link changes in a consistent way once the user has visited it ("Designate used links," Guideline 10.7, http://www.usability.gov//pdfs/chapter10.pdfs, 2009).

- *How do you make the names of the links meaningful to the user?* As with the choice of command names in menus, it is important to make the wording of text links meaningful to the user. For example, one of our team of authors recently visited a museum site that had a link called "Visiting?" in the navigation bar and another link called "What's on?" It was not at all clear what the difference was between these links, nor what might be found by following either of them. It helps if the wording of a text link closely reflects the users' goals. Thus, for the museum site, it turned out that "Visiting?" led to a page with the directions to the museum, so a link title like "How to find us" would have been more appropriate.

You may wish to consider alternatives to text links:

- Buttons or selectable graphical images: The use of buttons is consistent with graphical user interfaces (GUIs), so your users will probably be familiar with them. Selectable graphics can be more of a problem, and research has shown that they have a relatively low success rate. If there is a selectable graphic with text by it, most users will select the text. You also need to consider the needs of visually impaired users who may be using a screen reader: the selectable graphic will be invisible to the screen reader unless it has a text label.
- Drop-down lists: With these lists, options are chosen from one or more list boxes and the required page is identified according to these choices. This approach tends to be less usable, as the available options are invisible until the list is selected. Also, unlike text links, the list items do not indicate when the particular page has been viewed previously. This makes it even more difficult for the user to develop a mental model of the site. However, list boxes do take up less space than multiple text links.

Users feel more confident in their use of the Web site if they can predict what lies behind a link before choosing it. Here are some factors to think about when picking the text for the link:

- *Should you provide additional information about what the user will find when he or she follows the link?* Figure 8.4 illustrates how small pieces of text can be used to give a flavor of the material that will be found by following the link. This stops users from wasting time jumping to pages that are of no use to them. How often have you followed links with names like "More info" only to be disappointed? As a designer, you want to ensure that the users' expectations of the pages being linked to are satisfied.

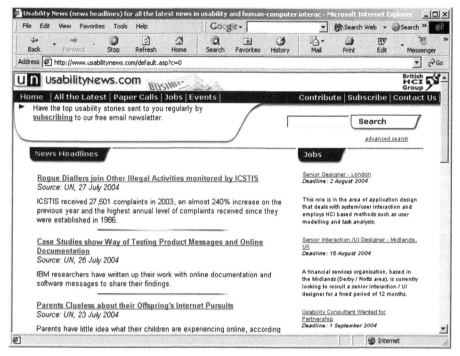

FIGURE 8.4
Augmenting links
with explanatory text.
(From http://www.
usabilitynews.com,
retrieved on July 29,
2004.)

- *Should you use link titles?* These are pop-up boxes that appear when the mouse pointer is over the link. They are particularly useful when there is insufficient room on the page to include additional information. Types of information they can contain include the name of the site being linked to, a summary of what the page contains, how it relates to the present page, and any potential difficulties, such as needing to register at the site.

Navigation Aids

Links are often combined into *navigation aids*. These provide users with an overview of the site structure and enable them to move around the site. Here are some useful navigation aids:

- Site map: Many sites offer a site map showing the site hierarchy condensed onto a single page (e.g., Fig. 8.5).
- Breadcrumb trail: In a breadcrumb trail, every level in the hierarchy from the top to your current position is listed from left to right. You can see this mechanism across the top of the Web page in Fig. 8.6, starting with "handbags" and finishing with "fabrics." In this way, it shows you both where you are and where you have come from. Every level is selectable, so you can move around very quickly.
- Geographical or visual maps: Links are contained within a visual metaphor. Figure 8.7 illustrates the use of a map to navigate a site; the user

FIGURE 8.5
A typical site map. (From http://www. latimes.com/services/ site/la-about-sitemap. htmlstory, retrieved on July 2, 2004.)

finds out about the different parts of Ireland by selecting the appropriate part of the map. If you take this approach, it is important to include textual labels that can be read by screen readers, so that the site may be used by the visually impaired. This metaphor can, however, increase the download time for a page.

- Navigation bars: Figures 8.5 through 8.7 all have variants of *navigation bars*, all of them in the L shape that is currently popular. The bar across the top can be shown visually as a simple list (as in Fig. 8.5), a single line of tabs (as in Fig. 8.7), or even rows of tabs (Fig. 8.6). At one point, Amazon.com had several rows of tabs but they turned out to be too confusing, and most sites now try to stick to a single row. The vertical bar is on the left-hand side in all of these examples, but it could be placed at the right if that seems to work better stylistically. Generally, the simpler styles (such as in Fig. 8.6 or Fig. 8.7) work better than the complicated multipurpose styles such as in Fig. 8.5.

- Drop-down lists: Some sites with large quantities of links use drop-down lists of associated links to organize them into sets while saving space. There is an example in Fig. 8.7, where the relatively long list of Irish counties has been compressed into a single drop-down list. This works best when the links in the list really are parallel, such as the counties, and where users really are likely to only want one of them at a time.

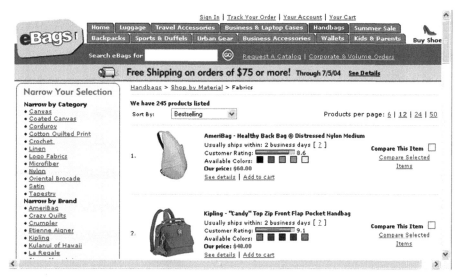

FIGURE 8.6
An e-commerce site with a typical breadcrumb trail. (From http://www. ebags.com, retrieved on July 2, 2004.)

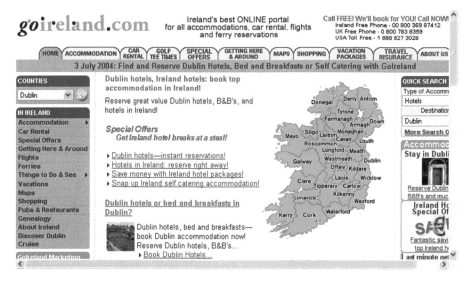

FIGURE 8.7
A geographic map exploits physical geography to organize links. (From http:// www.goireland.com, retrieved on July 2, 2004.)

DESIGNING HOME PAGES AND INTERIOR PAGES

We are going to look in detail at the two types of pages found on most Web sites: the home page and the interior pages. The home page is typically the first page you come to and the one to which you keep returning. The home page usually corresponds to container zero in the content diagram. Interior pages are those that you move on to after you have left the home page, but you have not left the site.

Designing the Home Page

Because it sets the scene for the whole site, the most challenging Web page to design is the home page. The home page has two main functions:

- It tells the users where they are.
- It tells the users what the site does.

How you achieve these functions varies greatly from site to site. However, most sites include some, or all, of the following items:

- The name or logo of the organization that owns the site. This is usually in the top-left corner. Unless your organization is as well known as Coca Cola or you wish to be obscure for stylistic reasons, it is usually a good idea to include a *tagline*, a few words of text that describe what your organization does.
- The name of the Web site. This is usually at the top of the screen. It should also be in the title bar for the browser window.
- A brief introduction to the site
- Some sort of navigation aid
- A summary of the latest news, promotions, or changes to the site. This is particularly useful for repeat visitors.
- A summary of the key content for first-time visitors
- A search facility. This should help the experienced Web users to find the information they need quickly (and is welcomed by less experienced users if your design fails to get them to their destination quickly).

An important part of telling the users where they are also involves making decisions about the choice of typeface, colors, and page layout.

We have chosen three contrasting home pages, all from Web sites owned by the CNN part of AOL Time Warner to illustrate different styles. These are all news sites and are likely to change rapidly, so you may want to look at the sites as they are today and compare them with our screenshots. The first one, Fig. 8.8, is the international edition of CNN's Web site. The majority of the page is filled with a big variety of links to different categories and types of news stories.

Figure 8.9 is a typical *splash page*, a Welcome page that exists to welcome the visitor and give minimal information about the brand.

Figure 8.10 has a style somewhere between the restrained, rich-link style of Fig. 8.8 and the minimalist, splash page style of Fig. 8.9. Much of the page is used for big, brand-driven images relating to specific facilities on the site.

Designing Interior Pages

Interior Web pages tend to have slightly different characteristics to the home page. Typically, they contain more content and less introductory and navigational information. It is important that they help orient the user, so it is still necessary to have information such as the name of the site and the company logo, but these perhaps should be smaller and less intrusive.

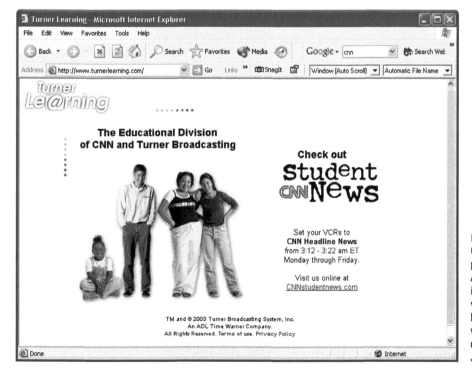

FIGURE 8.10
Contrasting home pages: a news site aimed at high school students. Much of the page is about branding and directing the visitor to one specific feature, the "weekly rewind." (From http://www. cnnstudentnews.cnn. com, retrieved on July 3, 2004.)

You should always include a link to the home page, as this will provide the necessary background information about the site. This is particularly important if the interior page does not contain the site navigation bar. It is also common to contain links to the other pages at the same level in the hierarchy.

Figures 8.11 and 8.12 show two interior Web pages, corresponding to the home pages illustrated in Figs. 8.8 and 8.10. Both the interior pages continue the design of the home page, but they simplify it so that the user can concentrate on the specific topic of the page.

DESIGN ISSUES FOR WEB PAGES

When you are designing Web pages, there are some basic principles and guidelines that you need to consider.

There are also a number of additional issues that you need to take into account when designing a Web page. We discuss some of the more important ones next.

Widgets on Web Pages

Web pages are a form of GUI and increasingly use a similar range of widgets. The issues we introduced in the section on the Lovely Rooms Hotel also need to be considered when you are using widgets on Web pages.

FIGURE 8.11
An interior page.
(From edition.cnn.
com, retrieved on
July 4, 2004.)

FIGURE 8.12
The same story
referred to on a
different site. (From
cnnstudentnews.cnn.
com, retrieved
on July 4, 2004.)

FIGURE 8.13
A home page that needs scrolling. (From http://www.candlemaking.org.uk, retrieved on July 6, 2004.)

Scrolling

The most important content should be visible without scrolling. Web designers talk about positioning content *above the fold*, a term taken from newspaper design. Broadsheet newspapers are displayed folded in racks, so the stories above the fold are the only ones visible to the potential purchaser. Similarly, the Web content above the fold has to sell the site to the visitor. There is a risk that readers will miss content that falls below the fold. Figure 8.13 illustrates a home page that requires scrolling to see important information, such as the purpose of the site and the internal links. The text does imply that the user needs to scroll down.

At one time, the phrase "users don't scroll" was frequently quoted as a design guideline, for example, in the 1996 column by Jakob Nielsen located at http://www.useit.com/alertbox/9606.html. However, since then users have become more adept in using the Web and designers have become more sensitive to the benefits and problems of longer Web pages. Recent advice has been more user-centered. For example, Koyani, Bailey, and Nall (2004) noted:

Guideline: Make page-length decisions that support the primary use of the Web page.

Comments: In general, use shorter pages for homepages and navigation pages, and pages that need to be quickly browsed and/or read online. Use longer pages to (1) facilitate uninterrupted reading, especially on content pages; (2) match the structure of a paper counterpart; (3) simplify page maintenance (fewer Web page files to maintain); and (4) make pages more convenient to download and print.

Scrolling horizontally, across the page, continues to be very unpopular with users as it interrupts the flow of reading on every line. Try to ensure that either the text wraps to the user's screen size or the line length is less than the anticipated screen size. Also, if the line length is more than about 60 characters (8–12 words), this will affect the legibility of the text.

Designing for Different Screens and Platforms

In conventional GUIs, it is possible to control the precise appearance of the screen. This is not possible for Web sites. Therefore, it can be difficult to completely address the scrolling issue. For example, the user may be viewing the site using a small screen on a handheld computer, which requires scrolling around extensively to find anything. Similarly, a visually impaired user may be using much larger type sizes, which means that both horizontal and vertical scrolling are almost inevitable.

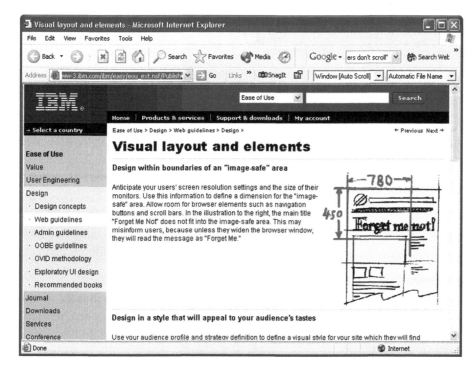

FIGURE 8.14
Important information
outside the image-
safe area. (From IBM
Ease of Use Web
Design Guidelines,
taken from http://
www-3.ibm.com/ibm/
easy/eou_ext.nsf/
Publish/602 on July 6,
2004.)

A partial solution is to ensure that the most important information is at the top-left of the screen. It is also useful to anticipate the typical screen size and resolution. This will enable you to specify *an image-safe area*. This is the area of the Web page that you assume will be visible to most users. Even this is not ideal, as those users with the appropriate screens may be viewing the page through a window that is smaller than the maximum screen size.

The maximum image-safe area will always be smaller than the size of the screen, because of tool bars, scroll bars, and other components of the browser window. For example, if your users mainly have 1024 × 768 pixel screens, then the image-safe area will be about 849 pixels (width) by 507 pixels (height) averaged across operating systems and browsers.

Figure 8.14 shows an example of what can happen if the important information on the screen does not fit into the image-safe area. In this case, the message "Forget me not!" will be read as "Forget me."

Another approach that is sometimes suggested is to have variants of your site. For example, you may have a variant designed to be accessed by users with handheld computers or mobile telephones, or a text-only variant aimed at people who prefer to avoid the download times associated with graphics or who are using a screen

TIP
The site http://www.
alistapart.com often has good articles
on designing flexible layouts.

reader. Unfortunately, some organizations have failed to maintain their variant alongside the main version or put promotions and special offers solely on the graphic-laden site, so text-only variants have become somewhat discredited. If you do opt for a variant-site policy, then make sure you put as much effort into maintaining it as the main site – and you may well find that it is less effort to design a single site that works flexibly and accessibly.

If you like want to maintain many different browsers, then http://www.thesitewizard.com/webdesign/multiplebrowsers.shtml says how to do it (visited May 16, 2009).

You should always try out your Web site on different browsers and operating systems to see what it really looks like to your users. A variety of commercial services will do this for you so that you do not have to maintain dozens of different combinations. These services come and go, but one that was flexibly priced and offered free trials in the summer of 2009 was http://www.browsercam.com.

Using the Screen Area Effectively

How often have you waited for a page to download only to find that it contains mainly advertisements, menu bars, and white space? White space can be useful for emphasizing the structure of information, and it is quick to download. However, users are interested in the content, so having so little can be frustrating. Ideally the content should represent at least 50 percent of the screen.

As with all aspects of the user interface (UI), no design is perfect. It is always necessary to make compromises. However, if the user has downloaded the site to access the content, then he or she expects to see it, so you need to make it worthwhile.

Improving the Download Time

Web sites are widely used to disseminate images, animations, sound clips, and video clips. Pages also often include Java and other types of code. The inclusion of any of these media will result in a page taking longer to download. Nielsen (2000) recommends that, to avoid the user's concentration being interrupted, Web pages need to download in less than one second. He also recommends 10 seconds as a compromise download time, because this is about as long as a user will wait without getting distracted by other thoughts or tasks.

For modem users, a download time of one second or less rarely happens, but it is a realistic target for users who have access from their office, as most offices have much faster Internet connections. Thus, the download time of your page depends on the users who are accessing it. You should aim to make the download time of your site acceptable for your particular users, which may involve making compromises over its content. It is interesting to note that many of the most frequently used Web sites are visually simple and fast to download.

The Web site in Fig. 8.15 uses white space and small images to convey a strongly design-led, artistic impression while keeping the download time short.

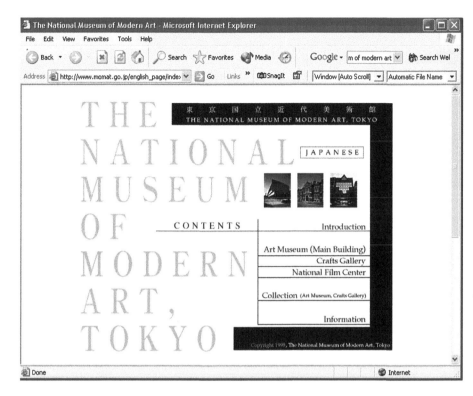

FIGURE 8.15
A Web site with a lot of white space. (From http://www.momat.go.jp/english_page/index_e.html, retrieved on July 5, 2004.)

The one in Fig. 8.16 is apparently similar in its design, but it takes much longer to download due to the presence of a flash animation and larger images.

When including larger files such as images, flash animations, or sound, you need to ask yourself: Is the benefit worth the extra download time? If not, it might be better to make them smaller or remove them altogether. It may be that the aesthetic effect that you want justifies the extra time. Or it may be that the user experience is much better. For example, sound will clearly enhance a site that sells CDs, as it will allow potential purchasers to listen to clips from the CD they are thinking of buying. However, having a continuous backing track to a site that provides information about a local tourist destination is unnecessary and irritating. It is often best to make the download of sound optional. Many users keep the sound switched off; if you use sound on your site, it is therefore a good idea to flag this visually, so that the user can opt to switch on the speakers.

If you need to include media that may take some time to download, it is courteous to warn your users, preferably telling them how long the download might take. Your visitor can then make an informed decision about whether to select the link.

As Web site managers hope to get repeat visitors, it makes sense to ensure that pages are built up on the screen so that header and navigation information is

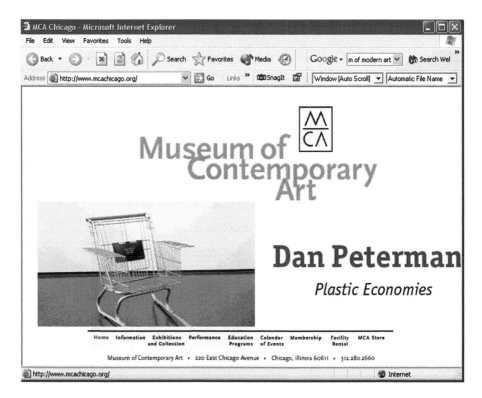

FIGURE 8.16
Similar Web site, much longer download time. (From http://www.mcachicago.org, retrieved on July 5, 2004.)

displayed first. The repeat visitor will then be able to select the required option without needing to wait for the graphics to download. This is also helpful for people using screen readers, as the text will be read before the images are in place.

Using Style Sheets

It is important for your site to have a consistent visual appearance. One way of achieving this is to use a *style sheet*. Style sheets also allow you to change the appearance of the whole site with relative ease. Thus, if you decide that the typeface used for titles should be changed, you simply alter the style sheet rather than changing every title by hand. A style sheet helps create the visual identity for a site. Style sheets are widely used in books, magazines, and newspapers. How do you know if you are reading the *Washington Post* newspaper? Probably because it looks like the *Post*, rather than like *USA Today* or the *Wall Street Journal*.

The Web site http://www.csszengarden.com has many designs that all appear different but are in fact the same content presented with differing style sheets. In Fig. 8.17 we have chosen four examples.

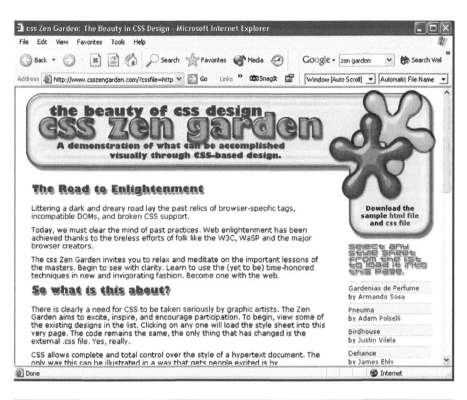

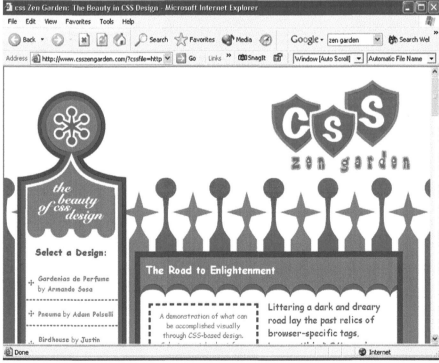

FIGURE 8.17
Styling with CSS (a) "No Frontiers!" by Michal Mokrzycki; (b) "Snack Bar" by Jay Wiggins Style (from http://www.csszen-garden.com, visited July 6, 2004).

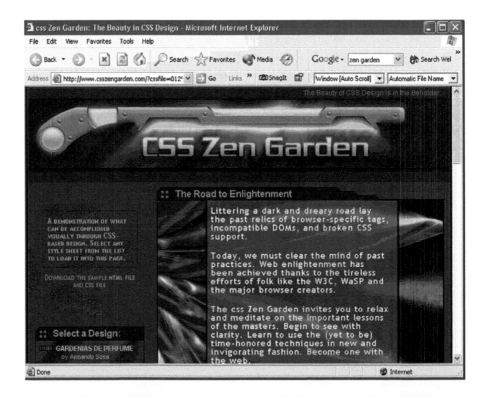

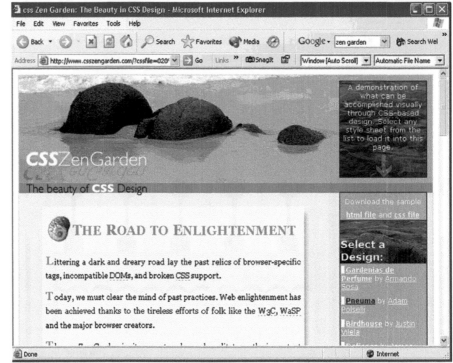

FIGURE 8.17
(c) "TechnOhm" by Josh Ambrutis, and (d) "Friendly Beaches" by Sophie G (from http://www.csszengarden.com, visited July 6, 2004).

A thoughtfully designed implementation of style sheets has great benefit for some users, especially people with impaired vision, if the design allows the user to override the style sheet with one that is more suitable for their needs. You will undo all your careful work in creating your style sheet if you then apply styles directly within the HTML markup.

Designing for Accessibility

The Web can provide tremendous benefits, but only if it can be accessed. Designing for accessibility has two parts: working within the appropriate guidelines for accessibility and ensuring that your design process includes users with disabilities. The World Wide Web Consortium's Web Accessibility Initiative describes how to decide whether your Web site conforms to their Web Accessibility Content Guidelines at http://www.w3.org/WAI/eval/Overview.html, and a big selection of tools that help you to do it is listed at http://www.w3.org/WAI/ER/existingtools.html.

Generally, going back over an existing Web site to amend it to conform to appropriate guidelines is a tedious and error-prone approach. Writing it to conform to the guidelines in the first place is much more likely to succeed.

WRITING THE CONTENT OF WEB PAGES

Even ugly, hard-to-navigate Web sites may still be successful if they have good enough content. When you go to see an action film, you may enjoy the explosions and other special effects but, if there is no plot, it soon gets boring. The same applies to Web sites: even though they may look impressive, if there is no content of interest to the users, then they will not revisit the site.

It is common for Web sites to contain a lot of text. This is partly because text is easy to handle and partly because English-speaking countries tend to be text-based societies. Good writing is good writing irrespective of the medium, but frequently we find that moving text to the Web brings its deficiencies into sharp focus.

The following guidelines will help you to write good content:

- Keep text to a minimum. You should probably include only about 50 percent of the text you would include in print form.
- Enable users to scan the text to pick out important points.
- Divide long blocks of text into separate sections.

We now look at each of these guidelines in more detail.

Keep Text to a Minimum

Most users do not enjoy reading long sections of text from the screen. This is largely because screen resolution is much lower than the resolution of paper. In time, this limitation will probably be overcome, but for the moment we find that many people prefer to print out anything that is longer than a couple of screens of text.

Thus, when you transfer the information to a Web page, aim to reduce the amount of text by about 50 percent. Perhaps surprisingly, this is often quite easy to achieve:

- Introductions are often difficult to write, and some writers take a long time to get going. Try deleting the introductory paragraphs and see whether they were really necessary.
- Make use of numbered or bulleted lists and tables to organize the information while also removing words.
- Check whether the text actually adds value from the user's point of view. "Marketese" and "waffle" are especially unpopular on the Web and may reduce the credibility of your Web site.

As you are likely to have a range of users, possibly from different countries, it is best to keep the language simple and to avoid jargon. Also, humor does not always cross cultures very well. Generally it is best to keep your content concise and factual. At the very least, you should ensure that your spelling and grammar are correct. Poorly checked Web sites can put users off completely, as they imply a lack of professionalism and care.

Journalists are taught an approach to writing called the *inverted pyramid method*. The idea behind this approach is to start by writing a brief conclusion and then slowly add detail. Thus, even if readers skim, they will still get the main points. This also meets the needs of users who are resistant to scrolling down the Web pages.

Help Users to Scan

Readers, in general, tend to scan and skip when they are on the hunt for the material that interests them. One reason for this is that users are often very busy, and there may be other sites that will meet their needs just as well. Thus, users want to establish if your site is the right one for them as quickly as possible. If it takes too long, then they may give up and move on.

The following guidelines will help you write text that can be easily scanned:

- *Use headings and subheadings as appropriate.* These help clarify the structure of the content. It is also useful for visually impaired readers with screen readers. For example, a site that sells books may have headings that indicate the different categories of books the user might be looking for.
- *Use meaningful headings that explain clearly what is in the section.* For example, a site selling computer-based products should not have a heading like "Other Gizmos" as this is not very clear – gizmos might be computer based, or they might not be. If, say, cell phones and personal organizers are the actual "gizmos" the term represents, then a better heading might be "Cell Phones and Personal Organizers."
- *Include bulleted and numbered lists.* Like this one!

- *Highlight and emphasize important issues and topics.* Links can help with this, as they make the linked words stand out. Avoid underlining normal text; because underlined text often indicates a link, users could become confused.

TIP

For more information on how people with visual impairments read Web sites, see Theofanos and Redish (2003), also available from http://www.redish.net/content/papers.html.

The wording of links is very important. It is quite common to see links like this: "For more information on link types click here." When you scanned this page, your eyes probably picked out the words "click here" because they look different. This is not very useful when you are scanning to get an overview of the page content, and it is especially unhelpful if you are using a screen reader to listen to the links, on their own, without the surrounding content. It would be better to write this as "Link types: more information." Users can then pick out the phrase "link types" when they scan the page. Putting the most helpful part of the link first ("link types") also helps people using screen readers, as many of them like to listen to just the first part of the link.

Dividing Long Blocks of Text into Separate Sections

Long blocks of text are difficult to read, so it is better to split such blocks into sections. These may either be on the same page and accessed by associative links or on separate Web pages. Splitting text is often done in a rather clumsy way, with pages being linked by buttons that say "Next Page." This is not very helpful, as it means the users still have to read all of the text and wait for pages to download at regular intervals. It also makes it more difficult to move around the text. In this situation, it might be better to have a long page containing associative links. This will have the additional benefit of allowing the users to print out all of the text so they can read it in the bath, on the bus, or wherever they want. A better approach is to split the text into chunks, each relating to a different topic.

SUMMARY

In this chapter, we have considered a variety of issues relating to the design of Web sites. In particular, we have considered the structure of a site, the design of individual pages, and the writing of content. As an illustration, we have looked in detail at an ongoing example based on a Web site for a hotel booking service. It is important to remember that in an actual design, you would carry out an iterative process, probably changing your design prototypes several times and involving the users at all stages to check the developing design.

PART 4

Evaluation, Analysis

CHAPTER 9

Final Preparations for the Evaluation

Debbie Stone, Caroline Jarrett, Mark Woodroffe, and Shailey Minocha

EDITOR'S COMMENTS

This chapter lays out important roles, procedures, and documents that you need before you begin your evaluation session with the participants. The best practices in this chapter are highly recommended for all facilitators, whether new to the field or a veteran of many years. One best practice described in this chapter is to prepare a script to ensure some consistency and rigor during the evaluation session. Some facilitators feel that a script is unnecessary, but this overconfidence can lead to errors and bias. Sometimes a single word can change how a participant reacts during a session. The same is true for pilot tests – they are essential for getting the bugs out of the test plan. You'll find useful checklists, tips on facilitation, and sage advice in this chapter.

INTRODUCTION

We are almost ready for an evaluation session. This chapter first describes the various roles and responsibilities of the evaluation team and then lays out essential activities (see Table 9.1) that include the following:

- Creating rules for observers
- Developing a script to ensure consistency across sessions
- Developing required forms (informed consent and nondisclosure agreements (NDAs)
- Planning a pilot test to check out the hardware, software, tasks, and procedures

Best practices and templates are provided so that you don't have to start from scratch.

Table 9.1	Final Preparations for the Evaluation	
What happens In a User Observation	**Your Strategic Choices**	**Preparations That May Be Needed**
You start by welcoming the participant and explaining the purpose of your evaluation and their role within it. Check that the participant is happy to continue, and ask for their consent on your planned use of the data you obtain.	What is the purpose of the evaluation?	Book the location.
	Which users will you choose?	Recruit participants.
	Where will you do the evaluation?	Assign roles for evaluators.
	What data do you need to collect?	Prepare briefings for evaluators.
		Create evaluation script.
		Create consent form.
		Create pretest interview plan or questionnaire.
If you are testing a commercial product before it is released, you may need to ask the participants to promise not to divulge anything they learn about the product during the evaluation. If you are testing an early prototype or partly developed system with defects, then you may need to ask the participants to avoid certain parts of it.	What product, system, or prototype are you testing?	Create nondisclosure form.
		Prepare the system or prototype.
		Check that you can do the tasks with the system or prototype.
You then proceed to the main part of the session: asking the participant to complete one or more tasks using your system, while you observe and record what you see.	What tasks will you ask the participant to try?	Create task descriptions.
		Create data collection form.
		Prepare technologies for data collection.
		Create forms for data analysis and interpretation.
Once the tasks are complete (or your time is up), you can ask the participants for their views on the experience in another interview or by asking them to complete a posttest questionnaire. The session closes with your final thanks for their help, possibly including an incentive.	Are there any specific concerns or questions that you want to ask the participants about?	Create posttest interview plan or questionnaire.
		Obtain incentives.

ROLES FOR EVALUATORS

For an evaluation session, you may be the sole person involved and therefore have to do everything. If other members of the team are also participating in the evaluation, several roles are available, and you can assign different roles to different people.

Facilitator

A good facilitator is the key to a good evaluation session. If the participants feel comfortable and welcomed, then they are more likely to relax and comment constructively on the interface. Snyder (2003) calls this the "flight attendant" role for the facilitator: looking after the well-being of the participant.

The second job for the facilitator is to try to keep the participant talking about what is going on. Snyder calls this the "sportscaster" role. It is definitely subordinate to the flight attendant role, but is especially valuable for the purposes of data collection.

The third job for the facilitator is to ensure that the purpose of the evaluation is fulfilled, the correct questions are asked, and that the questions are phrased in an objective manner. Snyder calls this the "scientist" role. It is also subordinate to the flight attendant role, but it is especially valuable for the validity and usefulness of the data that you collect.

EDITOR'S NOTE: WHAT MAKES A GOOD FACILITATOR?

The role of test facilitator is not easy. A good facilitator must:

- Be aware of possible biases, such as facial expressions, verbal reinforcement, and instructions or questions that can influence the participants' responses, that might affect the results. Dumas and Redish (1999, pp. 295–304) suggest that you "examine how you use adjectives and adverbs in your questions" (p. 298).
- Respond to a wide variety of participants. For example, a facilitator might have to deal with both very shy and very garrulous participants.
- Know when to intervene and when more can be learned by letting the users struggle.
- Know how to deal with unusual procedural and ethical situations. For example, when someone is clearly not a fit for a session, the facilitator must figure out how to dismiss that person without making him or her feel bad. How do you deal with someone who is hostile or even intimidating?
- Ensure privacy for the participants.
- Enforce best practices for the observers. For example, you don't want observers mocking the participants who are struggling or talking so loudly that their voices penetrate the walls of the testing room.
- Be reasonably consistent from session to session.

Notetaker

Someone needs to make a record of what is happening in the evaluation, a role that we call a *notetaker*.

> **EDITOR'S NOTE: NOTETAKING IS HARD!**
>
> The role of notetaker is a difficult one because you have to take notes on what people say during a usability evaluation and also record what they do without making interpretive judgements. For example, participants may state that they "hate this about a Web site" but actually have no problem completing a task. Notetakers have to consider what constitutes a "real" problem. For example, if a person hesitates for five seconds before making a choice without saying anything, does that indicate a problem? Notetakers have to be careful about injecting their interpretations onto the participant's behavior and generally record behavior ("the participant hesitated for several seconds before choosing the correct icon") versus recording an interpretation ("the participant is confused"). Good notetaking is difficult and requires training, practice, and feedback from an experienced user experience practitioner. There are various software tools for supporting notetaking, but the judgments about what to record and how to label events is still mostly human judgment.

Equipment Operator

If you have video or other recording equipment, then it helps to have someone on hand who is comfortable setting the equipment up and solving any problems that arise. If you are using a high-fidelity prototype or the actual system, you may need to arrange to have the system reset to its initial or unvisited state between participants.

Observer

Observing a usability evaluation is an excellent way to help stakeholders understand the importance of user-centered design.

> Usability testing is often the first or only time that many designers, developers, writers, and managers see actual users working with their site. Usability testing is a dose of reality that many need to see (www.usability. gov/methods/who_else.html, visited July 17, 2004).

Gaffney (2001) suggests these rules for briefing the observers. He uses the term "test administrator" where we say "facilitator."

INTRODUCTION

Usability testing can be very stressful for participants. Having observers present can add to this stress. Participants may be nervous and uncomfortable. Therefore please follow these guidelines.

RESPECT

At all times, we must treat participants with respect.

- Be quiet. Keep noise levels to a minimum to avoid disrupting the test.
- Do not discuss the personal attributes of the participants. It is inappropriate to discuss participants in any way that is not directly related to the work we are carrying out.
- Do not include participant names in any notes that you make.
- Refrain from joking and laughing, as this may be misinterpreted as being directed at the test participant.
- The test administrator is in charge of the visit. At any stage the administrator may request that any observer leave the area. If this happens, please comply immediately and without further discussion.

WAIT FOR THE RESULTS

You may see behavior that suggests particular design elements do not work well.

However, please refrain from making design changes until all the participants have been seen and the data analyzed.

Meeter and Greeter

A *meeter and greeter* is the person who meets the participants when they arrive for the evaluation. The meeter and greeter is generally responsible for all the domestic arrangements such as:

- Ensuring that the participant has access to the toilets if necessary
- Offering refreshments if appropriate
- Keeping the participant entertained if the evaluations are running late or the participant arrives early

Recruiter

The *recruiter* is the person or organization who finds the participants for the evaluation and who gets permission to go to the participant's home or work environment if this is a field study.

The Lone Evaluator

If you are doing it all by yourself, then you may want to make the evaluation sessions a little longer and allow extra time between sessions to keep yourself organized.

CREATING AN EVALUATION SCRIPT

One way of making sure that you pick the right level of questioning and introduce each task accurately is to write an *evaluation script* (also called a *test script* or *discussion guide*). Opinion varies among usability practitioners about whether or not to stick closely to an evaluation script at all times. For example, Clifford Anderson (Anderson, 2004) and Gerry Gaffney (Gaffney, 2003) are both clear on the view that you should always have a formal script. Anderson notes:

> I am famous for my extremely detailed test scripts. These typically include the scenario I will give the user and detailed steps for the correct and any logical alternate paths (whether correct or incorrect). The scripts also include possible interactions and interventions for each step. Though no test will ever go so neatly as my test scripts, thinking ahead what you are going to say in this manner can help ensure that each user will hear the same open-ended, non-directive questions.

Gaffney says:

> You should read a formal script to each participant in order to ensure that all participants receive the same information.
>
> Avoid the temptation to run usability testing without a script – it is very easy to give too much or too little information without one.

But Snyder (2003) takes a different point of view when talking about testing paper prototypes:

> **Wean yourself from scripts**. In a script, you write down everything you will say to the users and read it to them at the proper time. Scripts are useful in usability testing when it's important to control all the interactions you have with the users. For example, if you were testing two competing software packages, you'd want your introductions of them to use equally neutral wording. But in paper prototype testing, it's unlikely that you need this degree of scientific rigor – when an interface is rapidly changing, a detailed script can become more trouble to maintain than it's worth....Although scripts are okay when you're starting, as soon as you gain confidence in usability test facilitation, I recommend that you pare them down into checklists.

Our view is that an evaluation script is essential when you do your first evaluation, and it is beneficial for quite a few evaluations after that. Our objective as evaluators is that our participants should leave the evaluation session feeling no worse than when they arrived, and better if possible. You have many steps to cover, and it is easy to forget something that might be important to your participants. Although reading from a script may seem artificial, we find that the benefit of thoroughness outweighs the formality.

An Example of an Evaluation Script

Table 9.2 is an example of a typical script. We have added an extra column showing how the sentences in the script align with the stages in the evaluation. The evaluator reads from the script, apart from the *instructions in italics*.

Table 9.2	An Evaluation Script for a Web Site Evaluation

First, thank you for coming here today. I have a script here that I'll read to you. This may seem very formal, but it ensures that all participants receive the same information.	Welcome the participants.
Pause/offer opportunity for questions after each paragraph.	
The purpose of today's activity is to test a Web site that has been developed for Project X. We want to find out whether the Web site works well for people who are not familiar with the project. Based on what we learn, we will advise the developers on how to improve it.	Brief the participants.
I am going to ask you to try some tasks. We want to find out if the site makes them easy or difficult. It's important to emphasize that we are not testing your abilities in any way. We will be finished in about an hour.	
I will be taking notes all the time, and I will ask you to complete a short questionnaire about yourself. I will also ask for your comments. The information you give us is confidential, and your name will not be stored with this information.	
Can you please read this consent form, and sign it if you agree. The wording is a bit formal, so you are welcome to ask me about anything that is not completely clear.	Obtain consent.
Give the participants the consent form, and allow time for him or her to read and sign it.	
Thank you.	
Before we start, I would like to ask you to complete a brief questionnaire about yourself. Once again, let me point out that your name is not stored with this information.	Pretest the questionnaire.
Give the participants the questionnaire, and allow time for him or her to complete it.	
Thank you.	
We will now move on to the tasks. For each task, I will give you a card that has the task written on it. I would appreciate it if you can give me a running commentary on what you are doing, because I cannot see the screen very easily from where I am sitting.	Offer training or explain the task.
You may find that the Web site makes it difficult to do a task. If you get stuck because of this, that's fine. Just let me know, and we will skip that task and move on. If you want to take a break at any stage, let me know and we can do so.	

(continued)

Table 9.2 An Evaluation Script for a Web Site Evaluation (*Continued*)	
Are you ready to begin? *Administer each task in turn by offering the task card to the participants.* *Take notes of participants' comments and your observations.* That completes the tasks. It has been really helpful to know that some of them have been a bit difficult. That will give the developers some ideas about what to do to improve the site.	During the session, observe the participants and record your observations.
I would now like to ask you some general questions about the Web site. *Work through the postsession interview.*	Begin the postsession questionnaire or the interview.
That completes the session. Thank you for giving your time today. *Escort participants from the test area.*	Offer final thanks.
Collect notes and any other materials from the observers, if any, and tidy the test area. Reset the computer/Web site to ensure that the visited links are cleared and temporary data in cookies are deleted.	If data collection forms have been used, collect them from all involved.

FORMS TO USE WHEN ASKING FOR PERMISSION TO RECORD

You need the agreement of the participants to take part in the evaluation, and you may also need their permission to record the evaluation. Burmeister (2000) has listed 10 principles relating to informed consent in usability testing:

2.1.1 Minimal risk (P1)

Usability testing should not expose participants to more than minimal risk. Though it is unlikely that a usability test will expose participants to physical harm, psychological or sociological risks do arise. If it is not possible to abide by the principle of minimal risk, then the usability engineer should endeavor to eliminate the risk or consider not doing the test.

2.1.2 Information (P2)

Informed consent implies information is supplied to participants. Information...can be summarized as: the procedures you will follow; the purpose of the test; any risks to the participant; the opportunity to ask questions; and, the opportunity to withdraw at any time.

2.1.3 Comprehension (P3)

The facilitator needs to ensure that each participant understands what is involved in the test. This must be done in a manner that is clear. It must also be done so as to completely cover the information on the form. The procedure for obtaining consent should not be rushed, nor made to seem unimportant....Clearly one possible outcome of applying this principle is that the person involved may choose not to participate. However, not to permit such opportunities may adversely affect their ability to make an informed choice...

2.1.4 Voluntariness (P4)

...Coercion and undue influence should be absent when the person is asked to give their consent to participate in the test. Undue pressure might come in a number of subtle ways that one needs to be wary of – for instance, if you are in a position of authority over the participant such as employer to employee or teacher to student. Another subtle form of coercion is involved when participants receive payment for their participation. In the case of the latter it may be prudent to make the payment upfront, prior to the test. That way the participant will not feel pressured to have to stay to the end of the test (see P5 about the right to leave the test at any time)....

2.1.5 Participant's rights (P5)

Countries vary as to their recognition of human rights. Even where there is general agreement, definitions of those rights and interpretations of how they apply vary. Participants should have the right to be informed as to what their rights are....

2.1.6 Nondisclosure (P6)

When the product is under development or in any way confidential, participants need to be informed that they cannot talk about the product or their opinions of it....

2.1.7 Confidentiality (P7)

Confidentiality is different from the participant's right to privacy; it refers to how data about the participants will be stored [and used]....laws concerning privacy and confidentiality vary greatly. The legalities must be investigated in the context of where the test is taking place.

2.1.8 Waivers (P8)

Permission needs to be obtained from participants to use materials such as questionnaires, audio and video recordings (and their transcripts). In many countries they have the right to refuse to give waivers. Participants should be given the option...of having the data used for the [immediate] purposes of the test, or of also having it used in a wider context. If the latter, then the consent form should state in what further ways the data will be used, so that an informed decision can be taken by the participant. Such permission should state the purposes for which the material will be used. Several usability engineers the author corresponded with in researching the material for this paper gave anecdotal stories of near court cases and in one case an out of court settlement where material obtained during a usability test was subsequently used in very different settings; such as sales promotion of the product and for training purposes....

2.1.9 Legalese (P9)

...It is too tempting to have legal departments draft the consent form. Just as software engineering terminology and legal jargon can hinder the signing of forms, so in usability testing such language does not make for rapport building prior to the start of a usability test. Sensitive use on non-legal jargon should be made so that comprehension (P3) on the part of the participant is possible.

2.1.10 Expectations (P10)

Globalization and related issues to do with international differences in cultural and ethnicity lead to the notion of expectations. Each social grouping has its own means of resolving issues of power and hierarchy, turn taking, how interactions between people proceed, who can interrupt and contradict. There are expected behaviors. There are accepted behaviors. Cultures interact through expectations.... Misunderstandings arise due to differences in work practices and social class systems.

Burmeister (2000) points out that some of these principles are more important than others:

So which of these principles are mandatory and which are discretionary? Informed consent is about protecting the rights of all parties involved in a usability test. The first five principles are concerned with the rights of participants, the next four are concerned with the rights of the company that has organized the testing to take place. The last applies to both. On an international scale, all these principles are in the "discretionary" category, none are "mandatory." Given the heterogeneous nature of people involved in remote testing in particular, this is an inescapable reality. Yet in most Western societies, at least those that might be described as representing the European Anglo Celtic view, the first four principles fall into the "mandatory" category. That is, despite the differences in legal requirements, all these societies have value systems similar to each other.

Bearing all that in mind, decide whether you need to prepare a consent form for your evaluation or whether you prefer to cover the points listed in your evaluation script and just obtain the participant's verbal permission. Signing a form feels more formal and may add to the overall stress of the evaluation, but it may be essential if you have to obtain agreement from a legal department.

Nondisclosure Agreements

If your system is proprietary or confidential in any way, you may need to ask the participants to make some type of agreement to keep what they learn in the evaluation to themselves. These are usually known as *nondisclosure agreements* (NDAs). Generally, organizations that require NDAs also have legal departments with strong views as to how they should be worded. If possible, try to make sure that the NDA is worded in plain language and that you can both understand it and explain it to your participants. Box 1 presents an example of a combined NDA and consent form.

AN EXAMPLE OF A CONSENT FORM

Understanding Your Participation

Please read this page carefully.

Xerox Corporation is asking you to participate in evaluating a new product. By participating in this evaluation, you will help us improve this and other Xerox products.

We will observe you and record information about how you work with the product. We may also ask you to fill out questionnaires and answer interview questions.

We will videotape all or some of the interview and your work. By signing this form, you give your permission to Xerox to use your voice, verbal statements, and videotaped pictures for the purposes of evaluating the product and showing the results of these evaluations. We will not use your full name.

You will be working with a product that is still being developed. Any information you acquire about this product is confidential and proprietary and is being disclosed to you only so that you can participate in the evaluation. By signing this form, you agree not to talk about this product to anyone. You may tell them that you helped to evaluate new software.

If you need a break, just tell us.

You may withdraw from this evaluation at any time.

If you have any questions, you may ask now or at any time.

If you agree with these terms, please indicate your agreement by signing here:

Please print your name.

_____

Signature

_____

Date

_____

From www.stcsig.org/usability, retrieved July 17, 2004.

THE PILOT TEST

Before any actual evaluation sessions are conducted, you should run a *pilot test* as a way of evaluating your evaluation session and to help ensure that it will work. It is a process of debugging or testing the evaluation material, the planned time schedule, the suitability of the task descriptions, and the running of the session.

Participants for Your Pilot Test

You can choose a participant for your pilot test in the same way as for your actual evaluation. However, in the pilot test, it is less important that the participant is completely representative of your target user group and it is more important that you feel confident about practicing with him or her. Your aim in the pilot test is to make sure that all the details of the evaluation are in place.

Design and Assemble the Test Environment

Try to do your pilot test in the same place as your evaluation or in a place that is as similar as possible. Assemble all the items you need:

- Computer equipment and prototype, or your paper prototype. Keep a note of the version you use.
- Your evaluation script and other materials.
- Any other props or artifacts you need, such as paper and pens for the participants.
- The incentives, if you are offering any.
- If you are using video or other recording equipment, then make sure that you practice assembling it all for the pilot test. As you put it together, make a list of each item. There is nothing more aggravating than forgetting some vital part of your equipment.

Run the Pilot Test

Run the pilot participant through the evaluation procedure and all the supporting materials. The session should be conducted in the same way as the actual evaluation session. Ideally, the evaluator(s) who will conduct the actual evaluation session should participate in the pilot test. They should observe, take notes, and facilitate the pilot test, just as they would do in the actual session. For example, they should consider the following questions:

- Is the prototype functioning as required for the session?
- Is the introductory material clear enough to the evaluator(s) and the participants?
- Are the observation and data collection procedures working?
- Are the evaluator(s) aware of their roles and responsibilities for the evaluation session?
- Can the task descriptions be accomplished within the planned session time?

While observing the pilot participant, make a note of where the evaluation materials and procedures may need to be improved before conducting the actual usability evaluation sessions.

It is often helpful to analyze and interpret the data that you get from the pilot test. This often points out that an important facet of the evaluation has been overlooked and that some essential data, which you need to validate certain usability requirements, has not been collected.

If you are short of time, then you might consider skipping the pilot test.

If you do omit the pilot test, then you will find that you forget to design some details of the tasks or examples, discover that some item of equipment is missing, realize that your interview plan omits a topic of great importance to the participants, or find that your prototype does not work as you had intended. Doing a pilot test is much simpler than trying to get all these details correct for your first participant.

Often, the pilot test itself reveals many problems in the user interface (UI). You may want to start redesigning immediately, but it is probably best to restrain yourself to the bare minimum that will let the evaluation happen. If the changes are extensive, then it is probably best to plan another pilot test.

SUMMARY

In this chapter, we discussed the final preparations for evaluation:

- Assigning roles to team members (or adjusting the plan to allow extra time if you are a lone evaluator)
- Creating an evaluation script
- Deciding whether you need forms for consent and for nondisclosure
- Running a pilot test

Once you have completed your pilot test, all that remains is to make any amendments to your materials, recruit the participants, and run the evaluation.

CHAPTER 10
Usability Tests

Michael Kuniavsky

EDITOR'S COMMENTS

Think-aloud usability testing, where participants verbalize their reactions to a product as they work on a series of tasks, is a popular technique in the repertoire of usability practitioners because it is regarded as relatively easy to learn, straightforward to use, capable of generating useful data, convincing, and (relatively) inexpensive.

You can use think-aloud usability testing to follow with:

- Obtain first impressions of a product.
- Uncover features or components of the product that cause confusion.
- Reveal initial learning problems.
- Reveal clues about the user's mental model of a system.
- Reveal general likes and dislikes.
- Determine if the language is understood.
- Explore navigation and workflow efficiency.
- Uncover how users recover from errors.

This method is applicable from requirements analysis through product release. You can use the think-aloud testing method to get feedback on concept sketches, storyboards, wireframes, paper prototypes, existing products, working prototypes, and competitive products. The optimal time to use this method in new product development is generally in the exploratory stages of design when you are focused on high-level issues like overall navigation, major feature design, and high-level organization.

This chapter provides a detailed guide for planning and conducting a usability test. The author of this chapter, Michael Kuniavsky, is a very wise practitioner who provides a wealth of tips, tricks, and templates for a successful usability test.

USABILITY TESTS

A one-on-one usability test can quickly reveal an immense amount of information about how people use a prototype, whether functional, mock-up, or just paper. Usability testing is probably the fastest and easiest way to tease out showstopping usability problems before a product launches.

Usability tests are structured interviews focused on specific features in an interface prototype. The heart of the interview is a series of tasks that are performed by the interface's evaluator (typically, a person who matches the product's ideal audience). Tapes and notes from the interview are later analyzed for the evaluator's successes, misunderstandings, mistakes, and opinions. After a number of these tests have been performed, the observations are compared, and the most common issues are collected into a list of functionality, navigation, and presentation problems.

Using usability tests, the development team can immediately see whether people understand their designs as they are supposed to understand them. Unfortunately, the technique has acquired the aura of a final check before the project is complete, and usability tests are often scheduled at the end of the development cycle – after the feature set has been locked, the target markets have been determined, and the product is ready for shipping. Although testing can certainly provide insight into the next revision of the product, the full power of the technique remains untapped. They can be better used much earlier, providing feedback throughout the development cycle, both to check the usability of specific features and to investigate new ideas and evaluate hunches.

WHEN TO TEST

Because usability testing is best at seeing how people perform specific tasks, it should be used to examine the functionality of individual features and the way they're presented to the intended user. It is better used to highlight potential misunderstanding or errors inherent in the way features are implemented rather than to evaluate the entire user experience. During the early to middle parts of a development cycle, usability testing can play a key role in guiding the direction of functionality as features are defined and developed. Once the functionality of a feature is locked in and its interaction with other features has been determined, however, it's often too late to make any fundamental changes. Testing at that point is more an investment in the next version than in the current one.

Moreover, usability testing is almost never a one-time event in a development cycle for a product and should not be seen as such. Every round of testing can focus on a small set of features (usually no more than five), so a series of tests is used to evaluate a whole interface or fine-tune a specific set of features.

The first thing the development team needs to do is decide on the *target audience* and the *feature set to examine*.

This means that a good time to start usability testing is when the development cycle is somewhat underway, but not so late that testing prevents the implementation of extensive changes if it points to their necessity. Occasionally, usability testing reveals problems that require a lot of work to correct, so the team should be prepared to rethink and reimplement (and, ideally, retest) features if need be. In the Web world, this generally takes a couple of weeks, which is why iterative usability testing is often done in two-week intervals.

> **WARNING**
>
> Completely open-ended testing, or "fishing," is rarely valuable. When you go fishing during a round of user research – often prompted by someone saying, "Let's test the whole thing" – the results are neither particularly clear nor insightful. Know why you're testing before you begin.

A solid usability testing program will include iterative usability testing of every major feature, with tests scheduled throughout the development process, reinforcing, and deepening knowledge about people's behavior and ensuring that designs become more effective as they develop.

Example of an Iterative Testing Process: Webmonkey 2.0 Global Navigation

Webmonkey is a cutting-edge Web development magazine that uses the technologies and techniques it covers. During a redesign cycle, they decided that they wanted to create something entirely new for the main interface. Because much of the 1.0 interface had been extensively tested and was being carried through to the new design, they wanted to concentrate their testing and development efforts on the new features.

The most ambitious and problematic of the new elements being considered was a DHTML global navigational panel that gave access to the whole site (see Figs. 10.1 and 10.2) but didn't permanently use screen real estate. Instead, it would slide on and off the screen when the user needed it. Webmonkey's previous navigation scheme worked well, but analysis by the team determined that it was not used often enough to justify the amount of space it was taking up. They didn't want to add emphasis to it (it was, after all, secondary to the site's content), so they decided to minimize its use of screen real estate, instead of attempting to increase its use. Their initial design was a traditional vertical

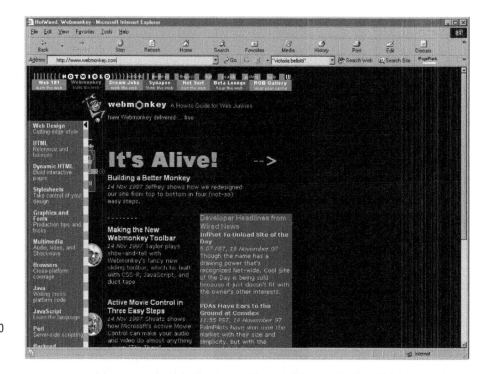

FIGURE 10.1
The Webmonkey 2.0
Navigation Panel
design (open).

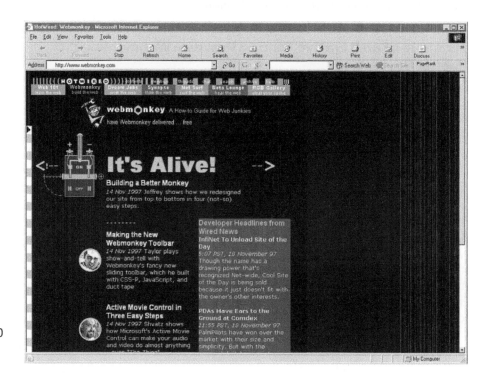

FIGURE 10.2
The Webmonkey 2.0
Navigation Panel
design (closed).

navigation bar, identical to that found in the left margin of the 1.0 site, but in its own panel. The panel was hidden most of the time but would reveal its contents when an arrow at the top of a striped bar on the left side was clicked. The target audience of Web developers would hopefully notice the striped bar and arrow and click on it out of curiosity.

Webmonkey developed on an iterative development cycle, so Web developers and sophisticated users were invited to a series of tests, with each test phase being followed by a design phase to incorporate the findings of the test. Although the purpose of the test was to examine the participants' entire user experience, the developers paid special attention to the sliding panel. In the first round of testing, none of the six evaluators opened the panel. When asked whether they had seen the bar and the arrow, most said they had, but they took the striped bar to be a graphical element and the arrow to be decoration.

Two weeks later, the visual design had not changed much, but the designers changed the panel from being closed by default to being open when the page first loaded. During testing, the evaluators naturally noticed the panel and understood what it was for, but they consistently had trouble closing it and seeing the content that it obscured. Some tried dragging it like a window; others tried to click inside it. Most had seen the arrow, but they didn't know how it related to the panel and so they never tried clicking it. Further questioning revealed that they didn't realize that the panel was a piece of the window that slid open and closed. Thus, there were two interrelated problems: people didn't know how the panel functioned and they didn't know that the arrow was a functional element.

A third design attempted to solve the problem by providing an example of the panel's function as the first experience on the page: a short pause after the page loaded, the panel opened and closed by itself. The designers hoped that showing the panel in action would make the panel's function clearer. It did, and in the next round of testing, the evaluators described both its content and its function correctly. However, none were able to open the panel again. The new design still did not solve the problem with the arrow, and most people tried to click and drag in the striped bar to get at the panel. Having observed this behavior, and (after some debate) realizing that they could not technically implement a dragging mechanism for the panel, the designers made the entire colored bar clickable so that whenever someone clicked anywhere in it the panel slid out (or back, if it was already open).

In the end, people still didn't know what the arrow was for, but when they clicked in the striped panel to slide it open, it did, which was sufficient to make the feature usable, and none of the people observed using it had any trouble opening or closing the panel thereafter.

HOW TO DO IT

Preparation

A full-on usability test (say six to 10 users) can easily take three to four weeks from conception to presentation of the results (see Table 10.1). You should start preparing for a usability testing cycle at least three weeks before you expect to need the results.

SETTING A SCHEDULE

Before the process can begin, you need to know whom to recruit and which features you want them to evaluate. Both of these things should be decided several weeks before the testing begins.

Table 10.1	A Typical Usability Testing Schedule
Timing	**Activity**
$t - 2$ weeks	Determine test audience; start recruiting immediately.
$t - 2$ weeks	Determine feature set to be tested.
$t - 1$ week	Write first version of script; construct test tasks; discuss with development team; check on recruiting.
$t - 3$ days	Write second version of guide; review tasks; discuss with development team; recruiting should be completed.
$t - 2$ days	Complete guide; schedule practice test; set up and check all equipment.
$t - 1$ day	Do a practice test in the morning; adjust guide and tasks as appropriate.
T	Test (usually 1–2 days, depending on scheduling).
$t + 1$ day	Discuss with observers; collect copies of all notes.
$t + 2$ days	Relax; take a day off and do something else; you will often be pressured to get a report out immediately, but this period of reflection is important for considering how small problems might be indicative of larger themes.
$t + 3$ days	Watch all tapes; take notes.
$t + 1$ week	Combine notes; write analysis.
$t + 1$ week	Present to development team; discuss and note directions for further research.

RECRUITING

Recruiting is the most crucial piece to start on early. It needs to be timed right and to be precise, especially if it's outsourced. You need to find the right people and match their schedules to yours. That takes time and effort. The more time you can devote to the recruiting process, the better (although more than two weeks in advance is generally too early since people often don't know their schedules that far in advance).You also need to choose your screening criteria carefully. The initial impulse is to recruit people who fall into the product's ideal target audience, but that's almost always too broad. You need to home in on the representatives of the target audience who are going to give you the most useful feedback.

Say you're about to put up a site that sells upscale forks online. Your ideal audience consists of people who want to buy forks.

In recruiting for a usability test, that's a pretty broad range of people. Narrowing your focus helps preserve clarity since different groups can exhibit different behaviors based on the same fundamental usability problems. Age, experience, and motivation can create seemingly different user experiences that are caused by the same underlying problem. Choosing the "most representative" group can reduce the amount of research you have to do in the long run and focus your results.

The best people to invite are those who are going to need the service you are providing in the near future or who have used a competing service in the recent past. These people will have the highest level of interest and knowledge in the subject matter, so they can concentrate on how well the interface works rather than on the minutia of the information. People who have no interest in the content can still point out interaction flaws, but they are not nearly as good at pointing out problems with the information architecture or any kind of content-specific features since they have little motivation to concentrate and make it work.

Say your research of the fork market shows that there are two strong subgroups within that broad range: people who are replacing their old silverware and people who are buying wedding presents. The first group, according to your research, is mostly men in their 40s, whereas the second group is split evenly between men and women, mostly in their mid-20s and 30s.

You decide that the people who are buying sets of forks to replace those they already own represent the heart of your user community. They are likely to know about the subject matter and may have done some research already. They're motivated to use the service, which makes them more likely to use it as they would in a regular situation. So you decide to recruit men in their 40s who want to buy replacement forks in the near future or who have recently bought some. In addition, you want to filter out online newbies, and you want to get people with online purchasing experience. Including all these conditions, your final set of recruiting criteria looks as follows:

- Men or women, preferably men
- 25 years old or older, preferably 35–50
- Have Internet access at home or work
- Use the Web five or more hours a week
- Have one or more years of Internet experience
- Have bought at least three things online
- Have bought something online in the last 3 months
- Are interested in buying silverware online

> **NOTE**
>
> Recruiters will try to follow your criteria to the letter, but if you can tell them which criteria are flexible (and how flexible they are) and which are immutable, it's easier for them. Ultimately, that makes it easier for you, too.

Notice that there is some flexibility in the age and gender criteria. This is to make the recruiter's life a little easier. You may insist that the participants be all male and that they must be between 40 and 50 years old, but if a candidate comes up who matches the rest of the criteria and happens to be 33 and female, you probably don't want to disqualify her immediately. Purchasing experience, on the other hand, requires precise requirements since getting people who aren't going to be puzzled or surprised by the concept of e-commerce is key to making the test successful. Testing an e-commerce system with someone who's never bought anything online tests the concept of e-commerce as much as it's testing the specific product. You rarely want that level of detail, so it's best to avoid situations that inspire it in the first place.

For this kind of focused task-based usability testing, you should have at least five participants in each round of testing and recruit somewhere from six to 10 people for the five slots. Jakob Nielsen has shown (in *Guerrilla HCI: Using Discount Usability Engineering to Penetrate the Intimidation Barrier*, available from http://www.useit.com/papers/guerrilla_hci.html) that the cost-benefit cutoff for usability testing is about five users per target audience. Larger groups still produce useful results, but the cost of recruiting and the extra effort needed to run the tests and analyze the results leads to rapidly diminishing returns. After eight or nine users, the majority of problems performing a given task will have been seen several times. To offset no-shows, however, it's a good idea to schedule a couple of extra people beyond the basic five. And to make absolutely sure you have enough people, you could double-book every time slot. This doubles your recruiting and incentive costs, but it ensures that there's minimal downtime in testing.

> **WARNING**
>
> You should strive to conduct a different test for each major user market since – by definition – each user market is likely to use the product differently.

In addition, Jared Spool and Will Schroeder point out that when you are going to give evaluators broad goals to satisfy, rather than specific tasks to do, you need more people than just five. However, in my opinion, broad goal research is less usability testing than a kind of focused contextual inquiry and should be conducted as such.

In addition, to check your understanding of your primary audience, you can recruit one or two people from secondary target audiences – in the fork case, for example, a younger buyer or someone who's not as Web savvy – to see whether there's a hint of a radically different perspective in those groups. This won't give you conclusive results, but if you get someone who seems to be reasonable and consistently says something contrary to the main group, it's an indicator that you should probably rethink your recruiting criteria. If the secondary audience is particularly important, it should have its own set of tests, regardless.

Having decided whom to recruit, it's time to write a screener and send it to the recruiter. Make sure to discuss the screener with your recruiter and to walk through it with at least two people in-house to get a reality check.

WARNING

If you're testing for the first time, schedule fewer people and put extra time in between. Usability testing can be exhausting, especially if you're new to the technique.

Then pick a couple of test dates and send out invitations to the people who match your criteria. Schedule interviews at times that are convenient to both you and the participant and leave at least half an hour between them. That gives the moderator enough slop time to have people come in late, for the test to run long, and for the moderator to get a glass of water and discuss the test with the observers. With 60-minute interviews, this means that you can do four or five in a single day and sometimes as many as six. With 90-minute interviews, you can do three or four evaluators and maybe five if you push it and skip lunch.

EDITOR'S NOTE: OVER-RECRUIT FOR SESSIONS WITH IMPORTANT OBSERVERS

For some important projects, you might have senior managers – vice presidents and directors – watching the session. For these very important person (VIP) sessions, consider recruiting an extra participant. It can be embarrassing to have VIPs ready to observe and then have the participant cancel or just not show up. This is a rare event if the recruiting was well done, but having senior people sitting around a lab with no participant can have a detrimental impact on your usability program, especially if it is relatively new. One approach is to invite a standby participant who is willing to be on-call for two sessions for an additional incentive.

CHOOSING FEATURES

The second step is to determine which features to test. These, in turn, determine the tasks you create and the order in which you present them. You should choose features with enough lead time so that the test procedure can be fine-tuned. Five features (or feature clusters) can be tested in a given 60–90-minute interview. Typical tests range from one to two hours. Two-hour tests are used for initial or broad-based testing, while shorter tests are most useful for in-depth research into specific features or ideas (though it's perfectly acceptable to do a 90-minute broad-based test).

Individual functions should be tested in the context of feature clusters. It's rarely useful to test elements of a set without looking at least a little at the whole set. My rule of thumb is that something is testable when it's one of the things that gets drawn on a whiteboard when making a 30-second sketch of the interface. If you would draw a blob that's labeled "nav bar" in such a situation, then think of testing the nav bar, not just the new link to the homepage.

The best way to start the process is by meeting with the development staff (at least the product manager, the interaction designers, and the information architects) and making a list of the five most important features to test. To start discussing which features to include, look at features that are:

- Used often
- New
- Highly publicized
- Considered troublesome, based on feedback from earlier versions
- Potentially dangerous or have bad side effects if used incorrectly
- Considered important by users
- Viewed with concern or doubt by the product team

A FEATURE PRIORITIZATION EXERCISE

This exercise is a structured way of coming up with a feature prioritization list. It's useful when the group doesn't have a lot of experience prioritizing features or if it's having trouble.

- Step 1: Have the group make a list of the most important things on the interface that are new or have been drastically changed since the last round of testing. Importance should not just be defined purely in terms of prominence; it can be relative to the corporate bottom line or managerial priority. Thus, if next quarter's profitability has been staked on the success of a new Fork of the Week section, it's important, even if it's a small part of the interface.
- Step 2: Make a column and label it "Importance." Look at each feature and rate it on a scale of 1–5, where 5 means it's critical to the success of the product and 1 means it's not very important.

Next, make a second column and label it "Doubt." Look at each feature and rate how comfortable the team is with the design, labeling the most comfortable items with a 1 and the least comfortable with a 5. This may involve some debate among the group, so you may have to treat it as a focus group of the development staff.

■ Step 3: Multiply the two entries in the two columns and write the results next to them. The features with the greatest numbers next to them are the features you should test. Call these out and write a short sentence that summarizes what the group most wants to know about the functionality of the feature.

TOP FIVE FORK CATALOG FEATURES BY PRIORITY

	Importance	Doubt	Total
The purchasing mechanism: Does it work for both single items and whole sets?	5	5	25
The search engine: Can people use it to find specific items?	5	5	25
Catalog navigation: Can people navigate through it when they don't know exactly what they want?	5	4	20
The fork of the week page: Do people see it?	4	4	16
The wish list: Do people know what it's for and can they use it?	3	5	15

Once you have your list of the features that most need testing, you're ready to create the tasks that will exercise those features.

In addition, you can include competitive usability testing. Although comparing two interfaces is more time consuming than testing a single interface, it can reveal strengths and weaknesses between products. Performing the same tasks with an existing interface and a new prototype, for example, can reveal whether the new design is more functional (or – the fear of every designer – less functional). Likewise, performing the same tasks, or conducting similar interface tours with two competing products, can reveal relative strengths between the two products. In both situations, however, it's very important not to bias the evaluator toward one interface over the other.

CREATING TASKS

Tasks need to be representative of typical user activities and sufficiently isolated to focus attention on a single feature (or feature cluster) of the product. Good tasks should have the following characteristics:

■ Reasonable: They should be typical of the kinds of things that people will do. Someone is unlikely to want to order 90 different kinds of individual forks, each in a different pattern, and have them shipped to 37 different addresses, so that's not a typical task. Ordering a dozen forks and shipping them to a single address, however, is.

- Described in terms of end goals: Every product, every Web site, is a tool. It's not an end to itself. Even when people spend hours using it, they're doing something *with* it. So, much as actors can emote better when given their character's motivation, interface evaluators perform more realistically if they're motivated by a lifelike situation. Phrase your task as something that's related to the evaluator's life. If they're to find some information, tell them why they're trying to find it. (Your company is considering opening an office in Moscow and you'd like to get a feel for the reinsurance business climate there. You decide that the best way to do that is to check today's business headlines for information about reinsurance companies in Russia.) If they're trying to buy something, tell them why (Aunt Millie's subcompact car sounds like a jet plane. She needs a new muffler.) they're trying to create something, give them some context. (Here's a picture of Uncle Fred. You decide that as a practical joke you're going to digitally put a mustache on him and e-mail it to your family.)
- Specific: For consistency between evaluators and to focus the task on the parts of the product you're interested in testing, the task should have a specific end goal. So rather than saying "Go shop for some forks," say, "You saw a great Louis XIV fork design in a shop window the other day; here's a picture of it. Find that design in this catalog and buy a dozen fish forks." However, it's important to avoid using terms that exist on the interface since that tends to tip off the participant about how to perform the task.
- Doable: If your site has forks only, don't ask people to find knives. It's sometimes tempting to see how they use your information structure to find something impossible, but it's deceptive and frustrating and ultimately reveals little about the quality of your design.
- Be in a realistic sequence: Tasks should flow like an actual session with the product. So a shopping site could have a browsing task followed by a search task that's related to a selection task that flows into a purchasing task. This makes the session feel more realistic and can point out interactions between tasks that are useful for information architects in determining the quality of the flow through the product.
- Domain neutral: The ideal task is something that everyone who tests the interface knows something about, but no one knows a lot about. When one evaluator knows significantly more than the others about a task, their methods will probably be different than the rest of the group. They'll have a bigger technical vocabulary and a broader range of methods to accomplish the task. Conversely, it's not a good idea to create tasks that are completely alien to some evaluators since they may not know even how to begin. For example, when testing a general search engine, I have people search for pictures of Silkie chickens: everyone knows something about chickens, but unless you're a Bantam hen farmer, you

probably won't know much about Silkies. For really important tasks where an obvious domain-neutral solution doesn't exist, people with specific knowledge can be excluded from the recruiting (e.g., asking "Do you know what a Silkie chicken is?" in the recruiting screener can eliminate people who may know too much about chickens).

- Reasonably long: Most features are not so complex that to use them takes more than 10 minutes. The duration of a task should be determined by three things: the total length of the interview, its structure, and the complexity of the features you're testing. In a 90-minute task-focused interview, there are 50–70 minutes of task time, so an average task should take about 12 minutes to complete. In a 60-minute interview, there are about 40 minutes of task time, so each task should take no more than seven minutes. Aim for five minutes in shorter interviews and 10 minutes in longer ones. If you find that you have something that needs more time, then it probably needs to be broken down into subfeatures and reprioritized (though be aware of exceptions: some important tasks take a much longer time and cannot be easily broken up, but they still need to be tested).

ESTIMATING TASK TIME

Carolyn Snyder, author of *Paper Prototyping: The Fast and Easy Way to Design and Refine User Interfaces* (Snyder, 2003), recommends a method for estimating how long a task will take.

- Ask the development team how long it takes an expert – such as one of them – to perform the task.
- Multiply that number by three to10 to get an estimate of how long it would take someone who had never used the interface to do the same thing. Use lower numbers for simpler tasks such as found on general-audience Web sites and higher numbers for complex tasks such as found in specialized software or tasks that require data entry.

For every feature on the list, there should be at least one task that exercises it. Usually, it's useful to have two or three alternative tasks for the most important features in case there is time to try more than one or the first task proves to be too difficult or uninformative.

People can also construct their own tasks within reason. At the beginning of a usability test, you can ask the participants to describe a recent situation they may have found themselves in that your product could address. Then, when the times comes for a task, ask them to try to use the product as if they were trying to resolve the situation they described at the beginning of the interview. Another way to make a task feel authentic is to use real money. For example, one e-commerce site gave each of its usability testing participants a $50 account and told them that whatever they bought with that account, they got to keep (in addition to the cash incentive they were paid to participate). This presented a much better incentive for them to find something they actually wanted than they would have had if they just had to find something in the abstract.

Although it's fundamentally a qualitative procedure, you can also add some basic quantitative metrics (sometimes called *performance metrics*) to each task to investigate the relative efficiency of different designs or to compare competing products. Some common Web-based quantitative measurements include the following:

- The speed with which someone completes a task
- How many errors they make
- How often they recover from their errors
- How many people complete the task successfully

Because such data collection cannot give you results that are statistically usable or generalizable beyond the testing procedure, such metrics are useful only for order-of-magnitude ideas about how long a task should take. Thus, it's often a good idea to use a relative number scale rather than specific times.

For the fork example, you could have the following set of tasks, as matched to the features listed earlier.

FORK TASKS

Feature	Task
The search engine: can people use it to find specific items?	Louis XIV forks are all the rage, and you've decided that you want to buy a set. How would you get a list of all the Louis XIV fork designs in this catalog?
Catalog navigation: can people navigate through it when they don't know exactly what they want?	You also saw this great fork in a shop window the other day (show a picture). Find a design that's pretty close to it in the catalog.
The purchasing mechanism: does it work for both single items and whole sets?	Say you really like one of the designs we just looked at (pick one) and you'd like to buy a dozen dinner forks in that pattern. How would you go about doing that?
	Now say it's a month later, you love your forks, but you managed to mangle one of them in the garbage disposal. Starting from the front door to the site, how would you buy a replacement?
The Fork of the Week page: do people see it?	This one is a bit more difficult. Seeing is not easily taskable, but it's possible to elicit some discussion about it by creating a situation where it may draw attention and noting if it

FORK TASKS *(Continued)*

Feature	Task
	does. It's a couple of months later, and you're looking for forks again, this time as a present. Where would be the first place you'd look to find interesting forks that are a good value?
	Asking people to draw or describe an interface without looking at it reveals what people found memorable, which generally correlates closely to what they looked at. [turn off monitor] Please draw the interface we just looked at, based on what you remember about it.
The Wish List: do people know what it's for?	While you're shopping, you'd like to be able to keep a list of designs you're interested in, maybe later you'll buy one, but for now you'd like to just remember which ones are interesting. How would you do that? [If they don't find it on their own, point them to it and ask them whether they know what it means and how they would use it.]

When you've compiled the list, you need to time and check the tasks. Do them yourself and get someone who isn't close to the project to try them. This can be part of the pretest dry run, but it's always a good idea to run through the tasks by themselves if you can.

In addition, you should continually evaluate the quality of the tasks as the testing goes on. Use the same guidelines as you used to create the tasks and see if the tasks actually fulfill them. Between sessions think about the tasks' effectiveness and discuss them with the moderator and observers. And although it's a bad idea to drastically change tasks in the middle, it's OK to make small tweaks that improve the tasks' accuracy in between tests, keeping track of exactly what changed in each session.

NOTE

Usability testing tasks have been traditionally described in terms of small, discrete actions that can be timed (such as "Save a file"). The times for a large number of these tasks are then collected and compared to a predetermined ideal time. Although that's useful for low-level usability tasks with frequent long-term users of dedicated applications, the types of tasks that appear on the Web can be more easily analyzed through the larger-grained tasks described here, because Web sites are often used differently from dedicated software by people with less experience with the product. Moreover, the timing of performance diverts attention from issues of immediate comprehension and satisfaction, which play a more important role in Web site design than they do in application design.

WRITING A SCRIPT

With tasks in hand, it's time to write the script. The script is sometimes called a "protocol," sometimes a "discussion guide," but it's really just a script for the moderator to follow so that the interviews are consistent and everything gets done.

This script is divided into three parts: the introduction and preliminary interview, the tasks, and the wrap-up. The one that follows is a sample from a typical 90-minute e-commerce Web site usability testing session for people who have never used the site under review. About a third of the script is dedicated to understanding the participants' interests and habits. Although those topics are typically part of a contextual inquiry process or a focus group series, it's often useful to include some investigation into them in usability testing. Another third is focused on task performance, where the most important features get exercised. A final third is administration.

Introduction (5–7 minutes)

The introduction is a way to break the ice and give the evaluators some context. This establishes a comfort level about the process and their role in it.

[Monitor off, Video off, Computer reset]

Hi, welcome, thank you for coming. How are you? (Did you find the place OK? Any questions about the non disclosure agreement (NDA)? Etc.)

I'm _____. I'm helping _____ understand how well one of their products works for the people who are its audience. This is _____, who will be observing what we're doing today. We've brought you here to see what you think of their product: what seems to work for you, what doesn't, and so on.

This evaluation should take about an hour.

We're going to be videotaping what happens here today, but the video is for analysis only. It's primarily so I don't have to sit here and scribble notes, and I can concentrate on talking to you. It will be seen by some members of the development team, a couple of other people, and me. It's strictly for research and not for public broadcast or publicity or promotion or laughing at Christmas parties.

When there's video equipment, it's always blatantly obvious and somewhat intimidating. Recognizing it helps relieve a lot of tension about it. Likewise, if there's a two-way mirror, recognizing it – and the fact that there are people behind it – also serves to alleviate most people's anxiety. Once mentioned, it shouldn't be brought up again. It fades quickly into the background, and discussing it again is a distraction.

Also note that the script is written in a conversational style. It's unnecessary to read it verbatim, but it reminds the moderator to keep the tone of the interview casual. In addition, every section has a duration associated with it so that the moderator has an idea of how much emphasis to put on each one.

> Like I said, we'd like you to help us with a product we're developing. It's designed for people like you, so we'd really like to know what you think about it and what works and doesn't work for you. It's currently in an early stage of development, so not everything you're going to see will work right.

No matter what stage the product team is saying the product is in, if it's being usability tested, it's in an early stage. Telling the evaluators it's a work-in-progress helps relax them and gives them more license to make comments about the product as a whole.

> The procedure we're going to do today goes like this: we're going to start out and talk for a few minutes about how you use the Web, what you like, what kinds of problems you run into, that sort of thing. Then I'm going to show you a product that _____ has been working on and have you try out a couple of things with it. Then we'll wrap up, I'll ask you a few more questions about it, and we're done.
>
> Any questions about any of that?

Explicitly laying out the whole procedure helps the evaluators predict what's going to come next and gives them some amount of context to understand the process.

> Now I'd like to read you what's called a statement of informed consent. It's a standard thing I read to everyone I interview. It sets out your rights as a person who is participating in this kind of research.
>
> As a participant in this research:
>
> - You may stop at any time.
> - You may ask questions at any time.
> - You may leave at any time.
> - There is no deception involved.
> - Your answers are kept confidential.
>
> Any questions before we begin?
>
> Let's start!

The informed consent statement tells the evaluators that their input is valuable, that they have some control over the process, and that there is nothing fishy going on.

> *Preliminary Interview (10–15 Minutes)*

The preliminary interview is used to establish context for the participant's later comments. It also narrows the focus of the interview into the space of the evaluator's experience by beginning with general questions and then narrowing the conversation to the topics the product is designed for. For people who have never participated in a usability test, it increases their comfort level by asking some "easy" questions that build confidence and give them an idea of the process.

In this case, the preliminary interview also features a fairly extensive investigation into people's backgrounds and habits. It's not unusual to have half as many questions and to have the initial context-setting interview last five minutes, rather than 10–15 minutes.

> [Video on]
>
> How much time do you normally spend on the Web in a given week?
>
> How much of that is for work use and how much of that is for personal use?
>
> Other than e-mail, is there any one thing you do the most online?
>
> Do you ever shop online? What kinds of things have you bought? How often do you buy stuff online?
>
> Do you ever do research online for things that you end up buying in stores? Are there any categories of items that this happens with more often than others? Why?
>
> Is there anything you would never buy online? Why?

When it's applicable, it's useful to ask about people's offline habits before refocusing the discussion to the online sphere. Comparing what they say they do offline and what you observe them doing online provides insight into how people perceive the interface.

> Changing gears here a bit, do you ever shop for silverware in general, not just online? How often?
>
> Do you ever do that online? Why?
>
> [If so] Do you have any favorite sites where you shop for silverware online?
>
> [If so] What do you like the most about [site]? Is there anything that regularly bothers you about it?
>
> *Evaluation Instructions (3 minutes)*

It's important that evaluators don't feel belittled by the product. The goal behind any product is to have it be a subservient tool, but people have been conditioned by badly designed tools and arrogant companies to place the blame on themselves. Although it's difficult to undo a lifetime of software insecurity, the evaluation instructions help get evaluators comfortable with narrating their experience, including positive and negative commentary, in its entirety.

In a minute, I'll ask you to turn on the monitor and we'll take a look at the product, but let me give you some instructions about how to approach it.

The most important thing to remember when you're using it is that you are testing the interface, the interface is not testing you. There is absolutely nothing that you can do wrong. Period. If anything seems broken or wrong or weird or, especially, confusing, it's not your fault. However, we'd like to know about it. So please tell us whenever anything isn't working for you.

Likewise, tell us if you like something. Even if it's a feature, a color, or the way something is laid out, we'd like to hear about it.

Be as candid as possible. If you think something's awful, please say so. Don't be shy; you won't hurt anyone's feelings. Because it's designed for people like you, we really want to know exactly what you think and what works and doesn't work for you.

Also, while you're using the product, I'd like you to say your thoughts aloud. That gives us an idea of what you're thinking when you're doing something. Just narrate what you're doing, sort of as a play-by-play, telling me what you're doing and why you're doing it.

A major component to effective usability tests is to get people to say what they're thinking as they're thinking it. The technique is introduced up front, but it should also be emphasized during the actual interview.

Does that make sense? Any questions?

Please turn on the monitor [or "open the top of the portable"]. While it's warming up, you can put the keyboard, monitor, and mouse where they're comfortable for you.

First Impressions (5–10 minutes)

First impressions of a product are incredibly important for Web sites, so testing them explicitly is always a good thing and quick to do. Asking people where they're looking and what they see points out the things in an interface that pop and provides insight into how page loading and rendering affects focus and attention.

The interview begins with the browser up, but set to a blank page. Loading order affects the order people see the elements on the page and tends to affect the emphasis they place on those elements. Knowing the focus of their attention during the loading of the page helps explain why certain elements are seen as more or less important.

Now that it's warmed up, I'd like you to select "Forks" from the "Favorites" menu.

[Rapidly] What's the first thing your eyes are drawn to? What's the next thing? What's the first thought that comes into your mind when you see this page?

> [After 1–2 minutes] What is this site about?
>
> Are you interested in it?
>
> If this was your first time here, what would you do next? What would you click on? What would you be interested in investigating?

At this point, the script can go in two directions. Either it can be a *task-based interview* – where the user immediately begins working on tasks – or it can be a *hybrid interview* that's half task-based and half observational interview.

The task-based interview focuses on a handful of specific tasks or features. The hybrid interview is useful for first-time tests and tests that are early in the development cycle. In hybrid interviews, the evaluator goes through an interface tour, looking at each element of the main part of the interface and quickly commenting on it, before working on tasks.

A task-based interview would look as follows.

> *Tasks (20–25 minutes)*
> Now I'd like you to try a couple of things with this interface. Work just as you would normally, narrating your thoughts as you go along.
>
> Here is the list of things I'd like you to do. [hand out list]
>
> The first scenario goes as follows:
>
> TASK 1 DESCRIPTION GOES HERE
>
> [Read the first task, hand out Task 1 description sheet]
>
> The second thing I'd like you to do is
>
> TASK 2 DESCRIPTION GOES HERE
>
> [Read the second task, hand out Task 2 description sheet] etc.

When there is a way to remotely observe participants, it is sometimes useful to ask them to try a couple of the listed tasks on their own, without the moderator in the room. This can yield valuable information about how people solve problems without an available knowledge source. In addition, it's a useful time for the moderator to discuss the test with the observers. When leaving the room, the moderator should reemphasize the need for the evaluator to narrate all of his or her thoughts.

Including a specific list of issues to probe helps ensure that all the important questions are answered. The moderator should feel free to ask the probe questions whenever it is appropriate in the interview.

Probe Questions (investigate whenever appropriate)

- Do the names of navigation elements make sense?
- Do the interface elements function as the evaluator had expected?
- Are there any interface elements that don't make sense?
- What draws the evaluator's attention?
- What are the most important elements in any given feature?
- Are there places where the evaluator would like additional information?
- What are their expectations for the behavior/content of any given element/screen?

A hybrid interview could look as follows. It begins with a quick general task to see how people experience the product before they've had a chance to examine the interface in detail.

First Task (5 minutes)

Now I'd like you to try something with this interface.

Work just as you would normally, narrating your thoughts as you go along.

The first scenario goes as follows:

TASK 1 DESCRIPTION GOES HERE

[Read the first task]

Interface Tour (10 minutes)
OK, now I'd like to go through the interface, one element at a time, and talk about what you expect each thing to do.

Go through:

- Most of front door
- A sample catalog page
- A shopping cart page

Focus on:

- Site navigation elements
- Search elements
- Major feature labels and behaviors
- Ambiguous elements
- Expectations

Per element probes [ask for each significant element, when appropriate]:

- In a couple of words, what do you think this does?
- What does this [label, title] mean?
- Where do you think this would go?
- Without clicking on it, what kind of page would you expect to find on the other side? What would it contain? How would it look?

Per screen probes [ask on each screen, when appropriate]:

- What's the most important thing on this screen for you?
- Is there any information missing from here that you would need?
- After you've filled it out, what would you do next?
- How would you get to the front door of the site from here? What would you click on?
- How would you get to [some other major section]?

Tasks (10 minutes)
The second thing I'd like you to do is:

TASK 2 DESCRIPTION GOES HERE

[Read the second task]

The last thing I'd like to try is:

TASK 3 DESCRIPTION GOES HERE

[Read the third task]

By the time all the tasks have been completed, the heart of the information collection and the interview is over. However, it's useful for the observers and analysts to get a perspective on the high points of the discussion. In addition, a blue-sky discussion of the product can provide good closure for the evaluator and can produce some good ideas (or the time can be used to ask people to draw what they remember of the interface as the moderator leaves the room and asks the observers if they have any final questions for the participant).

Wrap-up and Blue-Sky Brainstorm (10 minutes)
Please turn off the monitor, and we'll wrap up with a couple of questions.

Wrap-up
How would you describe this product in a couple of sentences to someone with a level of computer and Web experience similar to yours?

Is this an interesting service? Is this something that you would use?

Is this something you would recommend? Why/why not?

Can you summarize what we've been talking about by saying three good things and three bad things about the product?

Blue-Sky Brainstorm
OK, now that we've seen some of what this can do, let's talk in blue-sky terms here for a minute. Not thinking in practical terms at all, what kinds of things would you like a system like this to do that this one doesn't? Have you ever said, "I wish that some program would do X for me"? What was it?

> Do you have any final questions? Comments?
>
> Thank you, if you have any other thoughts or ideas on your way home or tomorrow, or even next week, please feel free to send an e-mail to _____. [hand out a card]

Finally, it's useful to get some feedback about the testing and scheduling process.

> And that's all the questions I have about the prototype, but I have one last question:
>
> Do you have any suggestions about how we could run these tests better, either in terms of scheduling or the way we ran it?
>
> Thanks. That's it, we're done.
>
> [Turn video off]

As with every phase of user research, the product stakeholders should have input into the testing script content. The complete script draft should still be vetted by the stakeholders to assure that the priorities and technical presentations are accurate. The first draft should be given to the development team at least a week before testing is to begin. A second version incorporating their comments should be shown to them at least a couple of days beforehand.

CONDUCTING THE INTERVIEW

There are two goals in conducting user interviews: getting the most natural responses from evaluators and getting the most complete responses. Everything that goes into the environment of a user interview – from the physical space to the way questions are asked – is focused on these two goals.

The Physical Layout

The physical layout should look as little like a lab as possible and as much like the kind of space in which the product is designed to be used. If the product is to be used at work, then it should be tested in an environment that resembles a nice office, preferably with a window. If it's for home use, then it should be tested in an environment like a home office. The illusion doesn't have to be all pervasive; it's possible to achieve the appropriate feeling with just a few carefully chosen props. For the home office, for example, soft indirect lighting and a tablecloth over an office desk instantly makes it less formal.

Often, however, the usability test must be performed in a scheduled conference room or a rented lab, where extensive alteration isn't possible. In those situations, make sure that the space is quiet, uncluttered, and as much as possible, unintimidating.

FIGURE 10.3
Picture-in-picture
video documentation.

Every interview should be videotaped, if possible. Ideally, a video scan converter (a device that converts computer video output to standard video) and a video mixer should be used to create a "picture-in-picture" version of the proceedings, with one image showing a picture of the person and the other of their screen (Fig. 10.3). The video camera should be positioned such that the evaluator's face and hands can be seen for the initial interview and so that the screen can be seen for the task portion of the interview. The moderator does not have to appear in the shot.

Accurate, clear audio is extremely important, so the video camera should have a good built-in microphone that filters out external noise, or you should invest in a lapel microphone, which the evaluator can clip onto his or her clothing, or a small microphone that can be taped to the monitor. The downside of lapel microphones is that although they capture the evaluator's comments, they don't always catch those of the moderator. An ideal situation is to have two wireless lapel microphones and a small mixer to merge the two sound sources or a single external microphone that is sensitive enough to capture both sides of the conversation without picking up the external noise that's the bane of built-in camera mics. But that's a lot of equipment.

If a two-way mirrored room is unavailable, closed-circuit video makes for good substitute. This is pretty easy to achieve with a long video cable and a television in an adjacent room (though the room should be sufficiently soundproof that observers can speak freely without being heard in the testing room). So, the final layout of a typical round of usability testing can look like Fig. 10.4.

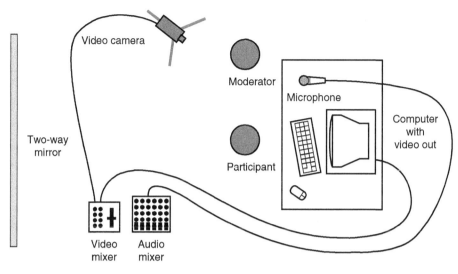

FIGURE 10.4
A typical usability testing configuration.

(Closed-circuit to remote viewing area)

EDITOR'S NOTE: USABILITY TESTING SOFTWARE WHEN YOU DON'T HAVE A FORMAL LAB

For relatively low cost ($1,000–3,000), you can purchase usability testing software such as Morae by TechSmith that can capture the participant's image, the screen, mouse clicks, and keystrokes. Remote conferencing tools such as GoToMeeting, WebEx, and LiveMeeting can be used to create virtual observation rooms where observers can see and hear the test participant.

MODERATION

The moderator needs to make the user feel comfortable and elicit useful responses at appropriate times without drastically interrupting the flow of the user's own narration or altering his or her perspective. The *nondirected interviewing* style should be used in all user interviews.

There are several things that moderators should do in all interviews.

- Probe expectations: Before participants click on a link, check a box, or perform any action with an interface, they have some idea of what will happen. Even though their idea of what will happen next may not be completely formed, they will always have *some* expectation. After the users have performed an action, their perception is forever altered about that action's effect. The only way to capture their view before it happens is to stop them as they're about to perform an action and ask them for their expectations of its effect. With a hyperlink, for example, asking the evaluators to describe what they think will happen if they click on a link can reveal a lot about their mental model of the functionality of the site.

Asking "Is that what you expected?" immediately after an action is also an excellent way of finding out whether the experience matches expectations.

- Ask "why" a lot: It's possible to learn a lot about people's attitudes, beliefs, and behaviors by asking simple, direct, unbiased questions at appropriate times. Five-year-olds do this all the time: they just ask "why" over and over again, digging deeper and deeper into a question without ever telegraphing that they think there's a correct answer. For example, when someone says, "I just don't do those kinds of things," asking "why" yields better information than just knowing that he or she does or doesn't do something.

- Suggest solutions, sometimes: Don't design during an interview, but it is OK to probe if a particular idea (that doesn't exist in the current product) would solve their problem. This is useful as a check on the interviewer's understanding of the problem, and it can be a useful way to sanity-check potential solutions. For example, a number of people in a test said they kept their personal schedule using Microsoft Outlook and their Palm Pilot. They weren't interested in online schedules since they felt it would involve duplicating effort even though they liked the convenience of a Web-based calendar. When the moderator suggested that their offline schedule could be synchronized with the online, they were universally excited and said that they would be much more likely to use the entire service if that feature were available.

- Investigate mistakes: When evaluators make mistakes, wait to see if they've realized that they've made a mistake and then immediately probe their thoughts and expectations. Why did they do something one way? What were they hoping it would do? How did they expect it to work? What happened that made them realize that it didn't work?

- Probe nonverbal cues: Sometimes people will react physically to an experience in a way that they wouldn't normally voice. When something is surprising or unexpected or unpleasant, someone may flinch, but not say anything. Likewise, a smile or a lean forward may signify satisfaction or interest. Watch for such actions and follow up, if appropriate. For example, "You frowned when that dialogue box came up. Is there anything about it that caused you to do that?"

- Keep the interview task centered: People naturally tend to tangent off on certain ideas that come up. As someone is performing a task, they may be reminded of an idea or an experience that they want to explore. Allowing people to explore their experiences is important, but it's also important to stay focused on the product and the task. When someone leans back, takes his or her hands off the keyboard, stops looking at the monitor, and starts speaking in the abstract, it's generally time to introduce a new task or return to the task at hand.

- Respect the evaluator's ideas: When people are off topic, let them go for a bit (maybe a minute or so) and see if they can wrap up their thoughts on their own. If they're not wrapping up, steer the conversation back to the task or topic at hand. If that doesn't seem to work, then you can be more explicit: "That's interesting and maybe we'll cover it more later, but let's take a look at the Fork of the Week page."

- Focus on their personal experience: People have a tendency to idealize their experience and to extrapolate it to others' needs or to their far future needs. Immediate experience, however, is much more telling about people's actual attitudes, needs, and behaviors and is usually much more useful than their extrapolations. When Peter says, "I think it may be useful to someone," ask him if it's useful to *him*. If Inga says that she understands it, but others may not, tell her that it's important to know about how *she* views it, not how it could be designed for others. If Tom says that something "may be useful someday," ask him if it's something that's useful to him *now*.

> **NOTE**
>
> Throughout this chapter, I have used the words "evaluator" and "participant" to refer to the people who are evaluating the interface, rather than "subject," "tester," "guinea pig," or whatnot. This is intentional. The people who you have recruited to evaluate your interface are your colleagues in this process. They are not being examined, the product is. It's tempting to set the situation up as a psychology experiment, but it's not. It's a directed evaluation of a product, not an inquiry into human nature, and should be treated as such on all levels.

MANAGING OBSERVERS

Getting as many members of the development team to observe the tests is one of the fastest ways to relate the findings of the test and win them over.

Make the appropriate staff watch the usability tests in real time, if possible. There's nothing more enlightening to a developer (or even a vice president of product development) than watching their interfaces misused and their assumptions misunderstood and not being able to do anything about it.

> **NOTE**
>
> Some researchers claim that it's possible to have multiple observers in the same room without compromising the quality of the observations. I haven't found that to be the case, nor have I chosen to have any in-room observers most of the time. It may well be possible to have a bunch of observers in the room and still have the participant perform comfortably and naturally – stage actors do this all the time, after all. However, I try to avoid the complications that this may introduce into the interpretation of people's statements by avoiding the question entirely.

The best way to get observers involved is through a two-way mirror or a closed-circuit video feed. Bring in plenty of food (pizza usually works). The team can then lounge in comfort and discuss the tests as they proceed (while not forgetting to watch how the participants are actually behaving). Because they know the product inside and out, they will see behaviors and attitudes that neither the moderator nor the analyst will, which is invaluable as source material for the analyst and for the team's understanding of their customers.

If neither a two-way mirror nor a closed-circuit feed is available, it's possible to have members of the team observe the tests directly. However, there should never be more than one observer per test. It's intimidating enough for the evaluator to be in a lab situation, but to have several people sitting behind them, sometimes scribbling, sometimes whispering, can be too creepy for even the most even-keeled. The observer, if he or she is in the room, should be introduced by name since this acknowledges his or her presence and gives the observer a role in the process other than "the guy sitting silently in the corner watching me."

Observers should be given instructions on acceptable behavior and to set their expectations of the process.

USABILITY TEST OBSERVER INSTRUCTIONS

1. Listen. As tempting as it is to immediately discuss what you're observing, make sure to listen to what people are really saying. Feel free to discuss what you're seeing, but don't forget to listen.
2. Usability tests are not statistically representative. If three of four people say something, that doesn't mean that 75 percent of the population feels that way. It does mean that a number of people may feel that way, but it doesn't mean anything numerically.
3. Don't take every word as gospel. These are just the views of a couple of people. If they have good ideas, great, but trust your intuition in judging their importance, unless there's significant evidence otherwise. So if someone says, "I hate the green," that doesn't mean that you change the color (though if everyone says, "I hate the green," then it's something to research further).
4. People are contradictory. Listen to how people are thinking about the topics and what criteria they use to come to conclusions, not necessarily the specific desires they voice. A person may not realize that two desires are impossible to have simultaneously, or he or she may not care. Be prepared to be occasionally bored or confused. People's actions aren't always interesting or insightful.
5. Don't expect revolutions. If you can get one or two good ideas out of each usability test, then it has served its purpose.
6. Watch for what people *don't* do or *don't* notice as much as you watch what they do and notice.

For in-room observers, add the following instructions:

7. Feel free to ask questions when the moderator gives you an explicit opportunity. Ask questions that do not imply a value judgment about the product one way or another. So instead of asking, "Is this the best-of-breed product in its class?" ask "Are there other products that do what this one does? Do you have any opinions about any of them?"
8. Do not mention your direct involvement with the product. It's easier for people to comment about the effectiveness of a product when they don't feel that someone with a lot vested in it is in the same room.

If the observers are members of the development team, encourage them to wait until they've observed all the participants before generalizing and designing solutions. People naturally want to start fixing problems as soon as they're recognized, but the context, magnitude, and prevalence of a problem should be known before energy is expended to fix it. Until the landscape of all the issues is established, solution design is generally not recommended.

TIPS AND TRICKS

- Always do a dry run of the interview a day or two beforehand. Get everything set up as for a real test, complete with all the appropriate hardware and prototypes installed. Then get someone who is roughly the kind of person you're recruiting, but who isn't intimately involved in the development of the product, and conduct a full interview with him or her. Use this time to make sure that the script, the hardware, and the tasks are all working as designed. Go through the whole interview, and buy the evaluator lunch afterward.
- Reset the computer and the lab in between every test. Make sure every user gets the same environment by clearing the browser cache, resetting the history (so all links come up as new and cookies are erased), and restarting the browser so that it's on a blank page (you can set most browsers so that they open to a blank page by default). Clear off any notes or paperwork from the previous person and turn off the monitor.
- If possible, provide both a Macintosh and a PC for your usability test, allowing the evaluator to use whichever one he or she is more comfortable with. You can even include a question about it in the screener and know ahead of time which one the participant typically uses.
- Don't take extensive notes during the test. This allows you to focus on what the user is doing and probe particular behaviors. Also, the participants won't associate their behavior with periods of frantic scribbling, which they often interpret as an indicator that they just did something wrong.
- Take notes immediately after, writing down all interesting behaviors, errors, likes, and dislikes. Discuss the test with any observers for 10–20 minutes immediately after and take notes on their observations, too.

HOW TO ANALYZE IT

Although some things are going to be obvious, a formal analysis is necessary to get to underlying causes and to extract the most value from the interviews. Analyzing the output is a three-stage process: collecting observations, organizing observations, and extracting trends from the observations.

> **NOTE**
>
> The moderator and analyst are referred to as separate people here, but in practice, the two roles are often performed by the same person.

Collecting Observations

There are three sets of observations to be collected: the moderator's, the observers', and the analyst's.

Collecting the moderator's and observers' notes is pretty straightforward. Get their notes (or copies), and have them walk you through them, explaining what each one means. In addition, interview them for additional observations that were not in their notes. These are frequently large-scale perspectives on the situation that the person made in the days or hours following the last test.

The analyst's notes are the most important and time-consuming part of the data collection process. The analyst should go through at least four of the videotapes and note down all situations where there were mistakes or confusion or where the evaluators expressed an opinion about the product or its features. He or she should note which features the evaluators had problems with, under what circumstances they encountered those problems, and provide a detailed description of the problem. The majority of the usability problems in the product will likely be found during this phase, as the patterns in people's behavior and expectations emerge.

Quantitative information, although not generalizable to the whole target market at large, is often useful when summarizing and comparing behavior (however, it's fraught with potential problems as people reading reports can latch on to largely meaningless numbers as some kind of absolute truth). To collect quantitative information, first create a measurement range for each question that everyone in the analysis team agrees upon. Don't use a stopwatch, and take exact numbers. The statistical error present in the small sample of people in a usability test swamps out the accuracy of a stopwatch. The most useful metrics are the ones that are the most general. Flow Interactive, Limited (http://www.flow-interactive.com), a U.K. user experience design and evaluation consulting company, uses the following range to measure how long people take to perform a task:

    0 – Fail
    1 – Succeed very slowly in a roundabout way
    2 – Succeed a little slowly
    3 – Succeed quickly

Most of the time, this is all the precision you need since an order-of-magnitude measure is all that's necessary to be able to make critical comparisons. Each scale should have three or five steps (don't use two, four, or six since it's hard to find a middle value; don't use more than five because it tends to get confusing) and a separate value for failure.

Make a grid for each participant consisting of the task metrics you're going to collect. As the videotapes are being watched, note the severity in each cell (when appropriate, define severity using the same language and scale that is used by the development team to define how serious code bugs are). For the fork tasks, the following table would reflect one person's performance.

MARLON'S TASK PERFORMANCE

User: Marlon	Time to Read	Errors	Time to Complete
Find Louis XIV	1	3	1
Buy replacement	3	1	2
Find similar forks	1	2	0
Key	0 – Don't read	0 – Fail because of errors	0 – Fail
	1 – Read very slowly	1 – Many errors	1 – Succeed very slowly in a roundabout way
	2 – Read moderately slowly	2 – Some errors	2 – Succeed a little slowly
	3 – Read quickly	3 – Few or no errors	3 – Succeed quickly

Then, when compiling the final analysis, create a table for each metric that summarizes the whole user groups' experience. For the completion time metric, the table could look as follows.

TASK PERFORMANCE TIME MEASURES

	Marlon	Eva	Marc	Barb	Jon	Avg.
Find Louis XIV	1	2	1	0	2	1.2
Buy replacement	2	3	2	1	1	1.8
Find similar forks	0	0	1	1	0	0.4

The average numbers, although not meaningful in an absolute context, provide a way to compare tasks to each other and between designs.

Note down feature requests and verbatim quotations from the evaluators, especially ones that encapsulate a particular behavior (e.g., "I don't understand what 'Forkopolis' means, so I wouldn't click there"). Feature requests are often attempts to articulate a problem that the evaluator can't express in any other way. However, they can also be innovative solutions to those same problems, so they should be captured, regardless.

2X VIDEO DECKS ARE COOL

To make the video review process go faster, I recommend using a video deck (or a digital video player) that can play back video and audio at 1.5 or 2 times natural speed. The

> speech is still understandable (although silly, since people sound like chipmunks unless the voice is pitch-shifted down, as it is done on Sony's professional-grade video hardware), and it's possible to make your way through a tape much faster.

If time and budget allow, a transcription of the whole session is helpful, but it should be used only as an aid in observing the tapes because it misses the vocal inflection and behavior that can really clarify some situations. For example, a confused pause of five seconds while an evaluator passes his pointer over every single visual element on the screen looking for somewhere to click is insufficiently conveyed by his statement of, "Aha! There it is."

Organizing Observations

First, read through all the notes once to get a feeling for the material. Look for repetition and things that may be caused by common underlying problems.

> **NOTE**
>
> Much as with analyzing contextual inquiry information or focus group observations, organizing usability testing information and extracting trends can be done in a group with the development team (and other stakeholders, as appropriate). This allows the group to use its collected knowledge to flesh out the understanding of the problem and to begin working on solutions.

Then put all the observations into a pile (literally, or in a single large document). Opening a separate document in a word processor, go through each observation and group it with other similar observations in the new document. Similarity can be in terms of superficial similarity ("Term not understood"), feature cluster ("Shopping cart problems"), or in terms of underlying cause ("Confusing information architecture"). Group the observations with the most broadly sweeping, underlying causes. Pull quotations out and group them with the causes that they best illustrate.

Extracting Trends

Having grouped all the observations, go through the groups and consolidate them, separating the groups of unrelated topics. Throw away those that only have one or two individual observations. For each group, try to categorize the problem in a single short sentence, with a couple of sentences to fully describe the phenomenon. Explain the underlying cause as much as possible, separating the explanation of the phenomenon from your hypothesis of its cause. Concentrate on describing the problem, its immediate impact on the user experience, and the place where the problem occurred. Be very careful when suggesting solutions. Ultimately, the development team knows more about the technology and the assumptions that went into the product, and the responsibility for isolating underlying causes and finding solutions is theirs. Your recommendations should serve as a guide of where solutions *could be* found, not edicts about what must be done.

WARNING

It's easy to confuse making user severity measures into priorities for the development of the project. This is generally inappropriate. What's most important to a user's success with the product is not necessarily what's most important to the product's success. The product team should be informed of problem severity from the user perspective and then use that to determine project priorities, but the two aren't the same.

Describe the severity of the problem from the user's perspective, but don't give observations numerical severity grades. If a shorthand for the characterization of observations is desired or requested, categorize the observations in terms of the effects they have on the user experience, rather than giving them an arbitrary severity. Such a scale could be "Prevents an activity," "Causes confusion," "Does not match expectations," "Seen as unnecessary."

Once all this is done, you should have a list of observations, hypotheses for what caused the phenomena, and quotations that reinforce and summarize the observations. You're ready to present your results to the team!

Example

This is a short report summarizing a test on another Webmonkey prototype for the site's development team. It builds on the previous testing that the site had gone through and focuses on the changes made to the front door and the renaming of various sections in the site.

EXECUTIVE SUMMARY

Five Web developers were shown the functional prototype for Webmonkey 4.0. In general, they liked it, especially the tutorials and the color scheme, but some of the organization confused them (specifically, the difference between the "Categories" and "Tutorials" sections). The new folderlike navigation metaphor made sense to everyone, and they wished that it was on every page. Everyone saw the "Cool Tools" section, but thought it was an ad and ignored it, and although they liked the "Inspiration" section, they expected it to be more than just animation in the long run.

Finally, a couple of people said that it would be cool to have Webmonkey link to good, useful external content in an unbiased way since it would be useful and would reinforce Webmonkey's street cred.

Executive summaries are very useful when communicating results. The vice president of product development may never read the report, but a couple of paragraphs giving 50 000 of the results of the usability test are likely to be read. When attaching the report in an e-mail, the executive summary should be included in the e-mail, while the rest of the report – including the executive summary – is included as an attachment.

PROCEDURE

Five people who spend a significant amount of time developing Web sites were invited. They were first asked some preliminary questions about their general net usage and where they went for developer information (both on the Web and in general).They were then shown the site prototype and asked to go through it in detail, concentrating on specific details, including the folder-style navigation, and the Cool Tools section. After giving their responses to the front door, they were asked to scroll down through one of the top stories, talking about their experience with the interface and their thoughts on the content. They were then asked to look for some specific content as a way of gauging their understanding of the layout of the site. Finally, they were asked some wrap-up and blue-sky questions, and the test was concluded.

A fast description of the procedure demystifies the process and provides important context for report recipients to be able to understand the results.

EVALUATOR PROFILES

Michael

Michael spends more than 40 hours a week on the Internet, 20 hours of which is spent making Web pages, including design, programming, and production. Of all the development sites, he likes Webmonkey because of its "broad range." He also regularly reads "Flash Zone" because it can give him tutorials that he can't get in print. For CGI work, he follows another site, "CGI Resources" (the "CGI Zone"? The specific site wasn't clear from the interview).

John

John spends 30 hours a week on the Internet, half of which is work related. He spends at least 10 hours a week making Web sites, including design, markup, and code. He uses reference books and Webmonkey for technical Web-related information. He also goes to "SGML University" and has never been to builder. com. Most of the time, he goes to these sites with specific questions. In general, he would like developer sites to be better organized by topic.

David

David spends 20–30 hours a week on the Internet, 75 percent of which is work related, and five to 10 percent is spent doing Web development, most of which is design. His main sources of technical information are Webmonkey and notes from school. He has never seen builder.com and goes to Webmonkey for both technology updates and to answer specific questions.

[Remaining profiles omitted]

Evaluator profiles are useful both to help the report reader understand the context in which people's statements were made and as a way to personify the participants to those who were unable to observe the tests. These profiles help personalize the abstract concept of a product's users and make the results much more immediate.

OBSERVATIONS

General Observations

1. People like tutorials above all else. All the evaluators were drawn to the tutorials, sometimes to the exclusion of other content. The tutorials section was often the first one mentioned when the evaluators were asked where they would click on next. It was also the section people preferred to go to for general information even though there was a broader range of content in the "Categories" section.
2. Almost everyone said they liked the color scheme. Without being asked about it, most of the evaluators volunteered that they really liked the color scheme on the homepage.
3. People generally come to development sites with specific questions in mind, not to see "the latest." When asked whether they go to sites like Webmonkey to catch up on the latest technology or to get answers to specific questions, people generally said that it was to answer specific questions.

Likewise, when asked how they preferred to navigate through sites like Webmonkey, people said that they preferred searching, rather than browsing, since that brought them closer to the specific information they were looking for.

Features

1. There was confusion between the content people would find in the "Categories" section and the "Tutorials" section (and, to a lesser extent, between the "Tutorials" section and the "Guides" section). Partially because of the ambiguity of the "Categories" name and partly because of the similar – but not completely identical – labels in the two sections, people were confused about what they would find in each section.

    📁 Categories
    📁 Tutorials
    📁 Guides
    📁 Jobs

    📁 About Webmonkey

    Whenever possible, include screenshots.

2. The "Cool Tools" section was noticed early by nearly everyone, but treated as a big ad and, thus, ignored by most. Until it was pointed out to a number of the evaluators that there was nonadvertising content in "Cool Tools," they did not appear to notice it. Most pointed to the picture and the price as indicators of why it was considered to be advertising content.

3. A couple of people saw and liked the idea behind the "First Time Here" link.
4. People didn't know to go to "Backend" for CGI topics and were unsure of what kinds of things would be found there. One person mentioned that he'd prefer it be called "Server Stuff" or something similar.
5. People didn't notice the reference pop-up on the main page at first, and when they did, they weren't sure about its relationship to the content accessible from the folders in the left-hand margin. However, most everyone found it to be a useful tool with contents that made sense (except for "ISO Entities"). A couple of people suggested that it be put in the left-hand margin along with the folders.

Navigation

1. Everyone understood the folder metaphor on the front door.
2. The inconsistent content and appearance of the left margin navigation was somewhat confusing. A number of people mentioned that they were surprised that the navigation in the left-hand margin changed from the front door to the subsections and the tutorials. Several mentioned that they would have preferred a continuation of the folder metaphor from the front door.
3. People generally understood the pathnamelike breadcrumb navigation at the top of the page though not everyone noticed it. The biggest disconnect came when people would jump to a "Tutorial" directly from the top page (thus expecting the path to be something like "home/ tutorial/javascript") and the path read "home/categories/javascript/tutorial," which did not match their expectation.

Naming

1. The "Categories" name wasn't clear. People weren't sure what "Categories" was referring to, and one person didn't even see it as a section to be clicked on.
2. "Guides" wasn't clear as a section title. There was confusion in most of the evaluators between the "Guides" section and the tutorials.
3. Likewise, "eBiz" wasn't clear. Although not everyone was asked about it, the couple of people who were didn't know what to expect on the other side.
4. "Heard on the Street" was ambiguous. Without looking at it, when the participants were asked to define what the "Heard on the Street" section was and how it was different from the other content sections, most people said that it was a "most recent" section or that it highlighted some news development.

CONCLUSION

The combination of the attraction of the concept of tutorials with the unclear wording of "Categories" caused people to frequently ignore the categories section entirely.

A lot of the confusion comes from the ambiguity of single-word names. "Categories" and "Guides," although they adequately describe the sections after people have already seen them, give people little information about them before they've seen them, since, as words, they're quite general. Thus, the naming of sections (and maybe everything on the site in general) has to be done with the user's context in mind. What may, in retrospect, make perfect sense may be confusing and ambiguous before a definition is produced.

QUOTATIONS
Michael

> "You know the functionality is out there, you just want to know how to put it together."

> "When I started going there, it was a beginning site, it was very good for that, but then it kind of stayed there and I moved on." [re: Builder.com]

> "I saw 'Cool Tool Pick,' and I thought that this would say GoLive and this would be Dreamweaver and this would be something else."

> "If one of them weren't there, it might be easier [to differentiate between them]." [re:"tutorials" vs."categories"]

John

> "It stands out without being the obnoxious Wired magazine look."

> "If I were coming here to find a specific answer on something, I would go to 'Tutorial.'"

> "'Categories' is everything and these are just subtopics."

> "I would prefer to see the latest tutorial [rather than Inspiration] at the top."

[Remaining quotations omitted]

A couple of sentences of evaluators' actual words often better illustrate the points you're trying to convey than a paragraph of explanation. The readers can then see the patterns you're trying to illustrate for them. When placed next to each point, they serve to reinforce each point as it's made. When presented all at once, they communicate the feel of a usability test.

Usability tests are one of the workhorses of user experience research. They can be done quickly and inexpensively, and provide a lot of immediately actionable information. Too often they're used as the only form of user feedback, but when used correctly, they're an invaluable tool.

CHAPTER 11

Analysis and Interpretation of User Observation Evaluation Data

Debbie Stone, Caroline Jarrett, Mark Woodroffe, and Shailey Minocha

EDITOR'S COMMENTS

The analysis and interpretation of data from evaluation sessions is influenced by a number of factors including:

- The amount of time you allocate for these activities. The consumers of the test report are usually anxious to get the results and there is pressure to provide "quick and dirty" reports. It is important to plan sufficient time in your schedule for unexpected interruptions, equipment failure, more data than you had expected and ambiguous data. A common shortcut for generating a test report is to give "fuzzy" numbers like "some users" or "many users," which can easily be questioned. Reports with fuzzy results can lack credibility.
- Training for observers. Taking notes is a difficult task. A coding scheme with problem categories can help, but notetakers still have to consider what they are seeing, what they are hearing, and whether they are recording data or making interpretations. Well-trained observers can make for better analysis and interpretation.
- Understanding what constitutes a "problem." This is sometimes obvious and sometimes very difficult. This chapter describes the general characteristics of a problem. What constitutes a problem is often determined by the context. If you have a Web form that a person uses once a month, then you might consider memorability as an issue. Do they remember what to do with the form? If the form is used 300 times a day, then anything that slows someone down (like the need to use the mouse to move to a different field) would be a problem. The same observation might yield a problem for the high-frequency users, but no problem for the occasional user who is not worried about the extra seconds required to move between fields.

This chapter describes best practices and suggestions for analyzing and interpreting your data and ensuring that you have a clear, persuasive, and useful report.

INTRODUCTION: HOW TO ANALYZE AND INTERPRET DATA FROM YOUR EVALUATION

An evaluation session generates a large amount of data. After the session, you will have at least some, if not all, of the following data items:

- Background data about the participant
- Notes made by the evaluator(s)
- Audio or video recordings
- Completed data collection forms
- Quantitative data on times, errors, and other usability metrics
- Quantitative (and possibly qualitative) data from pre- and post–session questionnaires
- Retrospective protocols
- A list of any usability problems identified during the observations

The process of analysis is concerned with turning the evaluation data collected into information from which you can make decisions. We will describe three steps in the analysis of evaluation:

- Collating the data
- Summarizing the data
- Reviewing the data to identify any usability problems

COLLATING THE DATA

There can be a surprisingly large quantity of pieces of paper after each evaluation session (see Fig. 11.1): your own notes, test materials, notes made by the participant, perhaps printed outputs, and (often) observers' notes. You may also want to back up the data entered by the participant. If you are testing a Web site, you could take screen shots or back up the log to show the participant's visited links before you reset the site for the next participant.

Paper forms are convenient if you want to record the results of discussing your findings in a debriefing meeting. If you have responses on questionnaires, then a database might be a good way to collate them. User observations usually produce so much qualitative data that it is worth typing it up in some way. A usability practitioner provided the following quote:

> I collect and number the notes and other forms from each participant immediately—between participants. I keep each set separately in a plastic wallet that is large enough to hold any videotape or backup as well. Then I try to type up the notes by the end of the next day at the latest. Even a week later it can be difficult to remember what I meant. But all I try to do is type up the raw notes. There is no need to do all the analysis at this stage, and usually I find that it is easier to make sense of the data if I do all the typing up first, then all the analysis together separately. That way, themes emerge more easily and I do not get sidetracked by one participant's experiences. It helps me to ensure that I have considered all the data before moving to recommendations.

FIGURE 11.1
There can be a surprisingly large quantity of pieces of paper after an evaluation.

Other practitioners have other methods for writing up notes. Some use index cards, with a point of interest on each; some use a spreadsheet, with an entry for each point of interest; others use a word processor, typing each comment.

Whatever method you choose, be sure to include a reference back to the original participant so that you can identify which participant inspired which comment. You should also be careful to note the difference between what a participant said and what you happened to notice. It is perfectly acceptable for you to form your own opinions about the user interface (UI) as you watch someone work on it, but you would not want to inadvertently quote your opinion as that of a user.

EDITOR'S NOTE: OBSERVATION VERSUS INTERPRETATION

Here are two notes from different observers of a usability test:

Observer 1: "Participant 1 moved the mouse back and forth across the menus several times. Then he opened the Modify menu, moving the mouse up and down the list of items. Then he clicked on the Insert menu and then he went to help and did a search...."

Observer 2: "The person is moving the mouse around a lot and looks very confused!"

> The first observer has described the participant's behavior and does not provide conclusions or interpretations of that behavior. The second observer provides a more general statement of what is happening, but then makes an interpretation. The participant might be confused, but might also be exhibiting exploratory behavior because he is unfamiliar with the software he is evaluating.
>
> Notetakers should be trained to record behaviors – the raw material from which interpretations can be made.

SUMMARIZING THE DATA

Summarizing the data involves extracting key comments from the collated data. It may also involve performing simple mathematical calculations (to compute averages of times spent on tasks and so on). For example, suppose your usability requirement was to validate the usability metric "Time spent to recover from an error," whose planned level is 30 seconds. During the evaluation session, you will record the start time of the task and the end time. You then subtract the start time from the end time to calculate the time spent on the task by the participant. That wasn't too hard, was it?

As the number of participants in most evaluations is small, complex statistical analysis is not applicable (Dray & Siegel, 1999), so we have not included details or methods for the statistical analysis of evaluation data.

REVIEWING THE DATA TO IDENTIFY USABILITY PROBLEMS

A key purpose of evaluation is to decide whether the interface has met the usability requirements and, if it has not, what to do about it. This entails reviewing the summarized evaluation data. If a review of the data shows that the usability requirements have been met, then no further analysis or interpretation of the data is required. If, however, incidents are revealed where, say, the participant has made an error, could not complete the task description, was unsure what to do next, or had to ask for or look up for further information, these incidents should be compiled into a list of usability problems. Usability problems are also referred to as usability defects in the literature; from this point on, we will adopt the term "usability defect."

A *usability defect* is a usability problem in the user interface. Usability defects can lead to confusion, error, delay, or outright failure to complete some task on the part of the user. They make the UI, and hence the system, less usable for its target users. To help you identify the usability defects, we have listed some of their characteristics in the box below (adapted from Chauncey Wilson, personal communication, 2001).

EDITOR'S NOTE: CHARACTERISTICS OF USABILITY DEFECTS

A usability defect has one or more of the following characteristics:

- It irritates or confuses the user.
- It makes a system hard to install, learn, or use.
- It causes mental overload of the user. (For example, the user may have to think a lot as the required action or feedback from the system may not be obvious or sufficient.)
- It causes poor user performance.
- It violates design standards or guidelines.
- It reduces trust or credibility of the system.
- It tends to cause repeated errors.
- It could make the system hard to market.

The usability defects identified from the summarized data can be recorded onto data analysis forms. We have suggested a template data analysis form for user observation in Table 11.1. Some sample data have been entered into the table for illustrative purposes.

Table 11.1	Data Analysis Form for User Observation	
Task Scenario No: 1 **Evaluator's Name: John** **Participant: Beth**	**Session Date: February 11** **Session Start Time: 9:30 a.m.** **Session End Time: 10:20 a.m.**	
Source of Evaluation Data (Video Clips, Audio Clips, Participant's Verbal Protocols, Observer's Notes, Retrospective Protocols, etc.)	Usability Defect Description	Evaluator's Comments
Verbal protocol	The user did not select the right menu item (Options) to initiate the task.	The user was not sure which menu the menu item Options was in.
Video	–	–

WORKING WITH QUANTITATIVE DATA

Quantitative data are more eye-catching for the readers of your evaluation report and are often regarded as more objective than qualitative data. If you have clearly defined usability metrics, then reporting is relatively simple as you can compare the results you got with the results you wanted. If you have not taken measurements during the evaluation, the qualitative data can still yield some numbers; for example, three out of five participants have made similar comments on some feature of the UI. Be particularly careful to avoid statistical language such as "significant result" unless you have enough data to undertake a statistical analysis that will support your claims.

There are three groups of methods for summarizing quantitative data:

- Tabulations, charts, and rankings that provide a visual representation of your data.
- Descriptive statistics such as mean, median, and mode that describe the data you have obtained.
- Inferential statistics such as tests of statistical significance that give the probability that a claim arising from your data can be applied to your user population as a whole.

In most evaluations, we look for information to help us decide what to do next with the UI, and small frequent tests are more helpful than a single, large-scale technique. We, therefore, usually opt for small numbers of participants in most usability evaluations. However, these small samples do not support the mathematics of most inferential statistics. For example, usually you need a random sample of 50–100 users as a minimum before calculating the significance. If you are contemplating large-scale quantitative techniques such as administering a questionnaire to a big group of users, then we suggest that you refer to one of the standard works on the topic.

TIP
Clegg (1983) is a good introduction to statistics. Huff (1991) explains how to use statistics appropriately.

Mathematically, you can use descriptive statistics on any sample size. For example, it is mathematically correct to take a task time of five seconds for one user, six seconds for the second user, and 55 seconds for the third, then calculate the average (mean) task time as (5 + 6 + 55)/3 = 22 seconds. From a mathematical point of view, including this average in your usability report does not claim anything for the likely task time for the user population as a whole. However, many readers of usability reports either do not have statistical training or are too busy to challenge your figures. They will assume that any descriptive statistics apply to the user population. If you include descriptive statistics in your report then consider whether they can or should apply to the user population. Is it likely that your users are all rather similar? Or might there be subgroups with very different profiles? Also, think about the conclusions that your readers might draw from the descriptive statistics.

EDITOR'S NOTE: MEAN VERSUS MEDIAN

Although not quite as common in usability reports, the use of the median would be more appropriate than the arithmetic mean in the above-mentioned example. Both the mean and the median are measures of central tendency. The mean is the sum of a set of values divided by the number of values. The median is the value that falls at the middle of the values when they are ordered from the lowest value to the highest (or vice versa). The median is less affected by a small number of extreme values. For example, the mean of $5 + 8 + 29 = 42/3$ or 14. The median of those same three values would be 8.

Tabular and visual representations of your data can provide a break from the narrative of your report and highlight the relevant material. For example, the Table 11.2, and Fig. 11.2 all have the same data. Which do you find easiest to understand?

Table 11.2	Example Data from an Evaluation	
Participant	**Experience Level**	**Task Time**
Participant 1	Experienced	5 seconds
Participant 2	Experienced	6 seconds
Participant 3	Novice	55 seconds
Target	–	4 seconds

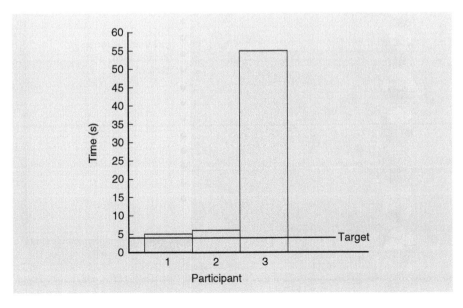

FIGURE 11.2
Example data from an evaluation.

EXAMPLE OF TASK TIMES

The task time for participant one (experienced) was five seconds, participant two (experienced) took six seconds, the third participant was a novice and took 55 seconds. The target for task time is four seconds.

WORKING WITH QUALITATIVE DATA

Quantitative data can show you that a defect exists, and perhaps the extent of its impact, but often it is qualitative data that give you the insights into the cause of the problem and what to do about it. For example, did a task take too long because the system response time was excessive or because the user found the interface confusing and chose incorrect options?

An Example of Data from Global Warming

One participant in a *Global Warming* evaluation provides a good example of the usefulness of qualitative data. He worked happily on the screen in Fig. 11.3, clicking on the different icons and reading the explanations that appeared on the Notebook page. Then he clicked on the "Move forward" arrow in the bottom right-hand corner and got to the screen in Fig. 11.4. There is a section from the evaluation notes in Fig. 11.5.

FIGURE 11.3
Explanation of each factor in the model.

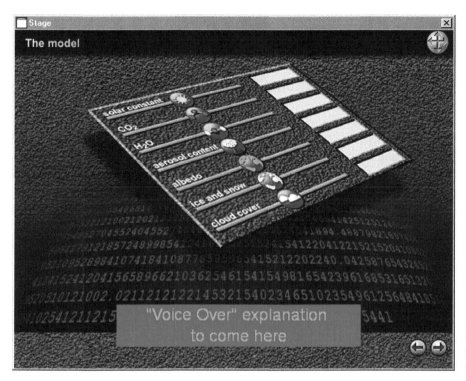

FIGURE 11.4
Voice-over explanation of how to interact with the factors.

Script	User's remarks
When screen appears, ask: Do you know what to do next? Do you recognize what to do, or did you have to recall what to do? What are you trying to do? *Ask user to take action.*	I have to skip on from that. Nothing happens when I click on these icons. I presume I'll have to click on the go forward button.

FIGURE 11.5
A section of notes from a *Global Warming* participant.

The middle of the screen shows a tilted view of the slide bars with round "factors" icons on them. The participant tried to click on the icons of these factors before going to the correct choice: the round button with an arrow in the bottom right-hand corner. This is a clear failure of "Easy to navigate," but do we know why?

In Fig. 11.3, the factor icons have an affordance for clicking and an instruction to click on an icon if you wish to know more. For example, clicking on the sun icon results in an explanation of the solar constant.

Figure 11.4 shows the same icons, with a reduced affordance for clicking because they are on a sloped image. It seems that the reduction in affordance was not enough to tell the participant that he should not click on these icons.

Making Decisions with Qualitative Data

Working with qualitative data is a process of making decisions that start with thinking about what to note in the evaluation (collecting the data), continues through the collation and review process, and then influences your summary (analysis and interpretation).

Those decisions need to be made in the light of the following factors:

- *The differences between the participants in your evaluation and the real users*. For example, your test participants might have more experience of the system than the real users, or they might lack specialist domain knowledge.
- *The differences between your test environment and the users' environment*. For example, you may have had to stop the test while you solved a configuration problem in the system, or the room where you conducted the test might be much quieter or noisier than the users' environment.

The same decisions apply to the data from your pilot test. It is even more likely that your pilot participant is different from your real users, so you need to be more cautious about drawing conclusions from the pilot data. The actual process of examining your qualitative data to identify usability defects depends very much on your user interface and on what happened in your evaluation. In practice, it is usually quite easy to spot the important problems and find the causes for them.

It often helps to speed up the work of reviewing your qualitative data if you establish a *coding scheme*. A coding scheme is any method of assigning a group, number, or label to an item of data. For example, you might look first for all the data about icons, then for everything about the meaning of labels, then for remarks about navigation. Some practitioners establish their coding schemes in advance, perhaps from a list of heuristics or from an inspection of the UI. Others derive a scheme from the pilot test. However, evaluations frequently surprise even the most experienced practitioner, and it is quite usual to find that the coding scheme needs to be modified somewhat when you start interpreting the data.

It is also typical to find that some of the data are inconclusive, cannot be retrieved, or have been badly written down. If your only data from an evaluation were derived from a video recording and the tape cannot be read, you have a disaster – which is why we place so much emphasis on taking paper notes of some kind along with any electronic data collection.

Generally, your chances of deciphering what a comment meant (whether from bad writing or clumsy phrasing) are much better if you do the analysis promptly and preferably within a day of the evaluation sessions.

INTERPRETATION OF USER-OBSERVATION DATA

Once you have analyzed your data – for example, by grouping them according to a coding scheme – your final step is interpretation: deciding what caused the defects that you have identified and recommending what to do about them. In Table 11.4, we suggest a template for gathering defects and interpretations. Again, some sample data have been entered into the table for the purposes of illustration. For the example task, because the defect is related to the first action of the task and the task cannot be accomplished until the user chooses the right menu item, we have assigned a *severity rating* of "High." Notice that this form carefully preserves the distinction between our observations and our comments on them.

Some practitioners prefer to gather the defects and the good points about the interface on a single form, whereas others prefer to deal with all the defects and all the good points in two separate passes. Choose whichever method you prefer.

Assigning Severities

The process of summarizing the data usually makes it obvious which problems require the most urgent attention. In our form in Table 11.3, we have included a column for assigning a severity to each defect.

Bearing in mind our comments about statistics, one important point to remember is that the weighting given to each participant's results depends very much on comparison with your overall user profile.

Recommending Changes

Some authorities stop here, taking the view that it is the responsibility of the development team to decide what to change in the interface. For example, the Common Industry Format for summative evaluation does not include a section for recommendations, taking the view that deciding what to do is a separate process when undertaking a summative evaluation:

Table 11.3 Data Interpretation Form for User Observations

Task Scenario No. 1 Evaluator's Name: John		Session Date: February 11 Session Start Time: 9:30 a.m. Session End Time: 10:20 a.m.	
Usability Observation	Evaluator's Comments	Cause of the Usability Defect, if There Is One	Severity Rating
The user did not select the right menu item (Options) to initiate the task.	The user was not sure which menu item Options was in.	The menu name is inappropriate, as it does not relate to the required action.	High
–	–	–	–

> Stakeholders can use the usability data to help make informed decisions concerning the release of software products or the procurement of such products. (http://zing.ncsl.nist.gov/iusr/documents/whatistheClF.html)

If your task is to improve the interface as well as to establish whether it meets the requirements, then you are likely to need to work out what to do next: recommending the changes.

So we suggest a template in Table 11.4 to record the recommendations. In the table, the "Status" column indicates what is being planned for the recommended change – when the usability defect will be rectified, if it has been deferred, or if it is being ignored for the time being.

It is hard to be specific about interpretation of results. Fortunately, you will find that many problems have obvious solutions, particularly if this is an exploratory evaluation of an early prototype.

Evaluations are full of surprises. You will find defects in parts of the interface that you thought would work well, and conversely you may find that users are completely comfortable with something that you personally find irritating or never expected to work. Equally frequently, you will find that during the analysis of the results you simply do not have the data to provide an answer. Questions get overlooked, or users have conflicting opinions. Finally, the experience of working with real users can entirely change your perception of their tasks and environment, and the domain of the user interface.

Your recommendations, therefore, are likely to contain a mixture of several points:

- Successes to build on
- Defects to fix
- Possible defects or successes that are not proven – not enough evidence to decide either way (these require further evaluation)
- Areas of the user interface that were not tested (no evidence) (these also require further evaluation)
- Changes to usability and other requirements

Table 11.4 Recommendations Form

Participant	Usability defect	Cause of the usability defect	Severity rating	Recommended solution	Status description
Beth	The user did not select the right menu item (Options) to initiate the task.	The menu name is inappropriate, as it does not relate to the required action.	The menu name should be changed to "Group."	High	Make change in next revision.
Mary	–	–	–	–	–

WRITING THE EVALUATION REPORT

Generally, you need to write up what you have done in an evaluation:

- To act as a record of what you did
- To communicate the findings to other stakeholders

The style and contents of the report depend very much on who you are writing for and why.

EDITOR'S NOTE: TIMELINESS CAN CAUSE TROUBLE: WHEN OBSERVATIONS BECOME "THE REPORT"

Be cautious about releasing preliminary results, including e-mails about the evaluation, that observers send to their teams after seeing a few sessions. By chance, observers might see sessions that are not representative of the overall results.

Development schedules have been shrinking over the last decade and there is often pressure to "get the data out quickly." In some cases, developers watch think-aloud sessions, discuss major problems at the end of the day and makes changes to the product (in the absence of any formal report) that sometimes appear in code even before the evaluation is complete. While fixing an obvious bug (e.g., a misspelled label) may be acceptable, changing key features without discussing the impact of the changes across the product may yield fixes that create new usability problems.

If you plan to release daily or preliminary results, err on the conservative side and release only the most certain findings with a caveat about the dangers of making changes before all the data are in. Caution observers that acting too hastily might result in fixes that have to be "unfixed" or political problems that have to be undone.

Here is an example of a typical report created for an academic journal.

EXTRACT FROM AN ACADEMIC PAPER ON THE GLOBAL WARMING EVALUATIONS

Abstract

The Open University [OU] has undertaken the production of a suite of multimedia teaching materials for inclusion in its forthcoming science foundation course. Two of these packages (*Global Warming and Cooling* and *An Element on the Move*) have recently been tested and some interesting general issues have emerged from these empirical studies. The formative testing of each piece of software was individually tailored to the respective designers' requirements. Since these packages were not at the same stage of development, the evaluations were constructed to answer very different questions and to satisfy different production needs. The question the designers of the *Global Warming* software wanted answered was: "Is the generic shell usable/easy to navigate through?"

This needed an answer because the mathematical model of *Global Warming* had not been completed on time but the software production schedule still had to proceed. Hence the designers needed to know that when the model was slotted in the students would be able to work with the current structure of the program.

2.0 Background

The multimedia materials for this Science Foundation course consisted of 26 programs. This first year course introduces students to the academic disciplines of biology, chemistry, earth sciences and physics and so programs were developed for each of these subject domains. The software was designed not to stand alone but to complement written course notes, videotapes, home experiments, and face to face tutorials.

The aims of the program production teams were to:

- Exploit the media to produce pedagogical materials that could not be made in any other way
- Produce a program with easy communication channels to
  i. the software itself via the interface
  ii. the domain knowledge via the structure and presentation of the program
- Provide students with high levels of interactivity
- Sustain students with a motivating learning experience

In order to test whether the programs would meet the above aims a framework for the developmental testing of the software was devised. A three-phased approach was recommended and accepted by the Science Team. This meant that prototypes which contained generic features could be tested at a very early stage and that the developers would aim, with these early programs, to actually make prototypes to be tested quickly at the beginning of the software's life cycle. This was known as the Primary Formative Testing Phase. The subjects for this phase would not need to be Open University students but people who were more "competent" computer users. We wanted to see if average computer users could navigate through a section and understand a particular teaching strategy without then having to investigate all the details of the subject matter. This would mean the testing could take place more quickly and easily with subjects who could be found on campus.

The Secondary Formative Testing Phase was aimed to test the usability and learning potential of the software. It would take place later in the developmental cycle and would use typical Open University students with some science background. Pre- to post-test learning measures would indicate the degree of learning that took place with the software. Testing the time taken to work through the programs was an important objective for this phase. It was agreed that the Open University students would be paid a small fee when they came to the university to test the software.

The Tertiary Testing Phase would include the final testing with pairs of Open University students working together with the software. In this way, the talk generated around the tasks would indicate how clearly the tasks were constructed and how well the students understood the teaching objectives of the program. (The framework is summarized in the table presented here.)

3.0 Framework for Formative Developmental Testing

3.1 The Testing Cycle

…The aim of the testing here was to evaluate some generic features, therefore all the pieces of the program did not have to be in place. In fact the aim of this evaluation study was to provide the developers with feedback about general usability issues, the interface and subjects' ease of navigation around the system…

3.2 Subjects

…Generic features were tested with "experienced users" who did not have scientific background knowledge and could easily be found to fill the tight testing schedule…. In order to understand if certain generic structures worked, "experienced users" were found (mean age = 32.6 years + 5). These consisted of 10 subjects who worked alone with the software and had already used computers for at least five years and had some experience of multimedia software. The reason these types of subjects were selected was that if these experts could not understand the pedagogical approach and use the interface satisfactorily, then the novice learners would have extreme difficulty too. Also these subjects were confident users and could criticize the software using a "cognitive walk through" methodology.

Evaluation type	Aims	Subjects
Primary Phase	Test design and generic features	Competent computer users
Secondary Phase	Test usability and learning potential of product	OU students with science background
Tertiary Phase	Test usability and whole learning experience	Pairs of OU students with science background

Framework for the Developmental Testing of the Multimedia Materials Produced for the Science Foundation Course

3.3 Data Collection Instruments

…In order to understand the students' background knowledge, they were given two questionnaires to complete which were about their computer experience and also a pre-test about the subject area which was going to be investigated. The pre-test was made up of eight to 10 questions which addressed the main teaching objectives of the software…

4.0 Evaluation Findings

…The *Global Warming* program introduced the students to a climatic model of the factors that change the earth's temperature. These variables, which include the solar constant, levels of carbon dioxide and water vapor, aerosol content, cloud cover, ice and snow cover, and albedo could all be changed by the student who could then explore these factors' sensitivities, understand the effects of coupling between factors by again manipulating them, and finally, to gain an appreciation of the variation of global warming with latitude and season.

There is a large cognitive overhead for the students using this software and they have to be guided through a number of tasks. It was, therefore, important to test the screen layout, interface and pedagogical approach very early in the developmental cycle and this was achieved by testing a prototype without the mathematical model being in place.

The "cognitive walk through" technique worked well here. Subjects said when they arrived at a stumbling block, *"I don't know what to do here."* The main difficulty experienced was when tabs instead of buttons suddenly appeared on the interface. The functionality of the tabs was lost on the subjects. A general finding here is not to mix these two different interface elements. Subjects liked the audio linkage between sections and the use of audio to convey task instructions. One subject enthusiastically mentioned that, *"This feels like I have a tutor in the room with me—helping me."* Other findings suggest that any graphical output of data should sit close to the data table. The simulation run button did not need an icon of an athlete literally running; however, the strategy of predict, look, and explain was a good one when using the simulation…

Conclusions

The two formative testing approaches proved to be effective evaluation techniques for two separate pieces of software. This was because the multimedia programs were in different phases of their developmental cycle. On the one hand, usability of a generic shell was the primary aim of the testing and experienced users, who could be found at short notice, were an important factor to the success of this evaluation. The ability of the subjects to confidently describe their experience became critical data in this instance.

Extracted from Whitelock (1998)

Should You Describe Your Method?

If you are writing a report for an academic audience, it is essential to include a full description of the method you used. An academic reader is likely to want to decide whether your findings are supported by the method and may want to replicate your work.

If you are writing for a business audience, then you will need to weigh up their desire for a complete record of your activities and the time that they have to read the report. Some organizations like to see full descriptions, similar to those expected by an academic audience. Others prefer to concentrate on the results, with the detailed method relegated to an appendix or even a line such as, "Details of the method are available on request."

Describing Your Results

"Description" does not need to be confined to words. Your report will be more interesting to read if you include screenshots, pictures, or other illustrations of the interface with which the user was working.

Jarrett (2004) gives two alternative views of the same piece of an evaluation report:

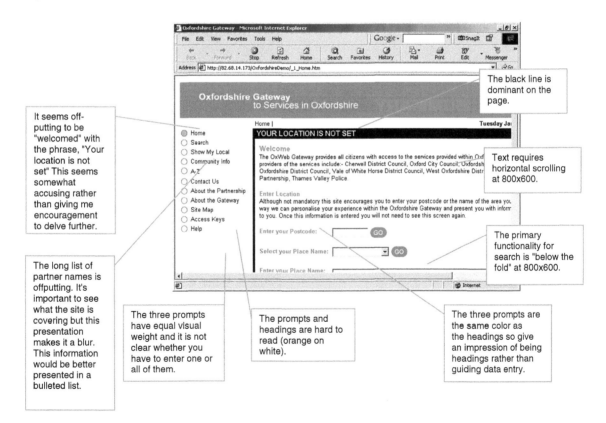

FIGURE 11.6

Findings presented with a screenshot. From Jarrett (2004).

We know that long chunks of writing can look boring, and we joke about "ordeal by bullet points" when we're in a presentation. But how often have we been guilty of the same sins in our reports?

Here are two ways to present the same information. First, as a block of text:

It seems off-putting to be "welcomed" with the phrase, "Your location is not set." This seems somewhat accusing rather than giving me encouragement to delve further. The long list of partner names is off-putting. It's important to see what the site is covering but this presentation makes it a blur. This information would be better presented in a bulleted list. The three prompts have equal visual weight and it is not clear whether you have to enter one or all of them. The prompts and headings are hard to read (orange on white). The three prompts are the same color as the headings so give an impression of being headings rather than guiding data entry. The primary functionality for search is "below the fold" at 800 × 600. Text requires horizontal scrolling at 800 × 600. The black line is dominant on the page. (p. 3)

Indigestible, right? Now look at the screenshot [in Fig. 11.6]. I preferred it, and I hope that you do too.

SUMMARY

In this chapter, we discussed how to collate evaluation data, analyze it, interpret it, and record recommendations. We introduced the concept of a severity rating for a usability defect: assigning severity ratings to usability defects helps in making decisions about the optimal allocation of resources to resolve them. Severity ratings, therefore, help to prioritize the recommended changes in tackling the usability defects. Finally, we started to think about how to present your findings. We will return to this topic in more detail, but first we will look at some other types of evaluation.

CHAPTER 12

Inspections of the User Interface

Debbie Stone, Caroline Jarrett, Mark Woodroffe, and Shailey Minocha

EDITOR'S COMMENTS

User interface inspections are the most commonly used tools in our efforts to improve usability. Inspections generally involve examining a user interface against a set of user interface standards, guidelines, or principles. This chapter describes heuristic evaluation, a method invented by Jakob Nielsen and Rolf Molich that was meant to be simple enough for developers and other members of a product team to use with limited training.

The primary goal of a heuristic evaluation is to reveal as many usability or design problems as possible at relatively low cost. A secondary goal of the heuristic evaluation is to train members of the product team to recognize potential usability problems so they can be eliminated earlier in the design process. You can use heuristic evaluation when:

- You have limited (or no) access to users.
- You need to produce an extremely fast review and do not have time to recruit participants and set up a full-fledged lab study.
- Your evaluators are dispersed around the world.
- You are looking for breadth in your review.
- Your clients have come to trust your judgment and for many issues do not require you to provide the results of user testing or other more expensive evaluation methods.

This chapter describes the procedure for heuristic evaluation and also provides several other inspection methods that practitioners can use, either individually or with groups, to eliminate usability defects from their products.

INTRODUCTION

Although user observation gives you a huge amount of insight into how users think about the user interface, it can be time consuming to recruit participants and observe them only to find that a large number of basic problems in the user interface could have been avoided if the designers had followed good practice in design. Undertaking an inspection of the user interface before (but *not* instead of) user observation can be beneficial to your evaluation.

> **NOTE**
>
> The contents of this section have been particularly influenced by the following sources: Virzi (1997), Nielsen (1994), and Nielsen (1993).

"Inspection of the user interface" is a generic name for a set of techniques that involve *inspectors* examining the user interface to check whether it complies with a set of design principles known as *heuristics*. In this chapter, we describe the *heuristic inspection* technique (also known as *heuristic evaluation*). Heuristic inspection was chosen as it is one of the most popular and well-researched inspection techniques for evaluation (Molich & Nielsen, 1990).

CREATING THE EVALUATION PLAN FOR HEURISTIC INSPECTION

Choosing the Heuristics

Your first task in planning a heuristic inspection is to decide which set of guidelines or heuristics you will use. If your organization has established a specific style guide, then that is one obvious choice. The advantage of using heuristics that you have used for design is that you can establish whether they have been applied consistently. Otherwise, the advantage of using a different set is that you get a fresh eye on the interface and may spot problems that would otherwise be overlooked.

One set of heuristics often used in inspections is the set proposed by Nielsen (1993), which we have included as Table 12.1.

We found that the humorous article on the usability of infants in the box below helped us to understand how these heuristics might be applied.

The Inspectors

Instead of recruiting a real or representative user to be your participant, you need to find one or more inspectors. Ideally, an inspector is an expert in human–computer interaction (HCI) and the domain of the system. These skills are rarely available in one person. It is also difficult for anyone, no matter how expert, to give equal attention to a variety of heuristics and domain knowledge. It is, therefore, more usual to find two or more inspectors with different backgrounds. The box below presents some ideas.

Table 12.1	Nielsen's Heuristics (1993)
Heuristic	**Description**
Visibility of system status	The system should always keep users informed about what is going on, through appropriate feedback within reasonable time.
Match between system and the real world	The system should speak the users' language, with words, phrases, and concepts familiar to the user, rather than system-oriented terms. Follow real-world conventions, making information appear in a natural and logical order.
User control and freedom	Users often choose system functions by mistake and will need a clearly marked "emergency exit" to leave the unwanted state without having to go through an extended dialog. Supports undo and redo.
Consistency and standards	Users should not have to wonder whether different words, situations, or actions mean the same thing. Follow platform conventions.
Error prevention	Even better than a good error message is a careful design that prevents a problem from occurring in the first place.
Recognition rather than recall	Make objects, actions, and options visible. The user should not have to remember information from one part of the dialog to another. Instructions or use of the system should be visible or easily retrievable whenever appropriate.
Flexibility and efficiency of use	Accelerators – unseen by the novice user – may often speed up the interaction for the expert user such that the system can cater to both the inexperienced and experienced users. Allow the users to tailor frequent actions.
Aesthetic and minimalist design	Dialogues should not contain information that is irrelevant or rarely needed. Every extra unit of information in a dialogue competes with the relevant units of information and diminishes their relative visibility.
Help users recognize, diagnose, and recover from errors	Error messages should be expressed in plain language (no codes), precisely indicating the problem, and constructively suggesting a solution.
Help and documentation	Even though it is better if the system can be used without documentation, it may be necessary to provide help and documentation. Any such information should be easy to search, focus on the user's task, list concrete steps to be carried out, and not be too large.

A HEURISTIC EVALUATION OF THE USABILITY OF INFANTS

For your consideration...

Results from a heuristic evaluation of infants and their user interface, based on direct observational evidence and Jakob Nielsen's list of 10 heuristics from http://www.useit.com. All ratings are from 1 to 10, with 1 being the worst and 10 being the best.

Visibility of System Status – 6: Although it is easy enough to determine when the infant is sleeping and eating, rude noises do not consistently accompany the other primary occupation of infants. Further, infants can multitask, occasionally performing all three major activities at the same time.

Match between System and the Real World – 3: The infant does not conform to normal industry standards of night and day, and its natural language interface is woefully underdeveloped, leading to the error message problems cited below.

User Control and Freedom – 2: The infant's users have only marginal control over its state. Although they can ensure the availability of food, diapers, and warmth, it is not often clear how to move the infant from an unfavorable state back to one in which it is content. When the default choice (data input) doesn't work, user frustration grows quickly.

Consistency and Standards – 7: Most infants have similar requirements and error messages, and the same troubleshooting procedures work for a variety of infants. Cuteness is also an infant standard, ensuring that users continue to put up with the many user interface difficulties.

Error Prevention – 5: Keeping the infant fed, dry, and warm prevents a number of errors. Homeostasis is, however, a fleeting goal, and the infant requires almost constant attention if the user is to detect errors quickly and reliably. All bets are off if the infant suffers from the colic bug or a virus.

Recognition Rather Than Recall – 7: The various parts of the infant generally match those of the user, though at a prototype level. The users, therefore, already have in place a mental model of the infant's objects. The data input and output ports are easily identifiable with a minimum of observation.

Flexibility and Efficacy of Use – 2: Use of the infant causes the user to conform to a fairly rigid schedule, and there are no known shortcuts for feeding, sleeping, and diaper buffer changing. Avoid buffer overflows at all costs, and beware of core dumps! Although macros would be incredibly useful, infants do not come equipped with them. Macro programming can usually begin once the infant attains toddler status.

Aesthetic and Minimalist Design – 5: As mentioned earlier, infants have a great deal of cuteness, and so they score well on aesthetic ratings. Balancing this, however, is the fact that the information they provide is rather too minimal. Infants interact with the user by eating, generating an error message, or struggling during buffer updates.

Help Users Recognize, Diagnose, and Recover from Errors – 1: Infants have only a single error message, which they use for every error. The user, therefore, is left to diagnose each error with relatively little information. The user must remember previous infant states to see if input is required, and the user must also independently check other routine parameters. Note the error message is not the same as a general protection fault. That is what resulted in the infant in the first place.

Help and Documentation – 1: Although some user training is available from experts, infants come with effectively no documentation. If users seek out documentation, they must sift through a great deal of conflicting literature to discover that there are very few universal conventions with regard to infant use.

Mean Score 3.9

This user has been up since 3:30 this morning (perhaps you can tell), and still has three to five months to go (he hopes) before stringing together eight hours of uninterrupted sleep.

McDaniel (1999, p. 44): This article was originally published in STC Intercom.

EDITOR'S NOTE: WHAT DO YOU CONSIDER WHEN CHOOSING HEURISTICS?

When you are choosing or developing heuristics, some of the issues to consider include the following:

- Relevance: Are the heuristics relevant to the domain and product? If you are evaluating a call center application where efficiency is a key attribute, you may need to include some domain-specific heuristics that are relevant to the call center environment and focus on high efficiency.
- Understandability: Will the heuristics be understood and be used consistently by all members of the analysis team?
- Their use as memory aids: Are the heuristics good mnemonics for the many detailed guidelines they are meant to represent? For example, does the heuristic "error prevention," prompt the novice or expert to consider the hundreds of guidelines regarding good labeling, input format hints, the use of abbreviations, explicit constraints on the allowable range of values, and other techniques or principles for actually preventing errors.
- Validity: Is there proof that a particular set of heuristics is based on good research? For example, the site, http://www.usability.gov, lists guidelines for Web design and usability and includes ratings that indicate the guidelines are based on research.

CHOOSING INSPECTORS FOR HEURISTIC EVALUATIONS

- Usability experts – people experienced in conducting evaluations
- Domain experts – people with knowledge of the domain (This may include users or user representatives.)
- Designers – people with extensive design experience
- Developers – people without any formal usability training, but who are keen to explore the usability defects that users might experience
- Nonexperts – people who are neither system domain experts nor usability experts, although they may be experts in their own particular domains (Nonexperts could be friends, colleagues, or family members who understand what you are doing and are willing to inspect the user interface to provide feedback.)

CONDUCTING A HEURISTIC INSPECTION

Because you know who the inspectors are, you usually do not need to ask them any questions about their background. Because the inspectors fill in the defect reports immediately, there is usually no need to record the session – there is little insight to be gained from watching a video of someone alternating between looking at a screen and filling in a form! However, you may want to record it if the inspector is verbalizing his or her thoughts while undertaking the inspection. If you want to record the inspection for later review, you will need to obtain permission from your inspector(s).

If your inspectors are domain or HCI experts, then they are unlikely to need any training before the session. If you have less experienced inspectors, it may be worthwhile to run through the heuristics with them and perhaps start with a practice screen so that everyone is clear about how you want the heuristics to be interpreted for your system.

Task Descriptions

You can prepare task descriptions just as you would for a user observation. The inspector then steps through the interface, reviewing both the task description and the list of heuristics, such as those shown in Table 12.1, at each step. This may make it easier to predict what users might do, but it has the disadvantage of missing out on those parts of the interface that are not involved in the particular task.

Alternatively, you might try to check each screen or sequence in the interface against the whole list of heuristics. It helps if you plan the sequence in advance, so that each inspector is looking at the same screen at the same time while undertaking the inspection.

The Location of the Evaluation Session

Generally, heuristic inspections are undertaken as controlled studies in informal settings that need have no resemblance to the users' environments. For example, Fig. 12.1 shows a usability expert, Paul Buckley, from a big UK

Table 12.2	Data Collection and Analysis Form for Heuristic Inspection		
Task Scenario No.: 1		Session Date: February 25	
Evaluator's Name: John		Session Start Time: 9:30 a.m.	
Inspector's Name: George		Session End Time: 10:20 a.m.	
Location in the Task Description	Heuristic Violated	Usability Defect Description	Inspector's Comments regarding the Usability Defect
New e-mail message arrives in the mailbox.	Visibility of system status	The user is not informed about the arrival of a new e-mail.	The user would like to be alerted when a new message arrives.
–	–	–	–

telecommunications company, British Telecom (BT), doing a heuristic inspection in the BT usability laboratory.

Collecting Evaluation Data

In Table 12.2, we have suggested a template for the collection of data during a heuristic inspection. You can see a similar form on the clipboard on the expert's lap in Fig. 12.1. Note that there is a column for recording the usability defects. This is because the inspectors will identify most of the usability defects as they walk through the interface during the evaluation session. This is different from the data collection form for user observation, where the usability defects are identified during the analysis of the data.

FIGURE 12.1
Heuristic inspection of a British Telecom (BT) user interface.

If more than one inspector is involved in the inspection, then each inspector should be encouraged to complete an individual data-collection form. Completing individual forms is useful at the time of specifying the severity ratings, because each individual inspector may want to specify his or her own severity ratings for the usability defects based on his or her own experience and opinions. Encourage the inspectors to be as specific as possible in linking the usability defects to the heuristics. This helps the inspectors concentrate on the heuristics to be checked.

ANALYSIS OF HEURISTIC INSPECTION DATA

The analysis of your data follows the same process as for the user observation. In theory, collating and summarizing data from a heuristic inspection is a relatively simple matter of gathering together the forms that the inspectors have used.

However, because inspectors do not always have the same opinion, you may want to get the inspectors to review each other's forms and discuss any differences between them, perhaps going back over the interface collectively to resolve any disagreements.

> **EDITOR'S NOTE: SHOULD HEURISTIC EVALUATIONS HIGHLIGHT POSITIVE ASPECTS OF A PRODUCT'S USER INTERFACE?**
>
> Heuristic evaluations are heavily focused on problems and seldom highlight positive aspects of a product's user interface. A guideline for usability test reports is that they highlight positive aspects of the product as well as negative aspects; heuristic evaluation reports could also highlight the major positive aspects of a product. Listing the positive aspects of a product has several advantages:
>
> - Evaluation reports that highlight positive and negative issues will be perceived as more balanced by the product team.
> - You might reduce the likelihood of something that works well being changed for the worse.
> - You may want to propagate some of the positive design features throughout the product.
> - Sometimes the positive features being mentioned actually bring focus to some of the very negative features being highlighted.

INTERPRETATION OF HEURISTIC INSPECTION DATA

The interpretation of your data follows the same process as for user observation. In Table 12.3, we have suggested a template for the interpretation of data during a heuristic inspection. When you produce your recommendations, you may want to invite the inspectors back to review your recommendations or the whole of your report to check that they agree with your interpretation.

BENEFITS AND LIMITATIONS OF HEURISTIC EVALUATIONS

In general, there are several benefits to conducting heuristic evaluations and inspections:

- Inspections can sometimes be less expensive than the user observation, especially if you have to recruit and pay participants for the latter.
- During an inspection, inspectors more often than not suggest solutions to the usability defects that they identify.
- It can be annoying to discover a large number of obvious errors during a usability test session. Inspecting the user interface (UI) first can help to reveal these defects.

Table 12.3	Interpretation Form for Heuristic Evaluation		

Task Scenario No.: 1
Evaluator: John
Inspector's Name: George **Review Meeting Date:**

Usability Defect	Inspector's Comments regarding the Usability Defect	Severity Rating	Recommendations
The user is not informed about the arrival of a new e-mail message.	The user would like to be alerted when a new message arrives.	High	Add sound or a visual indicator that alerts the user when a new e-mail message arrives.

There are, however, some limitations to conducting heuristic evaluations and inspections:

- As usability inspections often do not involve real or representative users, it is easy to make mistakes in the prediction of what actual users will do with the UI. However, real users can find the heuristics difficult to understand and the atmosphere of an inspection session to be unrealistic, thus limiting the data obtained.
- Inspectors often differ from real users in the importance they attach to a defect. For example, they may miss something they think is unimportant that will trip up real users, or they may be overly concerned about something that in fact only slightly affects the real users.
- Inspectors may have their own preferences, biases, and views toward the design of user interfaces or interaction design, which in turn may bias the evaluation data.
- The evaluation data from inspection is highly dependent on the skills and experiences of the inspectors. Sometimes, the inspectors may have insufficient task and domain knowledge. This can affect the validity of the evaluation data as some domain- or task-specific usability defects might be missed during an inspection.
- Heuristic reviews may not scale well for complex interfaces (Slavkovic & Cross, 1999).
- Evaluators may report problems at different levels of granularity. For example, one evaluator may list a global problem of "bad error messages" while another evaluator lists separate problems for each error message encountered.
- Lack of clear rules for assigning severity judgments may yield major differences; one evaluator says "minor" problem, whereas others say "moderate" or "serious" problem.

EDITOR'S NOTE: HOW DO YOU MEASURE THE SUCCESS OF A HEURISTIC EVALUATION?

In the usability literature, the focus is on how many problems of various severities are found. That is a start, but a more important measure might be how many problems are fixed. Sawyer, Flanders, & Wixon (1996) suggest that the results of heuristic evaluations and other types of inspections look at the impact ratio, which is the ratio of the number of problems that the product team commits to fix to the total number of problems found multiplied by 100 (p. 377). While the impact ratio provides a measure of how many problems are fixed, this measure still does not indicate how much more usable the product is as a result of the fixed problems.

VARIATIONS OF USABILITY INSPECTION

Participatory Heuristic Evaluations

If instead of HCI or domain experts you recruit users as your inspectors, then the technique becomes a *participatory heuristic evaluation* (Muller, Matheson, Page & Gallup, 1998). Muller and his colleagues created an adaptation of Nielsen's list of heuristics to make them accessible to users who are not HCI experts (see Table 12.4).

Table 12.4 Heuristics in Participatory Heuristic Evaluation (from Muller, et al., 1998, pp. 16–17)

System status

1. *System status.* The system keeps the users informed about what is going on through appropriate feedback within a reasonable time.

User control and freedom

2. *Task sequencing.* Users can select and sequence tasks (when appropriate), rather than the system taking control of the users' actions. Wizards are available but are optional and under user control.

3. *Emergency exits.* Users can
   - easily find emergency exits if they choose system functions by mistake (emergency exits allow the user to leave the unwanted state without having to go through an extended dialogue)
   - make their own decisions (with clear information and feedback) regarding the costs of exiting current work
   - access undo and redo operations

4. *Flexibility and efficiency of use.* Accelerators are available to experts but are unseen by the novice. Users are able to tailor frequent actions. Alternative means of access and operation are available for users who differ from the average user (e.g., in physical or cognitive ability, culture, language, etc.).

Table 12.4	Heuristics in Participatory Heuristic Evaluation (from Muller, et al., 1998, pp. 16–17) (*Continued*)

Consistency and relevancy

5. *Match between system and the real world.* The system speaks the users' language, with words, phrases, and concepts familiar to the user rather than system-oriented terms. Messages are based on the users' real world, making information appear in a natural and logical order.

6. *Consistency and standards.* Each word, phrase, or image in the design is used consistently, with a single meaning. Each interface object or computer operation is always referred to using the same consistent word, phrase, or image. Follow the conventions of the delivery system or platform.

7. *Recognition rather than recall.* Objects, actions, and options are visible. The user does not have to remember information from one part of the dialog to another. Instructions for use of the system are visible or easily retrievable whenever appropriate.

8. *Aesthetic and minimalist design.* Dialogues do not contain information that is irrelevant or rarely needed (extra information in a dialogue competes with the relevant units of information and diminishes their relative visibility).

9. *Help and documentation.* The system is intuitive and can be used for the most common tasks without documentation. Where needed, documentation is easy to search, supports a user task, lists concrete steps to be carried out, and is sized appropriately to the users' task. Large documents are supplemented with multiple means of finding their contents (tables of contents, indexes, searches, and so on).

Error recognition and recovery

10. *Help users recognize, diagnose, and recover from errors.* Error messages precisely indicate the problem and constructively suggest a solution. They are expressed in plain (users') language (no codes). Users are not blamed for the error.

11. *Error prevention.* Even better than good error messages is a careful design that prevents a problem from occurring in the first place. Users' "errors" are anticipated, and the system treats the "error" as either a valid input or an ambiguous input to be clarified.

Task and work support

12. *Skills.* The system supports, extends, supplements, or enhances the user's skills, background knowledge, and expertise. The system does not replace them. Wizards support, extend, or execute decisions made by the users.

13. *Pleasurable and respectful interaction with the user.* The user's interactions with the system enhance the quality of his or her experience. The user is treated with respect. The design reflects the user's professional role, personal identity, or intention. The design is aesthetically pleasing – with an appropriate balance of artistic as well as functional value.

14. *Quality work.* The system supports the user in delivering quality work to his or her clients (if appropriate). Attributes of quality work include timeliness, accuracy, aesthetic appeal, and appropriate levels of completeness.

15. *Privacy.* The system helps the user to protect personal or private information – that belonging to the user or to the user's clients.

Guideline Reviews

Guideline reviews are inspections that use a set of design guidelines, such as a corporate style guide, instead of one of the sets of heuristics we have included here.

Standards Inspections

A standards inspection uses a standard such as ISO 9241 as the reference rather than a set of heuristics.

Table 12.5 presents part of a sample data collection form (an applicability and adherence checklist) for evaluating a design with respect to part 12 of the ISO 9241 standard, which relates to the presentation of information.

Standards are written in a formal manner for practitioners, rather than being accessible for users. If you need to do a standards inspection, then you really should consider bringing in an expert who is familiar with the standard and its language as one of your inspectors. If that is impractical, then allow extra time during your preparation for becoming thoroughly familiar with it yourself.

A usability standard such as ISO 9241 is generalized to cater to a wide variety of user interfaces, so there may be some guidelines in the standard that are not applicable for the prototype you are evaluating (hence, the second column in Table 12.5 to record the applicability). The next column is for recording the adherence/nonadherence of the interface feature to the particular guideline of the standard. The inspector records his or her comments in the last column.

Cognitive Walkthrough

Cognitive walkthrough (CW) is a technique for exploring a user's mental processes while performing particular task(s) with a UI. The CW can be used for gathering requirements or evaluation. For evaluation, a CW may be used to

Table 12.5 Applicability and Adherence Checklist Used in Standards Inspection

Recommendations (An Example from ISO 9241, Part 12)	Applicability		Adherence		Evaluator's Comments
	Yes	No	Pass	Fail	
Labels	✓		✓		The label names are meaningful.
Labeling fields, items, icons, and graphs					
Fields, items, icons, and graphs are labeled unless their meaning is obvious and can be understood clearly by the intended users.					

assess the usability of a user interface design by examining whether a user can select the appropriate action at the interface for each step in the task. This can sound quite simple, and is, but you can gain a lot of information by using the CW technique for evaluation.

EDITOR'S NOTE: ADDITIONAL NOTES ON THE COGNITIVE WALKTHROUGH

The cognitive walkthrough (CW) is a usability inspection technique that focuses primarily on the ease of learning of a product. The CW is based on a theory that users often learn how to use a product through a process of exploration, not through formal training courses (Polson & Lewis, 1990). The CW was originally designed to evaluate "walk-up-and-use" interfaces (for example, museum kiosks, postage machines, and ATMs), but has been applied to more complex products (CAD systems, operating procedures, software development tools) that support new and infrequent users (Novick, 1999; Wharton, Bradford, Jeffries & Franzke, 1992). The CW is based on the concept of a hypothetical user and does not require any actual users. Rick Spencer (2000) proposed a simplified version of the CW that was more appropriate for fast-paced commercial software development (Spencer, 2000).

Peer Reviews

A peer review is an evaluation where a colleague, rather than an HCI or domain expert, reviews your interface. Early in the life cycle of designing and evaluating user interfaces, a simple approach is to ask someone to have a look at it. A peer review can be as informal as asking, "What do you think of this?" or you could go through the full process of a heuristic inspection. A degree of formality – such as booking a meeting; thinking carefully about which set of heuristics, standards, or guidelines you want to use; and taking notes – will help to ensure that you learn the most from the evaluation.

SUMMARY

In this chapter, we discussed how heuristic evaluation, one of the most widely applied inspection techniques, is conducted, and we considered the benefits and limitations of conducting inspections for evaluations. The procedure for conducting a heuristic evaluation can be applied to any other inspection, such as evaluating the user interface against a set of standards or guidelines or a customized style guide.

NOTE

For more information on standards inspection, guideline reviews, and other inspections, see Nielsen & Mack (1994), Yehuda & McGinn (2007), and Lewis & Wharton (1997).

Aldenderfer, M. S. & Blashfield, R. K. (1984). *Cluster analysis*. Sage University paper series on Quantitative Applications in the Social Sciences, No. 07-044. Beverly Hills, (CA): Sage.

Anderson, C. *How much interaction is too much?* (2004). <http://www.stcsig.org/usability/newsletter/0404-howmuchinteraction.html>.

Angiolillo, J. S. & Roberts, L. A. (1991). What makes a manual look easy to use? In: *Proceedings of the human factors society 35th annual meeting*, San Francisco, CA, 2–6 September, 222–224.

Arnowitz, J., Arent, M. & Berger, N. (2007). *Effective prototyping for software makers*. San Francisco, (CA): Morgan Kaufmann.

Attfield, J. (2000). *Wild things: The material culture of everyday life*. Oxford, UK: Berg Publishers.

Bardini, T. (2000). *Bootstrapping: Douglas Englebart, coevolution, and the origins of personal computing (CHI'03)*, 537–544.

Baxley, B. (2003). *Making the Web work: Designing effective Web applications*. Berkeley, (CA): New Riders.

Bel Geddes, N. (1932). *Horizons*. Boston, (MA): Little Brown & Company.

Berkun, S. *How to run a brainstorming meeting*. (2004). <http://www.scottberkun.com/essays/34-how-to-run-a-brainstorming-meeting/> Accessed 01.06.08.

Bernard, R. H. (2006). *Research methods in anthropology: Qualitative and quantitative approaches* (4th ed.). Lanham, (MD): Altamira Press.

Berry, D. C. & Broadbent, D. E. (1990). The role of instructions and verbalization in improving performance on complex search tasks. *Behavior & Information Technology, 9*(4), 175–190.

Bewley, W. L., Roberts, T. L., Schroit, D. & Verplank, W. L. (1983). Human factors testing in the design of Xerox's 8010 'Star' office workstation. In: *Proceedings of the ACM CHI'83 conference*, Boston, MA, 12–15 December, 72–77.

Beyer, H. & Holtzblatt K. (1998). *Contextual design: Defining customer-centered systems*. San Francisco, (CA): Morgan Kauffman.

Borchers, R. *Small group communication: Decision-making.* (1999). <http://www.abacon.com/commstudies/groups/decision.html> Accessed 21.10.05.

Brahm, C. & Kleiner, B. H. (1996). Advantages and disadvantages of group decision-making approaches. *Team Performance Management: An International Journal, 2*(1), 30–35.

Brewer, D., Garrett, S. B. & Rinaldi, G. (2002). Patterns in the recall of sexual and drug injection partners. *Advances in Medical Sociology, 8,* 131–149.

Brown, B. B. (1968). *A methodology used for the elicitation of opinions of experts.* Santa Monica, (CA): RAND Corporation.

Burmeister, O. K. (2000). Usability testing: Revisiting informed consent procedures for testing Internet sites. In selected papers from the second Australian institute conference on computer ethics (Canberra, Australia). In J. Weckert (Ed.) ACM international conference proceeding series, 7 (pp. 3–9) Darlinghurst, Australia: Australian Computer Society.

Camacho, M. L. & Paulus, P. B. (1995). The role of social anxiousness in group brainstorming. *Journal of Personality and Social Psychology, 68*(6), 1071–1080.

Card, S. K., English, W. K. & Burr, B. J. (1978). Evaluation of the mouse, rate-controlled isometric joystick, step keys, and text keys for text selection on a CRT. *Ergonomics, 21,* 601–613.

Card, S. K., Moran, T. P. & Newell, A. (1983). *The psychology of human-computer interaction.* Hillsdale, (NJ): Lawrence Earlbaum.

Carroll, J. M. & Rosson, M. B. (1987). Paradox of the active user. In J. M. Carroll. (Ed.), *Interfacing thought: Cognitive aspects of human-computer interaction* (pp. 80–111). Cambridge (MA): The MIT Press.

Carroll, J. M. & Thomas, J. C. (1988, January). Fun. *ACM SIGCHI Bulletin, 19*(3), 21–24.

Chin, J. P., Diehl, V. A. & Norman, K. L. (1988). Development of an instrument measuring user satisfaction of the human-computer interface. In: *Proceedings of the ACM CHI'88 conference,* Washington, DC, 15–19 May, 213–218.

Clegg, E. (1983). *Simple statistics.* Cambridge, UK: Cambridge University Press.

Clement, A. & Van den Besselaar, P. (1993). A retrospective look at PD projects. *Communications of the ACM, 36*(6), 29–37.

Coleman, W. D., Williges, R. C. & Wixon, D. R. (1985). Collecting detailed user evaluations of software interfaces. In: *Proceedings of the human factors society 29th annual meeting,* Baltimore, MD, 29 September–3 October, 240–244.

Cooper, A. (1999). *The inmates are running the asylum.* New York: Macmillan.

Cooper, A. & Reimann, R. M. (2003). *About face 2.0: The essentials of interaction design.* New York: Wiley.

Cooper, A., Reimann, R. & Cronin, D. (2007). *About face 3: The essentials of interaction design.* Indianapolis, (IN): Wiley.

Cordes, R. E. (1993). The relationship between post-task and continuous-vicarious ratings of difficulty. *International Journal of Human-Computer Interaction, 5*(2), 115–127.

Coskun, H. (2000). *The effects of outgroup comparison, social context, intrinsic motivation, and collective identity in brainstorming* (unpublished doctoral dissertation) University of Texas, Arlington.

Cotterman, W. W. & Kumar, K. (1989). User cube: A taxonomy of end users. *Communications of the ACM, 32*(11), 1313–1320.

Courage, C. & Baxter, K. (2005). *Understanding your users: A practical guide to user requirements methods, tools, and techniques.* San Francisco, (CA): Morgan Kaufmann.

CreatingMinds.org (n.d.). *Reverse brainstorming.* <http://www.creatingminds.org/tools/reverse_brainstorming.htm> Accessed 16.05.09.

Curtis, B (1981): Substantiating programmer variability. *Proceedings of the IEEE, 69*, 846.

Czaja, S. J. (1988). Microcomputer and the elderly. In M. Helander (Ed.), *Handbook of human-computer interaction* (pp.581–598). Amsterdam, The Netherlands: Elsevier Science Publishers.

Delbecq, A. L., Van deVen, A. H. & Gustafson, D. H. (1975). *Group techniques for program planners.* Glenview, (IL): Scott Foresman and Company.

Dennis, A. R. & Williams, M. L. (2003) Electronic brainstorming: Theory, research, and future directions. In P. B. Paulus and B. A. Nijstad (Eds.), *Group creativity: Innovation through collaboration* (pp. 160–178). London: Oxford University Press.

Diehl, M. & Stroebe, W. (1987). Productivity loss in brainstorming groups: Toward the solution of a riddle. *Journal of Personality and Social Psychology, 53*, 497–509.

Dillman, D. A. (2007). *Mail and Internet surveys: The tailored design method* (3rd ed.). Hoboken, (NJ): Wiley.

Doane, S. M., McNamara, D. S., Kintsch, W., Polson, P. G. & Clawson, D. M. (1992). Prompt comprehension in UNIX command production. *Memory & Cognition, 20*(4), 327–343.

Doane, S. M., Pellegrino, J. W. & Klatzky, R. L. (1990). Expertise in a computer operating system: Conceptualization and performance. *Human-Computer Interaction, 5*(2 and 3), 267–304.

Donoghue, K. (2002). *Built for use: Driving profitability through the user experience.* New York: McGraw-Hill.

Draper, S. W. (1984). The nature of expertise in UNIX. In *Proceedings of the IFIP INTERACT'84 first international conference human-computer interaction,* London, UK, 4–7 September, 465–471.

Dray, S. M. & Siegel, D. A. (1999). Penny-wise, pound-wise: Making smart tradeoffs in planning usability studies. *Interactions, 6*(3), 25–30.

Dreyfuss, H. (1955). *Designing for people.* New York: Simon & Shuster.

Dugosh, K. L., Paulus, P. B., Roland, E. J. & Yang, H. C. (2000). Cognitive stimulation in brainstorming. *Journal of Personality and Social Psychology, 79,* 722–735.

Dumas, J. S. (2003). User-based evaluations. In J. A. Jacko & A. Sears (Eds.), *The human-computer interaction handbook: Fundamentals, evolving technologies, and emerging applications.* Mahwah, (NY): Lawrence Erlbaum.

Dumas, J. & Redish, J. (1999). *A practical guide to usability testing* (Rev. ed.). Exeter, UK: Intellect.

Egan, D. E. (1988). Individual differences in human-computer interaction. In M. Helander (Ed.), *Handbook of human-computer interaction* (pp. 543–568). Amsterdam, The Netherlands: North-Holland.

Egido, C. & Patterson, J. (1988). Pictures and category labels as navigational aids for catalog browsing. In: *Proceedings of the ACM CHI '88 conference,* Washington, DC, 15–19 May, 127–132.

Epstein, R. (1996). *Creativity games for trainers: A handbook of group activities for jumpstarting workplace creativity.* New York: McGraw-Hill.

Fällman, D. (2003a). Design-oriented human-computer interaction. In: *Proceedings of the ACM-SIGCHI conference on human factors in computing systems (CHI'03),* 225–232.

Fällman, D. (2003b). *In romance with the materials of mobile interaction.* PhD Thesis, Department of Informatics, Umeå University.

Fowler, C. J. H. & Murray, D. (1987). Gender and cognitive style differences at the human-computer interface. In: *Proceedings of the IFIP INTERACT '87 second international conference human-computer interaction,* Stuttgart, Germany, 1–4 September, 709–714.

Fowler, F. J. Jr. & Mangione, T. W. (1990). *Standardized survey interviewing: Minimizing interviewer-related error.* Sage: Applied Social Research Methods Series No.18, Newbury Park, (CA): Sage.

Fowler, S. & Stanwick, V. (2004). *The Web application design handbook: Best practices for Web-based software.* Amsterdam: Morgan Kaufmann.

Francis, P., Firth, L. & Mellor, D. (2005). Reducing the risk of abandonment of assistive technologies for people with autism. In M. F. Costabile and F. Paternò (Eds.), *INTERACT 2005. LNCS 3585* (pp. 1104–1107). Berlin, Germany: Springer.

Freeman, E. & Gelernter, D. (1996). Lifestreams: A storage model for personal data. *SIGMOD Record, 25*(1), 80–86.

Gaffney, G. *Rules for briefing observers.* (2001). <http://www.infodesign.com.au/ftp/ObserverGuidelines.pdf>.

Gaffney, G. *Usability testing materials.* (2003). <http://www.infodesign.com.au/usabilityresources/evaluation/usabilitytestingmaterials.asp>.

Gantt, M. & Nardi, B. A. (1992). Gardeners and gurus: Patterns of cooperation among CAD users. In: *Proceedings of the ACM CHI '92 conference*, Monterey, CA, 3–7 May, 107–117.

Gedenryd, H. (1998). *How designers work: Making sense of authentic cognitive activities.* PhD dissertation, Lund University cognitive science. <http://asip.lucs.lu.se/People/Henrik. Gedenryd/HowDesignersWork/>.

Gibbons, M. & Hopkins, D. (1980). How experiential is your experience-based program? *The Journal of Experiential Education, 3*(1), 32–37.

Goel, V. (1995). *Sketches of thought.* Cambridge, (MA): The MIT Press.

Gomez, L. M., Egan, D. E. & Bowers, C. (1986). Learning to use a text editor: Some learner characteristics that predict success. *Human-Computer Interaction, 2*(1), 1–23.

Grawitch, M. J., Munz, D. C., Elliott, E. K. & Mathis, A. (2003). Promoting creativity in temporary problem-solving groups: The effects of positive mood and autonomy in problem definition on idea-generating performance. *Group Dynamics: Theory Research, and Practice, 7*(3), 200–213.

Green, A. J. K. & Barnard, P. J. (1990). Iconic interfacing: The role of icon distinctiveness and fixed or variable screen locations. In: *Proceedings of the IFIP INTERACT '90 third international conference human-computer interaction*, Cambridge, UK, 27–31 August, 457–462.

Greenbaum, J. M. & Kyng, M. (Eds.), (1991). *Design at work: Cooperative design of computer systems.* Mahwah, (NJ): Lawrence Erlbaum Associates.

Grudin, J. (1989). The case against user interface consistency. *Communications of the ACM, 32*(10), 1164–1173.

Grudin, J. (1992). Utility and usability: Research issues and development contexts. *Interacting with Computers, 4*(2), 209–217.

Grudin, J. (2006). Why personas work. In J. Pruitt & T. Adlin (Eds.), *The persona lifecycle: Keeping people in mind throughout product design.* San Francisco, (CA): Morgan Kaufmann.

Hakiel, S. R. & Easterby, R. S. (1987). Methods for the design and evaluation of icons for human-computer interfaces. In: *Proceedings of the IEE 2nd international conference command, control, communications and management information systems*, Bournemouth, UK, 1–3 April, 48–51.

Harrison, S., Back, M. & Tatar, D. (2006). It's just a method!: A pedagogical experiment in interdisciplinary design. In: *Proceedings of the 6th ACM conference on designing interactive systems*, University Park, PA, USA, June 26–28, 2006, DIS '06 (pp. 261–270). New York: ACM Press.

Heller, P. & Hollabaugh, M. (1992). Teaching problem solving through cooperative grouping. Pt. 2: Designing problems and structuring groups. *American Journal of Physics, 60,* 637–644.

Heskett, J. (1980). *Industrial design.* New York: Thames and Hudson.

Higgins, J. M. (2005). *101 Creative problem solving techniques: The handbook of new ideas for business.* Winter Park, (FL): New Management Publishing Company.

Hix, D. & Hartson, R. (1993). *Developing user interfaces: Ensuring usability through product & process.* New York: Wiley.

Holtzblatt, K., Wendell, J. B. & Wood, S. (2005). *Rapid contextual design: A how-to guide to key techniques for user-centered design.* San Francisco, (CA): Morgan Kaufmann.

Huff, D. (1991). *How to lie with statistics.* London: Penguin.

Hutchins, E. (1995). *Cognition in the wild.* Cambridge, (MA): The MIT Press.

Infinite Innovations Ltd. *Brainstorming toolbox.* (n.d.). <http://www.brainstorming.co.uk/toolbox/brainstormingtoolbox.html> Accessed 17.08.09.

Innovation Tools. *Brainstorming techniques resource center.* (n.d.). <http://www.innovationtools.com/resources/brainstorming.asp> Accessed 12.07.09.

Isaksen, S. G. (1998). *A review of brainstorming research: Six critical issues for inquiry.* Buffalo, (NY): Creative Research Unit, Creative Problem Solving Group.

Isen, A. M. (2000). Positive affect and decision making. In M. Lewis & J. M. Haviland-Jones (Eds.), *Handbook of emotions* (2nd ed., pp. 417–435). New York: Guilford Press.

Jacobson, I. (1987). Object-oriented development in an industrial environment. In: *Proceedings of the OOPSLA '87, SIGPLAN Notices, 22*(12), 183–191.

Jacobson, I., Christerson, M., Jonsson, P. & Övergaard, G. (1992). *Object-oriented software engineering: A use case driven approach.* Wokingham, England: Addison-Wesley.

Jarrett, C. (2004). Better reports: How to communicate the results of usability testing. In: *Proceedings of the 51st annual conference of the society for technical communication.* Baltimore, MD.

John, B. (1995). Why GOMS? *Interactions, 2*(4), 80–89.

John, B. E. & Kieras, D. E. (1996a). Using GOMS for user interface design and evaluation: Which technique? *ACM Transactions on Computer-Human Interaction, 3*(4), 287–319.

John, B. E. & Kieras, D. E. (1996b). The GOMS family of user interface analysis techniques: Comparison and contrast. *ACM Transactions on Computer-Human Interaction, 3*(4), 320–351.

Jones, J. C. (1992). *Design methods* (2nd ed.). New York: Van Nostrand Reinhold.

Kacmar, C. J. & Carey, J. M. (1991). Assessing the usability of icons in user interfaces. *Behaviour & Information Technology, 10*(6), 443–457.

Kay, R. H. (1989). A practical and theoretical approach to assessing computer attitudes: The computer attitude measure (CAM). *Journal on Research on Computing in Education,* 456–463.

Kelley, T. (2001). *The art of innovation: Lessons in creativity from IDEO, America's leading design firm.* New York: Doubleday.

Kieras, D. (1997). A guide to GOMS model usability evaluation using NGOMSL. In M. Helander, T. K. Landauer & P. Prabhu (Eds.), *Handbook of human-computer interaction* (2nd ed., pp. 733–766). New York: Elsevier.

Kolb, D. (1984). *Experiential learning: Experience as the source of learning and development.* Englewood Cliffs, (NJ): Prentice-Hall.

Koyani, S. J., Bailey, R. W. & Nall, J. R. (2004). *Research-based Web design & usability guidelines.* USA: Computer Psychology.

Krueger, R. A. & Casey, M. A. (2000). *Focus groups: A practical guide for applied research* (3rd ed.). Thousand Oaks, (CA): Sage.

Kuniavsky, M. (2003). *Observing the user experience: A practitioner's guide to user research.* San Francisco, (CA): Morgan Kaufmann.

Kyle, B. *SWOT analysis: Strengths, weaknesses, opportunities, and threats.* (2003). <http://www.marketingprofs.com/3/kyle1.asp> Accessed 03.11.05.

LaLomia, M. J. & Sidowski, J. B. (1990). Measurements of computer satisfaction, literacy, and aptitudes: A review. *International Journal of Human-Computer Interaction, 2*(3), 231–253.

LaLomia, M. J. & Sidowski, J. B. (1991). Measurements of computer attitudes: A review. *International Journal of Human-Computer Interaction, 3*(2), 171–197.

Lawson, B. (1997). *How designers think: The design process demystified* (3rd ed.). Amsterdam: Elsevier.

Lewis, C. & Wharton, C. (1997). Cognitive walkthroughs. In M. Helander, T. K. Landauer & P. Prabhu (Eds.), *Handbook of Human-Computer Interaction* (2nd ed., pp. 717–732). Amsterdam: Elsevier Science.

Lewis, S. (1991). Cluster analysis as a technique to guide interface design. *Journal of Man-Machine Studies, 10*, 267–280.

Lindgaard, G., Chessari, J. & Ihsen, E. (1987). Icons in telecommunications: What makes pictorial information comprehensible to the user? *Australian Telecommunication Research, 21*(2), 17–29.

Magyar, R. L. (1990). Assessing the icon appropriateness and icon discriminability with a paired-comparison testing procedure. In: *Proceedings of the human factors society 34th annual meeting*, Orlando, FL, 8–12 October, 1204–1208.

Mayes, J. T., Draper, S. W., McGregor, A. M. & Oatley, K. (1988). Information flow in a user interface: The effect of experience and context on the recall of MacWrite screens. In D. M. Jones & R. Winder (Eds.), *People and Computers IV* (pp. 275–289). Cambridge, UK: Cambridge University Press.

McDaniel, S. (1999). A heuristic evaluation of the usability of infants. *STC Intercom, 46*(9), 44.

McGee, D. (2004). The origins of early modern machine design. In W. Lefèvre, (Ed.), *Picturing machines 1400–1700* (pp. 53–84). Cambridge, MA: The MIT Press.

McGraw, K. & Harbison, K. (1997). *User-centered requirements: The scenario-based engineering process.* Mahwah, (NJ): Lawrence Erlbaum.

Michalko, M. (2006a). *Thinkertoys: A handbook of creative-thinking techniques* (2nd ed.). Berkeley, (CA): Ten Speed Press.

Michalko, M. (2006b). *Thinkpak: A brainstorming card deck* (Rev. ed.). Berkeley, (CA): Ten Speed Press.

Milliken, F. J., Bartel, C. A. & Kurtzberg, T. R. (2003). Diversity and creativity and work groups: A dynamic perspective on the affective and cognitive processes that link diversity and performance. In P. B. Paulus & B. A. Nijstad (Eds.), *Group creativity: Innovation through collaboration* (pp. 32–62). New York: Oxford University Press.

Milliken, F. J. & Martins, L. (1996). Searching for common threads: Understanding the multiple effects of diversity in organizational groups. *Academy of Management Review, 21*, 402–433.

MindTools. Reverse brainstorming. (n.d.). <http://www.mindtools.com/pages/article/newCT_96.htm> Accessed 16.05.09.

Molich, R. & Nielsen, J. (1990). Improving a human-computer dialogue. *Communications of the ACM, 33*, 338–348.

Morville, P. & Rosenfeld, L. (2006). Information architecture for the world wide Web (3rd ed.). Sebastopol, (CA): O'Reilly.

Muller, M. J. (2003). Participatory design: The third space in HCI. In J. A. Jacko & A. Sears (Eds.), *The human-computer interaction handbook: Fundamentals, evolving technologies, and emerging applications* (pp. 1051–1068). Mahwah, (NJ): Lawrence Erlbaum Associates.

Muller, M. J., Matheson, L., Page, C. & Gallup, R. (1998). Methods & tools: participatory heuristic evaluation. *Interactions, 5*(5), 13–18.

Mulligan, R. M., Altom, M. W. & Simkin, D. K. (1991). User interface design in the trenches: Some tips on shooting from the hips. In: *Proceedings of the ACM CHI'91 conference*, New Orleans, LA, 28 April–2 May, 232–236.

Mullins, P. M. & Treu, S. (1991). Measurement of stress to gauge user satisfaction with features of the computer interface. *Behaviour & Information Technology, 10*(4), 325–343.

Mycoted. Negative brainstorming. (2006). <http://www.mycoted.com/Negative_Brainstorming> Accessed 16.05.09.

Nardi, B. A. & Miller, J. R. (1991). Twinkling lights and nested loops: Distributed problem solving and spreadsheet development. *International Journal of Man–Machine Studies, 34*(2), 161–184.

NetMBA. SWOT analysis. (n.d.). <http://www.netmba.com/strategy/swot/> Accessed 16.05.09.

Nielsen, J. (1989a). What do users really want? *International Journal of Human-Computer Interaction, 1*(2), 137–147.

Nielsen, J. (1989b). The matters that really matter for hypertext usability. In: *Proceedings of the ACM Hypertext' 89 Conference*, Pittsburgh, PA, 5–8 November, 239–248.

Nielsen, J. (1990). *Hypertext and hypermedia.* Boston: Academic Press.

Nielsen, J. (1993). *Usability engineering.* San Francisco, (CA): Morgan Kaufmann.

Nielsen, J. (1994). Heuristic evaluation. In J. Nielsen & R. L. Mack (Eds.), *Usability Inspection Methods* (pp. 25–62). New York: Wiley.

Nielsen, J. (2000). *Designing Web usability: The practice of simplicity.* Indianapolis, (IN): New Riders Press.

Nielsen, J. & Levy, J. (1994). Measuring usability: Preference vs. performance. *Communications of the ACM, 37*(4), 66–75.

Nielsen, J. & Mack, R. (Eds.), (1994). *Usability inspection methods.* New York: Wiley.

Nielsen, J., Mack, R. L., Bergendorff, K. H. & Grischkowsky, N. L. (1986). Integrated software in the professional work environment: Evidence from questionnaires and interviews. In: *Proceedings of the ACM CHI '86 conference*, Boston, MA, 13–17 April, 162–167.

Nielsen, J. & Phillips, V. L. (1993). Estimating the relative usability of two interfaces: Heuristic, formal, and empirical methods compared. In: *Proceedings of the ACM INTERCHI'93 conference*, Amsterdam, The Netherlands, 24–29 April, 214–221.

Nielsen, J. & Sano, D. (1994). *SunWeb: User interface design for Sun Microsystem's internal web*, Chicago, IL, 17–20 October, 547–557.

Nielsen, L. (2003). *Constructing the user. Human computer interaction international 2003– Theory and practice.* Crete: Lawrence Erlbaum Associates.

Nieters, J. & Dworman, G. (2007). *Comparing UXD business models.* <http://www.uxmatters.com/MT/archives/000206.php> Accessed 12.07.09.

Nijstad, B. A., Diehl, M. & Stroebe, W. (2003). Cognitive stimulation and interference in idea generating groups. In P. B. Paulus and B. A. Nijstad (Eds.), *Group creativity: Innovation through collaboration* (pp. 137–159). New York: Oxford University Press.

Nolan, P. R. (1989). Designing screen icons: Ranking and matching studies. In: *Proceedings of the human factors society 33th annual meeting,* Santa Monica, CA, 8–12 October, 380–384.

Nolan, P. R. (1991). The design of keyboard templates. In: *Proceedings of the human factors society 35th annual meeting,* San Francisco, CA, 2–6 September, 486–490.

Norman, D. (2004). *Emotional design: Why we love (or hate) everyday things.* New York. Basic Books.

Novick, D. G. (1999). Using the cognitive walkthrough for operating procedures. *Interactions, 6*(3), 31–37.

OED Online. Definition of brain-storm. (n.d.).<http://www.oed.com> Accessed 01.06.08.

Osborn, A. F. (1963). *Applied imagination: Principles and procedures of creative problem-solving* (3rd Rev. ed.). New York: Charles Scribner's Sons.

Paulus, P. B. & Brown, V. R. (2003). Enhancing ideational creativity in groups: Lessons from research on brainstorming. In P. B. Paulus & B. A. Nijstad (Eds.), *Group creativity: Innovation through collaboration* (pp. 110–136). Oxford, UK: Oxford University Press.

Paulus, P. B. & Dzindolet, M. T. (1993). Social influence processes in group brainstorming: The illusion of group productivity. *Journal of Personality and Social Psychology, 64,* 575–586.

Paulus, P. B. & Nijstad, B. A. (Eds.) (2003). *Group creativity: Innovation through collaboration.* Oxford, UK: Oxford University Press.

Polson, P. G., Muncher, E. & Engelbeck, G. (1986). A test of a common elements theory of transfer. In: *Proceedings of the ACM CHI '86 conference,* Boston, MA, 13–17 April, 78–83.

Polson, R. G. & Lewis, C. (1990). Theory-based design for easily learned interfaces. *Human-Computer Interaction, 5,* 191–220.

Potosnak, K. M., Hayes, P. J., Rosson, M. B., Schneider, M. L. & Whiteside, J. A. (1986). Classifying users: A hard look at some controversial issues. In: *Proceedings of the ACM CHI '86 conference*, Boston, MA, 13–17 April, 84–88.

Pruitt, J. & Adlin, T. (2006). *The persona lifecycle: Keeping people in mind throughout product design.* San Francisco, (CA): Morgan Kaufmann.

Raskin, J. (2000). The humane interface: New directions for designing interactive systems. Reading, (MA): Addison-Wesley.

Rhenius, D. & Deffner, G. (1990). Evaluation of concurrent thinking aloud using eye-tracking data. In D. Woods & E. Roth, (Eds.) *Proceedings of the human factors society 34th annual meeting* (pp. 1265–1269). Santa Monica: CA.

Rogers, Y. (1986). Evaluating the meaningfulness of icon sets to represent command operations. In M. D. Harrison & A. F. Monk (Eds.), *People and computers: Designing for usability* (pp. 586–603). Cambridge, U.K: Cambridge University Press.

Romesburg, C. H. (1984). *Cluster analysis for researchers.* Belmont, (CA): Life-time Learning Publications (Wadsworth).

Rönkkö, K., Hellman M., Kilander B. & Dittrich Y. (2004). Personas is not applicable: Local remedies interpreted in a wider context. In: *Proceedings of the participatory design conference 2004.* Toronto, Canada.

Root, R. W. & Draper, S. (1983). Questionnaires as a software evaluation tool. In: *Proceedings of the ACM CHI '83 conference*, Boston, MA, 12–15 December, 83–87.

Rosenberg, M. J. (1969). The conditions and consequences of evaluation apprehension. In R. Rosenthal and R. L. Rosnow (Eds.), *Artifact in behavioral research* (pp. 279–349). New York: Academic Press.

Rosenfeld, L. & Morville, P. (2007). *Information architecture for the world wide web: Designing large-scale Web sites* (3rd ed.). Sebastopol, (CA): O'Reilly.

Rosson, M. B. (1984). Effects of experience on learning, using, and evaluating a text-editor. *Human Factors, 26*(4), 463–475.

Salasoo, A. (1990). Towards usable icon sets: A case study from telecommunications engineering. In: *Proceedings of the human factors society 34th annual meeting*, Orlando, FL, 8–12 October, 203–207.

Sandberg, J. (2006). Brainstorming works best if people scramble for ideas on their own. *The Wall Street Journal.* Retrieved June 1, 2008 from http://online.wsj.com/article/SB1150155518018078348-email.html.

Sawyer, P., Flanders, A. & Wixon, D. (1996). Making a difference—the impact of inspections. In M. J. Tauber (Ed.), *Proceedings of the SIGCHI conference on human factors in computing systems: common ground* (pp. 376–382). Vancouver, British Columbia, Canada, April 13–18, 1996. New York: ACM.

Schleifer, L. M. (1990). System response time and method of pay: Cardiovascular stress effects in computer-based tasks. *Ergonomics, 33*(1), 1495–1509.

Scott, B. & Neil, T. (2009). *Designing Web interfaces: Principles and patterns.* Sebastopol, (CA): O'Reilly Media.

Sein, M. K. & Bostrom, R. P. (1989). Individual differences and conceptual models in training novice users. *Human-Computer Interaction, 4*(3), 197–229.

Shackel, B. (1991). Usability—Context, framework, definition, design and evaluation. In B. Shackel & S. Richardson (Eds.), *Human factors for informatics usability* (pp. 21–37). Cambridge, UK: Cambridge University Press.

Shklar, L. & Rosen, R. (2009). *Web application architecture: Principles, protocols and practices.* Chichester, England: Wiley.

Sinha, R. (2003a). Beyond cardsorting: Free-listing methods to explore user categorizations. *Boxes and arrows.* <http://www.boxesandarrows.com/view/beyond_cardsorting_free_listing_methods_to_explore_user_categorizations> Accessed 01.06.08.

Sinha, R. (2003b). Persona development for information-rich domains. In: *Proceedings of CHI 2003.* New York: ACM Press.

Slavkovic, A. & Cross, K. (1999). Novice heuristics evaluation of a complex interface. In: *Extended abstracts of the ACM CHI 1999 conference on human factors in computing systems.* New York: ACM Press, 304–305.

Smith, B. L. (1993). Interpersonal behaviors that damage the productivity of creative problem-solving groups. *Journal of Creative Behavior, 27*(3), 171–187.

Snodgrass, A. & Coyne, R. (2006). *Interpretation in architecture: Design as a way of thinking.* London: Routledge.

Snyder. C. (2003). *Paper prototyping: The fast and easy way to define and refine user interfaces.* San Francisco, (CA): Morgan Kaufmann.

Spencer, R. (2000). The streamlined cognitive walkthrough method, working around social constraints encountered in a software development company. In: *Proceedings of ACM CHI 2000 conference on human factors in computing systems* (pp. 353–359). New York: ACM Press.

Spreng, K. P. (2007). Enhancing creativity in brainstorming for successful problem solving. *HOT Topics, 6*(11). Retrieved June 1, 2008 from <http://hot.carleton.ca/hot-topics/articles/brainstorming>.

Stammers, R. B. & Hoffman, J. (1991). Transfer between icon sets and ratings of icon concreteness and appropriateness. In: *Proceedings of the human factors society 35th annual meeting*, 354–258.

Stasser, G. & Birchmeier, Z. (2003). Group creativity and collective choice. In P. B. Paulus & B. A. Nijstad (Eds.), *Group creativity: Innovation through collaboration* (pp. 85–109). Oxford, UK: Oxford University Press.

Stewart, D. W., Shamdasani, P. N. & Rook, D. W. (2007). *Focus groups: Theory and practice* (2nd ed.). Thousand Oaks, (CA): Sage.

Sutherland, I. (1963). *Sketchpad: A man-machine graphical communication system.* PhD Thesis, MIT, Cambridge, MA. Available at <http://www.cl.cam.ac.uk/techreports/UCAM-CL-TR-574.html>

Suwa, M. & Tversky, B. (1996). What architects see in their sketches: Implications for design tools. In: *Proceedings of the ACM-SIGCHI conference on human factors in computing systems (CHI'96) conference companion,* 191–192.

Suwa, M. & Tversky, B. (2002). External representations contribute to the dynamic construction of ideas. In M. Hegarty, B. Meyer & N. H. Narayanan (Eds.), *Diagrams 2002* (pp. 341–343). New York: Springer-Verlag.

Teaching Effectiveness Program. (n.d.). *Leading a discussion using the nominal group technique.* <http://tep.uoregon.edu/services/newsletter/year95–96/issue30/nominal.html> Accessed 12.07.09.

Teasley, B., Leventhal, L., Blumenthal, B., Instone, K. & Stone, D. (1994). Cultural diversity in user interface design: Are intuitions enough? *ACM SIGCHI Bulletin, 26*(1), 36–40.

Telles, M. (1990). Updating an older interface. In: *Proceedings of the ACM CHI'90 Conference,* Seattle, WA, 1–5 April, 243–247.

Theofanos, M. F. & Redish, J. (2003). Bridging the gap: between accessibility and usability. *Interactions, 10*(6), 36–51.

Tretiack, P. (1999). *Raymond Loewy and streamlined design.* New York: Universe.

Trotter, R. (1981). Remedioas caseros: Mexian-American home remedies and community health problems. *Social Science and Medicine,* 15B: 107–114.

Trotter, R. & Schensul, J. J. (1998). Methods in applied anthropology. In H. R. Bernard (Ed.), *Handbook of methods in cultural anthropology* (pp. 691–735). Walnut Creek, (CA): AltaMira Press.

Tullis, T. S. (1985). Designing a menu-based interface to an operating system. In: *CHI '85 Proceedings,* San Francisco, CA, 79–84.

Tullis, T. & Wood, L. (2004). How many users are enough for a card-sorting study? In: *Proceedings of the usability professionals' association 2004 conference,* Minneapolis, MN, 7–11 June, CD-ROM.

Tversky, B. (2002). What do sketches say about thinking? In: *Proceedings of AAAI spring symposium on sketch understanding,* 148–151.

VanGundy, A. B. (1984). *Managing group creativity*. New York: American Management Association.

Väyrynen, S., Röning, J. & Alakärppä, I. (2006). User-centered development of video telephony for servicing mainly older users: Review and evaluation of an approach applied for 10 years. *Human Technology, 2*(1), 8–37.

Vincente, K. J. & Williges, R. C. (1988). Accommodating individual differences in searching a hierarchical file system. *International Journal of Man-Machine Studies, 29*(6), 647–668.

Virzi, R. A. (1989). What can you learn from a low-fidelity prototype? In: *Proceedings of the human factors society 33rd annual meeting*, Denver, CO, 16–20 October, 224–228.

Virzi, R. A. (1991). A preference evaluation of three dialing plans for a residential, phone-based information service. In: *Proceedings of the human factors society 35th annual meeting*, San Francisco, CA, 2–6 September, 240–243.

Virzi, R. A. (1997). Usability inspection methods. In M. Helander, T. K. Landauer & P. Prabhu (Eds.), *Handbook of human-computer interaction* (2nd ed., pp. 705–715). Amsterdam: Elsevier Science.

Vora, P. (2009). *Web application design patterns*. Burlington, (MA): Morgan Kaufmann.

Waldrop, M. (2001). *The dream machine: J.C.R. Licklider and the revolution that made computing personal*. New York: Viking Penguin.

Wastell, D. (1990). Mental effort and task performance: Towards a psychophysiology of human computer interaction. In: *Proceedings of the IFIP INTERACT '90 third international conference on human–computer interaction*, Cambridge, UK, 27–31 August, 107–112.

Wharton, C., Bradford, J., Jeffries, J. & Franzke, M. (1992). Applying cognitive walkthroughs to more complex user interfaces: Experiences, issues and recommendations CHI '92, pp. 381–388.

Whitelock, D. (1998). Matching measure for measure? A route through the formative testing of multimedia science software. In M. Olver (Ed.), *Innovation in the evaluation of learning technology*. London: University of North London.

Whiteway, M. (2001). *Christopher Dresser 1834–1904*. Milan: Skira Edinore.

Wikipedia. *SWOT analysis*. (n.d.). <http://en.wikipedia.org/wiki/SWOT_analysis> Accessed 16.07.09.

Wodtke, C. (2002). Information architecture: Blueprints for the Web. Berkeley: New Riders.

Wright, R. B. & Converse, S. A. (1992). Method bias and concurrent verbal protocol in software usability testing. In: *Proceedings of the human factors society 36th annual meeting*, Atlanta, GA, 12–16 October, 1220–1224.

Yehuda, H. & McGinn, J. (2007). Coming to terms: comparing and combining the results of multiple evaluators performing heuristic evaluation. In: *CHI '07 Extended abstracts on human factors in computing systems*, San Jose, CA, USA, April 28–May 03, 2007, pp. 1899–1904. New York, NY: ACM Press.

Zavod, M. J., Rickert, D. E. & Brown, S. H. (2002). The automated card-sort as an interface design tool: A comparison of products. In: *Proceedings of the human factors and ergonomics society 46th annual meeting*, Baltimore, MD, 30 September–4 October, 646–650.

Zwaga, H. J. (1989). Comprehensibility estimates of public information symbols: Their validity and use. In: *Proceedings of the human factors society 33rd annual meeting*, San Francisco, CA, 2–6 September, 979–983.

Focus groups
  advantages of, 46
  composition of, 52–53
  conducting, 46, 53
  facilitator, 51–52
  facilities for, 51
  mockups, reviewing, 48
  number of, 52
  preparing for, 49
  worksheet for, 50
Fork task, 302–303
Foundation document,
    191–192, 194, 196, 205
  definition of, 191, 204
  example of statements in,
    197
  persona characteristics in,
    192–194
Free listing, 119–120
  benefits of, 120
  drawbacks of, 121
  probes in
    alphabetic, 120
    semantic, 120
  questions, 78–79, 120
  for user-centered design,
    119
  use of, 119–120
Functional specifications,
    30–31

G

Gestation
  definition of, 156
  process, 157–158
Global warming evaluation,
    334–336, 339–342
Goals
  business, 28, 30
  usability, 18, 28
  user, 28, 30, 58, 169
GOMS analysis, 63
  uses of, 64
Graphical user interfaces
    (GUIs), 254, 260, 262
Group brainstorming, 109, 111

documents for, 133–134
  fundamental principles for,
    108–109
  procedure for, 107–108
  social issues in, 128–129
Group card sorting, 75
Guideline reviews, 356

H

Heterogeneous sampling, 40
Heuristic evaluation. *See*
    Heuristic inspection
Heuristic inspection
  benefits of, 352
  of British Telecom (BT) user
    interface, 351
  choosing inspectors for, 350
  conducting
    by collecting data, 351
    by locating evaluation
      session, 350–351
    by task descriptions, 350
  data analysis of, 351–352
  goal of, 345
  of infants, 348–349
  interpretation of data of,
    352
  ISO 9241 standards, 356
  issues in developing, 349
  limitations of, 353
  participatory, 354–355
  of user interface, 348–349
Hierarchical task analysis,
    58–60
  for Web site design, 60
Home pages, designing,
    258–260
HOME-RUN, 246–249
Human-error-tolerant design
  error management
    detection and identification,
      71
    mitigation, 71
    prevention, 71
    recovery, 71–72
    reduction, 71

Human factors (HF), 4
Hybrid interview, 308, 309
Hypertext system, 249

I

Icon usability, 14–17
Individual card sorting, 75
Information architecture (IA),
    56, 73, 74, 173
Inspection, heuristic
  benefits of, 352
  of British Telecom (BT) user
    interface, 351
  choosing inspectors for, 350
  conducting
    by collecting data, 351
    by locating evaluation
      session, 350–351
    by task descriptions, 350
  data analysis of, 351–352
  goal of, 345
  of infants, 348–349
  interpretation of data of,
    352
  ISO 9241 standards, 356
  issues in developing, 349
  limitations of, 353
  participatory, 354–355
  of user interface, 348–349
Instrumented browsers, 62
Intellectual property law, 44
Interface consistency, 66
Interface memorability, 10
Interviews
  advantages of, 46
  audio recordings in, 48–49
  conducting, 46, 53
  hybrid, 308, 309
  mockups, reviewing, 48
  note-taking approach for, 51
  for organizations, 49
  preliminary, 304, 306
  preparing for, 49, 51
  structured *vs.* unstructured,
    47
  survey, 47

techniques for
  contextual inquiry, 62
  decompose procedure, 63
  instrumented browsers, 62
  interviews and focus
    groups, 61
  standard operating
    procedures, 61
  user observation, 61
  think-aloud protocol, 61
  training materials, 61
  usability testing, 299–303
Test script. *See*
    Evaluation script
Text, scanning of, 270–271
Text links, 253–254
Think-aloud protocol, 61
Think-aloud usability testing,
    289
Three-click rule, testing, 29
Thumbnail sketches, 145
  use of, 146
Tree diagram, 87, 88
Trade-offs, usability, 17–18

U

UCD. *See* User-centered design
UI. *See* User interface
Unstructured interviews, 47
Usability, 4–6
  attributes, 6–7
    efficiency, 6, 9
    error tolerance and
      prevention, 6, 10–11
    learnability, 3, 6, 7–8
    memorability, 6, 9–10
    satisfaction, subjective, 6,
      11–14
  definition of, 6
  dimensions, 3
  goals, 18, 28
  of icon, 14–17
  trade-offs, 17–18
Usability defects, 330, 336, 351
  changes in, 337–338
  characteristics of, 331

severity rating for, 337
Usability inspection, variations
    of, 354–357
Usability measures, 7
Usability practitioners, 3, 23,
    279, 328
Usability testing, 278, 290
  choosing features, 298–299
  configuration, 313
  creating tasks, 299–303
  development cycle, 290
  iterative, 291–293
  observer instructions, 316
  principles relating to
    informed consent in,
    282–284
  recruiting, 295–297
  scheduling for, 294
Use cases, 57–58, 64–65
Usefulness, 5
User category labels, 179
  User-centered design
    (UCD), 119, 120, 278
  activities, 158
  examples of use of SWOT
    analysis in, 125
  free listing questions for, 119
User experience practitioners,
    3, 278
User friendly systems, 4
User interface (UI), 4, 19,
    264
  accelerators, 17
  consistency, 67
  elements, 14, 17, 19
  heuristic evaluation of,
    346–351
    participatory, 354–355
  positive aspects of, 352
User interface design (UID),
    18, 20
User interface designer, 151
User interviews
  analysis of
    collecting observations,
    318–320

extracting trends, 320–321
  organizing observations,
    320
  conducting, 311–317
    physical layout, 311
    moderators in, 313–315
    nondirected interviewing
      style in, 313
    tips and tricks for, 317
User-level goals and
    procedures, 58
User needs analysis
  activities of, primary, 24
  functional specifications of,
    30–31
  objectives of, 24
  research methods on, 31
    competitive analysis,
      43–46
    interviews and focus
      groups, 46–53
    survey, 32–43
  stakeholders, 25
  usability objectives, 28, 29
User observations data
  analysis of evaluation of
    collating, 328–329
    reviewing, 330–331
    summarizing, 330
  interpretation of, 337–339
  qualitative, 334–336
  quantitative, 332–333
Users
  casual, 9–10
  efficiency of, 6, 9
  goals of, 28, 30, 58, 169
  individual characteristics
    and differences of, 18–21
  needs and functionality of,
    47–48
  noncatastrophic errors, 6,
    10–11
  performance improvements
    of, 66–69
  primary and secondary
    targets of, 189

Edwards Brothers Malloy
Ann Arbor MI. USA
April 12, 2016